THE BIG BOOK OF
SERIAL
KILLERS

150 Serial Killer Files of the World's Worst Murderers

An Encyclopedia of Serial Killers

JACK ROSEWOOD

REBECCA LO

ISBN-13: 978-1-64845-099-0

FREE BONUS!

CONTENTS

INTRODUCTION

For hundreds of years, serial killers have walked the streets in all four corners of the world. *The Big Book of Serial Killers* has brought one hundred fifty of the most depraved, sadistic, and terrifying murderers from Russia, America, Germany, Australia, Korea, China, Denmark, and the UK together in one giant encyclopaedia.

From Elias Abuelazam to the Zodiac Killer, this A-Z reference book contains information on the classification of each killer, their background, victims, method of killing, arrest, trial, and punishment. Dates are included, such as when they started killing, their arrest, and (where relevant) their execution.

This encyclopedia is a concise and factual educational tool for those who wish to learn more about the men and women who kill.

Please use the table of contents to navigate to the serial killer you wish to read about, or just take them as they come. At the end of the book, after the Zodiac Killer chapter, you will find more information about the mug shots and references used for this book.

ELIAS ABUELAZAM

Date of birth: August 29, 1976

Aliases/Nicknames: Elias Abullazam

Characteristics: Racial attacks

Number of victims: 5

Date of murders: March of 2009 - August of 2010

Date of arrest: August 11, 2010

Murder method: Stabbing

Known Victims: David Motley, 31; Emmanuel Abdul Muhammad, 59; Darwin Marshall, 43; Frank Kellybrew, 60; Arnold Minor, 49

Crime location: Michigan, Virginia, and Ohio

Status: Sentenced to life imprisonment without parole.

Background

Abuelazam was born into a well-off Arab Christian family in Ramla, Israel, and the family relocated to America when he was a young child. His mother had married again and managed to obtain a green card, but she was never granted citizenship.

Abuelazam spent some time working as a mental health technician at the Piedmont Behavioral Health Center, now known as North Spring Behavioral Healthcare. He worked there until 2008, and it is this experience that may have given him the idea to plead insanity when he was later arrested and charged with murder.

On July 30, 2004, Abuelazam married Jessica Hirth. But the marriage did not last long. They divorced in 2007, and Jessica's parents were later shocked by his criminal activities. Her mother thought he was a "nice man." Jessica's father, however, claimed Abuelazam was abusive toward his wife and that was why she divorced him.

Murders

The crimes Abuelazam committed, and is suspected of committing, took place between the months of May and August, 2010. It is alleged he would drive his Chevrolet TrailBlazer around at night and target small-statured men who happened to be alone.

Abuelazam would come up with a ruse such as needing directions or help with his vehicle, and then he would stab them, aiming mainly for the stomach and chest. The majority of his victims were black, so authorities suspected the attacks were motivated by racial hatred.

By August 4, 2010, it was clear that the large number of stabbings that had occurred since May were likely the actions of one perpetrator, and a task force was created to investigate the crimes. Within a few days, the Leesburg Police were able to connect three attacks on black men in their area as the work of one man. Descriptions of the suspect had been given by the victims, and video surveillance footage of each attack was located and analyzed.

The police were in the process of narrowing down their suspects when Abuelazam happened to be arrested on August 5, in Arlington, Virginia. During a routine traffic stop, he was found to have an outstanding warrant for a previous assault. Though he was released on bond, his information was entered in the system and police were able to piece the puzzle together and identify him as their main suspect.

Arrest and Trial

On August 11, 2010, Abuelazam was arrested at Hartsfield-Jackson Atlanta International Airport as he waited to board a flight to Tel Aviv. He was given the option to appeal extradition to Michigan, which he declined. He was therefore transported to Flint, Michigan on August 26. Because of the nature of his alleged crimes, he was held without bond and placed in solitary confinement while he awaited his trial.

Abuelazam was eventually charged with a number of crimes, including the following:

June 26, 2010 - Bill Fisher, forty-two. Charged with assault with intent to murder.

July 12, 2010 - Antoine Jackson, twenty-nine. Charged with assault with intent to murder.

July 19, 2010 - Richard Booker. Charged with assault with intent to murder.

July 26, 2010 - Darwin Marshall, forty-three. Charged with murder.

July 27, 2010 - Antwoine Marshall, twenty-six. Charged with assault with intent to murder.

July 29, 2010- Davon Rawls, twenty. Charged with assault with intent to murder.

July 30, 2010 - Frank Kellybrew, sixty. Charged with murder.

August 1, 2010 - Etwan Wilson, eighteen. Charged with assault with intent to murder.

August 2, 2010 - Arnold Minor, forty-nine. Charged with murder.

August 7, 2010 - unnamed fifty-nine-year-old man. Indictment for this case.

He is also suspected of committing the following crimes:

May 24, 2010 - David Motley, thirty-one. Found murdered.

June 21, 2010 - Emmanuel Abdul Muhammad, fifty-nine. Found murdered.

July 23, 2010 - Stabbing of an unnamed twenty-one-year-old man.

July 29, 2010 - Stabbing of an unnamed fifty-nine-year-old man.

July 30, 2010 - Stabbing of an unnamed twenty-eight-year-old man.

August 3, 2010 - Attack of an unnamed teenager.

August 5, 2010 - Stabbing of an unnamed sixty-seven-year-old man.

August 6, 2010 - Attack of an unnamed man with a hammer.

The first trial began on May 8, 2012, for the Arnold Minor murder case. In an unusual turn of events, the judge allowed evidence from the other cases to be submitted during the trial. One important piece of evidence was a blood drop found on Abuelazam's pants, which was found to belong to Arnold Minor.

Fifty witnesses were called by the prosecution, including an uncle of Abuelazam who had assisted in the arrest. Faced with an overwhelming amount of evidence, the defense team put forward a plea of insanity. Only one expert witness testified regarding Abuelazam's mental state, and the credibility of this psychiatrist was questioned by the prosecution, specifically because this doctor's expertise was in drug and alcohol addiction, not mental illness.

Two psychologists were brought forward by the prosecution who claimed that, although Abuelazam likely suffered from some sort of personality disorder, there was no evidence that he was insane at the time of the murders. Abuelazam did not fit the legal criteria of insanity.

The jury began their deliberations on May 22, 2012, and just one hour later, they had made their decision. They found Abuelazam guilty of the murder of Arnold Minor.

Outcome

Abuelazam was sentenced on June 25, 2012, to serve life imprisonment without the possibility of parole.

STEPHEN AKINMURELE

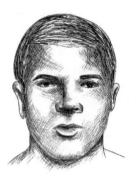

Date of birth: 1977

Aliases/Nicknames: Cul-de-sac killer

Characteristics: Ageist murder, robbery

Number of victims: 5

Date of murders: 1995 - 1998

Date of arrest: November 1, 1998

Murder method: Strangulation, bludgeoning

Known Victims: Eric Boardman, 77; Joan Boardman, 74; Jemmimah Cargill, 75; Dorothy Harris, 68; Marjorie Ashton, 72

Crime location: Blackpool and Lancashire, England

Status: Committed suicide by hanging while incarcerated awaiting trial.

Background

Not a great deal is known about Akinmurele's early life. His mother was from the Isle of Man and his father was Nigerian. At the age of six, he moved to the Isle of Man with his mother, and he was raised by both his mother and his grandmother.

He was considered a friendly boy at school but often got into trouble. He suffered from some unspecified mental health issues as a child, but there was no mention of any major incidents or concerns. By the time he was eighteen, he was living on the mainland and working as a civil servant in the Department of Benefits. He supplemented his income by working as a barman at a local bar called Rumours.

Murders

In October of 1998, the bodies of an elderly couple were found murdered in their home in Blackpool. Eric Boardman, seventy-seven and his wife Joan, seventy-four, were found by their daughter after they had been bashed to death. At the scene, a homemade cosh (a thick heavy stick or bar) had been located, and investigators were able to lift a fingerprint from it. That fingerprint matched Akinmurele.

Earlier, Jemmimah Cargill, seventy-five, was suspected to have died in a apartment fire in the same resort the Boardmans resided in. Once detectives discovered Akinmurele had also shared the apartment with Jemmimah Cargill, however, they determined the case to be another murder rather than an accidental death.

But it wasn't over yet. Akinmurele was also linked to the murder of Dorothy Harris in February of

1996, back on the Isle of Man. She too had died in a fire at her home. Although initially considered a terrible accident, it was now being deemed a homicide.

The more investigators looked, the more the number of potential victims increased. Marjorie Ashton had been strangled to death in her home in 1995, and Akinmurele could also be linked to this death.

Arrest and Trial

Akinmurele was arrested and subsequently charged with the murders of the Boardmans, Jemmimah Cargill, and Dorothy Harris. During questioning, it was found that Akinmurele's demeanor would change quite rapidly. Polite and quiet one minute, he could easily fly into a rage so terrifying that one of the detectives labeled him "one of the most dangerous men I have ever met."

While awaiting trial, Akinmurele was remanded in prison. During this time, he attacked a doctor, causing him injury; he also issued many threats to cause harm to others. Akinmurele even claimed he had committed another murder. But although his story seemed plausible, it was later determined his confession was not true.

Akinmurele seemed to show a hatred of elderly people, and this, combined with his mental state, led investigators to take another look at similar crimes that had happened both in the immediate area and back on the Isle of Man. They researched cases going back to 1994, and found many that could potentially be linked to Akinmurele.

Outcome

On August 28, 1999, Akinmurele was found hanging in his cell. He had crafted a ligature from his clothing which he attached to a window to hang himself. His trial was only weeks away, and he left a suicide note for his mother which said, "I couldn't take any more of feeling like how I do now, always wanting to kill."

As per protocol, an inquest was held. During this time, a number of issues were brought to the surface regarding the judiciary system. Not only had Akinmurele tried to kill himself twice before, his girlfriend had also warned the authorities that he was a danger to himself and had stated he did not want to go to trial.

During his prison stay, Akinmurele had been interviewed by a number of specialists, including doctors and a forensic psychiatrist. According to the psychiatrist, Akinmurele claimed to be "haunted by the images of [his] victims,"—they were always on his mind.

Following an attempted suicide while in the segregated unit, Akinmurele was moved to the health-care ward of the prison. However, he had managed to make a weapon out of a toothbrush and claimed to fantasize about taking one of the female staff members hostage. As a result, he was moved back to the segregated section. He was placed on suicide watch, but still managed to kill himself just two days later.

Trivia

Quote:

> "I can't help the way I feel, what I did was wrong - I know that and I feel for them - but it doesn't mean I won't do it again."

CHARLES ALBRIGHT

Date of birth: August 10, 1933

Aliases/Nicknames: The Dallas Ripper, The Dallas Slasher, The Eyeball Killer

Characteristics: Removal of victim's eyes

Number of victims: 3

Date of murders: December of 1990 - March of 1991

Date of arrest: March 22, 1991

Murder method: Shooting

Known Victims: Shirley Williams; Mary Lou Pratt; Susan Peterson

Crime location: Texas

Status: Sentenced to life imprisonment without parole.

Background

Albright was adopted by Fred and Delle Albright after they discovered him in an orphanage. Fortunately for Albright, Delle was a schoolteacher and he was able to jump two grades at school due to her diligence and help with his education. She was a strict parent, but also overprotective.

As a teenager, Albright began shooting small animals with a gun, and he showed some interest in taxidermy. His mother, wanting to encourage him in his hobby, would help him stuff the dead animals. By the time he was thirteen, Albright had already been arrested for aggravated assault and was known to be a petty thief. Yet his accelerated education enabled him to finish school at fifteen and enroll in a university. Though he had planned to become a doctor, was unable to complete his premed training.

He was arrested by the police again at the age of sixteen, for theft, and this time he was sent to prison for a year. Upon his release, he enrolled in a teacher's college, majoring in premed studies. But he was thrown out of the college when stolen property was found in his possession.

It was at this time that Albright embarked on a career in forgery. He created false documents showing he had attained both bachelor's and master's degrees, and he began forging signatures. He married his girlfriend from college, and they welcomed a daughter. Albright continued to forge checks, and while he was working as a teacher at a high school, his forgery was discovered, and he was put on probation.

The couple divorced in 1974. Albright was caught stealing merchandise from a hardware store worth hundreds of dollars, and was sent to prison again, this time for two years. However, he was released after serving only six months.

Upon his release, he made friends with his neighbors, and he became a trusted babysitter for children in the neighborhood. During a visit to a friend's home in 1981, Albright was caught molesting their nine-year-old daughter. At court, he plead guilty and was placed on probation. Albright later said he wasn't guilty but had said he was to avoid hassles.

In 1985, Albright was living in Arkansas when he met a lady named Dixie, who quickly moved in with him. Before long, Dixie was supporting him and paying the bills. Early in the mornings, however, Albright would deliver newspapers. That wasn't all he was doing though– Unbeknownst to Dixie, he was also visiting prostitutes.

Murders

Albright's first murder took place on December 13, 1990. The body of prostitute Mary Lou Pratt was discovered in the Oak Cliff neighborhood of Dallas. She had been killed by a gunshot to the back of the head from a .44 caliber firearm. The victim was wearing only a T-shirt and bra, and both had been pushed up to expose her breasts. Mary Lou's eyes were shut, and her face and chest were covered in bruises. When the medical examiner lifted her eyelids, he discovered that both of her eyes had been removed and taken from the scene.

On February 10, 1991, the body of another prostitute was found, and she also was almost completely nude. Susan Peterson had been shot once through the top of her head, once in the back of her head, and once in her left breast. Her body was found just outside of the city limits of South Dallas. She too, was missing her eyes.

Shirley Williams was the third prostitute found dead in the area. She had been shot twice - once through the top of her head and once in the face. She had also suffered a beating, with multiple bruises on her face and a broken nose. Like the other two victims, her eyes had been removed.

Timeline of murders:

December 13, 1990 - Mary Lou Pratt, thirty-three

February 10, 1991 - Susan Peterson

March 10, 1991 - Shirley Williams

Arrest and Trial

Albright was arrested and charged with three counts of murder on March 22, 1991. The trial started on December 13, 1991. At first, it seemed the prosecution's case was going to collapse, as most of the evidence was only circumstantial. However, there was also strong forensic evidence, as hairs from the murder scene of Shirley Williams were matched to Albright.

By December 18, 1991, the jury had already adjourned to deliberate. They quickly returned with a verdict of guilty, but only for the murder of Shirley Williams.

Outcome

As a result of the conviction, Albright was sentenced to life imprisonment without parole. He will spend the rest of his natural life in prison.

Trivia

- He removed the eyes from his victims, all of whom were prostitutes.
- He was, they said, a kind of Renaissance man – fluent in French and Spanish, a masterful painter, and able to woo women by playing Chopin preludes on the piano or reciting poetry by Keats.

RODNEY ALCALA

Date of birth: August 23, 1943

Aliases/Nicknames: Dating Game Killer, John Berger, John Burger

Characteristics: Rape and murder

Number of victims: 5 – 100 +

Date of murders: 1977 - 1979

Date of arrest: July 27, 1979

Murder method: Strangulation, beating

Known Victims: Robin Samsoe, 12; Jill Barcomb, 18; Georgia Wixted, 27; Charlotte Lamb, 32; Jill Parenteau, 21

Crime location: California

Status: Sentenced to death, awaiting execution.

Background

Rodrigo Jacques Alcala Buquor was born in San Antonio, Texas. In 1951, his parents, Raoul and Anna Maria Gutierrez, moved the family to Mexico. His father abandoned the family just three years later. When Alcala was about eleven years old, he moved to Los Angeles with his mother and siblings.

In 1960, at the age of 17, Alcala enlisted in the US Army, and became a clerk. Things started to go very wrong though in 1964, when Alcala went AWOL from the Army and hitchhiked to his mother's house. A military psychiatrist was tasked with assessing Alcala, and he determined he was suffering from antisocial personality disorder. Subsequently, he was medically discharged from the Army.

Alcala went on to study at the UCLA School of Fine Arts, from which he graduated. He first came under police scrutiny in 1968, following the rape of an eight-year-old girl. He had been seen luring the girl into his apartment, but was able to flee before the police got there, leaving the girl beaten. Alcala then enrolled in the NYU Film School and studied under Roman Polanski, using the name John Berger to put the police off his trail.

Over the next several years, Alcala continued to get arrested for a number of crimes, including assault on a young girl and drug possession. And he later admitted to knocking a fifteen-year-old girl unconscious and raping her, while posing as a professional photographer.

Although he had been convicted of rape and was therefore a registered sex offender, he still managed to become a contestant in 1978 on *The Dating Game*, a televised dating show. It is believed he had already murdered two women by this time. The show's host described him as a photographer who liked motorcycling and skydiving. Remarkably, Alcala won the date with the bachelorette, Cheryl Bradshaw, but she thought he was creepy and refused to go out with him.

Murders

Jill Barcomb was a runaway from New York when she disappeared in 1977. Her body was discovered in a Los Angeles ravine, and she had been "rolled up like a ball." At first, investigators thought she may have been a victim of the Hillside Strangler, but DNA evidence later showed Alcala to be responsible for her death.

Also murdered in 1977 was Georgia Wixted, who had been bludgeoned to death inside her apartment in Malibu. Charlotte Lamb was murdered in the laundry room of her apartment complex after being raped and strangled. Jill Parenteau was also killed in her apartment in Burbank. These four murders were all linked to Alcala through DNA.

Another murder that took place in 1977 was that of Pamela Jean Lambson. Pamela had gone missing after traveling to Fisherman's Wharf where she had arranged to meet a photographer. Her body was found near a hiking trail in Marin County, naked and battered.

Christine Ruth Thornton disappeared in 1977 in Wyoming. Her body wasn't found until 1982, and her remains were unidentified until DNA testing was done with samples from her relatives. An autopsy showed she had been around six months pregnant when she was murdered. Alcala later claimed that he did take photographs of Christine, but he denied murdering her.

Twelve-year-old Robin Samsoe disappeared on June 20, 1979, somewhere between her ballet class and a visit to the beach. Her body was discovered several days later, dumped in the Los Angeles foothills.

Timeline of known murders:

1971   Cornelia Crilley

1977   Ellen Hover

1977   Jill Barcomb

1977   Georgia Wixted

1977   Pamela Jean Lambson

1977   Christine Ruth Thornton

1978   Charlotte Lamb

1979   Jill Parenteau

1979   Robin Samsoe

Suspected of the following murders:

July 1977 - Antoinette Wittaker, thirteen

February 1978 - Joyce Gaunt, seventeen

Arrest and Trial

Detectives had been circulating a composite sketch of the man suspected of killing Robin Samsoe, and, as a result, Alcala was identified by his own parole officer. Officers searched his mother's home, during which they located a receipt for a storage locker belonging to Alcala in Seattle. When they went through the locker, they discovered hundreds of photographs of young girls, many of which were nude, and a pair of earrings identified as belonging to Robin Samsoe, as well as another pair that would later be traced back to Charlotte Lamb through DNA testing.

Alcala was arrested on July 27, 1979 and charged with Robin Samsoe's murder. He went to trial and was found guilty, receiving a death sentence in 1980. In 1984, the sentence was overturned because the jury had been informed of his previous crimes, which wasn't allowable. It was overturned a second time in 1986, as a result of claims that a witness had been hypnotized!

In 2003, Alcala was linked to two more murders through DNA. By 2010, he had stood trial for five murders - Robin Samsoe, Georgia Wixted, Jill Barcomb, Charlotte Lamb, and Jill Parenteau. Alcala was found guilty of all five murders and remained on death row. In 2011, he was indicted for the murders of Ellen Hover and Cornelia Crilley in New York, and he pled guilty to both in December of 2012.

There are numerous other cases Alcala is a suspect in, but many won't be prosecuted because he has already received the maximum sentence possible - death.

Outcome

Posing as a photographer was the main component of Alcala's MO, and investigators found over one hundred photographs in his possession following his arrest. They released one hundred twenty of these to the media in the hopes that the public might be able to help identify the women and young girls in them. Police wanted to know if any of them were also murder victims.

In the first weeks of the photographs being made public, around twenty-one women came forward to identify themselves. In 2013, a family member recognized a woman in one of the photographs and identified her as Christine Thornton, twenty-eight, who had been found murdered in Wyoming in 1982. Alcala was eventually charged with the murder but was unable to travel to Wyoming to stand trial due to ill health.

An additional nine hundred photographs from Alcala's collection were too sexually explicit to be shown to the public.

Trivia

- Serial killer Rodney Alcala represented himself at trial, and during questioning he morphed into two people. He interrogated himself on the stand for five hours, using a deep voice and calling himself "Mr. Alcala," then answering in his normal voice.
- After being sentenced to death in California, he received another twenty-five-year sentence in New York for killing two women.
- Filed a lawsuit against California for a slip-and-fall incident while incarcerated.
- Filed a lawsuit against California for failing to provide him with a low-fat diet while incarcerated.
- Allegedly has an IQ of 160.

DANIEL CAMARGO BARBOSA

Date of birth: January 22, 1930

Aliases/Nicknames: Manuel Bulgarin Solis, The Sadist of Chanquito

Characteristics: Murder and Rape

Number of victims: 72 - 150

Date of murders: 1974 - 1986

Date of arrest: February 26, 1986

Murder method: Stabbing and strangulation

Known Victims: Unnamed young girls

Location: Colombia, Ecuador

Status: Murdered in prison, November 13, 1994.

Background

When Barbosa was a young boy, his mother died. His father, who was described as being emotionally distant, yet overbearing, remarried. Barbosa's stepmother was apparently abusive. She punished him regularly and would dress him up in girls' clothes to humiliate him in front of other children.

As an adult, Barbosa had a live-in relationship with a woman named Alcira, and they went on to have two children together. However, Barbosa then fell in love with Esperanza; they had planned to get married until he discovered she wasn't a virgin. Barbosa somehow managed to convince Esperanza that he would stay in a relationship with her, provided she helped him find girls who were virgins that he could have sex with, and she agreed.

Esperanza would lure the young girls to the apartment and then drug them with sleeping pills so Barbosa could rape them. Five young girls were raped in this manner, but they were all released without any further harm. The fifth girl, however, reported the rape to the authorities, and both were arrested. Barbosa was charged with sexual assault and sentenced to three years in prison. But another judge was brought in and converted his sentence to eight years. After serving the full term, he was released back in to society.

Barbosa was arrested in Brazil in 1973, for not having correct documentation. (He was traveling and living under a false name, which led to his criminal records being delayed from Colombia, and he was subsequently deported.) On his return to Colombia, he began selling televisions on the street in Barranquilla. Not long after this, he embarked on his reign of murderous terror.

Murders

Shortly after he returned to Colombia in 1973, Barbosa was walking past a school one day and kidnapped a nine-year-old girl. He raped her and then murdered her so she would not be able to tell the police. This was his first known murder, but it most certainly wouldn't be his last. He was caught and convicted of this murder after returning to the scene of the crime to retrieve a television, and he was sentenced to twenty-five years in prison. In December of 1977, he was sent to a prison located on Gorgona, an island off of Colombia.

Barbosa spent quite a bit of time studying the ocean's currents, and he escaped in November of 1984 using a crudely built boat. After his escape, the authorities assumed he had either been eaten by sharks or had died at sea. However, he managed to make his way to Quito in Ecuador. From there, he traveled to Guayaquil around December 5. On December 18, he kidnapped another nine-year-old girl. The following day he kidnapped a ten-year-old girl.

Between the years of 1984 and 1986, it is estimated Barbosa committed a minimum of fifty-four rapes and murders in Guayaquil. Because of the high number of victims, the authorities initially thought the crimes were being committed by a group or a gang and didn't consider it could be the work of just one person.

To lure his young victims outside the main part of town, Barbosa often pretended to be a foreigner who was looking for a church. He would flash large amounts of money in front of them and offer to pay them if they showed him how to get to the church. His victims were always young, helpless, and poor, many of whom would be out on the streets trying to find some work. Once Barbosa had convinced them, he would tell them he knew of a shortcut through the woods. If they seemed hesitant or wary, he would let them go, as there were always plenty of other possible victims out there for him to try to lure. When they were out of sight of potential witnesses, he would rape and then kill them, usually by strangling or stabbing them. Often, the bodies were dismembered using a machete.

When Barbosa was later asked why he preferred children, he explained he liked to hear them cry.

Arrest and Trial

On February 26, 1986, Barbosa was arrested just minutes after he had murdered a little girl. He had been approached by two policemen who thought he was acting suspiciously, and when they got close to him, they discovered he was carrying a bag that contained the bloodstained clothes of his victim and a part of her genitals.

He initially told the police his name was Manuel Bulgarin Solis, but a surviving rape victim later identified him as Barbosa. While interviewed, he claimed to be responsible for the murders of seventy-two girls in Ecuador. He then showed the authorities where he had dumped many of the bodies, most of which had been dismembered. He was convicted in 1989, but received only twenty-five years' imprisonment as his sentence, which is the maximum in Ecuador. He was sent to the Garcia Moreno de Quito jail, which also housed Pedro Alonso Lopez.

Outcome

Barbosa was murdered in prison in November of 1994. His murderer, Luis Masache Narvaez, was the cousin of one of his many victims.

Trivia

- For interviews with journalists, Barbosa tried to demand an expensive fee for the privilege of talking to him.
- He claimed he chose young girls as victims because they "cried," which made the act of killing them more satisfying.
- Barbosa killed because he "hated" women for "not being what [he] believed women were supposed to be."

ROBERT BERDELLA

Date of birth: January 31, 1939

Aliases/Nicknames: Kansas City Butcher, The Bondage Killer

Characteristics: Torture, rape, murder, bodies not found

Number of victims: 6

Date of murders: 1984 - 1987

Date of arrest: April 2, 1988

Murder method: Drug overdose and asphyxiation

Known Victims: Robert Sheldon, 18; Jerry Howell, 20; Mark Wallace, 20; James Ferris, 20; Todd Stoops, 21; Larry Pearson, 20

Crime location: Kansas City

Status: Life imprisonment without parole; died in prison of natural causes in 1992.

Background

In 1939, Berdella was born into a Catholic family; his father was a die setter at the Ford Motor Company while his mother stayed at home. Berdella suffered from severe nearsightedness and so, at the age of five, was given thick glasses to wear. Berdella did well at school, although his teachers had difficulty teaching him. He was often bullied by other schoolchildren, most likely because of his glasses.

His father died suddenly at the age of thirty-nine, when Berdella was sixteen years old. Not long afterwards, his mother remarried, which made Berdella angry and resentful. Around this time, Berdella had been working at a local restaurant, and he later claimed that he had been sexually assaulted by one of his male co-workers.

In 1967, Berdella began to study at the Kansas City Art Institute. He had hoped to become a professor. During his time at the institute he began torturing animals, including a dog, chicken, and duck. It was also at this time that he began selling drugs and drinking alcohol, and when he was nineteen he was arrested for possession of marijuana and LSD. Luckily for Berdella, he was released five days later due to a lack of evidence.

Berdella was eventually expelled from the college following the murder of a dog, supposedly for the sake of his art. He then went on to train as a chef, and he became rather successful at it. He even helped set up a training program for other aspiring chefs and was a member of the local chefs' association. Ironically, Berdella was also a member of his local neighborhood watch and crime-prevention associations.

By the time Berdella was thirty-two years old, he was openly gay. After quitting his work as a chef, he opened an antique type store called Bob's Bizarre Bazaar. For a while, he was in a relationship with a Vietnam veteran, but when this ended he started spending his time with male prostitutes. He would befriend them and try to help them get out of the prostitution world. But there was much more to Berdella's interest in male prostitutes than simply trying to help them have a better life.

Murders

In July of 1984, Berdella drugged his friend Jerry Howell, who was a sex worker, and kept him captive in the basement of his home overnight. During this time, he raped him repeatedly and then finally ended the torture by asphyxiating him. Less than a year later, Berdella drugged another friend, Robert Sheldon, and kept him in the basement. He experienced a moment of guilt at one point and took Sheldon to a doctor for treatment. But then he took him back to the basement and kept him there until he killed him on April 15.

Berdella found Mark Wallace hiding in his shed during a storm in June and invited him to shelter inside his house. Once inside, he was drugged like the others and then raped and tortured before he was killed. In September, Berdella went to a gay bar and met James Ferris. Berdella took James back to his place and held him captive for weeks, repeatedly raping and torturing the young man until he finally murdered him.

In June of 1986, male prostitute Todd Stoops was lured back to Berdella's house, which wasn't difficult because they had known each other for a while. He was kept captive for six weeks until he died from blood loss and an infection. The following year, Larry Pearson was bailed out of jail by Berdella and ended up locked in Berdella's basement. When Berdella tired of Pearson, he bludgeoned him until he was unconscious. Then he put a bag over his head and suffocated him using a ligature around his neck.

The last known victim of Berdella was Chris Bryson, a prostitute, who was abducted in March of 1988. Although he too had been locked in the basement, he managed to escape and ran to the house next door and raised the alarm.

Timeline of murders:

July 5, 1984 - Jerry Howell, twenty - held captive for twenty-eight hours

April 12, 1985 - Robert Sheldon, eighteen

June 22, 1985 - Mark Wallace, twenty

September 26, 1985 - Walter James Ferris, twenty-five

June 17, 1986 - Todd Stoops, twenty-one - torture included electric shocks to his eyelids

June 23, 1987 - Larry Wayne Pearson, twenty - held captive for six weeks

Arrest and Trial

On April 2, 1988, Berdella was arrested. When his home was searched, officers discovered written logs of the torture Berdella had inflicted on his victims, as well as vast numbers of Polaroid photographs of them. Some of the torture included punching his fist into their anal cavity, administering electrical shocks, injecting drain cleaner into the vocal cords, and using cotton swabs to put bleach in their eyes. He also tried to gouge out the eyes of a victim just to "see what would happen."

Berdella had kept two skulls buried in his backyard for a while, then dug them up and placed them in a closet with the teeth in envelopes nearby. All of his victims had been dismembered, put into trash bags, and left on the curb for the trash collectors to take to the local landfill. Because of this, the bodies of his victims were never located.

Without the bodies as evidence, it was going to be very difficult for the prosecution to get a guilty verdict in court. Therefore, they made a deal with Berdella: If he confessed to his crimes and gave the details of each murder, they wouldn't seek the death penalty - he would receive only a life sentence. Berdella, unaware of the lack of evidence, agreed to the deal and pled guilty after confessing. He was sentenced to life imprisonment without the possibility of parole.

Outcome

In 1992, Berdella wrote letters to a minister where he claimed the prison officials were preventing him from receiving his heart medication. Not long afterwards, Berdella died from a heart attack.

Trivia

- He had a collection of Polaroids of his victims and their torture.
- A month before he was arrested, Robert Berdella received a ride home by fellow patrons at a bar when they realized he was too drunk to drive. On the way home, he "confessed" to torturing and killing six men, but no one took him seriously, given his level of intoxication.
- Larry Wayne Pearson's head was buried in Berdella's garden.

DAVID BERKOWITZ

Date of birth: June 1, 1953

Aliases/Nicknames: Son of Sam, Richard David Falco (birth name), The .44 Caliber Killer

Characteristics: Neighbor's dog ordered him to kill

Number of victims: 6

Date of murders: 1976 - 1977

Date of arrest: August 10, 1977

Murder method: Shooting

Known Victims: Donna Lauria, 18; Christine Freund, 26; Virginia Voskerichian, 21; Valentina Suriani, 18; Alexander Esau, 20; Stacy Moskowitz, 20

Crime location: New York City

Status: Sentenced to three life sentences without parole.

Background

David Berkowitz (whose birth name was actually Richard David Falco) was born in New York in 1953, to Elizabeth Broder and her married lover Joseph Klineman. Bizarrely, his mother chose to give him the surname Falco, which was the name of her ex-husband. Nobody really knows why she decided to do this, but theories have included that Klineman may have threatened her not to use his surname since he was already married.

Berkowitz was given up for adoption. A couple named Nathan and Pearl Berkowitz, who owned a hardware store in the Bronx and had been unable to have their own children, adopted him. They decided to keep his names but reversed the order, so he became David Richard Berkowitz. As he grew up, it was noted that his intelligence was above average, but he didn't want to learn. Instead, he became fascinated with pyromania and petty theft.

Because of his bullying and difficult behavior, his parents sought the advice of a psychotherapist, but no legal intervention was ever undertaken and no particular diagnosis was recorded. When Berkowitz was just fourteen, his adoptive mother passed away from breast cancer, and when his adoptive father remarried, he developed a dislike toward his stepmother.

When he was eighteen, Berkowitz enrolled in the US Army. And he ended up serving in South Korea in 1971. He was honorably discharged in 1974, and at this time he tracked down his birth mother, Elizabeth. They started visiting together, and before long she informed him of the illegitimacy of his birth, which greatly disturbed him. Eventually, Berkowitz stopped communicating with Elizabeth, but he continued talking to his half sister Roslyn for a while longer.

It is believed that learning the circumstances of his birth, including a birth father who wasn't interested in him and his parents' scandalous relationship, served as the crisis point in his already-troubled life. It was as though this discovery destroyed his own sense of identity.

Murders

Berkowitz's first attempt at murder took place on Christmas Eve, 1975, when he attacked two women with a knife. One of these women was Michelle Forman, who was just a teenager at the time. Although her injuries weren't life-threatening, she was hospitalized. Shortly after this failed attempt, Berkowitz moved to Yonkers in New York.

On July 29, 1976, Jody Valenti and Donna Lauria were sitting in Valenti's car, talking about their evening. It was just after 1:00 a.m., and when Lauria opened the door to leave, she saw a man coming toward the car. The man was Berkowitz, and he pulled a pistol out of the paper bag he had in his hand. He crouched down, aimed the gun with both of his hands, and fired at the two young women. Lauria was killed instantly and Valenti was shot in the thigh. Berkowitz quickly left, without saying anything.

Carl Denaro and Rosemary Keenan were sitting in Keenan's car on October 23, 1976, when all of a sudden the windows of the vehicle shattered. Acting instinctively Keenan started the car and drove off at high speed. They didn't realize they'd been shot at until they noticed Denaro had received a gunshot wound to the head; it eventually needed to be repaired with a metal plate.

The next shooting occurred just after midnight on November 27. Joanne Lomino and Donna DeMasi were walking home after seeing a movie, and when they reached Lomino's home, they stood on the front porch to talk for a while. A man dressed in military fatigues walked up to them and started to ask for directions. Then he pulled out a gun and shot the two girls. Lomino was shot in the back and was left a paraplegic and DeMasi received an injury to her neck.

Christine Freund and her fiancé John Diel had just been to see a movie and were sitting in Diel's car getting ready to drive to the local dance hall. At around 12:40 a.m., shots were fired into the car, and Diel drove off in a panic. Freund had been shot twice, and she succumbed to her injuries several hours later. Diel was uninjured.

Virginia Voskerichian was walking home from Columbia University at 7:30 p.m. on the night of March 8, 1977, when a man carrying a gun confronted her. She tried to protect herself using her textbooks, but her efforts failed. She was shot in the head and killed.

The next victims were Alexander Esau and Valentina Suriani. They were sitting in Suriani's car not far from her home at around 3:00 a.m. on April 17, when a man came out of nowhere and shot them both twice. Suriani died from her wounds at the scene, and Esau died hours later at the hospital.

On June 26, 1977, Sal Lupo and Judy Placido were sitting in Lupo's car at around 3:00 a.m. when shots were fired into the vehicle. Lupo received a wound to his forearm; Placido was more severely injured, with gunshots to her temple, shoulder, and neck. Remarkably, they both survived the attack. Later, they said they had just been talking about the "Son of Sam" attacks minutes before they were shot.

The last shootings took place in the early hours of July 31, 1977. Once again, a young couple, Stacy Moskowitz and Robert Violante, were sitting in their parked car near a park. While they were kissing, a man came up to the passenger's side of the car and fired four shots. Both were shot in the head. Moskowitz died later that day in hospital; Violante lost one eye and suffered serious damage to the vision in his other eye.

This attack was witnessed by a number of people, including a young man named Tommy Zaino, who had been sitting in a car parked three cars ahead of Violante's. Zaino had seen the man approaching Violante's car and was able to get a good look at him thanks to the streetlight and the brightness of the moon that night. Now the police had a clear description of the man who had been terrorizing the neighborhood.

Timeline of murders:

July 29, 1976 - Donna Lauria, eighteen

January 30, 1977 - Christine Freund, twenty-six

March 8, 1977 - Virginia Voskerichian, nineteen

April 17, 1977 - Alexander Esau, twenty

April 17, 1977 - Valentina Suriani, eighteen

July 31, 1977 - Stacy Moskowitz, twenty

Arrest and Trial

Four days after the shooting of Moskowitz and Violante, another witness contacted the police to inform them of what she had seen and heard that night. Cecilia Davis had seen a car being ticketed as it was parked near a fire hydrant on the street, and she recognized the officer as Michael Cataneo. A man walked past her and looked at her as though he were studying her. Unsettled, she ran home. As she ran, she heard gunshots behind her.

Her statement enabled the police to check every vehicle that had been ticketed on that street that night. One of those cars belonged to Berkowitz - a yellow four-door Ford Galaxy. Investigators asked the local police to arrange an interview with Berkowitz. The Yonkers police had been suspicious about Berkowitz, and they informed the investigators of their concerns Berkowitz was in fact "Son of Sam."

On August 10, police were outside the home of Berkowitz. Looking through his car windows, they noticed a rifle in plain view. They searched the car, despite not having a warrant, and found more items of interest related to the case. They urgently requested a formal search warrant, but Berkowitz emerged before it arrived. The police felt they had no choice but to arrest Berkowitz, and they did so at gunpoint.

The detective asked Berkowitz, "Who have I got?" And Berkowitz replied, "You know." The detective said he didn't know and asked him to explain who he was. Berkowitz turned to look at him and stated, "'I'm Sam."

It only took around half an hour for Berkowitz to confess to the shootings, and he was keen to plead guilty. However, he claimed during the interview that he had been told by the neighbor's dog to kill because it wanted "the blood of pretty girls." The name "Sam" belonged to his former neighbor, Sam Carr, and it was his dog that Berkowitz claimed to be possessed by a demon.

Despite his strange and disturbing delusions, Berkowitz was deemed fit to stand trial by three separate mental health examiners. The defense team wanted to plead not guilty by reason of insanity, but Berkowitz wouldn't agree to it. On May 8, 1978, Berkowitz stood up in court and plead guilty to all of the murders.

After further bizarre behavior at his first sentencing appearance, Berkowitz was given another psychiatric examination. But, once again, he was found to be sane. Therefore, on June 12, 1978, he was sentenced to twenty-five years to life for each murder, and the sentences were to be served consecutively. Incredibly, he was eligible to apply for parole after twenty-five years because of the terms set when he pled guilty.

Outcome

Following his sentencing, Berkowitz spent two months at a psychiatric facility before being sent to Attica prison, one of the toughest correctional facilities in the United States. He stayed there until 1990, when he transferred first to Sullivan Correctional Facility, and eventually to Shawangunk Correctional Facility.

In 1979, Berkowitz was attacked by an inmate, which resulted in a slash to the side of his neck. The wound was so severe it needed more than fifty sutures just to close the gaping laceration. Berkowitz would not identify the person who had attacked him. He instead said he was grateful, that it was a "punishment [he] deserved."

Berkowitz first applied for parole in 2002, which was denied. He tried again in 2016. Despite reports that he was a "model prisoner," his parole was denied again. He remains in prison.

Trivia

Quotes:

- "There are other Sons out there, God help the world."
- "A 'possessed' dog in the neighborhood won't let me stop killing until he gets his fill of blood."
- "I am a monster. I am the Son of Sam. I love to hunt."
- "I always had a fetish for murder and death."
- "I have several children who I'm turning into killers. Wait till they grow up."
- "I didn't want to hurt them, I only wanted to kill them."
- "I was literally singing to myself on my way home, after the killing. The tension, the desire to kill a woman had built up in such explosive proportions that when I finally pulled the trigger, all the pressures, all the tensions, all the hatred, had just vanished, dissipated, but only for a short time."
- "The demons wanted my penis."

PAUL KENNETH BERNARDO

Date of birth: August 27, 1964

Aliases/Nicknames: Paul Jason Teale; The Scarborough Rapist; The Schoolgirl Killer

Characteristics: Rape and murder

Number of victims: 3

Date of murders: December of 1990 - April of 1992

Date of arrest: February 17, 1993

Murder method: Strangulation and drug poisoning

Known Victims: Tammy Homolka, 15; Leslie Mahaffy, 14; Kristen French, 15

Crime location: Ontario, Canada

Status: Sentenced to 25 years, classified as dangerous, so unlikely to be released.

Background

As a young child, Bernardo was often described as a happy boy who was always smiling, despite the chaos surrounding him in his family life. His father Kenneth had been arrested and charged with the molestation of a young girl, and it was found he had also been sexually abusing his daughter. On learning of her husband's deeds, Bernardo's mother fell into a deep depression. Withdrawing herself from the family life around her, she moved into the basement of their house.

When Bernardo was sixteen years old, his mother told him, following an argument she had with his father, that he was the result of an extramarital affair. Bernardo was disgusted by this and began to call his mother terrible names (such as "whore") out in the open, never worrying about who would hear.

After graduating from the Sir Wilfred Laurier Collegiate Institute, Bernardo started working for the company Amway. He became quite fascinated with the motivational tapes and sales culture, and would often practice his selling techniques on women he met in bars. Bernardo started attending the University of Toronto Scarborough. By then he was immersed in dark sexual fantasies, often beating the women he went out with, and he would also enjoy humiliating women out in public.

His path crossed with a young woman named Karla Homolka in October of 1987, and they had an instant sexual attraction. Even better for Bernardo, Karla encouraged his dark fantasies and sadistic sexual behavior. Now he could do what he wanted and indulge in the fantasies that resided in his twisted mind.

Murders

An already established serial rapist, Bernardo's crimes became even more vicious in 1990, with the murder of his sister-in-law. Tammy Homolka was the younger sister of Karla, Bernardo's fiancé, and he flirted with her all the time. He became rather obsessed with the younger girl, and went from looking through her window to going into her bedroom while she was sleeping and masturbating. Karla, eager to please, actually broke the catches on the windows in Tammy's room to make it easier for Bernardo to enter.

On the night of July 24, 1990, Karla cooked dinner and served Tammy's food laced with crushed Valium tablets. She quickly became unconscious, and Karla watched while Bernardo raped her. But this wasn't to be the end of the attacks on Tammy.

The night of December 23, 1990, Tammy was given a rum-eggnog cocktail laced with sleeping pills. Tammy, fifteen, fell quickly into unconsciousness again. But this time, after they had undressed her, Karla placed a cloth soaked with Halothane, an anesthetic, over her nose and mouth. The couple then set up a video camera and filmed themselves as they raped the unconscious girl. At one point, Tammy started vomiting. When attempts to revive her failed, Karla and Bernardo finally called emergency services. But, first, they made sure she was dressed and placed in another room to hide any evidence of what they had done. Tammy never woke up. A few hours later, she was pronounced dead.

Six months later, on June 15, 1991, Bernardo was driving through Burlington when he came across Leslie Mahaffy, fourteen. It was the early hours of the morning and because she had missed her curfew, Leslie had been locked out of the house. Bernardo approached her, and she asked if he had a cigarette. She followed him back to his car and was quickly blindfolded and forced into it.

When they reached Bernardo and Karla's house, the couple began to play out the same ritual they had done with Tammy. They tortured and raped Mahaffy, videotaping the whole event. Her hands were tied, and the blindfold was still in place. But, at one point, she stated the blindfold was slipping, which meant she could see Bernardo and Karla. They continued to rape and torture her through the night.

The next day, Mahaffy was given a lethal dose of the drug Halcion, which (according to Bernardo) was administered by Karla. But Karla had a different story - she claimed the young girl was actually strangled to death by Bernardo. Either way, they now had to dispose of the body. The couple decided to dismember her body and seal the pieces in cement. The next day, Bernardo purchased bags of cement and stupidly kept the receipts.

Using Bernardo's grandfather's circular saw, Mahaffy was cut up and put into cement blocks. They then transported the blocks to Lake Gibson to dump them, making several trips. Some of the blocks were quite heavy. Despite their best efforts, one remained close to the shore, and it was found on June 29, 1991, by a man who was fishing with his son.

The next murder took place on April 16, 1992. The couple was now scouring the streets looking for potential victims, and on this afternoon they saw Kristen French, fifteen, walking along the street. Carrying a map, Karla approached the girl under the ruse of being lost and needing directions. As French attempted to help Karla, Bernardo attacked her from behind at knifepoint and forced her into the car.

French's ordeal lasted longer than the others: She was raped, sodomized, and tortured throughout the three days of Easter weekend. To help subdue her, she was forced to drink vast amounts of alcohol. All of this was videotaped by the couple once again. This time they didn't bothered with a blindfold, so it seemed their intention was to kill her right from the start.

French was executed the next day. Bernardo later claimed Karla had beaten her with a rubber mallet and that French had been accidentally strangled by a noose around her neck that was tied to a chest. Karla, however, claimed Bernardo spent seven minutes strangling the girl while she watched.

When French's nude body was found on April 30, 1992, it was clear that she had been washed and that someone had cut off her hair. Her body was found in a ditch on the side of the road in Burlington. Investigating officers originally thought the hair was cut so the killer could keep a trophy, but Karla later explained it was to try to slow down the identification of the body.

Timeline of murders:

December 23, 1990 - Tammy Homolka, fifteen

June 15, 1991 - Leslie Mahaffy, fourteen

April 16, 1992 - Kristen French, fifteen

Arrest and Trial

Bernardo and Karla had both previously been interviewed by the police on numerous occasions for a variety of reasons, including the death of Tammy, the Scarborough rapes, and Bernardo's habit of stalking women. A report was filed on May 12, 1992, that Bernardo should be interviewed again for the death of French. He was briefly interviewed, with the officers thinking he wasn't likely to be their suspect.

The Green Ribbon Task Force was created three days later to investigate the murders of Mahaffy and French. Bernardo and Karla applied to have their names legally changed to the surname Teale, which was the name of a fictional serial killer from a movie. In December, Karla was beaten by Bernardo and ended up requiring treatment at the local hospital; she decided to press charges against him. Bernardo was arrested but released and Karla went to stay with relatives. By now, DNA testing was being done on the evidence from the crime scenes and samples Bernardo had provided two years prior.

The DNA testing came back as a match, and investigators started surveillance of Bernardo. They interviewed Karla on February 9, 1993, telling her of their suspicions of his involvement in the rapes and murders, but she said nothing—until later that night, when Karla finally confessed everything to the uncle and aunt she had been staying with. Two days later, Karla met with a lawyer and sought full immunity in exchange for her cooperation. But, on February 13, it was decided that full immunity was not a possibility given the level of her involvement.

Bernardo was finally arrested on February 17, 1993. Because of the limitations and specifications of the search warrants, it took investigators seventy-one days to fully search Bernardo's house. They desperately tried to find the videotapes Karla had mentioned but only managed to locate a short tape of Karla involved in oral sex with an unidentified woman. Karla was offered a plea bargain on May 5, 1993, which meant she would only receive a sentence of twelve years if she gave evidence against her husband. She agreed.

Bernardo went to trial in 1995 for the murders of Mahaffy and French. Despite trying to convince the jury that Karla was the actual murderer, or that the deaths had been accidental, he was found guilty on September 1, 1995, of two counts of first-degree murder and two counts of aggravated sexual assault. He was sentenced to life in prison, with the possibility of parole after twenty-five years. However, he was declared a "Dangerous Offender," which means it is unlikely he will ever be paroled.

Outcome

While in prison, Bernardo has been subjected to a number of attacks. He was subsequently moved into a segregation unit for his own safety. Due to the nature of his crimes, it is unlikely that he will ever be released from prison.

Trivia

–   Bernardo was once an Amway salesman
–   Bernardo scored 35/40 on the Psychopathy Checklist
–   Has a degree in accounting
–   While incarcerated, Bernardo wrote and published a book on Amazon in November of 2015 called *A MAD World Order*. It was a graphically violent thriller and, due to public complaints, it was removed from Amazon after becoming a bestseller.

MARIE BESNARD

Date of birth: August 15, 1896

Aliases/Nicknames: The Good Lady of Loudun

Characteristics: Poisoning for financial gain

Number of victims: 0 - 12

Date of murders: 1927 - 1949

Date of arrest: July 21, 1949

Murder method: Arsenic poisoning

Suspected and Known Victims: Auguste Antigny, 33 (her first husband); Marie Lecomte, 86; Toussaint Rivet, 64; Blanche Rivet, 49; Pierre Davaillaud, 78 (her father); Louise Gouin, 92 (her maternal grandmother); Marcellin Besnard, 78 (her stepfather); Marie-Louise Besnard, 68 (her stepmother); Lucie Bodin, 45; Pauline Bodineau, 88; Virginie Lalleron, 83; Marie-Louise Davaillaud, 71 (her mother)

Crime location: Loudun, France

Status: Subsequently acquitted following three trials.

Background

In 1896, Marie Joséphine Philippine Davaillaud was born in Loudun, France. Her parents were considered frugal, and she attended a convent school for her education. Those who went to school with Marie described her as immoral, vicious, a thief, and a girl who ran wild with the boys.

In 1920, Marie married Auguste Antigny, her cousin, and they remained married until his death in 1927. Marie quickly went on to marry Léon Besnard in 1928. The couple soon realized that any chance of gaining a fortune was out of their hands until their relatives died. How surprising it was that, not long afterwards, various relatives died, leaving their wealth to Marie and Léon.

Murders

Not long after Léon's parents inherited a lot of money, they were invited to live with Léon and Marie. Soon after, Léon's father died of poisoning, supposedly from eating the wrong kind of mushrooms. Just three months later, his mother also died; the cause was given as pneumonia.

The couple ended up subletting some rooms to a couple who were wealthy and without children. The Rivets, Toussaint and Blanche, were friends of Léon's. On July 14, 1939, Toussaint died from pneumonia, and in December of 1941, Blanche died due to aortitis. In their will, Marie was listed as their only heir.

Marie was also named beneficiary on the wills held by her cousins Pauline Bodineau and Virginie Lalleron. On July 1, 1945, Pauline, who was eighty-eight, apparently mistook a bowl of lethal lye for a bowl of dessert and died. A week later, Virginie suffered an identical fate when she allegedly did exactly the same thing. Six months later, on January 16, 1946, Marie's mother, Marie-Louise Davaillaud also died.

At one point, Marie discovered Léon had been having an affair with another woman. Léon claimed to a friend that he thought Marie was poisoning him. He asserted that she had served him soup one night but there was already liquid in the bowl before she poured the soup. Shortly afterwards, on October 25, 1947, Léon was dead. The cause given was uremia.

Because of the claims of poisoning Léon had made, the gendarmerie ordered an investigation and an autopsy was conducted. The forensic surgeon found that Léon's body contained 19.45 mg of arsenic. Marie was promptly arrested and all other suspicious deaths associated with her were exhumed and re-examined. This led to Marie being charged with thirteen counts of murder.

Arrest and Trial

The autopsy reports showed that each victim had been poisoned by arsenic slowly over a period of time. At that time though, it was difficult to prove this. Toxicology was a relatively new science and Beroud, the forensic surgeon, had difficulty explaining his results and defending them when questioned on the stand by the defense lawyers. For this reason, the first two trials resulted in no conviction.

Besnard was placed on trial a third time in 1961. However, the defense was once again successful in undermining the relevance of the arsenic evidence, and Marie was acquitted of all of the murders.

Outcome

Although in today's legal system Marie would most likely have been convicted based on the autopsy findings, it wasn't the case in 1961. It may seem that she shouldn't be considered a serial killer without a conviction, but the evidence suggests otherwise, and she has therefore earned her place in this book.

Marie Besnard died in 1980, presumably from natural causes. She remained a free woman until her death.

KENNETH ALESSIO BIANCHI AND ANGELO BUONO

Date of birth: May 22, 1951; October 5, 1934

Aliases/Nicknames: The Hillside Strangler

Characteristics: Kidnapping, torture, rape, murder

Number of victims: 12

Date of murders: 1977 - 1979

Date of arrest: January 13, 1979; October 22, 1979

Murder method: Strangulation

Known Victims: Yolanda Washington, 19; Judith Ann Miller, 15; Lissa Kastin, 21; Jane King, 28; Delores Cepeda, 12; Sonja Johnson, 14; Kristin Weckler, 20; Lauren Wagner, 18; Kimberley Martin, 17; Cindy Lee Hudspeth, 20; Karen Mandic, 22; Diane Wilder, 27

Crime location: Los Angeles County, California

Status: Life in prison for Bianchi, and life without parole for Buono. Buono died in prison on September 21, 2002, due to natural causes.

Background

Kenneth Alessio Bianchi

As half of what would later become a well-known killing duo, Kenneth Alessio Bianchi was born in Rochester New York, in 1951. His mother was a prostitute and an alcoholic, and he was given up for adoption when he was less than two weeks old. Within a few months, he was adopted by Nicholas Bianchi and Frances Scioliono-Bianchi, who was the sister of Angelo Buono's mother.

From a very young age, Bianchi was described as being a compulsive liar, and his mother would say "he had risen from the cradle dissembling." According to witnesses, Bianchi would go into a trancelike state, where he would be unresponsive and his eyes would roll back. He was subsequently diagnosed with petit mal epilepsy. He also had a problem with urination and was subjected to a number of doctors' visits and physical examinations, where his genitals were scrutinized, poked, and prodded, which Bianchi found humiliating.

Bianchi suffered from terrible "fits of anger," and his behavior led to multiple appointments with a psychiatrist. When he was ten years old he was diagnosed with a form of passive-aggressive personality disorder. A year later, his IQ was measured and found to be 116, which was above average. Even so, he underachieved at school and did not get along with his teachers, which led to him changing schools twice.

When his father died in 1964, Bianchi showed no emotion. The loss of her husband meant that Bianchi's mother had to go to work, and often she would keep him home for extended periods of time. However, he still managed to graduate from high school in 1971.

Bianchi married not long after he graduated, but his wife left him after several months. He enrolled in college but only managed one semester before dropping out. From there, he drifted from job to job, until he landed work at a jewelry store as a security guard. This job enabled him to steal, and his girlfriends and the prostitutes he frequented were often the recipients of the valuables he lifted.

In 1977, Bianchi moved to Los Angeles, where he began to spend a lot of his time with his cousin, Angelo Buono. Buono was a lot older than Bianchi, and the younger man was impressed by the clothes and jewelry his cousin wore, as well as his ability to date many women. The men decided to work together as pimps, but this was only the beginning of what was yet to come.

Angelo Buono

Like Bianchi, Buono was born in Rochester, New York. His parents were first-generation immigrants from Italy. They eventually divorced, and Buono moved to Glendale, California with his mother. From a young age, Buono developed a loathing toward women, though it is unknown why. Despite this, he married several women, and sired numerous children. Buono displayed shocking brutality toward the women in his life.

In 1975, Buono had a successful auto-upholstery business, and he used this to help him lure young girls so he could rape them. When his cousin Bianchi turned up on his doorstep, they quickly discovered that they had similar fantasies about raping and murdering women.

Murders

On their own, both men were dangerous individuals. But together, they made a terrifying, sadistic, and lethal combination. They would drive around the Los Angeles streets at night, pretending to be undercover police officers, and showing their fake badges to women they came across. Then, they would demand the women get into Buono's car, which they claimed was an unmarked police car, and take them back to Buono's home under false pretenses.

Their victims came from all walks of life, and the youngest was just twelve years old when they murdered her. Both men took great joy in sexually abusing and torturing their victims before ending their lives, usually by strangulation. Their victims were subjected to vile and sadistic torture, including electric shocks, injections with chemicals, and poisoning with carbon monoxide gas.

While Bianchi and Buono were picking women up and murdering them, Bianchi actually applied to be a police officer. He had even been on several "ride-alongs" with officers to gain experience and insight into the job. Some of these trips even involved the search for the Hillside Strangler. If only the authorities had known he was sitting in the back seat of their police car the whole time.

One evening, after they had already successfully murdered ten women, Bianchi told Buono about the ride-alongs he had been on with the police, and how he was actually being questioned about the murdered women. Buono was furious and told Bianchi that if he didn't move to Bellingham, he would kill him. So, Bianchi moved to Bellingham in 1978.

In Bellingham, Bianchi worked as a security guard. On January 11, 1979, he lured two young female students to a house he was meant to be guarding. He made the first woman go down the stairs, where he promptly strangled her, and then he repeated the process with the second victim.

But Bianchi wasn't as clever as Buono, and he left a lot of clues at the scene. This evidence led to his arrest the following day. Once under arrest, Bianchi opened his mouth and confessed that he and Buono had once tried to abduct a woman but had let her go. Now he had alerted the police to Buono's involvement.

Timeline of murders:

October 17, 1977 - Yolanda Washington, nineteen

October 31, 1977 - Judith Lynn Miller, fifteen

November 6, 1977 - Lissa Kastin, twenty-one

November 10, 1977 - Jane King, twenty-eight

November 13, 1977 - Dolores Cepeda, twelve

November 13, 1977 - Sonja Johnson, fourteen

November 20, 1977 - Kristina Weckler, twenty

November 29, 1977 - Lauren Wagner, eighteen

December 9, 1977 - Kimberley Martin, seventeen

February 16, 1978 - Cindy Lee Hudspeth, twenty

January 11, 1979 - Karen Mandic, twenty-two

January 11, 1979 - Diane Wilder, twenty-seven

Arrest and Trial

Buono was arrested based on Bianchi's confessions, and their trials for the murders were set. Bianchi, trying to convince the authorities that he had another personality, pleaded not guilty by reason of insanity. He claimed this other personality, "Steve Walker," was the one who had committed the murders. Initially, psychiatric assessments led to the conclusion that he was indeed suffering from a multiple personality disorder.

The investigators then brought in another psychiatrist to assess Bianchi and he came up with a different opinion. While speaking with Bianchi, the psychiatrist told him that people with multiple personality disorder usually have three or more personalities. Immediately, Bianchi created another personality and his ruse was blown. When confronted, he admitted he had faked it all. He was, however, later diagnosed with antisocial personality disorder.

During his trial, the defense team brought forward Veronica Compton, whom Bianchi had started a relationship with while he was in prison. She lied, telling a false story about the crimes in an effort to show Bianchi was innocent. At one point, she admitted she wanted to buy a mortuary along with another convicted murderer so they could indulge in necrophilia. Compton went so far as to try to strangle a woman in a motel room in an attempt to make authorities think the Hillside Strangler was still out on the loose. She had even been given some semen by Bianchi to plant on the victim. But, all of her attempts failed. The woman survived, and she herself ended up being convicted and imprisoned for attempted murder.

In an effort to make his sentence more lenient, Bianchi agreed to testify against his cousin Buono. But, when it came time to testify, he made the whole process as difficult as possible, contradicting himself and being downright uncooperative. He was convicted of the murders and received a life sentence.

Buono's trial became one of the longest in legal history in the United States, and ran from November of 1981 to November of 1983. Despite Bianchi's efforts to help get the charges against Buono dismissed, or to at least get him a lighter sentence, Buono was convicted of committing nine murders. He was sentenced to life imprisonment without the possibility of parole.

Outcome

Bianchi tried to sue a woman in 1992 for using his face on a trading card. He claimed that his face was his trademark. Therefore, he wanted $8.5 million in compensation. The case was dismissed, and the judge stated that "if Bianchi had been using his face as a trademark when he was killing women, he would not have tried to hide it."

Bianchi was eligible for parole in 2010, but it was denied on August 18. He can apply for parole again in 2025.

On September 21, 2002, Buono was found deceased in his cell, having suffered a fatal heart attack.

Trivia

Bianchi:

- Bianchi wed a Louisiana pen pal in September of 1989 in a prison chapel ceremony.
- Actors who have portrayed him include: Billy Zane, C. Thomas Howell, Clifton Collins Jr., and Jeff Marchelletta.
- Has a measured IQ of 116, signifying above-average intelligence.

Buono:

- In 2007, Christopher Buono, his grandson, shot and killed his grandmother and then committed suicide. Christopher hadn't known who his grandfather actually was until 2005.
- Actors who have portrayed Buono include: Dennis Farina, Nicholas Turturro, and Tomas Arana.
- Buono married Christine Kizuka in 1986 while he was incarcerated.
- His hero and role model was the famed criminal, Caryl Chessman.

BIBLE JOHN

Date of birth: Unknown
Aliases/Nicknames: Bible John
Characteristics: Rape, beating, murder
Number of victims: 3
Date of murders: February 22, 1968 – October 31, 1969
Date of arrest: Unknown suspect
Murder method: Strangulation
Known Victims: Patricia Docker, 25; Jemima McDonald, 32; Helen Puttock, 29
Crime location: Glasgow, Scotland
Status: Unsolved

Background

Between the years of 1968 and 1969, three young women were murdered in Glasgow, Scotland, after attending the Barrowland Ballroom. Although it was quickly established that these murders were the work of just one man, there were no clues left behind at the scenes to indicate who the murderer could be. There have been a number of suspects over the years, and one man in particular was at the top of the suspect list. However, Bible John's true identity has never been uncovered, and the case remains a mystery.

Murders

The nude body of Patricia Docker, twenty-five, was found in a lane by a man on his way to work, on February 23, 1968. She was only meters away from her home. The night before she had told her parents she was going to a dance at the Majestic Ballroom, a club on Hope Street in Glasgow, Scotland. But, she also went to the Barrowland Ballroom which was hosting a twenty-five-and-older night. Her autopsy showed she had been raped and strangled, and it was believed she may have met her killer at the Barrowland. Despite extensive searching, her clothes and bag were never found.

How the next victim's body was found is truly tragic. Jemima McDonald was a thirty-two-year-old mother of three children who had gone to the Barrowland Ballroom on Friday, August 15, 1969. The next day, her sister Margaret heard children talking about a body they had seen in an old building. At first, she didn't pay too much attention. But on Monday, there was still no sign of her sister, so Margaret decided to investigate the rumors she had heard from the children. Inside the building, she found the fully clothed body of her sister Jemima. Her autopsy showed she had been raped, beaten, and strangled.

Witnesses came forward saying they had seen Jemima leaving Barrowland around midnight that Friday with a young man who was slim, tall, and had red hair. Further investigations uncovered a witness who claimed she had heard screaming coming from the old building the night Jemima was killed, but she was unable to say what time she had heard it, so the police didn't consider it important.

The third known victim was Helen Puttock, twenty-nine, who was found in her own back garden on October 31, 1969. Like the others, she had also attended the Barrowland Ballroom on the night she was killed. She and her sister Jean had met two men there, one of whom was called John and was supposedly from Castlemilk. The other man didn't disclose who he was or where he was from. When they left the ballroom, John went off to catch a bus, and the other man joined Helen and Jean in getting a taxi. According to Jean, the man was very well-spoken and liked to quote from the Bible, which is why the killer ended up being called "Bible John." Jean was dropped off at her home in Knightswood and the taxi headed for the direction of Helen's home in Scotstoun.

Helen had been raped and strangled, just like the others. Her handbag had been upended nearby, the contents scattered, but the bag itself was missing. She had grass stains on her feet, which showed she most likely tried to get away from her killer. There was also a human bite mark on one of her legs.

Each of the women killed was menstruating at the time of their murder. The killer had placed sanitary napkins or tampons either on the bodies or near them.

Suspects

Jean's description of the man in the taxi:

- Well-dressed and well-spoken
- Slim
- Red/fair hair
- Said his name was "John Templeton" or "Sempleson"
- Quoted from the Bible
- Aged between twenty-five to thirty
- Height around five feet ten inches

But, the bouncers who had been working at the Barrowland Ballroom that night gave a completely different description of the man who had left in the taxi with Helen and Jean. Their description was:

- Short
- Well-spoken
- Jet-black hair

The police were inclined to believe the description given by the bouncers because Jean had been intoxicated at the time. She denied being drunk during the taxi ride and stood by her description of the man she believed attacked and killed her sister. There actually was a sighting of a man matching Jean's description who got off a bus at Gray Street around 1:30 a.m. that morning. He was described as looking disheveled, and it seemed he had scratch marks on his face.

One suspect the police considered later was John Irvine McInnes. He had served with the Scots Guards and committed suicide in 1980. In 1996, his body was exhumed so DNA testing could be carried out, but the results came back as inconclusive. It's not clear why he was considered a suspect. In the end, the authorities deemed there was not enough other evidence to pin the murders on McInnes.

In 2004, a DNA sample taken from a minor crime scene came back as an 80 percent match to the sample obtained from Bible John's murders. This led police to consider that the person responsible for the murders was most likely related to the man charged with the minor crime. However, nothing further has come from this angle.

The most well-known suspect is Peter Tobin, who is mentioned in this book. He came to light as a potential suspect after being arrested and charged with murder in 2007. The reasons why he is suspected are as follows:

Early photos of Tobin are very similar to the Identi-Kit picture of Bible John

Tobin's ex-wives all claimed to have been throttled, raped, and beaten by him

Tobin had been living in Glasgow at the time and moved away in 1969

He used to frequent the Barrowland Ballroom

Tobin met his first wife at the ballroom at the same time the murders stopped

Tobin had strong religious views and was a Roman Catholic

Tobin became enraged by a woman's menstrual cycle

During the police investigation Operation Anagram, a woman came forward and claimed she had met Tobin at the Barrowland in 1968 and he had raped her. In 2010, another woman came forward and said she had met Tobin at the Barrowland and it was a "threatening experience." He persistently tried to get her to accompany him to a party in Castlemilk, but she refused. When she saw pictures of Tobin in 2010, she was certain that he was Bible John.

Unfortunately, it is unlikely there will ever be a DNA match with Tobin. According to police, the original samples from the crime scenes hadn't been stored correctly and had deteriorated. Helen's sister Jean, who provided the most widely accepted description of Bible John, passed away in 2010, never knowing who really killed her sister.

Trivia

- There are fifty thousand witness statements in the files, over one thousand suspects have been interviewed, and one hundred plus detectives have been on the case.

RICHARD BIEGENWALD

Date of birth: August 24, 1940

Aliases/Nicknames: The Thrill Killer

Characteristics: Robbery and murder

Number of victims: 6 - 9 +

Date of murders: 1958; 1981-1982

Date of arrest: January 22, 1983

Murder method: Shooting, stabbing

Known Victims: Stephen Sladowski, 47 (store owner); Maria Ciallella, 17; Deborah Osborne, 17; Betsy Bacon, 17; Anna Olesiewicz, 18; William J. Ward, 34 (drug dealer); John P. Petrone, 57

Crime location: New York, New Jersey

Status: Death sentence commuted to life. Died in prison on March 10, 2008, due to natural causes.

Background

Richard Biegenwald had a terrible start in life at the hands of his alcoholic father. Born in Rockland County, New York, Biegenwald was regularly beaten by his father. By the time he was five years old, serious problems were starting to emerge. It was at this age that Biegenwald set fire to the family home and was sent to the Rockland County Psychiatric Center for observation.

Biegenwald was not only gambling by the age of eight, but also drinking alcohol. He continued to receive psychiatric treatment, and when he was nine years old, he was subjected to electroshock therapy at Bellevue Hospital in New York. Following this treatment, he was sent to the State Training School for Boys, also in New York. He was no model student. While there, he was accused of inciting escape attempts among the other inmates and was frequently accused of theft.

Biegenwald would steal money from his mother when he visited her, and during a visit when he was eleven, he set himself on fire. At the age of sixteen, he was released from the State Training School so he could attend regular high school. This lasted only a few weeks before he dropped out. Not long afterwards, he moved to Nashville, Tennessee.

During the two years he lived in Nashville, Biegenwald stole a car and was arrested by federal agents in Kentucky for driving a stolen vehicle across state lines. When he was released by the authorities in Kentucky, he went to Staten Island, where he proceeded to steal another car. This time, he drove it to a grocery store in Bayonne, New Jersey, and attempted to rob the business. It was during this robbery that Biegenwald committed his first murder.

Murders

The first murder took place in Bayonne, New Jersey on December 18, 1958, during a robbery. Biegenwald and an accomplice held up a grocery store, and Biegenwald shot and killed Stephen Sladowski, the proprietor. Despite fleeing the state immediately after the murder, Biegenwald was tracked down two days later and arrested. He was taken back to New Jersey and subsequently convicted of murder, for which he was given a life sentence. But, after seventeen years of good behavior, Biegenwald was released in 1975.

Between the years 1978 and April of 1982, there were at least three more murders, but Biegenwald wasn't linked to these until much later on. In June of 1978, John P. Petrone, a former police informant and ex-convict, was shot to death at an old abandoned airport in Flemington, New Jersey. On November 1, 1981, Maria Ciallella was murdered by Biegenwald and buried at his mother's property. Then, on April 8, 1982, Biegenwald stabbed Deborah Osbourne to death. Her body was buried on top of Ciallella's at Biegenwald's mother's home.

On August 28, 1982, Anna Olesiewicz was walking along the boardwalk in Asbury Park when she came across Biegenwald. He lured the young woman into his car and shot her four times in the head. Her body was dumped in a wooded area behind the local Burger King on Route 35 in January of 1983, where it was then found by a group of children.

Biegenwald was also suspected of killing Virginia Clayton, a seventeen-year-old girl who was abducted and murdered on September 8, 1982. Three days later her body was found, just four miles away from where Petrone had been buried. Although suspected, Biegenwald has never been charged with this murder.

William Ward also went missing in September of 1982. A friend of Biegenwald's, Ward was a prison escapee and a drug dealer. His body was found in a shallow grave at a cemetery; he had been shot four times in the head.

Known victims:

1958 - Stephen Sladowski—shot to death after a robbery attempt in Bayonne, New Jersey.

June of 1978 - John P. Petrone—shot to death at an abandoned airport in Flemington, New Jersey.

November 1, 1981 - Maria Ciallella—shot and dismembered. She was buried at Biegenwald's mother's house.

April 8, 1982 - Deborah Osbourne—stabbed to death. She was buried on top of Ciallella's body at Biegenwald's mother's house.

August 28, 1982 - Anna Olesiewicz— shot four times in the head after being lured away from the Asbury Park boardwalk. Her body was left behind a Burger King in Ocean Township, NJ.

September of 1982 -William Ward—drug dealer shot and killed by Biegenwald at his home in Asbury Park.

Arrest and Trial

Biegenwald came under investigation after a friend of his wife's reported to the police that he had shown her a dead woman's body in his garage in Asbury Park. On January 22, 1983, police surrounded the home Biegenwald shared with his friend Dherran Fitzgerald. They created a ruse to get Biegenwald out of the house. Once he stepped out, officers grabbed him. Fitzgerald tried to hide in one of the rooms, but police found him and arrested him as well.

While Fitzgerald was being interviewed, he told officers that Biegenwald had shown him the dead body of a young woman in his garage. The body was then taken to the area behind the Burger King and dumped. He also admitted to helping Biegenwald take another body to his mother's house. They had buried it in the basement and, during this dig, they unearthed another body that had been there a while. All in all, Fitzgerald showed police where to find three other victims, as well as the two buried at Biegenwald's mother's house.

Despite there being nine known victims, there was only enough evidence to charge Biegenwald with five counts of murder in the first degree. At his trial, he was convicted on all counts and sentenced to death. However, his sentence was later overturned, and he was instead sentenced to four life sentences without the possibility of parole.

Outcome

On March 10, 2008, Biegenwald was transferred from the penitentiary to a local medical center, where he died of natural causes. An autopsy determined he had suffered from kidney and respiratory failure.

ARTHUR GARY BISHOP

Date of birth: September 29, 1952

Aliases/Nicknames: Roger Downs, Lynn Jones

Characteristics: Pedophilia

Number of victims: 5

Date of murders: 1979 - 1983

Date of arrest: July 24, 1983

Murder method: Drowning, beating with hammer

Known Victims: Alonzo Daniels, age 4; Kim Peterson, age 11; Danny Davis, age 4; Troy Ward, age 6; Graeme Cunningham, age 13

Crime location: Salt Lake City, Utah

Status: Executed by lethal injection on June 9, 1988

Background

Bishop was born in Hinckley, Utah, and would become the eldest of six brothers. The children were raised in a devout Latter-day Saint (also known as Mormon) household, and when Bishop was nineteen, he served as a religious missionary in the Philippines.

This former honor student and Eagle Scout was first arrested in 1978 for embezzlement. He received a five-year suspended sentence, but he skipped his parole and took off to Salt Lake City. While there, he assumed the alias Roger Downs. Following his conviction for the embezzlement, Bishop was excommunicated by the Latter-day Saints church.

As Roger Downs, Bishop joined the "Big Brother" program, where adult men take on the role of big brother to underprivileged children, or those who need a good male role model. There were never any suspicions that Bishop may have been abusing the children he cared for in the program. But, when he was later arrested for murder, dozens of these children came forward and accused him of abuse.

Murders

Bishop's first victim, Alonzo Daniels, was killed on October 14, 1979, after Bishop had lured the young boy away from his apartment. At the promise of candy, Alonzo willingly went into Bishop's apartment. Bishop tried to assault the boy sexually, then drowned him in the bathtub. He buried the boy's body in the desert.

Bishop used a similar method to lure Kim Peterson to his apartment. Kim, eleven, had been at a skating rink trying to sell a pair of roller skates, and Bishop feigned interest in buying them. Once they were at his apartment, Bishop killed Kim by bludgeoning him to death. His body was buried in the same area as Alonzo Daniels. Bishop was questioned about this disappearance as a matter of routine, but he wasn't considered a suspect.

On October 20, 1981, Bishop managed to lure another very young boy away from a supermarket. Danny Davis, who was just four years old, went with Bishop back to his apartment. His disappearance resulted in a massive search and manhunt, but witnesses could only give vague descriptions of the man they had seen with Danny.

Troy Ward, six, was abducted by Bishop on June 22, 1983. He was taken from a park to Bishop's apartment. Again, witnesses saw the man with Troy but couldn't identify him. Like the other boys, Troy was sexually assaulted, bludgeoned, and then drowned in the bathtub.

Suddenly, Bishop's killing escalated. He claimed his next victim just a month after Troy's murder. On July 14, Graeme Cunningham, thirteen, disappeared from his neighborhood. This time, Bishop made a critical error. It was known that Graeme was about to go on a camping trip with a friend, and they had a male chaperone coming with them - Arthur Bishop. This led police to take a closer look at Bishop. They discovered that he had lived in the vicinity of four of the missing children and that he was also friends with Graeme's parents.

Timeline of murders:

October 14, 1979 - Alonzo Daniels, four

November 8, 1980 - Kim Peterson, eleven

October 20, 1981 - Danny Davis, four

June 22, 1983 - Troy Ward, six

July 14, 1983 - Graeme Cunningham, thirteen

Arrest and Trial

Bishop was brought to the police station for questioning, but he was led to believe that he was simply helping the police with their inquiries into the disappearance of Graeme Cunningham. At the time, Bishop had been using the name "Roger Downs." Once they were able to convince him to give them his real name, it didn't take long for him to make his confession.

Bishop confessed to killing all five children. The day after his arrest, he took police to the desert area of Cedar Fort where three of the bodies were buried, and to Big Cottonwood Creek where he had buried the other two bodies. Bishop told the police that he enjoyed killing because it gave him a thrill, and he would do it again.

His trial began on February 27, 1984. The trial lasted until March 19, 1984, and Bishop was found guilty of five counts of aggravated murder, five counts of aggravated kidnapping, and one count of sexually abusing a minor. Bishop was sentenced to death, and he requested that his execution be done by lethal injection.

Outcome

On June 10, 1988, Bishop was executed by lethal injection at the Utah State Prison. Just before he was put to death, he professed his remorse for the crimes he had committed. He spent his last day reading Mormon scriptures, resting, and meeting with his lawyer, a biographer, a psychologist, and a bishop. He refused his last meal, deciding to fast on his last day on earth.

Bishop was taken into the execution chamber about thirty minutes before midnight, and by 12:15 a.m. he was pronounced dead. Unlike most other death row inmates, Bishop was tired of all the tediousness involved in trying to get his sentence commuted. He had stopped all final appeals and was ready to die.

Trivia

- Bishop tried to claim that his addiction to child pornography had led him to act out his violent fantasies.
- Final statement before his execution: "Jesus, thou Son of God, have mercy on my soul."
- He said to a prison psychologist: "I don't want to die, but I think it's necessary."

Portion of letter written by Bishop to explain why he committed the murders:

"I am a homosexual paedophile convicted of murder, and pornography was a determining factor in my downfall. Somehow, I became sexually attracted to young boys and I would fantasize about them naked. Certain bookstores offered sex education, photographic, or art books which occasionally contained pictures of nude boys. I purchased such books and used them to enhance my masturbatory fantasies... Finding and procuring sexually arousing materials became an obsession. For me, seeing pornography was lighting a fuse on a stick of dynamite. I became stimulated and had to gratify my urges or explode. All boys became mere sexual objects. My conscience was desensitized, and my sexual appetite entirely controlled my actions."

LAWRENCE SIGMUND BITTAKER AND ROY LEWIS NORRIS

Date of birth: September 27, 1940; February 2, 1948

Aliases/Nicknames: The Tool Box Killer, Pliers

Characteristics: Kidnap, torture, rape, murder

Number of victims: 5

Date of murders: June - October of 1979

Date of arrest: November 20, 1979; November 23, 1979

Murder method: Strangulation by ligature

Known Victims: Cindy Schaeffer, 16; Andrea Hall, 18; Jacqueline Lamp, 13; Jackie Gilliam, 15; Shirley Ledford, 16

Crime location: California

Status: Bittaker was sentenced to death, awaiting execution. Norris received a sentence of 45 years to life.

Background

Lawrence Sigmund Bittaker

Following his birth in 1940, Bittaker was placed in an orphanage by his parents, who had never wanted to have children. He was adopted as an infant by George Bittaker and his wife. Because of his adoptive father's work in aircraft factories, the family moved around regularly throughout Bittaker's childhood.

The first time Bittaker came to the attention of the police was at twelve years of age, when he was caught and arrested for shoplifting. During the next four years, he would be arrested multiple times for the very same crime. Bittaker would later claim that all the thefts he committed as a child were a way to make up for the lack of love and affection from his parents.

Bittaker was very intelligent, but he found school to be a bore. So, in 1957 he dropped out. The family was now living in California. Within a year of dropping out of high school, he had been arrested for a hit and run, auto theft, and evading arrest. He was subsequently sent to the California Youth Authority and would remain there until he turned eighteen.

When Bittaker was released, he discovered that not only had his adoptive parents moved to another state, but they had also disowned him. He never saw them again.

Roy Norris

Norris was born out of wedlock in Colorado in 1948, though his parents later married. At that time in society there was a lot of negative stigma surrounding illegitimate births, so the marriage was a way of saving face for the parents and, ultimately, the child.

The entire family lived very close together thanks to Norris's grandfather who was involved in real estate. His mother was a drug-addicted housewife, and his father worked in a scrapyard. Norris was frequently placed in the care of foster families throughout his childhood, but he did live with his parents from time to time.

When Norris was sixteen, during one of the periods he was living with his parents, he was visiting a female family member and started to talk to her in a sexually suggestive manner. Upset, she made him leave the house and promptly informed Norris' father of what had happened. His father threatened to beat him. In response, Norris took his father's car, made his way into the Rocky Mountains, and tried to commit suicide by using a syringe to inject air into his artery. Of course, his attempt failed, and he was later found by police as a runaway and returned to his parents.

After he dropped out of school, Norris enlisted with the Navy and was stationed in San Diego from 1965 to 1969. When he was twenty-one he was deployed to Vietnam, but he did not see any active combat during his four months there. He did, however, experiment with marijuana and heroin in Vietnam, and he became a regular marijuana user from then onward.

Murders

Bittaker and Norris made several trips picking up female hitchhikers and then letting them go, so they could perfect their techniques for when the time came to carry out their murderous fantasies. They outfitted their van by building a bed in the back which had tools, clothes, and a cooler with drinks and beer in it underneath. On the day of June 24, 1979, they had been hanging out at the beach, smoking marijuana and drinking beer and trying to flirt with the girls there.

That evening, they saw Lucinda Schaefer walking down a side street after leaving a church meeting. They tried to convince her to get in the van by offering her a lift home or some marijuana, but she refused. They drove a little ways ahead of her, and then Norris got out and waited for her to walk past. He then grabbed her and dragged her into the van. While Norris tied up her arms and legs and gagged her, Bittaker increased the radio's volume to drown out any sounds coming from the back.

Disturbingly, Bittaker kept a written record of what transpired that night. He wrote the following about Lucinda's demeanor in the van: "displayed a magnificent state of self-control and composed acceptance of the conditions of which she had no control. She shed no tears, offered no resistance and expressed no great concern for her safety ... I guess she knew what was coming."

Norris was the first to rape Lucinda while Bittaker went for a walk. When Bittaker returned, he raped her while Norris went for a walk. When it came time to decide what to do with her, they apparently argued, with each one later giving a different story as to who wanted to kill her and who wanted to let her go. Regardless, Norris tried to strangle her, but he couldn't handle the look in her eyes; he ended up running off and vomiting. Bittaker strangled her until she collapsed, but she was convulsing and still not dead. He then took a wire coat hanger and twisted it around her neck with a pair of vise-grip pliers until she stopped convulsing. Bittaker and Norris wrapped Lucinda's body in a plastic shower curtain and then threw her over a canyon. According to Norris, Bittaker told him the wild animals would eat her so there would be no evidence.

While driving along the Pacific Coast Highway on July 8, 1979, Bittaker and Norris came across Andrea Joy Hall hitchhiking. They slowed down, planning to offer her a ride, but they were beaten to it by someone else. This didn't stop Bittaker and Norris though. They continued to follow the vehicle until they got to Redondo Beach and she got out of the car.

While Norris was hiding in the van, Bittaker offered her a soft drink and told her it was in the cooler in the back of the van. As she got the drink, Norris pounced on her. Although she put up a good fight, he was able to subdue her by twisting her arm behind her back. She was then gagged and tied at the ankles and wrists, and they drove to a secluded area in the San Gabriel Mountains.

Andrea was raped twice by Bittaker and once by Norris. At one point, Norris thought he saw car headlights coming toward them. Bittaker quickly dragged her into the bushes and Norris drove off to see if he could find the car. Having no luck, he returned and they decided to travel to another location in the mountains. Andrea was forced to walk up a hill, completely naked, and perform oral sex on Bittaker. He then forced her to pose for some photographs.

They moved on to a third location, and she was made to walk up another hill with Bittaker. In the meantime, Norris went to a store nearby and bought some alcohol. When he came back, Bittaker was by himself. He showed Norris two more photographs he had taken of Andrea after he had told her he was going to kill her. He rammed an ice pick into her ear, piercing her brain, and then turned her over and did the same in the other ear. He actually stomped on the ice pick until the handle broke, but, remarkably, she was still alive. So he then had to strangle her to death before he threw her body over a cliff.

Jacqueline Leah Lamp and Jackie Doris Gilliam were sitting at a bus stop when Bittaker and Norris noticed them. It was September 3, and the two girls had been hitchhiking before they decided to take a rest at the bus stop. When Bittaker and Norris pulled up to the girls and offered them a ride, they got into the van. Almost immediately, Norris offered them some marijuana, and they didn't say no. However, they noticed Bittaker was heading in a different direction than what they had discussed and the girls started to protest.

Jacqueline tried to open the sliding door of the van, but was hit on the head by Norris with a bag of lead weights. She was knocked unconscious—but only briefly. He then gained control of Jackie. As Norris was gagging and tying her up, Jacqueline woke up and again tried to get out of the van. He dragged her back in, and Bittaker—aware the struggle could potentially be seen by witnesses—stopped the van and jumped in the back to help Norris finish gagging and tying up the two girls.

For two days, the girls were repeatedly raped and physically abused. At one point, Jackie's breasts were stabbed with an ice pick, and a pair of vise-grip pliers was used to tear off part of her nipple. Once again, Bittaker walked one of the girls, Jacqueline, up a hill and made her pose for nude photographs. He also allegedly made a tape recording of himself as he raped Jackie, and he forced her to say she was his cousin.

Then it came time to murder their captives. Jackie had an ice pick rammed into each ear and was subsequently strangled. Jacqueline was struck on the head by a sledgehammer wielded by Norris as Bittaker strangled her. At one point, Bittaker thought she was dead. But she opened her eyes, so he strangled her again while Norris struck her multiple times with the sledgehammer. Like the other girls before them, the bodies of Jackie and Jacqueline were thrown over an embankment.

Timeline of murders:

June 24, 1979 - Lucinda "Cindy" Schaefer, sixteen

July 8, 1979 - Andrea Joy Hall, eighteen

September 3, 1979 - Jackie Doris Gilliam, fifteen

September 3, 1979 - Jacqueline Leah Lamp, thirteen

October 31, 1979 - Shirley Lynette Ledford, sixteen

Arrest and Trial

Norris met up with a former prison inmate, Jimmy Dalton, in November of 1979, and confided in him about the murders he had committed with Bittaker. Dalton talked to his attorney about now being privy to this information and he was advised to notify the police. The information was then passed on to the Redondo Beach police, and detectives set about investigating the claims Norris had made.

An investigator visited a rape survivor who quickly identified the mug shots of Bittaker and Norris. They placed the men under surveillance, and Norris was arrested on November 20, for parole violation. At the same time, Bittaker was arrested for the rape of a woman called Robeck.

On November 30, Norris ended up confessing to the rate at a preliminary hearing. He told the court how they lured the girls to the van and then how they killed them, but he insinuated that the main culprit was Bittaker, and that he was just an accomplice.

Norris pleaded guilty to four counts of first-degree murder in March of 1980, as well as two counts of rape, and one of robbery. Norris was sentenced to forty-five years to life on May 7, 1980, with the possibility of parole in 2010.

Bittaker was arraigned on April 24, 1980, for twenty-nine charges of kidnapping, sodomy, murder, and rape, as well as charges regarding possession of a firearm and criminal conspiracy. On February 17, 1981, the jury found him guilty of five counts of murder, five charges of kidnapping, nine charges of rape, two charges of forcible oral copulation, one charge of sodomy, one charge of conspiracy to commit murder, and three charges of unlawful possession of a firearm.

Bittaker was subsequently sentenced to death for his crimes.

Outcome

Bittaker was originally meant to be executed on December 29, 1989, but this date was suspended after he appealed the decision. The Supreme Court upheld the death penalty and a new date was scheduled for July 23, 1991. Once again, Bittaker appealed and he was granted a stay on July 9, 1991. He is currently awaiting his execution while he remains incarcerated in San Quentin State Prison.

Trivia

Bittaker

- Described by FBI Special Agent John Douglas as the most disturbing individual upon whom he has ever performed a criminal profile.
- Before being convicted of murder, he served time for robbery, assault, motor vehicle theft, and a hit and run.
- While on death row in San Quentin Prison, he made friends with the likes of Sunset Strip murderer Doug Clark and serial killer William Bonin.
- Signs his fan mail "Pliers."
- Has a measured IQ of 138.
- FBI agent John Douglas made Scott Glenn (the actor who plays Jack Crawford in *Silence of the Lambs*) cry when Glenn was at the Behavioral Sciences Unit in Quantico, Virginia. Douglas played an audio tape of Bittaker and Norris torturing, raping, and killing young girls in the back of their van. Before then, Glenn was firmly against capital punishment.

ROBERT BLACK

Date of birth: April 21, 1947
Aliases/Nicknames: Smelly Bob
Characteristics: Pedophilia, rape, murder
Number of victims: 4
Date of murders: 1969 - 1990
Date of arrest: July 14, 1990
Murder method: Strangulation
Known Victims: Susan Maxwell, 11; Caroline Hogg, 5; Sarah Harper, 10; Jennifer Cardy, 9
Crime location: Scotland, Ireland, Britain
Status: Sentenced to life imprisonment. Died in prison on January 12, 2016, due to a heart attack.

Background

Black was born an illegitimate child in Grangemouth, Scotland, to mother Jessie Hunter Black and an unnamed father. His mother planned to put him up for adoption before moving to Australia, but she never completed the formal proceedings. Instead, Black was placed with foster parents Jack and Isabel Tulip when he was six months old. At the time, he was given their surname.

From a very early age, Black showed aggressive and antisocial tendencies. He had only a few friends, and he was prone to throwing tantrums. Black was bullied by his peers, which lead to him becoming a bully himself toward younger children. Despite his mother's insistence on being clean, Black had no interest in hygiene. This led to the nickname "Smelly Bob Tulip."

When he was five years old, Black and a little girl of the same age showed each other their genitalia. For some reason, this experience made Black believe he should have been born a girl. He became deeply interested in his genitals, those of female children, and various body orifices. From the age of eight upwards, he would insert objects into his anus, and he continued this into adulthood.

People in the community would often see Black with bruises on his face and body, leading to speculation that he was being physically abused by his foster parents. But, Black later claimed he couldn't remember how he got the bruises.

By 1958, both of his foster parents had died, and Black was sent to live with another foster family. Soon after, he committed his first sexual assault on a young girl in a public restroom. Black's foster mother found out about the incident and reported it to social workers, demanding he be sent elsewhere. He was subsequently placed in a children's home where both male and female children lived.

Black would frequently expose his genitals to girls in the home, and once he forcibly removed a girl's underwear from her body. It was then decided he needed to be sent to the Red House Care Home in Musselburgh, a male-only home. Not long after arriving there, Black was subjected to repeated sexual abuse from a male member of the staff. The abuse went on for three years, until the staff member happened to die from natural causes.

Black left the home in 1963, and moved to Greenock. He became a delivery boy for the local butcher, and would later admit to how he would sexually fondle young girls he found alone in the homes he delivered to. One evening that same year, Black came across a seven-year-old girl playing in the local park alone. He managed to lure her to an old air-raid shelter with the promise of seeing kittens. Once inside, he grabbed her by the throat and she eventually passed out. He then masturbated over her unconscious body.

Black was arrested and charged the following day, and he was made to undergo a psychiatric assessment before he attended court. The report stated the incident was an isolated one and he did not require any treatment. He was reprimanded and released, and he moved to Grangemouth, lodging with an elderly couple. He later started dating Pamela Hodgson, and she would become his only known girlfriend. Black claimed he proposed. Pamela not only declined, she also ended the relationship, supposedly because of his odd sexual demands. Black was devastated.

A pattern was definitely forming. Black's landlords discovered he had been molesting their nine-year-old granddaughter. Not wanting to subject the young girl to a police interrogation, they did not report it. But they did order Black to leave the home. He moved back to Kinlochleven and found lodging with a couple who happened to have a six-year-old girl. They too found he had been molesting their daughter. This couple did report him, and he was charged and found guilty of three counts of indecent assault.

Black was sent to Borstal, where he would receive specialized training and rehabilitation. Interestingly, Black would later be very upfront about every aspect of his childhood and his life, except for the time he spent at Borstal. This has led many to speculate that perhaps he suffered some kind of brutality while he was there. It was his experiences at Borstal that made Black determined he would never be imprisoned ever again.

Murders

On August 12, 1981, nine-year-old Jennifer Cardy was riding her bicycle from her home to a friend's house in Country Antrim when she was abducted. It wasn't until later in the day when she hadn't returned home that her parents became worried. Her bicycle was found hours after she had been reported missing; someone had covered it with leaves and branches to try and hide it. The authorities were now convinced she had been kidnapped.

Her body was found by two hunters six days later. She was in a reservoir close to a rest stop, sixteen miles from her home. The autopsy revealed she had been sexually abused, drowned, and most likely strangled by a ligature. Her watch had stopped working at 5:40 p.m., which indicated she had been killed just four hours after she was abducted.

Susan Claire Maxwell, eleven, was abducted by Black on July 30, 1982. She had been walking home after playing tennis, and was last seen at 4:30 p.m. as she crossed the bridge over River Tweed. She was reported missing, and a major search went underway the next day. Nearly three hundred police officers were involved in investigating her disappearance.

On August 12, a truck driver discovered her dead body hidden beneath undergrowth. She was still clothed, but her underwear and shoes were removed from her body. She had been bound and gagged, and her underwear was folded and placed underneath her head. It was clear she too had been sexually assaulted before she was killed.

Black's third victim was also his youngest. Caroline Hogg was just five years old when she was taken outside her home early in the evening of July 8, 1983. Her family searched the neighborhood when she hadn't come inside at 7:15 p.m. One young boy told the family he had seen Caroline with a man on the drive nearby, so they searched that area thoroughly before reporting her missing to the police.

The search was enormous. Over two thousand volunteers helped about fifty members of the Royal Scots Fusiliers look for young Caroline. Despite there being nine known pedophiles living in the area at the time of her disappearance, all were eliminated from the inquiry. A description of a man seen following Caroline that evening was given, and one teenage girl overheard her saying "yes please" to the man, whom she had assumed was the girl's father.

Many people came forward saying they had seen Caroline with the balding bespectacled man at the nearby fair. When they left the fair it seemed the little girl was frightened, but nobody had suspected anything sinister. Caroline's body was found on July 18, in a ditch near the M1 motorway in Twycross, three hundred ten miles away from her home. Her body was naked, and in the advanced stages of decomposition, so it was difficult to determine how she was killed. It was thought that she had been in the ditch since at least July 12.

Sarah Harper, ten, had been on her way to a store one hundred yards away from home to buy some bread on March 26, 1986. The store's owner later stated she had been in the store and made her purchases around 7:55 p.m.; a balding man, who had entered the store just after her, left as Sarah paid for the bread. She was last seen by two girls as she walked down an alley that led to her home. By 8:20 p.m., her mother was searching the streets looking for Sarah. She then reported her daughter missing to the police.

Sarah's body was found on April 19 in the River Trent, seventy-one miles away from her home, near Nottingham. She was bound, gagged, and partially dressed. The autopsy later showed she had most likely been killed within five to eight hours of her kidnapping. She had received numerous injuries to her face head, neck, and forehead, and she had been killed by drowning. Sarah had been sexually assaulted for an extended period of time before her death, which resulted in terrible internal injuries as well.

Also suspected of the following murders:

United Kingdom:

April 8, 1969 - April Fabb, thirteen - Fabb was last seen bicycling from Metton toward her sister's home in Roughton, Norfolk. Her remains have never been found.

May 21, 1973 - Christine Markham, nine - Disappeared while walking to school. Her body has never been found. Black was questioned about the case, but it remains unsolved.

August 19, 1978 - Genette Tate, thirteen - Disappeared while delivering newspapers. Her body has never been found. Black was known to be in the area at the time of the disappearance, and he died before formal charges could be made in this case.

July 22, 1979 - Suzanne Lawrence, fourteen - Disappeared after leaving her sister's home in Harold Hill, near London. Her body has never been found.

June 16, 1980 - Patricia Morris, fourteen - Disappeared from school grounds. Her body was found still fully clothed in Hounslow Heath two days after she had disappeared. She had been strangled with a ligature.

November 4, 1981 - Pamela Hastie, sixteen - She was bludgeoned and strangled; her body was found in Johnstone, Renfrewshire, in November of 1981. An eyewitness identified Black as the man seen running from the scene, but police were unable to find evidence he had been in the area.

Ireland:

March 18, 1977 - Mary Boyle, six - Disappeared in Ballyshannon during a visit with her grandparents. Her body has never been found. It was discovered Black was in County Donegal at the time of her disappearance.

Germany:

June 20, 1985 - Silke Garben, ten - Was on her way to a dental appointment when she disappeared. Her body was discovered in a stream the following day. She had been sexually assaulted and strangled. Black was known to be nearby delivering posters when Garben was murdered.

Netherlands:

August 5, 1986 - Cheryl Morriën, seven - Disappeared while walking to her friend's home in the Dutch city of Ijmuiden. Her body has never been found. Black traveled to nearby Amsterdam regularly to purchase child pornography.

France:

May 5, 1987 - Virginie Delmas, ten - Abducted from Neuilly-sur-Marne. Her body was found in an orchard in Paris on October 9. She had been strangled, but it couldn't be determined if she had been sexually assaulted due to the state of decomposition. Black made several deliveries in and around Paris on the date of Delmas's disappearance.

May 30, 1987- Hemma Greedharry, ten - Her body was discovered in the Paris suburb of Malakoff two hours after she was last seen alive. She had been raped and strangled. Black regularly traveled along the same road where the body was found while he was making deliveries in northern France.

June 3, 1987 - Perrine Vigneron, seven - Disappeared on her way to buy a Mother's Day card in Bouleurs. She had been strangled, and her body was discovered on June 27 in a rapeseed field in Chelles. A van similar to the description of Black's was seen in the area at the time of the murder.

June 27, 1987 - Sabine Dumont, nine - She had been strangled and sexually assaulted, and her body was discovered the next day in the commune of Vauhallan. Black was named as a prime suspect in Dumont's murder in 2011, but the case is still unsolved.

Arrest and Trial

On July 14, 1990, retired postmaster David Herkes was outside his house in Stow, tending to his garden, when he noticed what appeared to be an abduction taking place. A blue transit van had stopped across the road, and he saw the driver get out of the vehicle at the same time he noticed his neighbor's six-year-old girl walking past his line of sight. All of a sudden, the little girl's feet lifted off the ground. Herkes stood up just in time to see the driver push the girl into the van.

Herkes noted the van's registration number as it sped off, then ran to the girl's home to tell her mother. The police were called immediately. After the officers arrived, Herkes spotted the van and shouted that the man was actually driving toward them. One of the officers jumped out in front of the van, forcing it to stop. The driver, Black, was pulled out and handcuffed and held down on the pavement.

The father of the abducted girl was one of the officers who had raced to the scene. On arriving, he got into the back of the van and called out for his daughter, who was in a sleeping bag placed near the separating partition. Her wrists and legs were tied and a sticking plaster was gagging her mouth. A hood had also been tied over her head. When a doctor examined her, it was discovered she had been sexually assaulted.

During his interview at the police station, the investigating officer noticed the similarities between this child's abduction and the murders that had previously taken place. He contacted the officer in charge of the murder investigations who then came and interviewed Black. Although Black's answers weren't terribly helpful, the officer was convinced he was responsible.

The trial for the abduction and sexual assault on the young girl from Stow began on August 10, 1990. Black pled guilty of all charges, so the trial lasted only a day. When it came to sentencing, the judge took into consideration the opinions of the two psychiatrists who had assessed Black and claimed he would forever be a danger to children. Judge Ross therefore sentenced Black to life imprisonment.

After his sentencing, Black was interviewed at length regarding the murders of the three young girls, Susan Maxwell, Caroline Hogg and Sarah Harper. But, he refused to confess to the crimes. It was decided they needed more evidence, and the inquiry team continued to search for any proof or evidence they could find. They had a reasonable amount of circumstantial evidence, including receipts that placed Black near the abductions. In May of 1991, everything they had found was submitted to the Crown.

In March of the following year, it was decided by the Crown that there was enough evidence to try Black for the murders, as well as an attempted abduction. The trial began on April 13, 1994, and Black pleaded not guilty to the counts of murder, kidnapping, attempted kidnapping, and preventing the lawful burial of a body.

Black was found guilty of all charges on May 19, and received a life sentence for each, with a minimum of thirty-five years to be served on each of the murder counts. As Black was led out of the courtroom, he turned to the detectives who had been involved in the murder investigations and said, "Tremendous. Well done, boys."

Black went to trial again on September 22, 2011, for the sexual assault and murder of Jennifer Cardy. Although he agreed he may have been in the area at the time, he pleaded not guilty. This trial went on for six weeks, and at the end of it, the jury only needed four hours to deliberate. Once again he was found guilty of all charges. He received another life sentence, with a minimum of twenty-five years to be served.

Outcome

While imprisoned in Wakefield Prison in July of 1995, Black was attacked by two fellow inmates. He was bludgeoned with the leg of a table, stabbed in the neck, stabbed in the back, and had a mixture of boiling water and sugar thrown over him. Despite the brutality of the attack, Black was not seriously injured.

On January 12, 2016, Black died as a result of a heart attack. His body was cremated, but no family members or friends attended. A short service was held by the prison chaplain, and in February, his ashes were scattered at sea. He never admitted to killing the girls.

Trivia

Quotes by Black:

- "I'm not exactly proud of the way I feel towards young girls."
- "There's a part of me that knows I'm wrong, that knows it's wrong, that I shouldn't be doing things like that, I shouldn't even be thinking things like that.
- "But there's the other part that says, 'you like it, go on.'"

TERRY BLAIR

Date of birth: September 16, 1961

Aliases/Nicknames: Nil

Characteristics: Rape and murder

Number of victims: 7 +

Date of murders: 1982 - 2004

Date of arrest: September 10, 2004

Murder method: Strangulation

Known Victims: His pregnant ex-girlfriend, Angela Monroe; Sheliah McKinzie, 38; Anna Ewing, 42; Patricia Wilson Butler, 45; Darci I. Williams, 25; Carmen Hunt, 40; Claudette Juniel, 31

Crime location: Kansas City, Missouri

Status: Sentenced to life imprisonment without parole.

Background

As far as families go, Terry Blair was born into one which would become well-known to the authorities for a number of violent crimes. Blair was the fourth child to be born out of ten, and his mother had little education and issues with mental illness.

When Blair's brother Walter was incarcerated, he met a fellow inmate who was willing to pay him six thousand dollars to murder his rape victim, Katherine Jo Allen. Walter agreed, and when he was released, he abducted her from her apartment. He then took her to a vacant lot and shot her to death. He was arrested and charged, and subsequently convicted of her murder. In 1993, Walter Blair was executed.

Blair had a half brother named Clifford Miller who he abducted a woman from a bar. He shot her in the arm and took her to an empty house where he then repeatedly raped her. Clifford beat the woman into unconsciousness. In addition to the gunshot wound to her arm, she suffered a fractured skull, jaw, and cheek bones. Clifford was arrested and convicted and sentenced to two life sentences, plus two hundred forty years.

Blair's mother Janice wasn't innocent either. She shot and killed Elton E. Gray, though little is known about the circumstances surrounding this incident. She was arrested and charged. But, after entering an Alford plea, she was sentenced only to probation. (This plea acknowledges there is enough evidence to convict, so the defendant pleads guilty. But, they are still able to claim they are innocent.)

With a family such as this, it's no surprise that Terry Blair also turned to violence in his adult life.

Murders

Angela Monroe, the mother of Blair's two children, was pregnant when he killed her. Blair claimed he had been angry with her because she had been performing prostitution acts. He was sent to prison and served twenty-one years before being released.

Timeline of known murders and how they were committed:

1982 - Angela Monroe

2003 - Nellia Harris, thirty-three

July 14, 2004 - Anna Ewing, forty-two, strangled and neck broken.

September 2, 2004 - Patricia Wilson Butler, fifty-eight, strangled.

September 2, 2004 - Sheliah McKinzie, thirty-eight, strangled and neck broken.

September 4, 2004 - Darci I. Williams, twenty-five, strangled and neck broken.

September 4, 2004 - Carmen Hunt, forty, strangled.

September 4, 2004 - Claudette Juniel, thirty-one, strangled and neck broken.

Unknown date - Sandra Reed, forty-seven

Arrest and Trial

Blair was arrested on October 15, 2004, and charged with eight counts of first-degree murder, three counts of forcible rape, and one count of first-degree assault. Facing the death penalty, Blair waived his right to a jury trial to avoid being sentenced to death. At the end of the trial, he was sentenced to six terms of life imprisonment, with no possibility of parole.

Outcome

Blair is currently incarcerated at the Potosi Correctional Center, located in Mineral Point, Missouri.

Trivia

Statement by Blair:

"They took me to police headquarters, and they put me in an isolation area of the jail. I asked one of the jailers that came around there why I was put in that area, and she stated, "They don't want you to see the news," and I asked her, I said, "What's on the news?", and she said, "You".

WILLIAM BONIN

Date of birth: January 8, 1947

Aliases/Nicknames: The Freeway Killer

Characteristics: Rape and murder

Number of victims: 14 - 44

Date of murders: 1972 - 1980

Date of arrest: June 13, 1980

Murder method: Strangulation, stabbing

Known Victims: Dennis Frank Fox, 17; Glenn Barker, 14; Russell Rugh, 15; Lawrence Sharp, 17; Marcus Grabs, 17; Donald Hyden, 15; David Murillo, 17; Charles Miranda, 15; James McCabe, 12; Ronald Gatlin, 19; Harry Todd Turner, 14; Steven Wood, 16; Darin Lee Kendrick, 19; Steven Jay Wells,18; Thomas Lundren, 13; Harold Tate, 15 (not killed)

Crime location: California

Status: Executed by lethal injection on February 23, 1996.

Background

Bonin was the middle child of three boys born to parents Robert and Alice. Robert was a compulsive gambler who was often physically abusive toward his family. Both parents were alcoholics, and the children were often neglected. Neighbors would take pity on the boys and feed them and clothe them. At times they were sent to stay with their grandfather, who happened to be a convicted child molester. The grandfather had apparently molested their mother when she was young, and it has been established that he also molested his three grandsons.

In 1953, the boys were sent to an orphanage—an attempt by their mother to shield them from their abusive father. The orphanage was known to discipline the children in a severe manner over minor offenses. Disciplinary measures included severe beatings, partial drowning in water-filled sinks, and being placed in stress positions. Later in life, Bonin refused to talk about what happened at the orphanage, apart from admitting that he would consent to the older males' sexual advances, provided they tied Bonin's hands behind his back first.

The boys were sent back to their parents when Bonin was nine. When he was ten years old, he was caught stealing vehicle license plates and was sent to a juvenile detention center. Here, he was allegedly abused (sexually and physically) by multiple people, one of whom was his counselor.

The family decided to move to California in 1961, largely due to the inevitable foreclosure on their home. Not long after the move, Bonin's father died due to liver cirrhosis. Bonin went on to molest not only his younger brother, but also many children in the neighborhood. He would make false promises of supplying alcohol and lure them to the house.

Bonin graduated from high school in 1965 and became engaged soon after. This engagement was largely due to his mother's insistence, as she was concerned about her son's sexual preference for males; she thought that by marrying a woman, those preferences would go away. Bonin joined the air force the same year he graduated and was eventually sent to serve active duty in the Vietnam War. As an aerial gunner, Bonin logged over seven hundred hours of patrol and combat time while in Vietnam.

During the war, Bonin once risked his life to save a fellow airman who was wounded. As a result, he received the Good Conduct Medal. However, he later claimed that his experiences in Vietnam made him believe that human life was overrated. Bonin claimed he engaged in sexual relations with both females and males while in Vietnam. He also asserted that he sexually assaulted two soldiers at gunpoint during the Tet Offensive.

After three years' service with the Air Force, Bonin was honorably discharged in 1968. He moved back to his mother's home and married his fiancée soon after. The marriage wasn't to last though, and they divorced not long afterwards.

That same year, Bonin embarked on a series of sexual assaults against five youths aged twelve to eighteen years. In the early part of 1969, he was arrested and charged with multiple offenses against the five youths. He pled guilty and was sent to the Atascadero State Hospital, as he was considered to be a mentally disordered sexual offender who could respond to treatment.

During his time in the hospital, numerous assessments and examinations showed that he had a higher than average IQ; he also exhibited traits of manic depression. Furthermore, staff discovered that he had damage to the prefrontal cortex of his brain, which meant he was unable to restrain himself from violent impulses. Throughout his stay in the hospital, Bonin repeatedly engaged in forced sexual activities with fellow male inmates. Deemed untreatable, he was sent to prison.

In 1974, believing he no longer presented a danger to himself or to others, the authorities released Bonin from prison. But in 1975, Bonin would prove them wrong. He picked up a fourteen-year-old hitchhiker, David McVicker and, as soon as the boy entered the car, Bonin asked him if he was homosexual.

McVicker was stunned by this and asked Bonin to stop the car. Instead, Bonin pulled out a gun, drove to a field, and made McVicker undress. He then raped and beat him. Afterwards, Bonin attempted to strangle McVicker with a T-shirt. But when the boy started screaming, Bonin stopped, apologized, and drove McVicker home. As soon as he left, the boy told his mother what had happened, and the police were notified.

Charged and convicted, Bonin spent more time in prison. Following his release, he found work as a truck driver; he also developed a reputation around town among the young boys that he allowed teenagers to party at his house with alcohol. Through a neighbor, Bonin met a twenty-one-year-old man named Vernon Butts, and Gregory Miley, an eighteen-year-old. Butts would later state that he was terrified yet fascinated by Bonin, and that he enjoyed watching Bonin inflict torture and then murder his victims. Miley would also sometimes accompany Bonin on his murderous outings; he too participated willingly.

Murders

Schoolboys, young men hitchhiking, and male prostitutes were usually the victims Bonin targeted. He would either force or lure his victims into his Ford Econoline van, where they would quickly be overpowered and secured at the hands and feet by wire, handcuffs, or some sort of cord. Bonin would then sexually assault the victim and beat them severely around the head, face, and genitals. He would inflict terrible torture, and then strangle them, often using their own shirt as a ligature.

Sometimes though, he would stab or beat the victim to death. Darin Kendrick was killed when Bonin forced him to drink hydrochloric acid. Three others were killed from having an ice pick rammed into their ears, and Mark Shelton actually died from shock. Bonin had outfitted his van to prevent his victims from escaping. All of the internal door handles on the passenger side and in the back of the van were removed. He kept a supply of tools and equipment to use against his victims, including knives, ligatures, and a variety of regular household tools. The victim would normally be killed in the back of the van, then dumped along the southern California freeways.

Bonin didn't always work alone; he was usually accompanied and assisted by one of his four accomplices. It was later discovered that each murder he committed displayed an escalated level of brutality and violence, almost as though he needed a bigger thrill from each kill.

His first known victim, Thomas Lundren, was just thirteen years old when he was enticed, or captured, by Bonin on May 28, 1979 in Agoura. He left his home at around 10:50 that morning, and it was the last time he was seen alive. His battered body was discovered the same day; he was clothed except for his underwear and pants, which were missing. These items were later found in a field nearby, along with his genitals, which had been severed.

The autopsy showed he had multiple fractures of his skull, he had been stabbed multiple times, his throat had been slashed, and he had finally been strangled to death.

On August 4, 1979, Bonin abducted Mark Shelton, seventeen, in Westminster. The young man had been on his way to the cinema when he crossed paths with Bonin. Screaming was heard near his home at the time of his disappearance, which led investigators to believe he was kidnapped by violent force. In the back of the van a variety of objects were forced into his rectum, including a pool cue. This caused Mark Shelton's body to go into shock, and he died. His body was dumped on the side of the freeway in San Bernardino County.

The next day, Markus Grabs, seventeen, was hitchhiking along the Pacific Coast Highway when he was abducted by Bonin. He was tied up with a combination of ignition wire and cord and taken back to Bonin's house. Inside the house, Markus was beaten, sodomized, and stabbed seventy-seven times until he was dead. His nude body was found the next day in Malibu Creek.

Donald Ray Hyden, fifteen, was abducted on August 27, at around 1:00 a.m., after walking along the Santa Monica Boulevard. Construction workers discovered his body in a dumpster later that morning. The autopsy showed he had been tied up, beaten, and sodomized; his head had been bludgeoned and his neck stabbed. An attempt had been made to cut off his testicles, and he had been slashed across the throat. His death was caused by ligature strangulation.

On September 9, Bonin and his accomplice Vernon Butts abducted David Murillo, seventeen, as he was riding his bicycle to the theaters in La Mirada. They had lured Murillo into the van, where he was quickly bound and subdued. The boy was then raped repeatedly and beaten about the head by a tire iron. Finally, he was strangled with a ligature. His body was dumped alongside Highway 101 and thrown over an embankment. Just eight days later, Bonin abducted and killed Robert Wirostek, eighteen, as he rode his bicycle to a grocery store. His battered body was found alongside Interstate 10 on September 27.

The next known murder committed by Bonin occurred on November 1, when, along with Butts, they abducted an unidentified young man. Like the other victims, this John Doe had also been violently beaten, raped, and strangled to death. His body was left in a ditch alongside State Route 99, near Taft, Kern County. Bonin later admitted he had shoved an ice pick into this victim's nose and ear before he was killed.

Bonin abducted seventeen-year-old Frank Dennis Fox in Bellflower on November 30. His body, found alongside the Ortega Highway two days later, showed evidence of a violent and extensive beating to the head and face. His wrists and ankles had marks from ligatures. On December 13, the body of a young boy was discovered in an area of Rialto. The victim (not identified until August of 1980) was John Kilpatrick, fifteen, of Long Beach, who had disappeared while heading off from home to meet some friends.

On New Year's Day, 1980, Michael McDonald, sixteen, was abducted. He was beaten, brutalized, and strangled, and his fully clothed body was found two days later alongside Highway 71 in San Bernadino County. He would remain a John Doe until March 24, when he was finally identified.

The next murder Bonin committed was undertaken with the help of Gregory Matthews Miley, his eighteen-year-old acquaintance. Charles Miranda, fifteen, had been hitchhiking along Santa Monica Boulevard when he was approached by Bonin and Miley. Miley later claimed that Bonin and Miranda had consensual sex in the van while Miley drove the van around. Bonin then whispered the "kid's going to die" in Miley's ear, at which point they quickly bound Miranda. They robbed Miranda of the six dollars he had in his wallet, and Bonin then raped him. Miley attempted to rape Miranda but was unable to maintain an erection, which lead to him assaulting Miranda with sharp objects out of frustration. Miranda was then beaten and strangled by Bonin as Miley jumped on top of his chest. Unlike the others, Miranda's body was found in an alleyway near East Second Street.

Within a few hours, Bonin and Miley were searching for another victim; Bonin stated he was still "horny" and wanted to attack and kill again. At Huntington Beach they came across James Macabe, twelve, who was waiting at a bus stop. They offered the boy a ride to Disneyland and drove to a local grocery store, parking in the lot. Bonin got in to the back of the van, and Miley took over driving. He could hear the boy crying as Bonin raped and beat him. Later, Miley got into the back and helped Bonin beat the boy. They used a tire iron to crush his neck, and then Bonin strangled him to death. Three days later, Macabe's body was found near a dumpster in Walnut.

Bonin spent a month in jail for breaching his parole conditions and was released on March 4. Just ten days later, he claimed his next victim. Ronald Gatlin, eighteen, was abducted after he left his friend's home in Van Nuys. Like the others, he was sodomized and beaten, and an ice pick was driven into his ear and neck multiple times. Finally, Bonin used a ligature to strangle him, and the body was found in Duarte the next day.

Fourteen-year-old Glenn Barker was lured into Bonin's van on March 21 when he was hitchhiking to school. He was raped and beaten and burnt on the neck multiple times with a burning cigarette. Numerous foreign objects had been forced into his rectum, and he was eventually strangled with a ligature. The very same day, Russell Rugh, fifteen, was kidnapped from a bus stop in Garden Grove; he was subjected to terrible violence over an eight-hour period. The bodies of both young boys were found in the Cleveland National Forest on March 23.

Bonin met William Ray Pugh, seventeen, one night in March after they left Everett Fraser's house. Bonin offered Pugh a ride, and almost as soon as they drove away, Bonin propositioned Pugh for sex. Pugh was supposedly shocked. After a few minutes of silence, he tried to get out of the van while they were slowed at a light. Bonin grabbed Pugh by the collar, pulling him back across the seat, then told Pugh how he liked to kidnap young males and kill them. He told Pugh, as he dropped him off at home, that he hadn't been killed because people had seen them leave Fraser's home together.

Pugh became an accomplice to Bonin, and on March 24 they abducted Harry Todd Turner, fifteen, from the street after Turner had run away from a boys' home. They offered the boy twenty dollars for sex and lured him into the van. Turner was bound, then sodomized and bitten. Pugh was ordered by Bonin to beat the boy, and then Bonin strangled him. They left his body outside the rear delivery door of a business. His autopsy showed his skull had been fractured eight times, and his genitals had been mutilated.

Steven Wood, sixteen, was abducted on April 10 as he walked to school after a dentist appointment. He received the same treatment as the other victims, and was also strangled to death by ligature. His body was left in an alleyway in Long Beach. On April 29, Bonin, assisted by Butts, lured an employee of the Stanton supermarket into the van. The victim, Darin Kendrick, nineteen, was told they could sell him drugs. He willingly got in and they drove to Butt's apartment.

Once inside the apartment, Kendrick was overpowered and bound, then sodomized. They strangled him, but not completely, which was another form of torture. Then they forced him to drink hydrochloric acid. The acid caused horrific burns to his mouth, chin, chest, and stomach. Butts rammed an ice pick into his ear so violently that it caused a fatal injury to his spinal cord. When his body was found behind a warehouse near the Artesia Freeway, the ice pick was still sticking out of his ear canal.

Lawrence Sharp, seventeen, an acquaintance of Bonin's, was killed on May 17 simply because Bonin was sick of him hanging around. He was also tied up and sodomized, beaten severely around the head and body, and strangled. His body was found the next day, dumped behind a Westminster gas station. Two days later, Bonin wanted Butts to help him with another killing but Butts refused. Alone, Bonin abducted Sean King, fourteen, from a bus stop in Downey. His body was found in Live Oak Canyon.

Several days later, James Michael Munro, eighteen, was invited by Bonin to move into the apartment he shared with his mother. Munro was a homeless drifter, and he accepted Bonin's offer without hesitation. They began a sexual relationship even though bisexual Munro preferred to have sex with women. At first, Munro thought Bonin was a "good guy," until Bonin told him on June 1 that he wanted Munro to help him abduct and kill a young hitchhiker.

Bonin and Munro came across Steven Wells, eighteen, on June 2. Wells was waiting at a bus stop when he was lured into the van. When Bonin found out Wells was bisexual, he offered him two hundred dollars to come back to his house and be bound before they had sex. Wells agreed. Once he was in the apartment, he was bound, raped, and beaten by both men. Before he was strangled, Bonin informed Wells he was about to be murdered. His body was put into a cardboard box and transported to the home of Butts.

Bonin encouraged Butts to look at the body they had in the van. Then he allegedly asked Butts where the best place to dump the body would be, and Butts suggested a gas station or where they had "dumped the last one." Wells' body was eventually left behind an old gas station in Huntington Beach. Even though the station was no longer used, his body was still found quickly - just five hours after it was dumped.

Confirmed victims:

May 28, 1979 - Thomas Lundgren, thirteen

August 4, 1979 - Mark Shelton, seventeen

August 5, 1979 - Markus Grabs, seventeen

August 27, 1979 - Donald Ray Hyden, fifteen

September 9, 1979 - David Murillo, seventeen

September 17, 1979 - Robert Wirostek, eighteen

November 1, 1979 - John Doe, nineteen to twenty-five

November 30, 1979 - Frank Dennis Fox, seventeen

December 10, 1979 - John Kilpatrick, fifteen

January 1, 1980 - Michael McDonald, sixteen

February 3, 1980 - Charles Miranda, fifteen

February 3, 1980 - James Macabe, twelve

March 14, 1980 - Ronald Gatlin, eighteen

March 21, 1980 - Glenn Barker, fourteen

March 21, 1980 - Russell Rugh, fifteen

March 24, 1980 - Harry Todd Turner, fifteen

April 10, 1980 - Steven Wood, sixteen

April 29, 1980 - Darin Lee Kendrick, nineteen

May 17, 1980 - Lawrence Sharp, seventeen

May 19, 1980 - Sean King, fourteen

June 2, 1980 - Steven Wells, eighteen

Arrest and Trial

Pugh had been arrested for stealing a car in May of 1980. While in jail, he admitted to a counselor that he recognized the modus operandi of the murders on the news as those described to him previously by Bonin. This information was passed on to the police, who then interviewed Pugh. He denied any involvement in the actual murders but claimed Bonin was the Freeway Killer. When police looked into Bonin's background, they discovered he had an extensive criminal history involving the sexual assault of young boys. He was therefore put under surveillance.

While under surveillance, police noticed Bonin driving randomly throughout Hollywood on June 11. He seemed to be trying to lure teenage boys into his van. After failing four times, he finally convinced a boy to get in, and the police followed Bonin until he parked in a parking lot near the Hollywood Freeway. Police approached stealthily, and when they heard muffled screaming and banging sounds coming from inside, they forced their way in to the van. Bonin was in the process of raping Harold Tate.

Following his arrest, investigators searched his van and his home and found numerous items suggesting he was the Freeway Killer. In addition to restraints, binding materials, knives, pliers, and a tire iron, they found that parts of his house and the inside of his van were stained heavily with blood. There was even a scrapbook with news clippings about the murders in the van's glove box.

Although he tried to deny having any part of the many murders, Bonin eventually gave in and confessed. Interviewed over the course of several days, he admitted to the abduction, rape, and murder of twenty-one young men and boys. He showed no remorse, other than what he felt at being caught. He quickly acknowledged Butts, Munro, and Miley as his accomplices.

Bonin was eventually charged with sixteen counts of murder on July 29, 1980. He was also charged with one count of sodomy, eleven counts of robbery, and one count of mayhem. Butts was charged at the same time, with six murders and three counts of robbery. On November 14, Butts received three more murder charges and was scheduled to go to trial on July 27, 1981.

Munro was arrested on July 31, 1980, and charged with murdering Steven Wells. He pleaded not guilty to all charges. Miley was arrested on August 22 and charged with the murders of James Macabe and Charles Miranda. A phone conversation he had with a friend had been recorded, and during the call he admitted his guilt. He initially pleaded not guilty but subsequently changed his plea to guilty.

Bonin's first trial came to an end on January 6, 1982, at which point he was found guilty of committing ten of the murders. Consideration of sentencing continued until January 20, when Bonin was given the death penalty. Later, he went to trial in Orange County and was charged with four murders. This trial would last six weeks. On August 2, 1983, a guilty verdict was given in all four murders, along with three counts of robbery. Again, he was sentenced to death.

On January 11, 1981, before he went to trial, Butts committed suicide by hanging himself in his cell. Munro was given fifteen years to life for the murder of Steven Wells. Miley received a sentence of twenty-five years to life in February of 1982, for the murder of Charles Miranda. He also received a twenty-five-year term for the murder of James Macabe. On May 25, 2016, Miley died as the result of injuries he'd sustained two days earlier when another inmate attacked him.

William Pugh received a sentence of six years after being found guilty of voluntary manslaughter in the murder of Harry Todd Turner. He spent only four years in prison and was released back into the community in 1985.

Outcome

Bonin spent fourteen years waiting on death row before his execution date was finally scheduled. Initially, Bonin was meant to be executed by the gas chamber. But, because of issues with a previous execution, this was changed to lethal injection. His last meal consisted of two large pizzas, three pints of ice cream, and eighteen cans of Coke. He had chosen five people to spend his last hours with, including a biographer, a chaplain, and his attorney.

He was taken to the gas chamber (where the injections would be given) at 11:45 p.m., and he was pronounced deceased at 12:13 a.m.

Trivia

– While on death row, made friends with several other serial killers, including Douglas Clark, Lawrence Bittaker, and Randy Kraft.
– Final Meal: Two large pepperoni-and-sausage pizzas, three pints of coffee ice cream, and three six-packs of regular Coca Cola.

Quote by Bonin:

"I would suggest that when a person has a thought of doing anything serious against the law, that before they did that they should go to a quiet place and think about it seriously."

BOSTON STRANGLER

Date of birth: September 3, 1931

Aliases/Nicknames: Albert Henry DeSalvo, The Green Man, The Measuring Man, The Mad Strangler of Boston

Characteristics: Rape and murder

Number of victims: 13

Date of murders: June 1962 - January 1964

Date of arrest: November of 1964

Murder method: Strangulation

Known Victims: Anna Slesers, 55; Mary Mullen, 85; Nina Nichols, 68; Helen Blake, 65; Ida Irga, 75; Jane Sullivan, 67; Sophie Clark, 20; Patricia Bissette, 23; Mary Brown, 69; Beverly Samans, 23; Evelyn Corbin, 58; Joann Graff, 23; Mary Sullivan, 19

Crime location: Boston

Status: Never convicted of murder, but was sentenced to life imprisonment for rape. Murdered in prison by stabbing, November 25, 1973.

Background

Although it has long been considered that Albert DeSalvo was the Boston Strangler, there has been some controversy in recent years that he may not have been responsible for all thirteen murders. All of the victims were female and had resided in the Boston area, and the killings took place during the early 1960s.

These murders were often referred to as the "silk stocking murders" because each of the victims appeared to have been strangled with a silk stocking. Even though there is doubt about Albert DeSalvo's role in these murders, they are still attributed to him.

DeSalvo was one of five children born into a household of alcoholism and violence. He began getting into trouble at a young age, largely for petty crimes and minor violence. He spent some time in the Army, but was eventually discharged for not obeying orders. Following his discharge he married German woman Irmgard Beck. Their first child was born handicapped, but despite their modest income and the added expense of the child, they managed to sustain themselves.

According to his wife, DeSalvo was "highly sexed." But she would try to avoid having sex with him out of fear of having another baby that was handicapped. She couldn't avoid him forever, however, and she subsequently gave birth to a healthy baby boy. DeSalvo had settled into the role of family man, and was well-liked by his employer and his work colleagues, even though he was an outrageous braggart.

During his younger years, DeSalvo would knock on women's doors claiming to be scouting for new models, and he managed to convince many of these women to let him into their homes. Once inside, he would proceed to "measure them up" under the pretense of checking to see if they would be suitable as models. This led to him being charged with sexually-oriented mischievousness, and he was sent to prison for eighteen months.

Murders

The first known victim of the strangler was Anna Slesers, fifty-five. She was found dead in her apartment in Back Bay, Boston on June 14, 1962. An object had been used to sexually assault her, and she had been strangled to death with the belt from her bathrobe.

According to DeSalvo, his next attempted attack took place on June 28, 1962. He had entered the apartment of Mary Mullen, who was eighty-five. When he grabbed her, she collapsed on the ground. He fled the building, unaware she had suffered a fatal heart attack.

On June 30, 1962, Nina Nichols, sixty-eight, was attacked in her home. She was sexually assaulted, and the strangler used Nina's nylon stockings to strangle her to death. The next victim of the strangler was Helen Blake, sixty-five, who was attacked on the same night. She too had been strangled with her own stockings after being sexually assaulted.

Ida Irga, seventy-five, was killed on August 19, after being sexually assaulted and strangled in her apartment in Beacon Hill, Boston. In Dorchester, on August 21, sixty-seven-year-old Jane Sullivan was sexually assaulted and strangled to death with her stockings. There are no further known murders until the killing of Sophie Clark, twenty, on December 5, 1962. Once again, the strangler had sexually assaulted his victim and then strangled her.

Patricia Bissette, twenty-three, was strangled with her nylon stockings on December 31, 1962. Her body was found in her home in Back Bay, Boston. The murder of Mary Brown occurred on March 6, 1963, and was a lot more violent than the previous murders. Mary had been raped, beaten, strangled, and stabbed in her own apartment in Massachusetts.

The next woman murdered was Beverly Samans, twenty-three. She was found at her home in Massachusetts on May 6, 1963. Unlike the others, who had been strangled, Samans was stabbed to death. On September 8, Evelyn Corbin, fifty-eight, was raped and strangled with her nylon stockings and found in her home in Salem, Massachusetts.

On November 23, 1963, Joann Graff, twenty-three, was found in her apartment after she'd been strangled with her stockings. There was a brief break following this murder, with the next occurring on January 4, 1964. Mary Sullivan, nineteen, was found dead in her apartment in Boston, after being sexually assaulted and strangled. This was the last known murder committed by the Boston Strangler.

Known victims:

June 14, 1962 - Anna E. Slesers, fifty-five - Her body was found in her apartment at 77 Gainsborough St., Back Bay, Boston.

June 28, 1962 - Mary Mullen, eighty-five - Her body was found in her apartment at 1435 Commonwealth Ave., Boston.

June 30, 1962 - Nina Nichols, sixty-eight - Her body was found in her home at 1940 Commonwealth Ave., Boston.

June 30, 1962 -Helen Blake, sixty-five - Her body was found in her home at 73 Newhall St., Lynn, Massachusetts.

August 19, 1962 - Ida Irga, seventy-five - Her body was found in her apartment at 7 Grove Street, Beacon Hill, Boston.

August 21, 1962 - Jane Sullivan, sixty-seven - Her body was found in her home at 435 Columbia Road, Dorchester, Boston.

December 5, 1962 - Sophie Clark, twenty - Her body was found in her apartment at 315 Huntington Ave., Back Bay, Boston.

December 31, 1962 - Patricia Bissette, twenty-three - Her body was found in her home at 515 Park Drive, Back Bay, Boston.

March 6, 1963 - Mary Brown, sixty-nine - Her body was found in her apartment at 319 Park Ave., Lawrence, Massachusetts.

May 6, 1963 - Beverly Samans, twenty-three - Her body was found in her home at 4 University Road in Cambridge, Massachusetts.

September 8, 1963 - Evelyn Corbin, fifty-eight - Her body was found in her home at 224 Lafayette St., Salem, Massachusetts.

November 23, 1963 - Joann Graff, twenty-three - Was strangled with her nylon stockings. Her body was found in her apartment at 54 Essex St., Lawrence, Massachusetts.

January 4, 1964 - Mary Sullivan, nineteen - Her body was found in her apartment at 44-A Charles St., Boston.

Arrest and Trial

A young woman let a stranger into her home on October 27, 1964, because the man had claimed to be a police detective. He attacked her, tied her to the bed, then sexually assaulted her. All of a sudden, after apologizing to the woman, he left. The woman was able to give police a good description of the man who attacked her, which led them to Albert DeSalvo.

Initially, DeSalvo was charged with the rape of the woman in October. But, while he was being held in jail, he confessed to fellow inmate George Nassar that he was responsible for the Boston Strangler murders. Nassar reported DeSalvo's claims to his attorney, who then informed the police. When DeSalvo was interviewed by the police, he gave a lot of information that wasn't public knowledge. However, not all of his claims matched the crime scenes of some of the murders. There was also no physical evidence tying him to the murders.

DeSalvo went on trial for a number of sexual offenses he had committed during the period he was referred to as "The Green Man" and the "Measuring Man," when he raped and assaulted women but did not kill them. His attorney tried to show he was insane by mentioning his confessions to the Boston Strangler murders, but that information was declared inadmissible by the judge.

Found guilty of the sexual assaults, DeSalvo was sentenced to life imprisonment in 1967. But, he was never charged with the murders. The same year he was sentenced, he escaped from Bridgewater State Hospital, where he was being held, with two other inmates. He handed himself over to the authorities the next day, and was sent to the Walpole State Prison, which was a maximum security facility.

Outcome

On November 27, 1973, DeSalvo was found murdered in the prison infirmary, having suffered stab wounds. Inmate Robert Wilson, who was associated with the Winter Hill Gang, was charged with the murder. But, because of a hung jury, he was never convicted.

For many years there was some speculation as to whether or not DeSalvo was in fact the Boston Strangler. The murder that triggered most of the controversy was that of Mary Sullivan. During his confession, DeSalvo claimed to have penetrated Sullivan sexually, yet the autopsy showed no evidence that any sexual activity had taken place.

A call was made for DNA testing from the fluid evidence found at Mary Sullivan's crime scene to determine once and for all if DeSalvo was the killer. On July 11, 2013, the Boston Police announced that there was a DNA link between Mary Sullivan and DeSalvo. They had used samples from

DeSalvo's nephew though. To conclusively solve the issue, a court order was made to exhume DeSalvo's body and test again. On July 19, it was announced that there was a definite link through DNA, proving that DeSalvo was in fact the man who had killed Mary Sullivan.

Trivia

- There is a Boston hardcore band named The Boston Strangler.
- The Rolling Stones released "Midnight Rambler" on the album *Let It Bleed* in 1969. The song is a loose biography of Albert DeSalvo.

Poem written by DeSalvo:

Here is the story of the Strangler, yet untold,
The man who claims he murdered thirteen women,
young and old.
The elusive Strangler, there he goes,
Where his wanderlust sends him, no one knows.
He struck within the light of day,
Leaving not one clue astray.
Young and old, their lips are sealed,
Their secret of death never revealed.
Even though he is sick in mind,
He's much too clever for the police to find.
To reveal his secret will bring him fame,
But burden his family with unwanted shame.
Today he sits in a prison cell,
Deep inside only a secret he can tell.
People everywhere are still in doubt,
Is the Strangler in prison or roaming about?

JERRY BRUDOS

Date of birth: January 31, 1939

Aliases/Nicknames: The Shoe Fetish Slayer, The Lust Killer

Characteristics: Fetishist, necrophiliac

Number of victims: 4

Date of murders: January 26, 1968 - April 27, 1969

Date of arrest: May 25, 1969

Murder method: Strangulation

Known Victims: Linda Kay Slawson, 19; Jan Susan Whitney, 23; Karen Elena Sprinker, 19; Linda Dawn Salee, 19

Crime location: Oregon

Status: Sentenced to life imprisonment. Died on March 28, 2006, of natural causes.

Background

When Brudos was born, his mother was disappointed because she had wanted a girl, not a boy. Because of this, she would ignore him and often belittle him. From the young age of five, Brudos developed a fetish for women's shoes, which would last throughout his lifetime. As a teenager, he would follow local women and attack them, either by choking them or knocking them down, and then he would run away with their shoes.

He spent a lot of time throughout his teens in state hospitals and psychotherapy. His disturbing behaviors escalated when he was seventeen, at which time he dug a hole and held girls as his sex slaves. When this was discovered, he was sent to Oregon State Hospital; he remained in the psychiatric ward for nine months. The assessments found that his fetish and sexual fantasies all revolved around thoughts of revenge and hatred toward his mother and women in general.

Despite all of this, Brudos was able to graduate from high school, and he trained to be an electronics technician. After he married in 1961, he and his wife moved to Portland, Oregon and settled down. But, he began to complain about having migraines and "blackouts." To relieve his symptoms, he would prowl the streets at night and steal lacy underwear and shoes.

Murders

Brudos' first murder took place on January 26, 1968. Linda Slawson, nineteen, had been selling encyclopedias in the same Portland neighborhood Brudos lived in when she disappeared. Her body has never been found, though Brudos later admitted he threw her into the Willamette River after killing her.

On November 25, 1968, Jan Whitney, twenty-three, went missing from Eugene. Her car was found at a rest stop on Interstate 5, between Salem and Albany. On July 27, 1969, her body was found in the Willamette River tied to a piece of iron from the railroad.

Karen Sprinkler, nineteen, was last seen alive in the parking lot of a store in Salem. Her body was found weighted down in the Long Tom River, near Monroe, on May 10, 1969. The last known murder occurred on April 23, 1969. Linda Salee, twenty-two, had last been seen at a business' parking lot in Portland, and her body was also found in the Long Tom River near Monroe. Like Karen Sprinkler, her body had also been weighted down before being tossed in the river.

At the time of the murders, Brudos was married and had two children. Sometimes he posed as a policeman, using a fake uniform and badge to lure young women into his vehicle. Once he had them in his vehicle, he would take them back to his house in Salem and kill them in his garage, all without his wife or children knowing a thing.

As his victims died, Brudos would take photographs of them. He liked to dress them in lingerie and have sex with them after they died. Often, he would cut off parts of their bodies, such as a foot he preserved and a breast he set in resin and used as a paperweight. He had a collection of high-heeled shoes, and he used to put the preserved foot in the shoes to "model" them.

Timeline of known murders:

January 26, 1968 - Linda Slawson, nineteen

November 25, 1968 - Jan Whitney, twenty-three

March 27, 1969 - Karen Sprinker, nineteen

April 23, 1969 - Linda Salee, twenty-two

Arrest and Trial

In May of 1969, Brudos attempted to abduct a twelve-year-old girl, who managed to escape. She gave a description of her attacker and, when shown a photo lineup, she identified Brudos. He was quickly arrested. At first, Brudos claimed to be innocent. Then, on June 27, just three days before he was meant to stand trial, Brudos confessed to killing Whitney, Sprinkler, and Salee.

Because he pleaded guilty, the trial was unnecessary, and Brudos was sentenced to life imprisonment.

Outcome

While he was in prison, Brudos wrote letters to companies selling shoes asking them for copies of their catalogs. He likened the shoe catalogs to "pornography" in his mind, and he had many of them in his cell.

On March 28, 2006, Brudos died as a result of cancer of the liver. At the time, he was the longest-serving inmate of the Oregon Department of Corrections, having served thirty-seven years.

Trivia

- Known as "The Shoe Fetish Slayer," he bludgeoned and strangled four women, taking body parts as trophies.
- His mother had wanted a daughter, so she dressed him in women's clothing.
- He was obsessed with women's shoes, and he cut off one victim's foot to model the shoes he'd stolen.

TED BUNDY

Date of birth: November 24, 1946

Aliases/Nicknames: Chris Hagen, Kenneth Misner, Officer Roseland, Richard Burton, Rolf Miller

Characteristics: Abduction, ambush, rape, and murder

Number of victims: 30 +

Date of murders: 1961 - 1978

Date of arrest: February 15, 1978

Murder method: Beating with heavy object, strangulation

Known Victims: Anne Marie Burr, 8 years old; Lonnie Trumbell, 20; Lisa Wick, 20; Joni Lenz, 18; Lynda Ann Healy 21; Donna Gail Manson, 19; Susan Elaine Rancourt, 19; Brenda Baker, 15; Roberta Kathleen Parks, 20; Brenda Carol Ball, 22; Georgeann Hawkins, 18; Janice Ott, 23; Denise Naslund, 18; Caryn Campbell, 23; Julie Cunningham, 26; Denise Lynn Oliverson, 25; Melanie Cooley, 18; Shelly Robertson, 24; Nancy Wilcox, 16; Melissa Smith, 17; Laura Aime, 17; Debby Kent, 17; Carol DaRonch, 18 (survived); Nancy Baird, 23; Sue Curtis, 15; Debbie Smith, 17; Rita Lorraine Jolly, 17; Vicki Lynn Hollar, 24; Karen Chandler, 21 (survived); Kathy Kleiner, 20 (survived); Lisa Levy, 20; Margaret Bowman, 21; Cheryl Thomas, 21 (survived); Kimberly Leach, 12; Lynette Culver, 13; Rita Curran, 24

Crime location: Washington, Colorado, Utah, Oregon, Florida, Idaho, Vermont

Status: Executed by electric chair on January 24, 1989.

Background

Theodore "Ted" Bundy was yet another illegitimate child born under a cloud of shame and secrecy. His mother, Eleanor Cowell, was brought up by parents who were very religious. Having a baby at twenty-two years old, and without a husband, was scandalous. So, Bundy was raised by his grandparents as an adopted baby. In his early years, he was led to believe his mother was his sister.

While still a toddler, Bundy and his mother moved to Tacoma, Washington. In 1951, she married Johnnie Bundy. They went on to have several children, and although it was a working-class family, they all seemed very content. But, as a young child, Bundy was already displaying odd fascinations with macabre topics. He showed an intense interest in knives at just three years old.

As a student, Bundy was intelligent and did well, but socially he had trouble with making friends. When he became a teenager, his behavior started to deteriorate. He enjoyed peeping in people's windows, and he often stole things that he wanted without any guilt.

Bundy enrolled in the University of Washington. While there, he met and fell in love with a young lady from California. A pretty girl, Bundy was attracted to the fact she had everything he desired - class, influence, and money. When she ended the relationship he was devastated. Later, it became apparent that many of his victims resembled her – they had long, dark hair and were attractive.

His later victims who survived the attacks described Bundy as charismatic and handsome. These characteristics, coupled with his ploy of pretending to be injured and needing help, enabled him to gain their trust.

Murders

Bundy was definitely one of the most depraved killers in the last century. He would often go back to the bodies after he had disposed of them and perform various sexual acts with the corpses. He would continue this until the bodies were so decomposed or damaged by wild animals that it was no longer possible to have physical contact with them.

At least twelve of Bundy's victims were decapitated, and some of the heads were kept in his apartment for a period of time. Like many serial killers who keep trophies, Bundy kept the heads. He undoubtedly got a great deal of enjoyment reliving his crimes simply by looking at or touching the severed heads of his victims.

Bundy's most brutal attack occurred on January 15, 1978, while he was on the run after escaping from prison. In the early hours of the morning, he made his way into the Florida State University Chi Omega sorority house. At around 2:45 a.m., he attacked Margaret Bowman, twenty-one, with a piece of firewood as she lay sleeping in her bed. He then used a nylon stocking to strangle her. Next, he went into Lisa Levy's bedroom. The twenty-year-old was beaten until she was unconscious, then strangled. Bundy tore off her nipple, bit her buttock, and assaulted her sexually with a bottle.

In the bedroom next door, Bundy attacked Kathy Kleiner and Karen Chandler. Kleiner had her jaw broken and her shoulder was lacerated; Chandler received a concussion, a broken jaw, a broken finger, and some of her teeth were knocked out. All four women were attacked within a period of about fifteen minutes.

After fleeing the sorority house, Bundy broke into an apartment and attacked Cheryl Thomas, a student from the university. Although she survived, she suffered a dislocated shoulder and a broken jaw; her skull was fractured in five places. The attack left her permanently deaf.

On the evening before he was due to be executed, Bundy discussed his victims with Bill Hagmaier, and his list was as follows:

Washington, eleven (Including parks; he abducted in Oregon, but killed in Washington. This includes three unidentified victims.)
Utah, eight (three unidentified)
Colorado, three
Florida, three
Oregon, two (both unidentified)
Idaho, two (one unidentified)
California, one (unidentified)

Timeline of known murders:

February 1, 1974 - Lynda Ann Healy, twenty-one - Bludgeoned while she was sleeping and then abducted. Her skull and mandible were discovered at Taylor Mountain.

March 12, 1974 - Donna Gail Manson, nineteen - Abducted while walking to a concert and murdered. Her body was left (according to Bundy) at Taylor Mountain, but it has never been found.

April 17, 1974 - Susan Elaine Rancourt, eighteen - Disappeared after attending an evening advisors' meeting at Central Washington State College. Her skull and mandible were found at Taylor Mountain.

May 6, 1974 - Roberta Kathleen Parks, twenty-two - Went missing from Oregon State University in Corvallis. Her skull and mandible were found at Taylor Mountain.

June 1, 1974 - Brenda Carol Ball, twenty-two - Disappeared after leaving the Flame Tavern in Burien. Her skull and mandible were found at Taylor Mountain.

June 11, 1974 - Georgann Hawkins, eighteen - Abducted from an alley behind her sorority house, UW. Skeletal remains recovered at Issaquah were identified by Bundy as being Hawkins.

July 14, 1974 - Janice Ann Ott, twenty-three - Abducted from Lake Sammamish State Park in broad daylight. Her skeletal remains were recovered at Issaquah.

July 14, 1974 - Denise Marie Naslund, nineteen - Abducted from the same park four hours after Ott. Her skeletal remains were recovered at Issaquah.

Utah, Colorado, Idaho

October 2, 1974 - Nancy Wilcox, sixteen - Ambushed, assaulted, and strangled in Holladay, Utah. According to Bundy, her body was buried near Capitol Reef National Park, two hundred miles (three hundred twenty km) south of Salt Lake City, but it has never been found.

October 18, 1974 - Melissa Anne Smith, seventeen - Vanished from Midvale, Utah. Her body was found in a mountain area nearby.

October 31, 1974 - Laura Ann Aime, seventeen - Disappeared from Lehi, Utah. Her body was discovered in American Fork Canyon by hikers.

November 8, 1974 - Debra Jean Kent, seventeen - Vanished after leaving a school play in Bountiful, Utah. According to Bundy, her body was left near Fairview, Utah, one hundred miles (one hundred sixty km) south of Bountiful. Only a patella bone was found, but it was never formally identified as belonging to Kent.

January 12, 1975 - Caryn Eileen Campbell, twenty-three - Disappeared from a hotel in Snowmass, Colorado. Her body was discovered dumped on a dirt road nearby.

March 15, 1975 - Julie Cunningham, twenty-six - Disappeared on the way to a tavern in Vail, Colorado. According to Bundy, her body was buried near Rifle, ninety miles (one hundred forty km) west of Vail, but it was never found.

April 6, 1975 - Denise Lynn Oliverson, twenty-five - Abducted while cycling to her parents' house in Grand Junction, Colorado. According to Bundy, her body was thrown into the Colorado River five miles (eight km) west of Grand Junction, but it has never been found.

May 6, 1975 - Lynette Dawn Culver, twelve- Abducted from Alameda Junior High School in Pocatello, Idaho. According to Bundy, her body was thrown into what authorities believe to be the Snake River, but it has never been found.

June 28, 1975 - Susan Curtis, fifteen - Disappeared during a youth conference at Brigham Young University. According to Bundy, her body was buried near Price, Utah, seventy-five miles (one hundred twenty-one km) southeast of Provo, but it has never been found.

Florida

January 15, 1978 - Margaret Elizabeth Bowman, twenty-one - Bludgeoned and then strangled as she slept at the Chi Omega sorority at Florida State University.

January 15, 1978 - Lisa Levy, twenty - Bludgeoned, strangled, and sexually assaulted as she slept at the Chi Omega sorority at Florida State University.

February 9, 1978 - Kimberly Diane Leach, twelve - Abducted from her junior high school in Lake City, Florida. Her skeletal remains were found near Suwannee River State Park, forty-three miles (sixty-nine km) west of Lake City.

Possible Victims

Bundy remains a suspect in several unsolved homicides, and he is likely responsible for others that may never be identified. During a conversation in 1987, he confided to Keppel that there were "some murders" that he would "never talk about," because they were committed "too close to home," "too close to family," or involved "victims who were very young."

August 31, 1961 - Ann Marie Burr, eight - Vanished from her home in Tacoma when Bundy was fourteen. Her house was on Bundy's newspaper delivery route. The victim's father was certain that he saw Bundy in a ditch at a construction site on the nearby UPS campus the morning his daughter disappeared. There was other circumstantial evidence suggesting Bundy was responsible, but he repeatedly denied responsibility. He even wrote a letter of denial to the Burr family in 1986. According to Keppel, Burr fits all three of Bundy's "no discussion" categories of "too close to home," "too close to family," and "very young." Forensic testing was done on material evidence from the crime scene in 2011, but the DNA samples were too degraded for analysis.

June 23, 1966 - Flight attendants Lisa E. Wick and Lonnie Trumbull, both twenty, were bludgeoned with a piece of wood as they slept in their apartment in Seattle's Queen Anne Hill district. This was near the Safeway store where Bundy was working, and the women were known to shop there. Trumbull died in the attack, but Wick survived. To date, there has been no proof Bundy was responsible, but the similarities between the crime and the later attack at the sorority were striking.

May 30, 1969 - Susan Davis and Elizabeth Perry, both nineteen, were stabbed to death while they were on vacation. Their car was found near the Garden State Parkway, Somers Point, New Jersey. Their bodies were found in nearby woods three days later. One victim was fully clothed, and the other was nude. Bundy told forensic psychologist Art Norman that his first murder victims were two women in the Philadelphia area. According to Julia, Bundy's aunt, he was wearing a leg cast due to a vehicle accident on the weekend Davis and Perry were killed. There was no record of the accident or of Bundy having to be in a leg cast, and it was later known that he would fake injuries to lure women to his car. Despite no firm evidence, he remains a suspect in this case.

July 19, 1971 - Rita Curran, twenty-four, was murdered in her apartment in Burlington, Vermont. She was bludgeoned, strangled, and raped. The crime had similarities to other murders Bundy committed, and there was a municipal record that stated a person named "Bundy" was bitten by a dog in that area the same week.

July 22, 1971 - Joyce LePage, twenty-one, disappeared from the campus of Washington State University. Her skeletal remains were found nine months later in a deep ravine south of Pullman, Washington. Bundy remains a suspect in this case.

June 29, 1973 - Rita Lorraine Jolly, seventeen, disappeared from West Linn, Oregon.

August 20, 1973 Vicki Lynn Hollar, twenty-four, disappeared from Eugene, Oregon. Bundy confessed to two homicides in Oregon but never identified the victims. Oregon detectives suspected that they were Jolly and Hollar, but they didn't get the opportunity to interview Bundy.

May 27, 1974 - Brenda Joy Baker, fourteen, had been hitchhiking near Puyallup, Washington. Her body was found in Millersylvania State Park the following month. Although Bundy was a suspect in this case, he denied responsibility.

July 1, 1974 - Sandra Jean Weaver, nineteen, disappeared from Salt Lake City. Her nude body was discovered the next day near Grand Junction, Colorado. It was believed by some that Bundy mentioned her name during his death row interview, but it couldn't be confirmed.

August 2, 1974 - Carol L. Valenzuela, twenty, disappeared while hitchhiking near Vancouver, Washington. Her remains were discovered in a shallow grave two months later, south of Olympia, along with the remains of another female victim later identified as Martha Morrison. Both women had long hair parted in the middle, like many other victims of Bundy. In August of 1974 Bundy had driven from Seattle to Salt Lake City, so he could have passed through Vancouver and Eugene en route.

September 1, 1974 - Martha Morrison, seventeen, was last seen in Eugene, Oregon.

April 15, 1975 - Melanie Suzanne "Suzy" Cooley, eighteen, disappeared after leaving her school in Nederland, Colorado, fifty miles (eighty km) northwest of Denver. Her body was discovered by road maintenance workers two weeks later in Coal Creek Canyon, twenty miles (thirty-two km) away. There is evidence (namely, gas receipts) that Bundy was in the area at the time of her murder. But, to date, the case remains unsolved.

July 1, 1975 - Shelly Kay Robertson, twenty-four, failed to show up for work in Golden, Colorado. Her remains were found by two mining students in August, five hundred feet (one hundred fifty m) inside a mine on Berthoud Pass near Winter Park Resort. There were gas receipts that put Bundy in the area at the time of the murder, but the case remains unsolved.

July 4, 1975 - Nancy Perry Baird, twenty-three, disappeared from the gas station where she worked in Farmington, Utah, twenty miles (thirty-two km) north of Salt Lake City. Her body was never found, and officially she is still listed as a missing person. During his death row interviews, Bundy denied any knowledge of, or responsibility for, the murder.

February 1976 - Debbie Smith, seventeen, disappeared from Salt Lake City. Her body was found near the Salt Lake City International Airport on April 1, 1976. Despite some publications listing Bundy as the perpetrator of this murder, the case remains unsolved.

Arrest and Trial

On August 16, 1975, Bundy failed to stop at a routine traffic stop and was caught and arrested by a Utah Highway Patrol officer in Granger, Salt Lake City. When he saw the passenger seat was missing from Bundy's car, the officer conducted a search and found a "murder kit." The items found included a mask made from pantyhose, a ski mask, handcuffs, rope, an ice pick, a crowbar, and trash bags, as well as a number of tools. Bundy tried to explain the items as being "household items," but the officer remembered the description of the car and suspect from a kidnapping in November the previous year. The details matched Bundy.

After Bundy was arrested, his apartment was searched, but nothing significant was found. Bundy was released and put on twenty-four-hour surveillance. During this period, detectives interviewed his previous girlfriend, Elizabeth Kloepfer, in Seattle. She said that before Bundy moved to Utah, she came across some odd items in her apartment and at Bundy's home. These included a bag of plaster of Paris, crutches, surgical gloves, a sack of women's clothing, and a meat cleaver.

Bundy's car, a Volkswagen Beetle, was located and retrieved from its new owner and put under forensic testing. Hairs were found that were matched to those of Caryn Campbell, Melissa Smith, and Carol DaRonch. Bundy was put in a lineup and identified by DaRonch as the man who had pretended to be "Officer Roseland."

Despite being charged with aggravated kidnapping and attempted criminal assault against DaRonch, he was let out on bail. Police continued to surveil Bundy. He went on trial in February of 1976 for the DaRonch case and was found guilty. He was sentenced to up to fifteen years in prison on June 30, 1976. In October the same year, he was found hiding among bushes on the prison grounds and was sent to solitary confinement for several weeks.

That same month he was charged with the murder of Caryn Campbell. He was transferred to Aspen for the trial and chose to represent himself in court, meaning he was excused from being handcuffed or shackled. At one point, he asked to visit the law library located in the courthouse so he could conduct research for his case. Bundy was given permission. Subsequently, he jumped out of the second-story window and escaped.

He was recaptured six days later. This wasn't to be the last time he would attempt an escape. He managed to create a hole in the ceiling of his cell and purposely lost weight so he could fit through it. At night, he would practice climbing through it and navigating the crawl space. His break for freedom occurred on December 30, 1977. Bundy piled books on his bed and covered them with a blanket so it would look like he was sleeping, then he climbed through the ceiling hole. Bundy dropped down into the chief jailer's apartment—he happened to be out for the night—stole his clothes, and walked out the front door.

Bundy committed additional murders while he was on the run. On February 15, he was pulled over once again by police. Checks on his vehicle showed Bundy's car was stolen, and when Officer David Lee informed him he was under arrest, Bundy kicked him and ran. Officer Lee fired off two warning shots then chased after him, tackling him. He subdued Bundy after a struggle, and placed him in his car for transport to jail.

By the time Bundy went to trial for his crimes, the evidence was insurmountable. It was no surprise that he was found guilty, and even less of a surprise that he received the death penalty.

Outcome

On January 24, 1989, Bundy was strapped into the electric chair. By 7:16 a.m., he was pronounced dead. His body was cremated and his ashes scattered over the Cascade Mountains in Washington.

He declined to order a special last meal; instead, he opted for the standard prison meal on offer. There were around forty-two witnesses to his execution, and many death penalty supporters lined the fences outside the prison, some holding placards that read "burn Bundy burn."

Trivia

– Bundy's 1968 Volkswagen Beetle was displayed in the lobby of the National Museum of Crime and Punishment in Washington D.C. until its closure in 2015. It is presently on exhibit at the Alcatraz East Crime Museum in Pigeon Forge, Tennessee.

Quotes by Bundy:

– "You learn what you need to kill and take care of the details... It's like changing a tire...The 1st time you're careful... By the 30th time, you can't remember where you left the lug wrench"
– "I'm the most cold-blooded sonofabitch you'll ever meet."

JOHN JUSTIN BUNTING

Date of birth: September 4, 1966

Aliases/Nicknames: The Snowtown Murders, The Bodies in Barrels Murders

Characteristics: Torture, cannibalism, murder

Number of victims: 11

Date of murders: 1992 - 1999

Date of arrest: May 19, 1999

Murder method: Strangulation, shooting

Known Victims: Clinton Trezise, 22; Ray Davies, 26; Michael Gardiner, 19; Barry Lane, 42; Thomas Trevilyan, 18; Gavin Porter, 29; Troy Youde, 21 ;Frederick Brooks, 18; Gary O'Dwyer, 29; Elizabeth Haydon, 37; David Johnson, 24

Crime location: Snowtown, South Australia

Status: Sentenced to 11 life sentences without parole.

Background

Bunting was born in Inala, Queensland, in 1966. At the age of eight, a friend's older brother sexually assaulted and beat him. By the time he was a teenager, he had developed a fascination with anatomy, weapons, and photography. In young adulthood, his opinion of homosexuals and pedophiles turned into a strong hatred. When Bunting was twenty-two years old, he was working at an abattoir, and he would brag about how he enjoyed slaughtering the animals.

In 1991, Bunting moved to Salisbury North, located in South Australia, and made friends with his neighbors Robert Wagner, Wagner's girlfriend Vanessa Laney, and Mark Haydon. This friendship would lead to Wagner assisting Bunting in committing the murders at a later date.

Also living with Bunting at the time were James Vlasskis, his mother, and his half brother. They also were drawn into Bunting's murderous acts.

Murders

In August of 1992, Clinton Trezise was invited over to Bunting's house for a visit. Once there, Bunting used a shovel to bash him to death, and he was buried in a shallow grave at Lower Light, South Australia. Bunting had claimed Trezise was a pedophile and, after the murder, would often refer to him as "Happy Pants." It would be two years before Trezise's body was found, and the case remained unsolved for some time after that.

In a caravan parked behind Suzanne Allen's house lived Ray Davies, an intellectually disabled man. Davies and Allen had once been in a relationship. Allen later claimed Davies had made sexual advances to her grandsons, and this led to his murder. He was killed by Bunting and Wagner and his disappearance was never reported. The caravan was cleaned and sold; police later found Davies' body buried in Bunting's backyard.

Wagner didn't like Michael Gardiner simply because he was a homosexual. He lived nearby in a house he shared with friends, and he was openly gay. After Bunting and Wagner had killed him, they got another friend, Frederick Brooks, to call Gardiner's friends and pretend to be the dead man so they could try to get access to his bank accounts. His body was found in one of the drums in Snowtown. They had cut off one of his feet so the lid would close properly.

Barry Lane, like Gardiner, was also a homosexual, and he was a known cross-dresser. Lane and Wagner had been in a relationship for more than ten years and they lived together. Bunting had heard that Lane had told others about the murder of Trezise. So, in October 1997, Bunting made Lane call his mother and say he was moving away. Afterward, Bunting killed Lane, dismembered his body, and placed him in the drum with the body of Michael Gardiner.

Also living with Lane was Thomas Trevilyan, whom many considered to have psychiatric problems. He only ever wore army-style clothes and would often go for very long walks with bare feet. Trevilyan had helped during the murder and dismemberment of Lane and, similarly, Bunting killed him because he had told others of the murder. Trevilyan was taken to an area of the Adelaide Hills where Bunting and Wagner forced him to stand on top of a box while they placed a noose around his neck. The box was kicked out from under him and he hanged.

In 1998, Gavin Porter was living in the same house as Bunting and Vlasskis. Porter was a heroin addict, and Bunting was infuriated when he was pricked by a used syringe when he sat on the couch. Bunting called Porter a waste and said he didn't deserve to live. Bunting and Wagner then killed him while he slept in his car in the driveway. His body was placed in a barrel that ended up at Snowtown.

Vlasskis told Bunting that his half brother, Troy Youde, had molested him when they were younger. In response, Bunting, Wagner, Vlasskis, and Haydon paid a visit to Youde in August of 1998. They dragged Youde from his bed and killed him, dismembered his body, and placed it in a barrel that was later taken to Snowtown.

Despite helping Bunting after the death of Gardiner, Frederick Brooks became the next victim on their list. The intellectually disabled man was killed on September 17, 1998. Another intellectually disabled man, Gary O'Dwyer, was killed some time in 1998. Bunting and Vlasskis made sure they got his personal banking and welfare information before they killed him so they could continue to access his welfare payments. Police discovered his body in Snowtown, covered with burn marks from electric shocks.

Elizabeth Haydon, Mark Haydon's wife, was the only female murdered by Bunting and Wagner. On November 20, 1998, while her husband and nephew were away for the day, she was murdered. Incredibly, her husband would later help try to conceal the crime. It was her murder that later led police to the old bank vault in Snowtown.

Vlasskis lured his stepbrother David Johnson to the bank in Snowtown on May 9, 1999. When Bunting said Johnson had to die, Vlasskis went along with it. Upon arriving at the building, Johnson was grabbed and handcuffed, then forced to read a script prepared by Bunting. He was also forced to give the PIN number for his bank account, and the whole spiel was recorded on a computer that had a microphone.

Vlasskis and Wagner tried to access Johnson's bank accounts, but they were unsuccessful. When they got back to Snowtown, they killed Johnson. His body was dismembered, and then Wagner and Bunting cooked up parts of his flesh and ate it.

August, 1992 - Clinton Trezise, twenty-two

December 1995 - Ray Davies

August 1997 - Michael Gardiner, nineteen

October 1997 - Barry Lane, forty-two

November 1997 - Thomas Trevilyan, eighteen

1998 - Gavin Porter, twenty-nine

August 1998 - Troy Youde, twenty-one

September 17, 1998 - Frederick Brooks, eighteen

1998 - Gary O'Dwyer, twenty-nine

November 20, 1998 - Elizabeth Haydon, thirty-seven

May 9, 1999 - David Johnson, twenty-four

Arrest and Trial

While investigating the disappearance of Elizabeth Haydon, police discovered the Snowtown location. Inside the disused bank they found the human remains of eight victims in six plastic barrels. On May 21, 1999, Bunting, Wagner, Vlasskis, and Mark Haydon were arrested for the murders.

Bunting and Wagner's trial became the longest trial in South Australian history. It lasted for nearly a year and, in December of 2003, Bunting was found guilty of committing eleven murders. Wagner was found guilty of committing ten murders, despite only confessing to three of them. Vlasskis plead guilty to four murders.

In 2004, Haydon was found guilty of assisting with five murders. As the ringleader of the group, Bunting was sentenced to eleven terms of life imprisonment without parole. Wagner received ten life sentences without parole, and Vlasskis was sentenced to four life sentences with a minimum of twenty-six years. Haydon received twenty-five years without parole for eighteen years.

Trivia

– Bunting was born with no sense of smell.

RICARDO CAPUTO

Date of birth: 1949
Aliases/Nicknames: The Lady Killer
Characteristics: Had visions and heard voices
Number of victims: 4
Date of murders: 1971 - 1977
Date of arrest: January 18, 1994
Murder method: Stabbing, strangulation
Known Victims: Natalie Brown, 19; Judith Becker, 26; Barbara Ann Taylor, 28; Laura Gomez, 23
Crime location: New York, California, Mexico
Status: Sentenced to 25 years. Died of a heart attack in prison, in October of 1997.

Background

Caputo was born in Mendoza, Argentina in 1949, and he spent his childhood there. He was described as an athletic boy who loved swimming and running. At one point, he had become quite an accomplished expert in martial arts. He was also very good at sketching. As an adult, he relied on this talent to make money when he traveled, often sketching customers in bars in exchange for a fee.

Caputo went to New York in 1970, on a six-month visa. At that time, his visa was granted because he had no prior history of criminal activity or mental health problems in his background. He began working as a waiter in various restaurants, and eventually he was hired by the Plaza Hotel as a custodian.

At a local bank, he met a teller named Natalie Brown, who was nineteen years old and lived on Long Island with her parents. Before long, they started dating. She was an attractive young lady, with long dark hair and a lovely smile. Her goal was to follow in her mother's footsteps and become a nurse. Brown's family lived a lifestyle opposite to Caputo: While he lived in cheap rented rooms and worked a menial job, her family was far more affluent.

They continued dating, however, and a year later, they traveled around Europe together. Upon their return to the United States, they announced their engagement. But a marriage would never take place, and the relationship was far from healthy.

Murders

Natalie Brown, nineteen, was found stabbed to death on July 31, 1971. Caputo was immediately suspected and arrested. He was deemed incompetent to stand trial, however, and was instead sent to Matteawan State Hospital for psychiatric treatment. There, he was under the care of Judith Becker, a psychologist at the prison hospital.

Caputo was moved to the Manhattan Psychiatric Center in October of 1973, and was occasionally given furloughs from the hospital. Often, he would turn up at Judith Becker's home, and she tried to be friendly with him. On October 21, 1974, her body was found beaten and strangled to death. Caputo was again an immediate suspect and police began to look for him.

Caputo went to San Francisco to evade capture, and there he killed another woman. Barbara Taylor was found beaten to death in 1975. Her boyfriend was suspected of the crime. When a photo of the man was circulated, it was found that he resembled Caputo, although a different name had been used.

Once again, Caputo went on the run. This time, he went to Mexico City. He killed Laura Gomez there in 1977, though little is known about this murder.

Timeline of known murders:

1971 - Natalie Brown, nineteen, Flower Hill, New York

1974 - Judith Becker, twenty-six, Yonkers, New York

1975 - Barbara Ann Taylor, twenty-eight, San Francisco

1977 - Laura Gomez, Mexico City

Other suspected victims:

1981 - Devan Green, Los Angeles

1983 - Jacqueline Bernard, sixty-four, New York City

Arrest and Trial

Caputo managed to stay undetected for almost twenty years, and he would have continued to get away with the murders if he hadn't turned himself in. On January 18, 1994, Caputo, while recalling his crimes, claimed he had an alternate personality and that he was terrified of this murderous personality coming back.

He was deemed fit to stand trial and was found guilty of committing two of the murders. He was sentenced to twenty-five years to life in prison.

Outcome

Caputo died in prison in 1997, after suffering a fatal heart attack. He was forty-eight years old.

Trivia

Quotes by Caputo:

- "I turned myself in in order to avoid any more killings."
- "When I did what I did, I was sick and I hope that I can be cured while I am incarcerated. That's all I have to say."

DAVID CARPENTER

Date of birth: May 6, 1930

Aliases/Nicknames: The Trailside Killer

Characteristics: Rape and murder

Number of victims: 7 +

Date of murders: 1979 - 1980

Date of arrest: May 14, 1981

Murder method: Shooting, stabbing

Known Victims: Heather Scaggs, 20; Ellen Hansen, 20; Richard Stowers, 19; Cynthia Moreland, 18; Shauna May, 25; Diana O'Connell, 22; Anne Alderson, 26; Anne Kelly Menjivas (suspected); Mary Frances Bennett, 23; Edda Kane (suspected);Barbara Schwartz (suspected)

Crime location: Santa Cruz and Marin Counties, California

Status: Sentenced to death, awaiting execution.

Background

Carpenter had a very difficult start to life, having an alcoholic father and a domineering mother, who both physically abused him. He developed a stutter, and by the age of seven it was so bad he was unable to socialize properly with other children. He was also forced to take part in violin lessons and ballet, which led to even more teasing by his peers.

As a child, Carpenter was a bed-wetter. Later, he enjoyed torturing animals. When he was seventeen years old, he was arrested and convicted for the molestation of two younger children who happened to be his cousins. He spent a year in prison before being released.

Carpenter continued to molest children until he married in 1955. The couple had three children of their own and, to support the family, Carpenter would take on a variety of work including working as a printer and salesman. He also was involved with the coast guard and was honorably discharged from the service.

Despite being married, Carpenter frequently stalked other women, and in 1960, he lured a woman into the woods. There she was tied up with a clothesline, beaten with a hammer, and stabbed in the hand. A military patrol officer came across the scene, and a gunfire exchange took place. Carpenter was shot and injured, and arrested. He was convicted of assault with intent to commit murder, as well as two counts of assault with a deadly weapon.

He was sentenced to fourteen years of imprisonment. While incarcerated, his wife divorced him. Carpenter was assessed by the prison psychiatrists, and they determined he was suffering from a sociopathic personality disorder. He only served nine years of his sentence and, upon release, he found another woman and remarried. This marriage would also fail.

From then, the attacks Carpenter made on women escalated, with many being abducted, raped, and beaten. In 1979, his attacks became even more violent, and he began to kill his victims.

Murders

Carpenter's first victim was Edda Kane, forty-four, who was killed on August 19, 1979. Her naked body was found on August 20, 1979, on a hiking trail in the Mount Tamalpais State Park. Her autopsy showed she had been killed "execution style" with a gunshot to the head while she had been kneeling.

On March 8, 1980, Barbara Swartz, twenty-three, went for a hike in the park and met a terrible fate. Her body was discovered the following day on a trail in the park. She had been stabbed multiple times in the chest while kneeling. Anne Alderson disappeared from the park on October 15, 1980. Her body was found the following day; she had been shot three times in the head while kneeling.

On November 27, Shauna May, twenty-five, was meant to meet with her lover at Point Reyes Park but never showed up. Her body was found in a shallow grave two days later. Next to her was the corpse of Diana O'Connell, who had disappeared in October. Both women had been shot in the head. Hours before these two victims were found, two other bodies had been discovered. Richard Stowers and Cynthia Moreland had gone missing in September, after telling people they were going for a hike in the park. They too had been killed execution style, with gunshot wounds to the head.

Carpenter attacked again on March 29, 1981, but this time the location was Henry Cowle State Park, near Santa Cruz. Stephen Haertle and Ellen Hansen were ambushed as they hiked, and when Carpenter said he was going to rape Hansen, she tried to warn him off. He opened fire on the couple, killing Hansen and seriously wounding Haertle, who managed to crawl for help. Haertle was able to give police a good description of Carpenter.

Carpenter's next murder would be his undoing. On May 1, 1981, Heather Scaggs went missing from San Jose after telling her boyfriend she was going to buy a car from David Carpenter, in San Francisco. She had said Carpenter told her to come alone. Her body was found on May 24, in the Big Basin Redwood State Park.

Timeline of known murders/dates bodies found:

August 19, 1979 - Edda Kane, forty-four

October 21, 1979 - Mary Frances Bennett, twenty-three

March 8, 1980 - Barbara Schwartz, twenty-three

October 11, 1980 - Richard Stowers, nineteen

October 11, 1980 - Cynthia Moreland, eighteen

October 15, 1980- Anne Alderson, twenty-six

November 28, 1980 - Diana O'Connell, twenty-two

November 28, 1980 - Shauna May, twenty-five

March 29, 1981 - Ellen Hansen, twenty

May 1, 1981 - Heather Scaggs, twenty

Arrest and Trial

Police visited Carpenter following the disappearance of Heather Scaggs, and noticed he resembled the description and composite sketches provided by Haertle. When Haertle was shown a lineup of mug shots, he picked out Carpenter as the man who'd attacked him and Hansen. Carpenter was arrested on May 14.

When police searched Carpenter's home, they were unable to find a weapon. But they did find a witness who claimed to have sold Carpenter a .45 caliber gun, and another witness also said he had bought a .38 revolver in June from Carpenter. The police located this weapon and, when it was tested, it was found to be the same gun that had been used in the attacks on Haertle, Hansen, and Scaggs.

Carpenter went to trial in April of 1984, in Los Angeles. The evidence was indisputable, and he was found guilty of the murders of Scaggs and Hansen. He was sentenced to death. On May 10, 1988, Carpenter was found guilty of first-degree murder in a San Diego court for the killing of Richard Stowers, Cynthia Moreland, Diana O'Connell, Shauna May, and Anne Alderson.

Outcome

Carpenter was sent to San Quentin to await his execution. The appeals process is still ongoing.

RICHARD TRENTON CHASE

Date of birth: May 23, 1950

Aliases/Nicknames: The Vampire of Sacramento

Characteristics: Necrophilia, mutilation, cannibalism, mentally ill

Number of victims: 6

Date of murders: December 1977 - January 1978

Date of arrest: January 27, 1978

Murder method: Shooting

Known Victims: Ambrose Griffin, 51; Teresa Wallin, 22 (three months pregnant); Evelyn Miroth, 38; her son, Jason, 6; her nephew, David, 22-months-old; and her friend, Dan Meredith, 51

Crime location: Sacramento, California

Status: Sentenced to death. Committed suicide, on December 26th, 1980, by overdosing on prescribed medication.

Background

A Sacramento native, Chase was born on May 23, 1950, into and abusive environment. Chase also suffered abuse at the hands of his mother. By the time he was ten years old, he was already displaying traits of the Macdonald triad - arson, enuresis (bed-wetting), and cruelty to animals. As he grew into adolescence, he was known to use both drugs and alcohol chronically.

Chase developed some bizarre beliefs and hypochondria as he got older. He believed his heart would stop beating at times. At one point, he even stated that "someone had stolen [his] pulmonary artery." Supposedly, he would hold oranges on top of his head because he believed his brain would absorb the vitamin C. According to Chase, the bones of his skull moved around and were separated, so he shaved off his hair so he could see the movement take place.

Chase eventually moved out of his mother's home because he was suspicious she was trying to poison him. He moved into an apartment with some friends, but they soon began complaining of his constant state of intoxication. He also had a habit of wandering around the apartment with no clothes on, even when visitors were present. The friends told Chase to move out, but he refused to go. So, they left the apartment instead.

Now that he had the apartment to himself, Chase was able to indulge in the macabre desires, fantasies, and interests that he had kept hidden. He would catch animals, kill them, and disembowel them. At times, he would eat the dead animals raw; other times, he placed the organs in a blender with some Coca-Cola and drank the awful concoction. When asked why he ate the animals, he said he believed that ingesting them would stop his "heart from shrinking."

In 1975, Chase injected the blood of a rabbit into his veins and was taken to hospital for treatment. Subsequently, he was committed to a mental institution against his will. While he was a patient there, staff discovered him with blood around his mouth. It turned out that he had been catching birds and drinking their blood.

Chase's behavior was downright bizarre, and his claims were too fantastic to be believed. He stated he had drained blood from a therapy dog and injected it to help him with his drug and alcohol addictions. He would also smear his own feces on the walls of his room, as well as on himself.

Chase was diagnosed with paranoid schizophrenia. He was released in 1976, after finding a suitable treatment regime with medication, because he was no longer considered a threat to society. He was put under his mother's care, but she weaned Chase off his medication and helped him get another apartment.

At some point in 1977, Chase was found on a reservation in Nevada and arrested. He had blood smeared all over his body, and in his truck was a bucket full of blood. The blood was determined to be cow's blood, however, and charges were dropped.

Murders

Chase's first victim was Ambrose Griffin, a father of two who became a random target when Chase drove by and shot him on December 29, 1977. In less than a month, he claimed his next victim, Teresa Wallin. On January 23, 1978, Chase surprised Wallin, who was pregnant, in her own home. He shot her three times, killing her, and then raped her as he stabbed her multiple times with a knife. Chase cut off her nipple and drank her blood. He also removed some of the internal organs from her body. He then collected up dog feces from outside and shoved it in to her mouth and throat.

A few days later, on January 27, Chase entered Evelyn Miroth's home. He came across her friend Danny Meredith, and shot him before sealing his car keys and wallet. He then shot and killed Evelyn, her son, and her nephew. Chase engaged in necrophiliac acts with Evelyn's body; he also indulged in cannibalism. A little girl, who had been invited over to play, then knocked on the door. Chase took off in Meredith's car, taking the body of twenty-two-month-old David Ferreira with him. A neighbor was alerted and the police called.

Timeline of known murders:

December 29, 1977 - Ambrose Griffin, fifty-one

January 23, 1978 - Teresa Wallin, twenty-two

January 27, 1978 - Danny Meredith, fifty-one

January 27, 1978 - Evelyn Miroth, thirty-eight

January 27, 1978 - Jason Miroth, six

January 27, 1978 - David Ferreira, twenty-two months

Arrest and Trial

When police investigated the crime scene at the Miroth house, they found perfect palm prints in the blood that led them directly to Chase. He was arrested and once he had been linked to the other murders, he was charged with six counts of murder. The defense tried to have the charges dropped to second-degree murder by referring to Chase's mental health history, but they were unsuccessful. On May 8, 1979, Chase was found guilty of six counts of first-degree murder and sentenced to death.

While in prison, other inmates were frightened of Chase because of the horrific nature of his crimes.

Some even tried to convince Chase to kill himself. During interviews with Robert Ressler, Chase exhibited bizarre beliefs and behavior. At one point, he gave Ressler a pile of macaroni and cheese he had been hoarding in his pockets.

Outcome

On Boxing Day 1980, a guard found Chase lying strangely on his bed. Upon inspection, it was found he had stopped breathing. An autopsy was conducted and it was determined that Chase had committed suicide by overdosing on antidepressant medication he had been stockpiling over a number of weeks.

Trivia

- Serial killer Richard Chase once attempted to enter the home of a woman but, finding that her doors were locked, walked away. Chase later told detectives that he took locked doors as a sign that he was not welcome, but that unlocked doors were an invitation to come inside.

Quote by Chase:

- "Magic is the envelopment and coercion of the objective world by the ego; it is a dynamic subjectivism. Religion is the coercion of the ego by gods and spirits who are objectively conceived beings in control of nature and man."

ANDREI CHIKATILO

Date of birth: October 16, 1936

Aliases/Nicknames: The Butcher of Rostov, The Forest Strip Killer, The Red Ripper, The Rostov Ripper

Characteristics: Necrophilia, cannibalism, mutilation, evisceration

Number of victims: 53 - 56

Date of murders: 1978 - 1990

Date of arrest: November 20, 1990

Murder method: Stabbing, strangulation

Known Victims: Lena Zakotnova, 9; Larisa Tkachenko, 17; Lyubov Biryuk, 13; Lyubov Volobuyeva, 14; Oleg Pozhidayev, 9; Olga Kuprina, 16; Irina Karabelnikova, 19; Sergey Kuzmin, 15; Olga Stalmachenok, 10; Laura Sarkisyan, 15; Irina Dunenkova, 13; Lyudmila Kushuba, 24; Igor Gudkov, 7; Valentina Chuchulina, 22; unknown woman (18-25); Vera Shevkun, 19; Sergey Markov, 14; Natalya Shalapinina, 17; Marta Ryabenko, 45; Dmitriy Ptashnikov, 10; Tatyana Petrosyan, 32; Svetlana Petrosyan, 11; Yelena Bakulina, 22; Dmitriy Illarionov, 13; Anna Lemesheva, 19; Svetlana Tsana, 20; Natalya Golosovskaya, 16; Lyudmila Alekseyeva, 17; unknown woman (20-25); Akmaral Seydaliyeva, 12; Alexander Chepel, 11; Irina Luchinskaya, 24; Natalya Pokhlistova, 18; Irina Gulyayeva, 18; Oleg Makarenkov, 13; Ivan Bilovetskiy, 12; Yuri Tereshonok, 16; unknown woman (18-25); Alexey Voronko, 9; Yevgeniy Muratov, 15; Tatyana Ryzhova, 16; Alexander Dyakonov, 8; Alexey Moiseyev, 10; Helena Varga, 19; Alexey Khobotov, 10; Andrei Kravchenko, 11; Yaroslav Makarov, 10; Lyubov Zuyeva, 31; Viktor Petrov, 13; Ivan Fomin, 11; Vadim Gromov, 16; Viktor Tishchenko, 16; Svetlana Korostik, 22

Crime location: Rostov Oblast, Russia

Status: Executed by gunshot to the head on February 16, 1994.

Background

In 1936, when Chikatilo was born, there was a massive famine in the Ukraine due to the forced collectivization of agriculture created by the ruler Joseph Stalin. Chikatilo's parents were collective farm laborers, which meant that instead of receiving monetary payment for their work, they were given the right to cultivate their own food on some land behind the one-bedroom hut the family lived in.

There was a huge shortage of food, and Chikatilo claimed he didn't eat bread until he was twelve years old. The family would often eat leaves and grass to rid themselves of hunger pains. His mother told him repeatedly that he had once had an older brother who was kidnapped when he was four years old and eaten by the neighbors. This has never been corroborated though, and it remains a mystery as to whether or not this ever happened.

His father was drafted into the Red Army during World War II and was, at one point, wounded and taken prisoner by the Nazis. When the Nazis occupied the Ukraine, Chikatilo claimed to have seen numerous horrifying incidents, including fires, bombings, and shootings, and he would hide with his mother to survive. They even had to watch their home burn down. Chikatilo had to sleep in a single bed with his mother. He was a chronic bed-wetter, and his mother would beat him each time he messed the bed.

In 1943, while his father was still away in the Army, his mother gave birth to a girl, Tatyana. There was much speculation as to who the father of the baby was, given her husband's absence. It was well-known that women were often raped by German soldiers during the occupation; perhaps Chikatilo had even witnessed it, given the tiny hut they were living in at the time.

Chikatilo was a good student at school, but he was shy and physically weak. He was constantly hungry due to the famine and would often faint at school and at home. He became a target for bullying given his obvious poverty, his small stature, and his shyness. At home, he was bullied by his mother, who berated him constantly. Tatyana, his sister, later stated that their mother was unforgiving and incredibly harsh toward her children, whereas their father was kind.

Murders

The murders Chikatilo committed were violently brutal and what he did to the bodies of his victims was incomprehensible. Chikatilo would often gouge out the eyes of his victims, believing they contained a "snapshot" of the last thing the victim saw. When he discovered this wasn't true, he stopped doing it.

The bodies were usually mutilated. Some had their noses bitten off, their stomachs eviscerated, and their genitals and tongues cut off or cut out. During the murder of one of his female victims, Chikatilo bit off her nipple and swallowed it, which resulted in him ejaculating. Before they were dead, he sometimes shoved leaves and mud into his victims' mouths to keep them quiet.

Timeline of known murders:

December 22, 1978 - Lena Zakotnova, nine - Chikatilo accosted the young girl while she was walking home from an ice-skating rink.

September 3, 1981 - Larisa Tkachenko, seventeen - Approached and killed by Chikatilo while she was waiting for a bus to take her back to boarding school.

June 12, 1982 - Lyubov Biryuk, thirteen - Abducted and murdered after a shopping trip in the village of Donskoi.

July 25, 1982 - Lyubov Volobuyeva, fourteen - Killed in an orchard near Krasnodar Airport. Her body was found on August 7.

August 13, 1982 - Oleg Pozhidayev, nine - This was the first male victim. Pozhidayev was killed in Adygea, and his body has never been found.

August of 1982 - Olga Kuprina, sixteen - Killed in Kazachi Lagerya. Her body was found on October 27.

September 12, 1982 - Irina Karabelnikova, nineteen - She was lured away from Shakhty station and murdered. Her body was found on September 20.

September of 1982 - Sergey Kuzmin, fifteen - A boarding school runaway, Kuzmin's body was found near Shakhty station in January, 1983.

December 11, 1982 - Olga Stalmachenok, ten - Olga was lured off a bus while riding home from her piano lessons in Novoshakhtinsk.

June of 1983 - Laura Sarkisyan, fifteen - Sarkisyan was from Armenia. Her body was never found.

July of 1983 - Irina Dunenkova, thirteen. Dunenkova's body was found in Aviators Park, Rostov, on August 8, 1983.

1983 - Lyudmila Kushuba, twenty-four - Killed in woodland near a Shakhty bus station. Her body was found on March 12, 1984.

August 9, 1983 - Igor Gudkov, seven - Gudkov was Chikatilo's youngest victim. He was the first male victim linked to the manhunt.

September of 1983 - Valentina Chuchulina, twenty-two - Her body was found on November 27, 1983, in woodland near Kirpichnaya station.

Between late September and early October of 1983 - Unknown woman, eighteen to twenty-five - Chikatilo claimed he encountered this victim while she tried to find a "man (client) with a car."

October 27, 1983 - Vera Shevkun, nineteen - Was murdered in a mining village near Shakhty. Her body was found on October 30.

December 27, 1983 - Sergey Markov, fourteen - Disappeared while returning home from work experience. His body was found on January 4, 1984.

January 9, 1984 - Natalya Shalapinina, seventeen - Shalapinina had been a close friend of Olga Kuprina, killed by Chikatilo in 1982.

February 22, 1984 - Marta Ryabenko, forty-five - Chikatilo's oldest victim, she was killed in Aviators Park, Rostov.

March 24, 1984 - Dmitriy Ptashnikov, ten - This boy was lured away from a kiosk selling stamps by Chikatilo, who pretended to be a fellow collector.

May 25, 1984 - Tatyana Petrosyan, thirty-two - Murdered at the same time as her daughter outside Shakhty. She had known Chikatilo since 1978.

May 25, 1984 - Svetlana Petrosyan, eleven - Svetlana saw Chikatilo murder her mother before he chased her and killed her with a hammer.

June of 1984 - Yelena Bakulina, twenty-two - Bakulina's body was found on August 27, in the Bagasenski region of Rostov.

July 10, 1984 - Dmitriy Illarionov, thirteen - Vanished in Rostov while on his way to get a health certificate, so he could attend summer camp.

July 19, 1984 - Anna Lemesheva, nineteen - Disappeared on her way to a dentist appointment. She was killed in Shakhty.

July of 1984 - Svetlana Tsana, twenty - Originally from Riga. Her body was found on September 9 in Aviators Park, Rostov

August 2, 1984 - Natalya Golosovskaya, sixteen - Vanished on a visit to Novoshakhtinsk, where she was to visit her sister.

August 7, 1984 - Lyudmila Alekseyeva, seventeen - A student lured from a bus stop by Chikatilo, who offered to direct her to Rostov's bus terminal.

Between August 7 and 13 of 1984 - Unknown woman, twenty to twenty-five - Killed in Tashkent by Chikatilo while on a business trip to the Uzbek SSR city.

August 13, 1984 - Akmaral Seydaliyeva, eleven - A runaway from Alma-Ata, Kazakhstan, Seydaliyeva was killed by Chikatilo in Tashkent.

August 28, 1984 - Alexander Chepel, eleven - Chepel was killed on the banks of the Don River, near where Alekseyeva had been killed.

September 6, 1984 - Irina Luchinskaya, twenty-four - A Rostov librarian, killed by Chikatilo in Aviators Park, Rostov.

August 1, 1985 - Natalya Pokhlistova, eighteen - Lured off a train by Chikatilo near Domodedovo Airport, Moscow Oblast. Her body was found on August 3.

August 27, 1985 - Irina Gulyayeva, eighteen - Killed in a grove of trees near Shakhty bus station. Her body was found the following day.

May 16, 1987 - Oleg Makarenkov, thirteen - Killed in Sverdlovsk, Ukraine, Chikatilo led police to his remains after his arrest.

July 29, 1987 - Ivan Bilovetskiy, twelve - Killed by Chikatilo on a business trip to Zaporizhya, Ukrainian SSR. His body was found on July 30.

September 15, 1987 - Yuri Tereshonok, sixteen - Was lured off a train in Leningrad Oblast and killed. Chikatilo led police to his remains after he was arrested.

Between late September of 1987 and early May of 1988 - Unknown woman, eighteen to twenty-five - Killed near Krasny Sulin train station. Her body was found on April 6.

May 14, 1988 - Alexey Voronko, nine - Voronko was killed near a train station in Ilovaisk, Ukraine: the Rostov–Ukraine rail route.

July 14, 1988 - Yevgeniy Muratov, fifteen - The first victim killed near Rostov since 1985. Muratov's body was found on April 10, 1989.

February 1989 - Tatyana Ryzhova, sixteen - A runaway from Krasny Sulin, she was killed in Chikatilo's own daughter's apartment.

May 11, 1989 - Alexander Dyakonov, eight - Killed in Rostov city centre the day after his eighth birthday. His body was found on July 14.

June 20, 1989 - Alexey Moiseyev, ten - Killed in the Vladimir region, east of Moscow. Chikatilo confessed to this murder after his arrest.

August 19, 1989 - Helena Varga, nineteen - A student from Hungary who had a child. She was lured off a bus and killed in a village near Rostov.

August 28, 1989 - Alexey Khobotov, ten - Vanished from outside a theater in Shakhty. Chikatilo led police to his remains after his arrest.

January 14, 1990 - Andrei Kravchenko, eleven - Lured from a cinema by Chikatilo. He was killed in Shakhty. Kravchenko's body was found on February 19.

March 7, 1990 - Yaroslav Makarov, ten - Lured from a Rostov train station by Chikatilo. He was killed in Rostov botanical gardens.

April of 1990 - Lyubov Zuyeva, thirty-one - Lured off a train near the Donleskhoz station near Shakhty. Her body was found on August 24.

July 27, 1990 - Viktor Petrov, thirteen - Killed in Rostov botanical gardens, a few yards from where Makarov had been murdered.

August 14, 1990 - Ivan Fomin, eleven - Killed at Novocherkassk municipal beach. His body was found on August 17.

October 17, 1990 - Vadim Gromov, sixteen - A student from Shakhty. Gromov vanished while riding the train to Taganrog.

October 30, 1990 - Viktor Tishchenko, sixteen - Killed in Shakhty. Tishchenko fought hard for his life; he was the victim who bit Chikatilo's finger.

November 6, 1990 - Svetlana Korostik, twenty-two - Chikatilo's last victim. Her body was found on November 13 in woodland near Donleskhoz station.

Arrest and Trial

In November of 1990, Chikatilo was stopped by police and questioned when he was found in the same area as one of his victims, Svetlana Korostik. On November 14, he was arrested and formally interviewed. What followed was a confession that lasted two weeks, as Chikatilo gave the details of fifty-six murders he claimed he had committed.

Chikatilo went on trial on April 14, 1992, during which he had to be kept inside a special iron cage to protect him from his victims' families. Throughout the trial his behavior was strange. At one point, he said he was lactating because he was pregnant, he yelled out that he wasn't a homosexual, and twice he pulled his pants down. While the final argument was being presented by the prosecutor, Chikatilo began to sing and had to be removed from the courtroom.

Despite his bizarre actions, Chikatilo was deemed to be sane by a number of psychiatrists. On October 14, 1992, he was found guilty of fifty-two murders and sentenced to death.

Outcome

Chikatilo made a number of appeals to the Russian Supreme Court to save his life, to no avail. His last appeal was sent to the president at the time, Boris Yeltsin, but this too was denied on January 4, 1994.

On February 14, 1994, Chikatilo was transferred from his cell to a soundproofed room within the prison. He was executed by a single gunshot to the head.

Trivia

Quotes by Chikatilo:

- "What I did was not for sexual pleasure. Rather it brought me some peace of mind."
- Before his execution - "When I used my knife, it brought psychological relief. I know I have to be destroyed. I was a mistake of nature."
- "The blood and the agony gave me relaxation and a certain pleasure."

THOR NIS CHRISTIANSEN

Date of birth: December 28, 1957

Aliases/Nicknames: Nil

Characteristics: Necrophilia, hitchhikers

Number of victims: 4

Date of murders: 1976 - 1979

Date of arrest: July 7, 1979

Murder method: Shooting

Known Victims: Jacqueline Anne Rook, 21; Mary Ann Sarris, 19; Patricia Marie Laney, 21; Laura Sue Benjamin, 22

Crime location: Santa Barbara and Los Angeles Counties, California

Status: Sentenced to life imprisonment. Stabbed to death in prison, March 30, 1981.

Background

Christiansen was born in Denmark, 1957. When he was five years old, the family immigrated to the United States; they eventually settled in Solvang, California. Christiansen was regarded as being an ordinary child, who did well at school. But, all that changed when he reached the age of sixteen.

Christiansen dropped out of high school and moved out of home, finding work as an attendant at a gas station. During this time, he began to gain a lot of weight; he went from being a slender young man to weighing around two hundred seventy-five pounds.

It was also around this time that his thoughts began to turn dark, and he would fantasize about killing women and sexually violating their bodies. Before long, these thoughts turned into actions, and Christiansen began to kill.

Murders

On December 6, 1976, Christiansen abducted Jacqueline Rook, twenty-one, from a bus stop in Goleta, Santa Barbara. The very same day, Mary Sarris, who was a waitress in Goleta, also went missing. On January 18, 1977, Patricia Laney, twenty-two, went missing from another bus stop in Goleta. Her body was discovered the next day in Refugio Canyon. Two days later, the body of Rook was found in the same area. On May 22, the body of Sarris was found in Drum Canyon.

On April 18, 1979, Linda Preston, twenty-four, was hitchhiking in Hollywood when she was picked up by Christiansen. They drove along for several blocks, then he pulled out a gun and fired into her ear.

Although she was bleeding badly, she was able to jump from his car and escape.

Laura Benjamin, twenty-three, was abducted and killed by Christiansen on May 26, 1979.

Known victims:

December 6, 1976 - Jacqueline Anne Rook, twenty-one - Isla Vista

December 6, 1976 - Mary Ann Sarris, nineteen - Isla Vista

January 18, 1977 - Patricia Marie Laney, twenty-one - Isla Vista

May 26, 1979 - Laura Sue Benjamin, twenty-three - Los Angeles County

Arrest and Trial

Preston, who had survived being shot by Christiansen, happened to see him in a tavern on July 11, and she immediately called the police. He was arrested and charged with the serious assault. While he was in custody, police noticed there were similar aspects between his attack on Preston and the unsolved murders of Rook, Sarris, and Laney. He was subsequently charged with three counts of first-degree murder; he was then charged with the murder of Laura Benjamin.

His first trial in early 1980 was for the murder of Benjamin. Initially, he tried to plead insanity, but he changed his mind and withdrew the plea. He went to trial in June of 1980 for the murders of Rook, Sarris, and Laney, and decided to plead guilty to all charges. He was sentenced to spend his life in prison.

Outcome

Christiansen was murdered in prison on March 30, 1981. He was found in the Folsom Prison exercise yard with a single stab wound to the chest. The murderer was never identified.

DOUG CLARK

Date of birth: March 10, 1948

Aliases/Nicknames: The Hollywood Slasher, The Sunset Strip Killer, The Sunset Strip Slayer

Characteristics: Necrophilia, pedophilia, decapitation

Number of victims: 7

Date of murders: June 1980 - August 1980

Date of arrest: August 12, 1980

Murder method: Shooting

Known Victims: Karen Jones, 24; Exxie Wilson, 21; Marnette Comer, 17; Jack Robert Murray, 45; Gina Narano, 15; Cynthia Chandler, 16; unknown girl

Crime location: Burbank and Los Angeles, California

Status: Sentenced to death, awaiting execution.

Background

Clark's family moved around a lot when he was a child, due to his father Franklin being a naval intelligence officer. It was later claimed that they had resided in thirty-seven countries during Clark's childhood. His father resigned from the Navy in 1958, and took an engineering position with a transport company in Texas. But this didn't keep the family settled, and before long they were on the move again.

At one point, Clark was sent to an exclusive school in Geneva, and he then attended the Culver Military Academy. Following his graduation in 1967, he enlisted in the air force. It was around this time that everything seemed to start unravelling, and he was eventually discharged from the force.

Over the next ten years, Clark drifted around. Sometimes he found work as a mechanic. But his real passion was to become a sexual athlete, and he often referred to himself as "the king of the one-night stand." He worked as a steam plant operator in Los Angeles, for the Los Angeles Department of Water and Power, based at the Valley Generating Station. But this didn't last, and one night he just decided to quit.

He then worked at the Jergens soap factory, located in Burbank, as a boiler operator. But this didn't last long either. He was often absent from work and had even made violent threats toward some co-workers, so he was fired.

In 1980, he met Carol Bundy in a local bar, and they became a couple. Soon after, Clark moved in with Bundy and he discovered that she had fantasies similar to his own.

Murders

Clark's first known victim was Marnette Comer, seventeen, who had been a runaway. Her body was found in the San Fernando Valley woods, and it appeared she had been killed at the beginning of June. On June 11, Clark picked up two teenagers, Gina Narano and Cynthia Chandler, on the Sunset Strip. He told them to perform oral sex on him, and then shot them both in the head. Afterwards, he took them to a garage and raped their corpses. Their bodies were found the next day near the Ventura Freeway.

Bundy was uncomfortable with Clark's story of the murders and called the police. She claimed she had some knowledge, but refused to give any clues as to who the murderer was. Clark had previously told Bundy that if they were ever caught, he would take the full blame so she wouldn't go to prison.

On June 24, Karen Jones and Exxie Wilson were lured into Clark's car. The two women were shot and killed before being dumped out in plain sight. Wilson's head was removed and kept in the fridge, and Bundy would put makeup on it before Clark used it for necrophiliac acts. Two days after the murders, the head was cleaned and put in a box before it was left in an alleyway.

Bundy then began to spend some time with John Murray, a man she knew before she'd met Clark. A part-time singer, Bundy was infatuated with Murray, and one night she told him what she and Clark had been doing. Murray was shocked, and gave the impression he was going to tell the police. On August 5, Bundy enticed Murray into his van to engage in sex. Instead, she shot him and cut off his head.

Two days after killing Murray, Bundy couldn't handle the stress of the situation and confessed to a co-worker that she had murdered him. The police were promptly called.

Timeline of known murders:

June 1, 1980 - Marnette Comer, seventeen

June 11, 1980 - Gina Narano, fifteen

June 11, 1980 - Cynthia Chandler, sixteen

June 24, 1980 - Karen Jones, twenty-four

June, 1980 - Exxie Wilson, twenty

July 25, 1980 - Jane Doe

August 5, 1980 - Jack Robert Murray, forty-five

Arrest and Trial

Bundy gave the police a complete explanation of the crimes she had committed with Clark, which led to his immediate arrest. Clark was charged with six counts of murder and Bundy was charged with two. When Clark went to trial, he tried to put all the blame on Bundy, making himself out to be an innocent fool. But, his attempts to lessen his own involvement in the crimes failed, and he was found guilty and sentenced to death.

In return for her testimony against Clark, Bundy made a plea bargain. She received a life sentence, avoiding the death penalty. Bundy died in prison on December 9, 2003, from heart failure.

Outcome

Clark is still sitting on death row awaiting his date with the executioner.

Trivia

- Clark's lawyer was allegedly intoxicated throughout the case, and several times he fell asleep while Clark was being cross-examined by the prosecution. He made the request to defend himself, but was denied any advisory counsel, co-counsel, or even the services of a law clerk. The judge told him to "go it alone," which was actually illegal.

THE CLEVELAND TORSO MURDERER

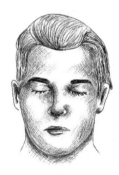

Date of birth: Unknown

Aliases/Nicknames: Mad Butcher of Kingsbury Run

Characteristics: Dismemberment, decapitation, castration, use of chemicals

Number of victims: 12- 20

Date of murders: 1935 - 1938

Date of arrest: Not captured

Murder method: Most likely decapitation

Known Victims: Edward Andrassy; Florence Genevieve Polillo; others unidentified

Crime location: Cleveland, Ohio

Status: Never identified, therefore not apprehended.

Background

The Cleveland Torso Murderer, who remains unidentified to this day, has been linked to up to twenty murders that took place between 1935 and 1938. There are at least twelve victims officially attributed to the work of this serial killer, and each had been dismembered. Those who worked on the Cleveland Torso Murderer case believe that there are other murders he may be responsible for, including some from the 1920s and 1950s.

This serial killer tended to target drifters. For this reason, some of the victims have never been identified. He murdered both men and women, seeming to have no preference for one gender over the other. It was the era of the Great Depression, and his victims all appeared to come from the lower classes of society.

Each victim was beheaded. In some cases, the torso was also cut in half, which lead to the moniker "The Cleveland Torso Murderer." The majority of the male victims had their genitals removed, and some victims displayed evidence of some sort of chemical treatment on their body. Most were discovered long after their deaths, and the advanced level of decomposition also made it difficult to identify the bodies. To add to this difficulty, many of the heads were never located.

Eliot Ness was the Public Safety Director of Cleveland during the period of the twelve official murders. Although he wasn't heavily involved in the investigation, he did assist with the interrogation of one suspect, Dr. Francis E. Sweeney. Ness also oversaw the burning of the Kingsbury Run area, which is where the killer abducted most of his victims.

Whoever the Cleveland Torso Murderer was, he seemed to delight in taunting Ness. At one point, he placed the dead remains of two of his victims directly in the line of sight of Ness' office.

Murders

The first victim attributed to the Torso Murderer was Edward Andrassy, found in the Jackass Hill area of Kingsbury Run. His body was found on September 23, 1935; he had been decapitated and his genitals removed. It was estimated he had been dead for two or three days. Around thirty feet away was the body of a John Doe, who also had been decapitated and castrated. The skin of his body had been exposed to some sort of chemical, which made it red in color and leathery. This victim was estimated to have been dead for three or four weeks.

Florence Genevieve Polillo was killed somewhere between January 26 and February 7, 1936. Her body was found in downtown Cleveland, and it had been dismembered. Her head was never found; it was believed she had been dead for two to four days.

The second John Doe was killed around June 5, 1936. It was believed he had still been alive when his head was cut off. Unlike Polillo, his head was found, and he had been dead for around two days when he was discovered. The next murder occurred around May of 1936. The body of a third John Doe was found on July 22, in the Big Creek area of Brooklyn. He too had been decapitated while still alive.

On September 10, 1936, half of a male torso was found in Kingsbury Run. This victim was unidentified, and there was nothing attached to the torso below the hips. The head was never located, and the man had been dead for about two days. The next body missing its head was found on February 23, 1937. The body was female and was never identified.

The body of a black Jane Doe was found on June 6, 1937, underneath the Lorain-Carnegie Bridge. The head had been removed along with a rib. This victim had been dead for about a year. The body of an unidentified male was found on July 6, 1937, in the Cuyahoga River. The head was never located.

A leg belonging to an unidentified female was found in the Cuyahoga River on April 8, 1938. The following month, a thigh was found in the river, and then a sack containing other body parts was discovered under the bridge. In all, the thighs, a foot, a lower leg, and a torso was found. This victim had drugs in her system, unlike the other victims.

The last two victims were discovered on August 16, 1938. An unidentified female and an unidentified male were found at the Lakeshore Dump. Both had been decapitated, though both heads were recovered.

Timeline of known murders:

September 23, 1935 - Edward Andrassy

September 23, 1935 - John Doe I

January 26/February 7, 1936 - Florence Genevieve Polillo

June 5, 1936 - John Doe II, "The Tattooed Man"

July 22, 1936 - John Doe III

September 10, 1936 - John Doe IV

February 23, 1937 - Jane Doe I

June 6, 1937 - Jane Doe II

July 6, 1937 - John Doe V

April 8, 1938 - Jane Doe III

August 16, 1938 - Jane Doe IV

August 16, 1938 - John Doe VI

Suspects

A Cleveland resident, Frank Dolezal, was arrested on August 24, 1939, under suspicion of being responsible for the death of Florence Polillo. Six weeks after he was arrested however, Dolezal died in prison. He was found to have six broken ribs, which weren't present before he was arrested. Although he had admitted at one point to killing Florence in self-defense, it is generally believed that he wasn't responsible for her murder or any of the others.

Another potential suspect was Dr. Francis E. Sweeney, a World War I veteran who had extensive experience with amputations in the field during the war. Sweeney was interviewed by Eliot Ness, the Cleveland Public Safety Director at the time, and was given two polygraph examinations, both of which he failed. Sweeney committed himself to a mental hospital, and there was no further evidence to suggest he was the killer.

CARROLL EDWARD COLE

Date of birth: May 9, 1938

Aliases/Nicknames: Nil

Characteristics: Cannibalism, dismemberment

Number of victims: 16

Date of murders: 1948, 1971 - 1980

Date of arrest: 1980

Murder method: Strangulation, drowning

Known Victims: Duane, 10; Essie Buck; Bonnie Sue O'Neil; Dorothy King; Wanda Roberts; Sally Thompson; Diana Pashal; Kathlyn Blum; Marie Cushman; Myrlene Hamer; others unidentified

Crime location: Nevada, Iowa, California

Status: Executed by lethal injection on December 6, 1985.

Background

Cole was born in Sioux City, Iowa. Not long after the birth of his sister in 1939, the family relocated to California. His father LaVerne was working in a shipyard when he was called up to fight in World War II. While he was away on active service, his wife Vesta embarked on a number of extramarital affairs. Cole would often accompany his mother when she committed adultery, and he was threatened with a beating if he told anyone what she was up to.

At school, Cole was teased a lot for having a "girls'" name. At times, his mother would even dress him up in girls' clothing and tease him. One of the bullies at school was a boy called Duane, who subsequently drowned in a local lake. This was considered a tragic accident until many years later when Cole confessed to murdering Duane.

Cole came into contact with the police numerous times throughout his teen years, largely for drunkenness, thefts, and petty crimes. Stealing became a habit, and after he joined the Army, he was discharged rather quickly for stealing guns.

In 1960, Cole was living in Richmond, California. One night, he attacked two couples he came across in parked cars on a "lover's lane." Shortly afterwards, he called the police and stated he was having violent fantasies about strangling women. Over the next three years, he spent a lot of time in and out of mental hospitals.

Cole was diagnosed with having an antisocial sociopathic personality, but was believed to be stable when he was released in April of 1963. He moved to Dallas and ended up marrying Billie Whitworth, an alcoholic stripper. Two years later, Cole burned down a motel because he was convinced his wife was having affairs with other men there. He was arrested, convicted of arson and sent to prison. His marriage ended.

Following his release, Cole tried to strangle an eleven-year-old girl. For this, he ended up with a five-year sentence in prison. He served his time and was released, and subsequently attempted to strangle two more women. This time, he admitted himself into a mental hospital. Although it was noted by the doctors that Cole had murderous fantasies, they still decided to release him, and he was sent back to San Diego.

Murders

On May 7, 1971, Cole picked up Essie Buck in a bar in San Diego. He killed her by strangulation and kept her body in the trunk of his car for a while before disposing of it. Two weeks after this murder, he killed another woman, who has remained unidentified. He buried this victim in the woods. Later, he claimed that both women were killed because they were unfaithful to their husbands, which reminded him of his mother.

Cole married Diana Parshal in July of 1973, but the relationship was troubled by her alcoholism and their constant fighting. On September 19, 1979, he strangled her to death. A neighbor became suspicious that she was missing and notified the police. When they investigated, they found her body in a closet, wrapped in a blanket. They decided she had died of alcoholism, however, and Cole wasn't charged.

After his wife's death, Cole moved around for a while. He claimed he killed a woman in Las Vegas before he moved back to Dallas. He allegedly murdered three women in November of 1980. And when he was found at the scene of the third killing, he was taken into custody.

Timeline of known murders:

May 7, 1971 - Essie Buck

May 23, 1971 - Woman known only as "Wilma"

May 30, 1971 - Unknown woman

After March of 1972 - Two unknown women killed

August of 1975 - Myrlene Hamer

May 14, 1977 - Kathlyn Blum

October of 1977 - Unknown woman

August 27, 1979 - Bonnie Sue O'Neil

September 19, 1979 - Diana Parshal

November 3, 1979 - Marie Cushman

Arrest and Trial

Cole was arrested at the scene of a murder in November of 1980. However, it was decided the victim had most likely died from natural causes. The authorities were about to release Cole from custody when he started to confess to the murder, as well as other crimes. According to Cole, he was responsible for the deaths of at least fourteen women over a nine-year period. But, there could have been others he couldn't remember due to his drunkenness.

Cole went to trial for the murders he had committed in Texas, and on April 9, 1981, he was found guilty of three murders. He received a life sentence. Following the death of his mother in 1984, Cole agreed to go to trial for murders he had committed in Nevada. This was surprising, given that Nevada had the death penalty.

Once again he was found guilty, and he was sentenced to death in October of 1984. Campaigners against the death penalty tried to get Cole's sentence commuted to life imprisonment, but Cole disagreed and didn't want the campaigners to fight on his behalf. When he was given his death sentence, he actually thanked the presiding judge.

Outcome

Cole was lead to the converted gas chamber on December 6, 1985, at 1:43 a.m., having been administered sedatives at 12:12 a.m. to keep him relaxed. He was strapped to the table and the needles inserted at 2:05 a.m. Following the administration of the lethal drug cocktail, Cole was seen to convulse before his body relaxed again at 2:07 a.m. Minutes later, he was pronounced dead. The execution lasted for five minutes.

Trivia

- Last meal before execution - jumbo shrimp, tossed salad with French dressing, Boston clam chowder, French fries, and the last of his supply of twenty-five lbs. of cookies and candy.
- Played cards with the prison priest during his last hours.

Quote by Cole:

- "I just messed up my life so bad that I just don't care to go on."

ADOLFO CONSTANZO

Date of birth: November 1, 1962

Aliases/Nicknames: The Godfather of Matamoros, The Witch Doctor

Characteristics: Human sacrifices and ritual torture

Number of victims: 16 +

Date of murders: 1986 - 1989

Date of arrest: Not apprehended due to his death

Murder method: Stabbing, shooting

Known Victims: Men - unnamed drug dealers, cult members

Crime location: Matamoros, Mexico

Status: Assisted suicide by gunfire, May 6, 1989.

Background

Constanzo's mother was a fifteen-year-old Cuban immigrant when she gave birth to him in Miami in 1962. She would go on to have more children, all to different fathers. After her first husband died, she moved to San Juan, in Puerto Rico. She met her next husband there and remarried.

Although Constanzo was baptized a Catholic, his mother would take him to Haiti on visits with her to learn about voodoo. This conflict of religions must have had some sort of impact on Constanzo. In 1972, the family returned to Miami. Not long afterwards, his stepfather died.

When Constanzo was a teenager, he became a sorcerer's apprentice in the religious practice of Palo Mayombe, and part of this practice involved the sacrifice of animals. His mother had remarried again, and Constanzo's new stepfather was also involved in Palo Mayombe; he was apparently involved in the drug trade too.

Along with his mother, Constanzo was arrested multiple times for theft, shoplifting, and vandalism. His mother believed Constanzo was psychic, and she claimed he had foretold the attempted assassination of President Ronald Reagan.

When Constanzo matured into an adult, he moved to Mexico City. There he met Martin Quintana, Omar Orea, and Jorge Montes, who would become his followers. They all became involved in a business where they would cast good luck spells, and this involved the sacrifice of animals such as lion cubs, zebras, goats, chickens, and snakes. The majority of their clientele were wealthy drug dealers and hitmen.

As a result of this business, Constanzo was introduced to other wealthy members of society, including corrupt Mexican policemen, who subsequently introduced him into the powerful drug cartels in the city. To successfully carry out his spell casting, Constanzo needed human bones, so he began raiding the local graveyards. Before long, however, he decided he would need live humans to sacrifice. This led him to commit sixteen (perhaps more) terrible murders.

Murders

Constanzo believed his "magic spells" enabled the cartels to be successful. So, he demanded he be a business partner with the Calzadas, one of the most powerful families around at that time. They refused his demands, and soon after, seven members of the family vanished. Later, when their bodies were found, they were incomplete. Some were missing ears, brains, fingers, and toes. One victim had their spine removed.

In 1988, after moving to Rancho Santa Elena, a house in the desert, Constanzo carried out a number of murders as part of his rituals. Some of the victims were drug dealers he considered rivals, while others were strangers who happened to cross paths with him.

Constanzo murdered a young premed student, Mark Kilroy, at the ranch on March 13, 1989. His henchmen had kidnapped Kilroy outside a bar and taken him to Constanzo at his ranch. Kilroy was an American citizen who was on holiday in Mexico at the time. Following his murder, Mexican police were put under a lot of pressure from authorities in Texas to solve the murder. As a result, the police arrested four followers of Constanzo, and the cult was uncovered.

Police learned that Constanzo had killed Kilroy because he needed a "superior" brain for a ritual spell. When officers raided Constanzo's ranch, they found a cauldron containing a human brain and a dead black cat. As they searched the ranch, they found fifteen corpses (all mutilated) buried there, including the body of Kilroy. According to witnesses, Kilroy had been killed by a strike to the back of the neck with a machete.

Arrest and Trial

Constanzo had a "death pact" with members of his followers. They had fled to Mexico City and were discovered when the local police were called to attend an unrelated dispute taking place at an apartment building. When the police officers neared Constanzo's hiding place, he thought they were coming for him and he opened fire on them with his machine gun. Now that he had attracted their attention, he was completely surrounded by the police. Constanzo was not prepared to go to prison, so he gave the gun to Alvaro de Leon and ordered him to shoot himself and Martin Quintana. They were both dead by the time the police entered the apartment.

Outcome

Police arrested Alvaro de Leon and Sara Aldrete at the apartment. Charges were laid against fourteen of the cult members. These charges ranged from drug-running and obstruction to murder. De Leon was convicted and sentenced to thirty years in prison. Sara Aldrete was convicted of committing multiple murders and sent to prison for more than sixty years. Two other members, Serafin Hernandez and Elio Hernandez, were also found guilty of multiple murders and sentenced to sixty years in prison.

There were a number of possible accomplices, though their exact involvement was never proven. They included:

- Rubén Estrada, aka "Patitas Cortas"
- Christian Campos, aka "El Panzas"
- Emmanuel Romero, aka "El Trompas"
- Saul Sánchez, aka "El Macaco"
- Ricardo Peña, aka "El Cepillín"

DEAN CORLL

Date of birth: December 24, 1939

Aliases/Nicknames: The Candy Man, The Pied Piper

Characteristics: Rape, mutilation

Number of victims: 27 +

Date of murders: 1970 - 1973

Date of arrest: Not arrested due to his death

Murder method: Shooting, Strangulation

Known Victims: Jeffrey Konen, 18; Danny Yates, 14; James Glass, 14; Jerry Waldrop, 13; Donald Waldrop, 15; Randell Harvey, 15; David Hilligiest, 13; Gregory Malley Winkle, 16; Ruben Watson, 17; Willard "Rusty" Branch Jr., 17; Frank Aguirre, 18; Mark Scott, 17; Johnny Delone, 16; Billy Baulch, 17; Steven Sickman, 17; Wally Jay Simoneaux, 14; Richard Hembree, 13; Richard Kepner, 19; Joseph Lyles, 17; Billy Ray Lawrence, 15; Ray Blackburn, 20; Homer Garcia, 15; John Sellars, 17; Michael "Tony" Baulch, 15; Marty Jones, 18; Charles Cary Cobble, 17 ; James Dreymala, 13

Crime location: Houston, Texas

Status: Shot to death by Elmer Wayne Henley before apprehension, August 8, 1973.

Background

Dean Corll was born in Fort Wayne, Indiana, as the first child of parents Arnold and Mary. Though his mother was protective of Corll, his father was a lot stricter with him as a child. The couple had an unhappy marriage, and they divorced in 1946. The family home was sold as a result, and they moved into a trailer in Memphis. Arnold had gone into the Air Force, and the parents wanted to keep contact between the children and their father.

As a child, Corll was described as being rather shy but serious, and he didn't interact much with other children. He did, however, show a lot of concern for others. When he was seven years old, he developed rheumatic fever. This wasn't diagnosed until he was eleven, however, after doctors discovered he had a heart murmur. It didn't affect him dramatically, but it meant he was unable to participate in sports at school.

Corll's parents tried to reconcile in 1950. But, this only lasted a few years, and they divorced again in 1953. The children were placed in the care of their mother, but still had a good relationship with their father.

Corll's mother married again, this time to Jake West, a traveling clock salesman. This led to the family moving to Vidor. His mother and stepfather were encouraged to start a small candy company, which they called "Pecan Prince." They started out operating from their garage, and Corll worked days and nights, even when he was still at school. Working in the family candy business led to him becoming known as the "Candy Man" later in life.

Murders

The majority of Corll's victims were abducted from Houston Heights in downtown Houston. Back then, the area was considered to be a low-income neighborhood. Corll brought in two accomplices to help him abduct young boys and men. Both Elmer Wayne Henley and David Owen Brooks were teenagers at the time, and many of the victims were friends with one or the other. Some victims were known to Corll prior to being kidnapped, and at least two victims had worked for Corll at his candy company.

The general method of abduction was to entice the victim into a vehicle with the promise of a ride somewhere or a party invitation. Once inside the vehicle, usually either a Ford Econoline van or a Plymouth GTX, they were then taken to Corll's house. The victim would be given drugs or alcohol until they passed out. Then they would either be grabbed forcefully or tricked into putting on handcuffs, stripped naked, and tied to a plywood board used for torture, or sometimes to Corll's bed.

Once the victim was secured, they would be subjected to vicious sexual assaults, beatings, and torture. When it was over, they would be either shot to death or strangled. Sometimes the victims would be kept alive for several days, enduring brutal attacks the whole time. The dead body would then be wrapped in plastic sheeting and buried in one of the four areas Corll used to dispose of his victims. These four locations were a beach on the Bolivar Peninsula, a boat shed, a beach in Jefferson County, and an area of woods near Lake Sam Rayburn.

In many cases, Corll forced his victims to write letters or make phone calls to their parents to make up excuses as to why they hadn't come home—thus preventing suspicion and the involvement of the authorities. Corll also liked to keep "trophies" from his victims, usually their keys.

Timeline of known murders:

September 25, 1970 - Jeffrey Konen, eighteen - Was hitchhiking when he was abducted. His body was buried at High Island Beach.

December 13, 1970 - James Glass, fourteen - Lured away from an evangelical rally by David Brooks, along with Danny Yates.

December 13, 1970 - Danny Yates, fourteen - Lured away from an evangelical rally by David Brooks, along with James Glass.

January 30, 1971 - Donald Waldrop, fifteen - Was abducted on the way to a bowling alley with his brother Jerry Waldrop.

January 30, 1971 - Jerry Waldrop, thirteen - Was abducted on the way to a bowling alley with his brother Donald Waldrop. Both were strangled and buried in the boat shed.

March 9, 1971 - Randell Harvey, fifteen - Was abducted on his way home from work. Shot in the head and buried in the boat shed.

May 29, 1971 - David Hilligiest, thirteen - A childhood friend of Elmer Wayne Henley. David was abducted along with his friend George Malley Winkle.

May 29, 1971 - Gregory Malley Winkle, sixteen - Was abducted on his way to a swimming pool. Winkle had been an employee of Corll Candy and was the boyfriend of the sister of Randell Harvey.

August 17, 1971 - Ruben Watson Haney, seventeen - Disappeared on his way to the cinema. Called his mother later and said he was staying with David Brooks for the weekend. Haney was strangled and buried in the boat shed.

February 9, 1972 - Willard "Rusty" Branch Jr., seventeen - Was shot, castrated, and buried in the boat shed. His father, a police officer, died of a heart attack while searching for his son.

March 24, 1972 - Frank Aguirre, eighteen - Was strangled to death and buried at High Island Beach. Aguirre was engaged to Rhonda Williams.

April 20, 1972 - Mark Scott, seventeen - Had been a friend of both Brooks and Henley. He was strangled and buried at High Island Beach.

May 21, 1972 - Johnny Delone, sixteen - Was abducted while walking to a store with a friend. After being shot in the head, Delone was strangled by Henley.

May 21, 1972 - Billy Baulch, seventeen - Had been an employee at Corll Candy. Was strangled to death by Henley and buried at High Island Beach.

July 20, 1972 - Steven Sickman, seventeen - Was abducted after leaving a party. Was strangled and several ribs were fractured. His body was buried in the boat shed.

October 3, 1972 - Wally Jay Simoneaux, fourteen - Was abducted on his way to high school. He tried to call his mother while he was being held at Corll's house, but the call disconnected. He was strangled to death and buried in the boat shed.

October 3, 1972 - Richard Hembree, thirteen - Was abducted from a grocery store. After being shot in the mouth, he was strangled.

November 12, 1972 - Richard Kepner, nineteen - Was abducted on his way to a pay phone. Kepner was strangled and buried at High Island Beach.

February 1, 1973 - Joseph Lyles, seventeen - Had been living on the same street as Brooks and knew Corll. Was buried at Jefferson County Beach.

June 4, 1973 - Billy Ray Lawrence, fifteen - A friend of Henley, Lawrence called his father from Corll's and asked if he could go fishing. Corll kept him alive for four days before killing him and burying his body at Lake Sam Rayburn.

June 15, 1973 - Ray Blackburn, twenty - Was abducted while hitchhiking to see his wife and new baby. Was strangled and buried at Lake Sam Rayburn.

July 7, 1973 - Homer Garcia, fifteen - Was an acquaintance of Henley. Was killed by a gunshot to the head and buried at Lake Sam Rayburn.

July 12, 1973 - John Sellars, seventeen - Was shot in the chest and buried at High Island Beach. Sellars was the only one fully clothed when his body was found.

July 19, 1973 - Michael "Tony" Baulch, fifteen - Was the younger brother of earlier victim Billy Baulch. Was strangled and buried at Lake Sam Rayburn.

July 25, 1973 - Marty Jones, eighteen - Was last seen walking with his friend Charles Cobble toward the apartment Corll shared with Henley.

July 25, 1973 - Charles Cary Cobble, seventeen - Was last seen walking with his friend Marty Jones towards Corll's apartment with Henley. He was shot in the head twice and buried in the boat shed. He had been a friend of Henley's at school.

August 3, 1973 - James Dreymala, thirteen - Was last seen in South Houston riding his bicycle. He phoned his parents and said he was at a party.

Arrest and Trial

In the early hours of August 8, 1973, Henley returned to Corll's home with Timothy Kerley and Rhonda Williams, whom he had been to a party with. Corll was enraged that a girl had been brought to the apartment, and he told Henley on the side that he had "ruined everything." Corll calmed down and gave them marijuana and alcohol, and Henley and Kerley were also sniffing paint fumes. Around two hours later, all three had passed out, with Corll watching them.

When Henley woke, his ankles were bound, there was tape on his mouth, and Corll was putting handcuffs on his wrists. Lying next to him were Williams and Kerley, also bound and gagged, and Corll had removed Kerley's clothes. Corll took the gag from Henley's mouth and again told him that he was angry at Henley for bringing a girl to his apartment. He said he was going to kill them all after he had finished assaulting and torturing Kerley. Corll kicked Williams in the chest and dragged Henley to the kitchen, placing a pistol against his stomach. Henley calmed Corll down and offered to participate in the torture of Kerley and the murder of him and Williams. Corll agreed and set Henley free from his bindings and handcuffs.

Henley helped Corll take the two young people into the bedroom and tie them both to the torture board. Corll told Henley to cut off William's clothes, which he started to do as Corll began assaulting Kerley. Williams asked Henley if what was happening was real. When he replied "yes," she asked him if he was going to do anything about it.

Henley asked if he could take Williams into the other room and Corll ignored him. Henley grabbed the pistol, shouting that Corll had "gone far enough." Corll got off Kerley and Henley told him he couldn't continue "any longer" and have him kill all his friends. Corll walked toward Henley, telling him to kill him. When Henley stepped back, Corll shouted, "You won't do it!" But, Henley fired the gun, shooting Corll in the forehead. Incredibly, the bullet didn't pierce the skull. As Corll lunged at him, Henley shot him again, in the shoulder. Corll tried to stagger out of the room, and Henley shot him three more times in the shoulder and back.

Corll died in the hallway where he had fallen, and Henley untied Williams and Kerley. As they got dressed, they talked about what they should do. At first, Henley suggested they leave, but Kerley stated they should call the police. At 8:24 a.m., Henley phoned the Pasadena Police. They then sat on the porch and waited.

While being questioned about Corll's death, Henley confessed that—for nearly three years—he, along with David Brooks, had helped to abduct teenage boys for Corll, who then raped, tortured, and murdered them. He also admitted he had taken part in the mutilation and torture of several victims before they were killed. Henley also explained how Corll had paid him and Brooks up to two hundred dollars for every victim they were able to get to Corll's apartment.

Initially, the police weren't convinced the story Henley was telling was real. Until he mentioned the names of some of the victims, and the police recognized them as being listed as missing persons. Henley went on to say where the bodies of the victims had been buried, and agreed to go with the police to the boat shed, where most of the bodies were located.

As they began to dig up the ground inside the boat shed, they uncovered the first body. They now knew that Henley's stories were true, and they continued to unearth more victims buried in the boat shed. Nearly all of the bodies had been wrapped in plastic sheeting, and some still had ligatures around their necks. By the time they had finished searching the boat shed, the police had found eight victims.

The same day, David Brooks arrived at the police station with his father and made a statement declaring he had nothing to do with any of the murders. But he did admit that he had known Corll had raped and killed two boys back in 1970. The following morning, Henley gave his full statement, including his own role of murderer in nine of the killings, and the level of involvement of Brooks in all but three murders.

Brooks finally confessed on the evening of August 9, and he went with police to High Island Beach to help them locate the bodies of the victims buried there. Henley accompanied the police to Lake Sam Rayburn to help find more bodies. On August 13, both Henley and Brooks went to High Island Beach again with police to locate the last of the victims. The final tally was twenty-seven.

Henley's trial took place on July 1, 1974, and he was charged with six murders. During the trial, the amount of evidence was extraordinary—eighty-two pieces were brought forward in court. It only took the jury ninety-two minutes to deliberate at the end of the trial. On July 16, Henley was found guilty and sentenced to six terms of ninety-nine years, to be served consecutively.

Henley appealed his conviction and a retrial began on June 18, 1979. This time the trial went on for nine days. Henley was again found guilty on June 27, 1979. He received the same sentence as before.

Brooks went on trial on February 27, 1975. Although he was indicted for four murders, he was charged only with the murder of William Ray Lawrence in June of 1973. The trial lasted for less than a week. After just ninety minutes of deliberation, the jury returned a guilty verdict. On March 4, 1975, Brooks was sentenced to life imprisonment.

Outcome

The local police came under heavy fire from families of the victims, who believed the police should have realized much sooner that there was a serial killer active in the area. The sheer number of boys and young men that were disappearing should have been a major clue to law enforcement.

Appeals lodged by both Henley and Brooks to reduce their sentences were declined.

Trivia

- In addition to providing transportation and shelter, Corll paid Henley and Brooks up to two hundred dollars to bring their friends, or other boys of a similar age, over to his apartment to rape and kill them.
- Corll drove a Ford Econoline van that he used to abduct and transfer his victims, both living and dead. The van had curtains across the windows and a peg board interior where Corll would be able to handcuff his victims and keep weapons and other torture devices. Boys would be lured into the van with drugs or the promise of a party. After they were murdered, they would also be transported to their burial site in the same vehicle.

ANTONE (TONY) CHARLES COSTA

Date of birth: August 2, 1944

Aliases/Nicknames: Nil

Characteristics: Necrophilia, dismemberment, mutilation

Number of victims: 4 - 8

Date of murders: 1966 - 1969

Date of arrest: March 6, 1969

Murder method: Shooting, drugging, drowning

Known Victims: Patricia H. Walsh; Mary Anne Wysocki; Susan Perry; Sydney Monzon; Bonnie Williams; Diane Federoff; Barbara Spaulding; Christine Gallant

Crime location: California, Massachusetts, New York

Status: Sentenced to life imprisonment. Committed suicide by hanging on May 12, 1974.

Background

Born in 1945, Costa was still just an infant when his father was killed in World War II. His mother later remarried, and when Costa was seven years old, he informed his mother that a man was coming into his bedroom at night. Upon questioning, he identified his stepfather as the nighttime visitor.

When he was sixteen, Costa entered an apartment in Massachusetts. He was leaning over a teenage girl who was asleep in her bed, when she suddenly awakened and screamed. Costa fled the scene. But, it wasn't the last time this girl would see him. Just three days later, he went back to the house and tried dragging her down the stairs. Luckily for the girl, the neighbors stopped him.

Costa was convicted of assault and burglary on January 4, 1962, and was given a one-year suspended sentence, along with three years of probation. In 1963, Costa married, and the relationship produced three children. His drug use, however, led to him displaying irresponsible and bizarre behavior that put a large strain on the marriage.

Costa brought two girls - Diane Federoff and Bonnie Williams - back to his house in June of 1966. He explained that he was going to drive them to Pennsylvania, and then he would continue on solo to California. Later, he claimed he had taken the girls to Hayward, California. But, they were never found. Ten days after the trip, Costa came back home to Massachusetts.

Costa and a female acquaintance were hiking in the Truro Woods in August of 1967, when an incident occurred. Costa shot his friend with an arrow. Later, he claimed it was an accident and apologized. By 1968, Costa's marriage was a mess. In late January, he moved to the Haight-Ashbury district in San Francisco.

Murders

Costa's first victim, Bonnie Williams, went missing in June of 1966, along with her friend Diane Federoff. His next victim was Barbara Spaulding, who disappeared during 1968. Her body has never been found.

On May 24, 1968, Sydney Monzon went missing from her home. Costa shot her, then removed the heart from her body. The autopsy revealed signs that Monzon had been sexually abused after her death. Christine Gallant was killed by Costa on November 23, 1968, but details of her murder are scarce. Susan Perry went missing on September 10, 1968. Her body was found on March 2, 1969.

Patricia Walsh and Mary Anne Wysocki went missing on January 24, 1969. Patricia and Mary had both been killed by gunshots, and their hearts had been removed from their bodies. The autopsy of each woman also showed signs of postmortem sexual abuse. Their bodies were found together, along with the body of Sydney Monzon.

Timeline of known murders:

June of 1966 - Bonnie Williams

June of 1966 - Diane Federoff

1968 - Barbara Spaulding

May 24, 1968 - Sydney Monzon

September 10, 1968 - Susan Perry

November 23, 1968 - Christine Gallant

January 24, 1969 - Patricia Walsh

January 24, 1969 - Mary Anne Wysocki

Arrest and Trial

On March 6, 1969, Costa was arrested and charged with multiple murders. His trial began on June 3, 1969, and he was arraigned for the murders of Mary Anne Wysocki, Patricia Walsh, Sydney Monzon, and Susan Perry. Costa was convicted in May of 1970, and sentenced to life imprisonment.

Outcome

On May 12, 1974, Costa was found hanging in his cell. His death was declared a suicide.

Trivia

- Costa wrote a book called *Resurrection* while he was in prison. In it, he described the murders of Wysocki and Walsh as being committed by his friend "Carl." He also claimed the deaths of Susan Perry and Sydney Monzon were due to drug overdoses, and that it was "Carl" who dismembered the bodies.

RICHARD COTTINGHAM

Date of birth: November 25, 1946

Aliases/Nicknames: The Torso Killer

Characteristics: Torture, rape, mutilation

Number of victims: 6 - claims up to 100

Date of murders: 1967, 1977 - 1980

Date of arrest: May 22, 1980

Murder method: Strangulation

Known Victims: Nancy Schiava Vogel, 29; Maryann Carr; Deedeh Goodarzi, 22, and "Jane Doe"; Valerie Street, 19; Jean Reyner

Crime location: New York, New Jersey

Status: Sentenced to life imprisonment.

Background

Cottingham was the eldest of three children. When he was twelve years old, the family moved to River Vale, in New Jersey. There, his mother stayed home to take care of the children while his father went to work for an insurance company.

Having to move to a new school at a young age proved challenging for Cottingham on a social level. He had difficulty making friends, and he spent most of his time with his mother and siblings at home. But, by the time he enrolled in Pascack Valley High School, things were starting to change, and he was able to make friends.

Following his graduation from high school, Cottingham joined his father at the insurance company Metropolitan Life, where he worked as a computer operator. Later in life, he worked as a computer operator for Blue Cross Blue Shield Association, located in New York. Cottingham was a good employee who was well-liked by his employers and co-workers.

In 1970, Cottingham married a woman named Janet, and they went on to have three children. The first child was born in 1973, the second in 1975, and the last in 1976. Just three years after the birth of their third child, Janet filed for divorce. She cited that her husband had been involved in extramarital affairs, and that he had been seen frequently at the local gay bars.

During the time Cottingham was committing murders, he had been arrested a few times for minor offenses. These crimes included shoplifting and driving while intoxicated. At no point was a connection made between him and the murders that had been taking place.

Murders

Nancy Schiava Vogel, Cottingham's first victim, disappeared after she left to play bingo at a church. Three days later, her strangled corpse was found in her car in Ridgefield Park, New Jersey. Her body was bound and naked.

The bodies of Deedeh Goodarzi and an unidentified woman were found by firemen on December 2, 1979, after they responded to a fire at a hotel close to Times Square in New York. The heads and hands had been removed from both bodies, and they had been set alight with the aid of lighter fluid, which had been poured on them.

On May 5, 1980, the body of Valerie Ann Street was discovered at a Quality Inn in Hasbrouck Heights, New Jersey. Her hands were handcuffed, her shins had been beaten, and her body was covered in bite marks. An examination of her body showed some sort of adhesive had been taped across her mouth, and she had been killed by asphyxiation. Just ten days later, Jean Reyner was found in the Seville Hotel, stabbed to death.

Timeline of known murders:

1967 - Nancy Schiava Vogel, twenty-nine

1977 - Maryann Carr

December 2, 1979 - Deedeh Goodarzi, twenty-two

December 2, 1979 - Jane Doe

May 5, 1980 - Valerie Ann Street, nineteen

May 15, 1980 - Jean Reyner

Arrest and Trial

Cottingham picked up a prostitute named Leslie Ann O'Dell, eighteen, on May 22, 1980. They agreed on one hundred dollars in exchange for sex, and they went to the same Quality Inn where Street's body had been found. While she was lying on her stomach awaiting a massage from Cottingham, he pulled out a knife and placed it against her throat. Cottingham handcuffed her and began to torture her. One of her nipples was almost bitten off, and O'Dell cried out in pain. Even though her voice was muffled, motel staff heard her and immediately called the police. They demanded Cottingham open the door to the room.

Cottingham was arrested in the hallway, as more police officers arrived. Searching the property he had with him, officers found a pair of handcuffs, two slave collars, a leather gag, replica pistols, a switchblade, and a large amount of prescription pills. Upon searching his house, they found a number of items he had taken from his victims.

Cottingham eventually went to trial, charged with the murder of Valerie Street. He was found guilty and sentenced to one hundred seventy-three to one hundred ninety-seven years in prison. Two more trials followed, and he was found guilty of four second-degree murders.

Outcome

Many people are pleased that Cottingham will never enter society again. Because of his long sentence, he will eventually die behind bars.

Trivia

- One month before his arrest, Cottingham's wife filed for divorce citing "extreme cruelty." She also claimed that he had refused sex with her since 1976.
- The only thing Cottingham admitted was, "I have a problem with women."

JEFFREY DAHMER

Date of birth: May 21, 1960

Aliases/Nicknames: The Milwaukee Cannibal

Characteristics: Rape, Cannibalism, Necrophilia, Dismemberment

Number of victims: 17

Date of murders: 1978 - 1991

Date of arrest: July 22, 1991

Murder method: Throat cutting, strangulation

Known Victims: Stephen Hicks, 19; Steven Tuomi, 26; James "Jamie" Doxtator, 14; Richard Guerrero, 25; Anthony Sears, 26; Eddie Smith, 36; Ricky Beeks, 27; Ernest Miller, 22; David Thomas, 23; Curtis Straughter, 19; Errol Lindsey, 19; Tony Hughes, 31; Konerak Sinthasomphone, 14; Matt Turner, 20; Jeremiah Weinberger, 23; Oliver Lacy, 23; Joseph Bradehoft, 25

Crime location: Ohio, Wisconsin

Status: Sentenced to 16 life sentences. Murdered in prison on November 28, 1994.

Background

Perhaps one of the most famous serial killers of the twentieth century, Jeffrey Dahmer was the first of two children born to Lionel Herbert and Joyce Annette Dahmer. Lionel was a student of chemistry at Marquette University, and Joyce worked as an instructor of teletype machines.

Both parents absolutely doted on Dahmer as an infant, but his mother was known to be a little difficult and hungry for attention. She would often get into arguments with her husband as well as the neighbors and was quite a tense person. When Dahmer started school, his mother spent more and more time lying in bed, supposedly recovering from "weakness." Because his father was away a lot due to his studies, Joyce constantly demanded his attention when he did come home.

Joyce would regularly work herself into an anxious state over small matters. At one point, she attempted suicide by overdosing on the medication she had become addicted to. Because of his mother's issues, Dahmer and his brother received little attention from either parent. Dahmer later stated that their home life was one of "extreme tension," especially between his parents who argued constantly.

As a student, Dahmer was described as timid and quiet. His demeanor gave the impression that he was neglected at home, and it was well-known that his mother had issues. Dahmer did, however, have a small group of friends while he was at school.

When Dahmer was around four years old, he watched as his father removed some animal bones from underneath their house. As he played with the bones, he seemed excited by the noise they made. From then onwards, he developed a fascination for collecting bones. He also collected a variety of butterflies, dragonflies, and large insects, which he stored in jars.

From there, he moved on to collecting animal carcasses that had been killed on the road. He would cut these bodies up, stating that he was curious to see how the animal fitted together. He was fascinated by the position of the bones in live animals as well. At one point, Dahmer placed the head of a dog on a stake behind the house.

When Dahmer's sibling was born in 1966, the family was living in Doylestown, Ohio. Dahmer was given the chance to choose his baby brother's name, and he chose David. By this time, his father Lionel had completed his degree and was working as an analytical chemist.

Two years later, the family moved again, this time to Bath, Ohio. In 1970, while the family was having chicken for dinner, Dahmer asked his father what would happen to the bones if they were put in a solution of bleach. Up until then, Lionel had been concerned about his elder son's quiet and rather solitary attitude, so was pleased to see him show an interest in science. He was happy to show Dahmer how to bleach and preserve animal bones, and Dahmer applied these methods on the collection of animal remains he still gathered.

Murders

The majority of Dahmer's victims were drugged with sedatives before they were strangled to death. Sometimes he bludgeoned them to death, as was the case with his first and second victims. Ernest Miller, who was murdered on September 2, 1990, died from blood loss and shock after Dahmer had cut his carotid artery.

A number of the victims killed in 1991 had holes drilled into their skull. Dahmer would then inject muriatic acid or boiling water through the holes into the brain. He did this to try to render the victim submissive and unable to resist. Although this wasn't intended to be a method of killing, three of Dahmer's victims died during the process.

On June 18, 1978, Steven Hicks was hitchhiking to Chippewa Lake Park to see a rock concert. He was picked up by Dahmer, who then used a dumbbell to bludgeon Hicks before strangling him. His body was cut into pieces, pulverized, and then scattered in the wooded area behind Dahmer's family home.

Steven Tuomi, twenty-five, was killed by Dahmer at the Ambassador Hotel. But, Dahmer claimed he couldn't remember actually killing him. He later said he must have been drunk when he beat the man to death. Tuomi's body was dismembered by Dahmer in his grandmother's basement, and the remains were put out in the trash.

Dahmer met James Doxtator, fourteen, outside a gay bar, and he lured the boy to his home with the promise of earning fifty dollars for some nude photos. Doxtator was strangled and his body kept in the basement for a week. He was then dismembered and discarded in the trash.

On March 24, 1988, Richard Guerrero was killed in Dahmer's bedroom. He had been drugged before Dahmer strangled him to death. His body was dismembered in the basement and the flesh put into acid to dissolve it. The bones went out in the trash, but Dahmer kept the skull for several months before getting rid of it.

The last victim to be drugged and killed at Dahmer's grandmother's house was Anthony Sears, twenty-four. Sears was killed on March 25, 1989, and after he was dismembered, Dahmer kept certain body parts. His genitals and his skull were preserved and later found in a filing cabinet in Dahmer's North Twenty-Fifth Street home.

Raymond Smith was killed on May 20, 1990; he was the first to be killed at Dahmer's new apartment. Dahmer had met Smith, a prostitute, at a bar, and invited him back to the apartment. He was drugged with sleeping pills, then strangled. Dahmer painted his cleaned skull red and kept it.

An acquaintance of Dahmer, Edward Smith, was last seen attending a party with Dahmer on June 14, 1990. After he was murdered, Dahmer used acid to destroy Smith's bones. He put the skull in the oven to try to dry it out but accidentally destroyed it in the process.

Dahmer met Ernest Miller outside a bookstore. A dancer, Dahmer found Miller's physique attractive. Back at his apartment, Dahmer cut Miller's carotid artery, and after he had bled to death, he dismembered his body in the bath. Miller's skeleton was cleaned and stored in the filing cabinet, and his biceps, heart, and parts of his legs were frozen so they could be eaten at a later date.

David Thomas, twenty-two, met Dahmer near the Grand Avenue Mall on September 24, 1990. Dahmer offered to pay him for some nude photos, and Thomas agreed, accompanying Dahmer back to his apartment. His drink was laced with drugs. Once he was unconscious, Dahmer decided he "wasn't my type" but killed him anyway. He took numerous photos of the body as he dismembered it.

Dahmer lured Curtis Straughter back to his apartment on February 18, 1991. The young man was drugged, handcuffed, and then strangled. He was dismembered in the bath, and Dahmer kept his skull, genitals, and hands.

On April 7, 1991, Errol Lindsey became the first victim Dahmer experimented on with his technique of drilling into the skull. After he had injected muriatic acid into Lindsey's brain, the young man awakened. So, Dahmer gave him a drink containing sedatives. He then strangled him to death and removed his skin, which he kept for several weeks. He also kept Lindsey's skull.

Dahmer used his usual offer of paying for nude photos to lure Tony Hughes to his apartment on May 24, 1991. Tony Hughes was deaf and mute, so Dahmer and Hughes communicated by written notes. Hughes was strangled and left on the floor of Dahmer's bedroom for three days. His body was then dismembered. Once again, Dahmer took photos of the process. His skull was kept and used for identification purposes later.

Konerak Sinthasomphone, fourteen, was drugged and put through the skull-drilling process—with acid then being injected into his brain—on May 27, 1991. Thinking the boy was incapacitated, Dahmer went to the store to buy some beer. When he got back, Sinthasomphone was out in the street, naked, and asking for help. When the police arrived, Dahmer told them the boy was intoxicated and that they were lovers. Incredibly, the police left him in Dahmer's care. More acid was then injected into his brain, which accidentally killed him. His body was dismembered, and Dahmer kept his head in the freezer.

Dahmer came across Matt Turner at a bus stop on June 30, 1991. As with the others, Dahmer used his photo ruse to lure him back to his apartment. Once inside, Turner was given a laced drink and then strangled. Afterwards, he was dismembered in the bath. His torso was put in a fifty-seven-gallon drum and his internal organs and head were kept in the freezer.

At a Chicago gay bar on July 5, 1991, Dahmer met Jeremiah Weinberger, who agreed to spend the weekend with Dahmer. After drugging Weinberger, Dahmer drilled into his skull and injected boiling water into his brain. Apparently, his eyes were open when he died. His head was cut off and his body left in the bath for a week before it was cut up. His torso also went into the drum.

The payment-for-photos ruse was used once again on Oliver Lacy, twenty-four, a bodybuilding enthusiast, on July 15, 1991. Lacy was drugged and then strangled with a leather strap. His head was cut off and placed in the refrigerator, along with his heart. Dahmer kept his skeleton as he was planning on using it to create a "shrine" of the skulls and bones he had collected.

Dahmer's last victim was Joseph Bradehoft. He was murdered on July 19, 1991, and left on Dahmer's bed for two days. His head was removed on July 21, and put into the refrigerator. As with Weinberger and Turner, his torso ended up in the drum.

Timeline of murders:

June 18, 1978: Steven Hicks, eighteen

November 20, 1987: Steven Tuomi, twenty-five

January 16, 1988: James Doxtator, fourteen

March 24, 1988: Richard Guerrero, twenty-two

March 25, 1989: Anthony Sears, twenty-four

May 20, 1990: Raymond Smith, thirty-two

June 14, 1990: Edward Smith, twenty-seven

September 2, 1990: Ernest Miller, twenty-two

September 24, 1990: David Thomas, twenty-two

February 18, 1991: Curtis Straughter, seventeen

April 7, 1991: Errol Lindsey, nineteen

May 24, 1991: Tony Hughes, thirty-one

May 27, 1991: Konerak Sinthasomphone, fourteen

June 30, 1991: Matt Turner, twenty

July 5, 1991: Jeremiah Weinberger, twenty-three

July 15, 1991: Oliver Lacy, twenty-four

July 19, 1991: Joseph Bradehoft, twenty-five

Arrest and Trial

On July 22, 1991, Dahmer talked to three men and offered them one hundred dollars to come back to his apartment to take some nude photos, hang out, and drink beer. Tracy Edwards, one of the men, agreed. When they got inside the apartment, Edwards noticed a terrible stench and multiple boxes of acid sitting on the floor. At one point, Dahmer told him to turn and look at his fish. As he did so, Dahmer put a handcuff on his wrist. He failed to handcuff both wrists, but was still able to convince Edwards to go into his bedroom with him to take the photos.

In the corner of the room was a large drum from which emanated a terrible smell. Dahmer made a number of threats toward Edwards and brandished a knife. Edwards continued to try to stop Dahmer from attacking him by appeasing him, all the while looking for a way to escape. At one point, he was able to convince Dahmer that they should go back out to the living room and have a beer. Edwards got up from the couch, stating he needed to use the bathroom. He noticed Dahmer wasn't holding the handcuffs or the knife and was distracted.

Edwards punched Dahmer in the face, which knocked him off-balance, and then ran straight out the front door of the apartment. On the street outside, Edwards flagged down two police officers. He asked them to remove the handcuffs on his wrist. When they were unable to, he took them up to Dahmer's apartment. Dahmer admitted he had put the handcuffs on Edwards but didn't explain why.

The officers were told that the key was in Dahmer's bedroom, and when they went in, the officers noticed a bunch of photos in an open drawer. The photos were of the dismembered bodies, and it was obvious they had been taken in Dahmer's apartment. Dahmer tried to fight with the officers but was overcome and arrested.

Upon searching his apartment after his arrest, the following items were found:

- Four severed heads
- Seven skulls
- Blood drippings on a tray in the refrigerator
- Two human hearts
- Part of an arm muscle
- A torso
- A bag of organs and flesh
- Two whole skeletons
- Two hands
- Two penises that had been preserved
- A scalp

- Three torsos in the drum
- Seventy-four photos of dismembered bodies

Dahmer was charged with sixteen counts of first-degree murder. Despite his history, he was found to be legally sane and able to stand trial. He was subsequently convicted and sentenced on February 15, 1992, to fifteen terms of life imprisonment. He was charged and convicted of a sixteenth murder later, for which he received another life sentence.

Outcome

At around 8:10 a.m. on November 28, 1994, Dahmer was found on the floor of the prison's gym bathroom. He had suffered horrific injuries to his head and face. He had been in the area with Jesse Anderson and Christopher Scarver as part of their usual work detail. Anderson was also critically injured. Both had been struck repeatedly by a twenty-inch metal bar, as well as struck against the wall multiple times.

Both men were still alive when they were discovered, but Dahmer died an hour later after being rushed to hospital. Anderson succumbed to his injuries two days later. Scarver, who had already been sentenced to life for a previous murder, informed the prison authorities immediately after returning to his cell that he had attacked both men. He claimed, "God told me to do it." He received two more life sentences for the murders of Dahmer and Anderson.

In 2015, Scarver changed his story and said that both men had poked him in the back and then laughed at him. He alleged Dahmer would taunt fellow inmates by shaping his food to look like body parts, and that Dahmer showed no remorse for his horrific crimes.

In Dahmer's will, he had requested that there be no funeral service for him and that he be cremated. His ashes were subsequently divided between his parents.

Trivia

- His IQ was estimated to be around 145, putting him close to being at genius level.

Quotes by Dahmer:

- "I carried it too far, that's for sure."
- "I've got to start eating at home more."
- "I made my fantasy life more powerful than my real one."
- "I think in some way I wanted it to end, even if it meant my own destruction."
- "I would cook it, and look at the pictures and masturbate."
- "My consuming lust was to experience their bodies. I viewed them as objects, as strangers. It is hard for me to believe a human being could have done what I've done."
- "I couldn't find any meaning for my life when I was out there, I'm sure as hell not going to find it in here. This is the grand finale of a life poorly spent and the end result is just overwhelmingly depressing... it's just a sick, pathetic, wretched, miserable life story, that's all it is. How it can help anyone, I've no idea."

KARL DENKE

Date of birth: August 12, 1870

Aliases/Nicknames: The Cannibal of Ziębice

Characteristics: Cannibalism

Number of victims: 42 +

Date of murders: 1909 - 1924

Date of arrest: December 21, 1924

Murder method: Killing by axe

Known Victims: Unnamed travelers and homeless men and women

Crime location: Munsterberg, Germany

Status: Committed suicide by hanging in his cell, one day after his arrest.

Background

Nothing is known about Denke's childhood, but as an adult, he ran a rooming house from 1918 to 1924. He was well-liked by his tenants, who often called him "papa." Denke was popular throughout the community, and he was the organ blower at his local church. Little did anyone know, this seemingly "good" man had been committing murders and eating his victims' flesh.

Murders

Denke's victims were mostly people who wouldn't be missed if they disappeared, and if they were, it would be a long time before they would be reported missing. He generally targeted tramps, beggars, and "journeymen"—men passing through on their way to their destinations.

A tenant of Denke's heard cries for help coming from his apartment on December 21, 1924. He raced down the stairs, thinking Denke may be injured somehow, and found a young man staggering down the corridor. There was blood streaming from his scalp, which had been cut open. As the young man collapsed, he claimed Denke had struck him with an axe. The tenant summoned the police immediately.

When the police searched Denke's flat, they found identification papers belonging to twelve journeymen. They also found a number of items of men's clothing. In the kitchen were two large tubs in which meat was pickling in brine. Officers estimated the tubs contained the flesh and bones of around thirty victims. Denke's ledger was found; in it, he had listed dates and names and the weights of victims that he had pickled since 1921.

Arrest and Trial

Denke was arrested and taken to the local jail on December 21, 1924. There, he was to be questioned about the attack on the young man, as well as the evidence of numerous murders found in his flat. Denke, however, never did explain himself to the police and face criminal charges. By morning, he was dead.

Outcome

On December 22, 1924, Denke was found dead in his cell. He had hanged himself.

After his death, police went to his apartment to secure all of his property. There, they made even more disturbing discoveries. Not only were there the two tubs of meat pickling in the kitchen, there were also several containers filled with pickled human flesh. Bones were found that had been prepared for processing, and there was also an apparatus for making soap.

Dozens of suspenders, shoelaces, and belts hung on the walls, all made from human skin. In the closet there was a lot of clothing stained with blood, including a skirt. Eventually, the pickled flesh was scientifically tested and found to be human. A total of twenty victims were eventually identified, but it is estimated he had killed and pickled more than forty people.

Trivia

–   In Munsterberg, Karl was known as a generous, caring, and devout local citizen. He was even referred to by some as "Vater Denke," or Father Denke. He carried the cross at evangelist funerals and played the organ during church services.

PAUL DENYER

Date of birth: April 14, 1972
Aliases/Nicknames: The Frankston Serial Killer
Characteristics: Transsexual, hatred of women
Number of victims: 3
Date of murders: June - July 1993
Date of arrest: July 31, 1993
Murder method: Stabbing, strangulation
Known Victims: Elizabeth Stevens, 18; Debbie Fream, 22; Natalie Russell, 17
Crime location: Melbourne, Australia
Status: Sentenced to three life sentences and is eligible for parole after 30 years.

Background

Not a lot of information is available about the early life and childhood of Paul Denyer, but the few things that are public knowledge are truly disturbing. According to his mother, he had an accident when he was a child and suffered some sort of injury to his head after rolling off a table.

Denyer took the family's kitten, cut it, and hung it from a tree. Killing and dissecting cats was well established in Denyer's history, and it is a common trait among sadistic serial killers. While Denyer was at school, an incident occurred where Denyer assaulted a fellow student. The victim of the assault happened to be chewing on a pen at the time, which became lodged in his throat.

Animal cruelty, social inadequacies, and assault on others were all warning signs through Denyer's childhood that perhaps something was wrong with him. If more attention had been paid to these traits, maybe what occurred later in life could have been prevented.

Murders

The body of Elizabeth Stevens, eighteen, was found on June 12, 1993, in Lloyd Park near Frankston. She had been staying with her aunt and uncle and was reported missing by them the night before. Her throat had been cut, and there were six stab wounds to her chest. Four cuts ran from her breasts to her navel, and there were four more running across her abdomen, creating a crisscross pattern. There were also several cuts and grazes on her face, and her nose was broken. The clothing on her upper body had been removed, and her bra was pushed up around her neck. Despite initial suspicions, the autopsy showed she hadn't been sexually assaulted.

Debbie Fream, twenty-two, went missing on July 8, 1993, after she drove to the local store to buy some milk. Her body was found four days later in a paddock near Carrum Downs. She had been stabbed twenty-four times in the head, neck, arms, and chest. Though she had been strangled, she hadn't been sexually assaulted.

The next victim was killed on July 30, 1993. Natalie Russell disappeared while riding her bicycle home from John Paul College. Her body was found in some bushes near a bicycle track, and her throat had been cut. She also had numerous stab wounds to her neck and face. There was no indication she had been sexually assaulted.

Timeline of known murders:

June 11, 1993 - Elizabeth Stevens, eighteen

July 8, 1993 - Debbie Fream, twenty-two

July 30, 1993 - Natalie Russell, seventeen

Arrest and Trial

A police officer happened to see a yellow Toyota Corolla near the bicycle track where Russell's body was found at around the time of her murder, and he had written down the registration number. When they put the number through the computer system, they discovered the same car had been seen in the same vicinity where Fream's body was found. A mailman had also reported seeing a man slumped down in the same car as though he was trying to hide himself.

The registration came back to Paul Denyer, and when detectives went to talk to him, he wasn't home. They left a card asking him to call. Instead, they received a call from someone else asking why the police wanted Denyer to get in touch. They explained it was a routine inquiry and they were interviewing everyone in the area. Within ten minutes of the phone call, detectives headed to Denyer's address.

Denyer opened the door when the detectives knocked and invited them in. While he was telling them where he was at the time of each murder, it was noticed that he had numerous cuts on his hands. To explain his injuries, Denyer claimed he had gotten his hands caught in an engine fan while working on a car. Suspecting they had their man, the detectives took Denyer back to the station for further questioning.

They interrogated Denyer into the early hours of the next morning, but he steadfastly denied responsibility for the killings. Until they asked him for a DNA sample. Denyer asked how long it would take to get DNA results back, and if they had evidence to compare to his DNA. Then he sat quietly for a bit before he declared he was the man who had killed the three women.

When Denyer went to trial for the three murders he pleaded guilty to all charges. A clinical psychologist explained to the court that Denyer was a sadist who found pleasure in killing women. He showed no remorse for what he had done to his victims or their friends and families.

Outcome

For the three murders, Denyer was sentenced to three life sentences. He also received an extra eight years for abducting another woman. Initially, he was denied the possibility of parole, and was expected to spend the rest of his life in prison. However, Denyer appealed to the Supreme Court of Victoria on July 20, 1994, and was granted a thirty-year non-parole period. Although he is unlikely to ever get parole, there is the possibility for him to apply after serving thirty years.

Trivia

- While imprisoned, Denyer has requested to be allowed to purchase and wear ladies cosmetics, a request which was denied.
- When asked why he had killed Elizabeth Stevens, Denyer replied: "Just wanted... just wanted to kill. Just wanted to take a life because I felt my life had been taken many times."
- Denyer also filed freedom of information requests to learn of the Victorian government's policy on gender reassignment surgery for prisoners, and he has sought evaluation to determine his suitability for such surgery, which was also rejected by medical specialists.

NANNIE DOSS

Date of birth: November 4, 1905

Aliases/Nicknames: The Giggling Nanny, The Giggling Granny, The Jolly Black Widow, The Lonely Hearts Killer, Lady Blue Beard

Characteristics: Killed for insurance money

Number of victims: 8 - 11

Date of murders: 1920 - 1954

Date of arrest: October of 1954

Murder method: Arsenic poisoning

Known Victims: Four of her husbands, her mother, her sister Dovie, her grandson Robert, and her mother-in-law, Arlie Lanning's mother

Crime location: Alabama, North Carolina, Kansas, Oklahoma

Status: Sentenced to life imprisonment. Died of leukemia on June 2, 1965, while incarcerated.

Background

Doss was one of five children born to James and Louisa Doss, in Blue Mountain, Alabama. Christened Nancy Hazel, Doss despised her father. So did her mother, who was said to have a nasty streak and was very controlling. James would make the children stay home from school and work on the family farm. As a result, Doss never learned to write or read very well.

The family went on a train trip to visit relatives when Doss was around seven years old. The train came to a sudden stop, making Doss strike her head on the metal bar on the back of the seat in front. The accident resulted in her suffering from terrible headaches and blackouts for many years, and she struggled with bouts of depression.

Although she didn't read well, Doss did like to immerse herself in her mother's romantic magazines. And, later in life, she enjoyed reading the lonely hearts columns. Doss and her sister were heavily restricted by their father from dressing like other girls their age and they certainly weren't allowed to wear makeup. The girls couldn't attend dances either. Despite all his efforts to protect his girls from the clutches of men, however, they both were molested on a number of occasions.

When she was sixteen years old, Doss married a man she met at work at the Linen Thread factory, named Charley Braggs. They only dated for four months before her father gave his consent for them to marry. Braggs' mother lived with the couple after they married, and she too was controlling. The young couple went on to have four children - all daughters.

Murders

Doss became stressed from the children and overbearing her mother-in-law and started drinking and smoking. Both Doss and her husband were guilty of committing adultery. Braggs would sometimes disappear for days, leaving Doss to manage the household. Tragedy then struck in 1927, when two of their daughters died—supposedly from food poisoning. Braggs suspected Doss had murdered the girls and fled the home, taking the eldest daughter with him and leaving the baby with Doss.

Not long after Braggs left, his mother, who was still in the house with Doss, also died. Eventually, in 1928, Braggs returned their daughter to Doss, and they divorced soon after. Doss took both of her children with her to live in her mother's house. She became fascinated by the lonely hearts columns once again, and sent many letters in response to men advertising. One of these men was Robert Franklin "Frank" Harrelson.

Frank started sending Doss poetry, and she replied by sending him a cake. They married in 1929 and lived in Jacksonville. Soon into the marriage, Doss discovered that Frank had a criminal record for assault and was an alcoholic. Despite this, they remained married for sixteen years, until Frank met an untimely death.

When Doss' eldest daughter Melvina gave birth to her second baby in 1945, the baby died soon after birth. Melvina had been given ether during her labor, which could cause hallucinations, and she thought she saw Doss stick a hatpin into the baby's head. She asked her husband and sister, who said Doss had told them the baby was dead. Doss happened to be holding a hairpin at the time.

Melvina's marriage disintegrated. After a while, she started dating a soldier whom Doss did not approve of. On July 7, 1945, Melvina left her son Robert in the care of Doss while she visited with her father, and the child died. Doctors diagnosed his cause of death as asphyxia from unknown causes. Doss had taken out life insurance on Robert valued at five hundred dollars, which she collected two months after his death.

When Japan surrendered at the end of World War II, Doss' husband Frank celebrated quite zealously. One night, while intoxicated, he raped Doss. When she found his whiskey jar buried in the garden the next day, she filled it up with rat poison. Frank died that night.

Single again, Doss found another suitor in the lonely hearts column, Arlie Lanning—another alcoholic and adulterer. During their marriage, Doss sometimes disappeared for months at a time. When she was at home though, she played the part of a doting wife. When Lanning died from heart failure, the whole town supported her. Not long afterwards, their house burnt down. It was insured, with Doss listed as the recipient. Soon after, Lanning's mother died, and Doss left North Carolina.

Doss went to stay at her sister Dovie's house. Dovie was bedridden and died not long after Doss arrived. Doss then met and married Richard L. Morton. This husband wasn't an alcoholic like the others, but he was a womanizer. He died in 1953, three months after Doss' mother died, supposedly from poison.

Doss' last husband was Samuel Doss from Tulsa, Oklahoma. They married in June of 1953, and being a clean, church-attending man, he didn't approve of the romance novels that Doss was so fond of. By September, he was in the hospital and the diagnosis was that he was suffering from an infection of the digestive tract. He was sent home on October 5. He died that very night. Because the death was so sudden, an autopsy was undertaken. This showed poor Samuel had a large amount of arsenic in his body, and Doss was arrested.

Arrest and Trial

After her arrest, Doss confessed to multiple murders, including four of her husbands, her mother, Dovie, Robert, and mother Lanning. The state focused on the murder of Samuel Doss, and she was found mentally fit to stand trial. She pleaded guilty on May 17, 1955. Doss received a sentence of life imprisonment; she managed to avoid the death penalty because she was female, and the state didn't want to pursue the execution of a woman.

Outcome

Suffering from leukemia, Doss succumbed to her illness and died, on June 2, 1965.

Trivia

- Her first husband--the only one she didn't kill--claimed he left her because she frightened him.
- When interviewed about her life in the McAlester prison in Tulsa, Doss complained that the only job she was allowed there was in the laundry, noting that her offer to work in the kitchen was politely declined.

JOSEPH E. DUNCAN III

Date of birth: February 25, 1963

Aliases/Nicknames: Nil

Characteristics: Kidnapping, rape, pedophilia

Number of victims: 5 - 7

Date of murders: July 6, 1996, April 4, 1997, May 16, 2005

Date of arrest: July 2, 2005

Murder method: Striking with hammer

Known Victims: Sammiejo White, 11; Carmen Cubias, 9; Anthony Michael Martinez, 10; Brenda Groene, 40; Mark McKenzie, 37; Slade Groene, 13; Dylan Groene, 9

Crime location: Washington, California, Idaho

Status: Received six life sentences without parole, and three federal death sentences.

Background

A violent sexual predator from a young age, Duncan committed his first recorded crime in 1978, when he was just fifteen years old. He had held a nine-year-old boy at gunpoint and raped him. A year later, he was arrested while driving a car that had been stolen. Because he was a juvenile, he was sent to the Dyslin Boys Ranch, where he would receive therapy. While there, he admitted that he had tied up and sexually assaulted six young boys. He also claimed he had already raped thirteen boys.

Duncan was released, and in 1980, he abducted a fourteen-year-old boy at gunpoint, using weapons he had stolen from a neighbor. The boy was sodomized, and Duncan was arrested and sentenced to serve twenty years in prison. He only served fourteen years, however, and was released on parole in 1994.

He was arrested for marijuana use in 1996, and was held in jail for several weeks. Eventually, he was released with further parole restrictions. In 1997, he violated his parole conditions and was returned to prison. He was released early in July of 2000, for good behavior, and he moved to North Dakota.

Duncan was arrested again in March of 2005, and charged with the molestation of two boys in 2004. His bail was set at fifteen thousand dollars, which was paid by a businessman Duncan had met previously. As soon as he was free, Duncan disappeared, and a federal warrant was issued. From here onwards, Duncan became even more violent, committing a number of murders.

Murders

In 1996, Duncan murdered Carmen Cubias and Sammiejo White while on parole after he'd been arrested for marijuana use. He also murdered Anthony Martinez in California in 1997. But, none of these murders were linked to Duncan until after he was arrested for the murder of Brenda Groene.

The bodies of Groene, Mark McKenzie, and Slade Groene were discovered in their home on May 16, 2005. Groene's other two children, Dylan and Shasta, were missing. The autopsies showed that all of the victims had died as a result of blunt trauma to the head after they had been bound. An Amber Alert went out and a major search was conducted to find the two missing children.

Early in the morning of July 2, 2005, witnesses saw Shasta at a Denny's restaurant with a man. Without the man knowing, staff and customers quietly called the police and placed themselves in various areas of the restaurant in case the man tried to leave with the young girl. He was quickly arrested, but there was no sign of young Dylan.

Responding to tips called in to the police, authorities began focusing their attention of the remote areas of the Idaho-Montana border in their search for Dylan. On July 4, his remains (positively identified by the FBI lab through DNA testing) were found in the Lolo National Forest near St. Regis, Montana.

Timeline of known murders:

July 6, 1996 - Carmen Cubias, nine

July 6, 1996 - Sammiejo White, eleven

April 1997 - Anthony Michael Martinez, ten

May 16, 2005 - Brenda Groene, forty

May 16, 2005 - Slade Groene, thirteen

May 16, 2005 - Mark McKenzie, thirty-seven

May 16, 2005 - Dylan Groene, nine

Arrest and Trial

After his arrest, Duncan became a suspect in a number of unsolved cases of missing or murdered children. He was linked to the murder of Anthony Martinez through fingerprints found on the body, and it was formally announced on August 3 that Duncan was responsible for the boy's murder. While in custody, Duncan confessed to killing Carmen Cubias and Sammiejo White.

Duncan was charged with murders in three courts - Idaho, for the murders of Groene, her son, and Mark McKenzie; California, for the murder of Anthony Martinez; and the United States District Court for the murder of Dylan, his kidnapping, and the kidnapping of his sister Shasta.

The first trial took place on July 13, 2005, but was deferred to a later date so more preparation could be done. The trial was then set for October 16, 2006. But, as soon as it began, Duncan pleaded guilty to all charges. He was sentenced to three life sentences for the kidnappings, but the sentencing for the murder charges was delayed, pending the results of the federal trial on the kidnapping and murder charges.

Duncan pleaded guilty to all charges against him in the federal trial on December 3, 2007. He reached a plea agreement, the details of which have not been released. The jury deliberated on sentencing for three hours on August 27, 2008, and came back with three death sentences. He was further sentenced to three life sentences for the kidnapping of Shasta and Dylan.

On January 24, 2009, Duncan was extradited to California to face charges for the murder of Anthony Martinez. He agreed to a plea deal and pleaded guilty on March 15, 2011. He was sentenced to two more life sentences, without the possibility of parole.

Outcome

In total, Duncan received three federal death sentences and six life sentences. While incarcerated, he has confessed to killing two girls in Seattle in 1996. But, no charges have been placed against him. He is still on death row awaiting his execution.

Trivia

- Before he was arrested, Duncan had published his thoughts and ideas on a website he called "The Fifth Nail." He named it as such because of the lore that, apart from the four nails used to crucify Jesus, there was a fifth nail that was hidden by the Romans.
- His blog and website talked about Duncan's life as a sex offender, but he denied that he was a pedophile.
- He also claimed he had been sexually abused as a young child.

WALTER E. ELLIS

Date of birth: June 24, 1960

Aliases/Nicknames: Milwaukee North Side Strangler

Characteristics: Rape and murder

Number of victims: 7

Date of murders: 1986 - 2007

Date of arrest: September 5, 2009

Murder method: Strangulation

Known Victims: Deborah L. Harris, 31; Tanya L. Miller, 19; Florence McCormick, 28; Sheila Farrior, 37; Jessica Payne, 16; Joyce Mims, 41; Ouithreaun C. Stokes, 28

Crime location: Milwaukee, Wisconsin

Status: Sentenced to seven life sentences without parole. Died of natural causes on December 1, 2013, while incarcerated.

Background

Ellis almost seemed to be a person who, during different periods in his life, could put forth a different personality. As a child, those who lived in his neighborhood described him as an angry boy who would threaten other young children he played with. As he reached his teens, he was known to have assaulted a number of youths in the area.

Yet as an adult, those same neighbors described him as more calm and subdued. He would drive around the streets selling shoes out of his car. He would often pull over on the side of the road and chat with various neighbors. Nobody who knew him then ever suspected he was capable of murder.

Ellis got into trouble with the law from a young age, and he had been arrested twelve times between the years 1981 and 1998. At one point, he served five years in prison for reckless endangerment. But, he was able to get away with his most heinous crimes for many years—until his DNA brought him down.

Murders

The body of Deborah L. Harris was found on October 10, 1986, in a Milwaukee river. Her autopsy showed she had been strangled. Just a day later, Tanya L. Miller was found strangled to death between a garage and a house.

The next murders occurred in 1995. The body of Florence McCormick was found in the basement of an empty house by workmen on April 24. Although the house was boarded up at the time, one of the windows was broken. Authorities assumed that was how she came to be in there. An autopsy showed she had been strangled.

On June 27, the body of Sheila Farrior, who had also been strangled, was found in an empty house when the owner visited to check on the work that had been done to it. Two months later, on August 30, the body of sixteen-year-old runaway Jessica Payne was found behind an empty house. Unlike the other victims, she had been killed by having her throat slashed.

Joyce Mims was found dead in a vacant house on June 20, 1997. Workers turned up to do renovations on the property and found her on the second floor. She had been missing for two days before she was found.

On April 27, 2007, city inspectors found the dead body of Ouithreaun C. Stokes inside a vacant house that had once been used as a rooming house. Like almost all of the other victims, the modus operandi was the same - the victim had been strangled.

Timeline of murders:

October 10, 1986 - Deborah L. Harris, thirty-one

October 11, 1986 -Tanya L. Miller, nineteen

April 24, 1995 - Florence McCormick, twenty-eight

June 27, 1995 -Sheila Farrior, thirty-seven

August 30, 1995 -Jessica Payne, sixteen

June 20, 1997 - Joyce Mims, forty-one

April 27, 2007 - Ouithreaun C. Stokes, twenty-eight

Arrest and Trial

Through DNA testing, authorities discovered that Ellis was the serial killer known as the North Side Strangler. He was arrested on September 7, 2009. When he appeared before court, he initially pleaded not guilty; he was also willing to defend himself, despite being represented by Attorney Russell Jones. The attorney subsequently withdrew from the case, and on February 18, 2011, Ellis pleaded no contest to seven murders.

Pleading no contest is not an admission of guilt; it simply means that the defendant knows the prosecution has enough evidence to prove the possibility of guilt. Ellis was convicted and sentenced on February 24, receiving seven life sentences without the possibility of parole.

Outcome

Ellis was transferred from prison to a hospital in South Dakota, where he subsequently died on December 1, 2013, from unspecified natural causes.

KENNETH ERSKINE

Date of birth: July 1963

Aliases/Nicknames: The Stockwell Strangler

Characteristics: Rape, sodomy, possible gerontophilia

Number of victims: 7 +

Date of murders: April - July of 1987

Date of arrest: July 28, 1987

Murder method: Strangulation

Known Victims: Eileen Emms, 78; Janet Cockett, 67; Valentine Gleim, 84; Zbigniew Strabawa, 94; William Carmen, 84; William Downes, 74; Florence Tisdall, 83

Crime location: Stockwell, England

Status: Incarcerated at Broadmoor Mental Hospital.

Background

Erskine was one of four children born to Charles and Margaret Erskine. Charles was Antiguan and Margaret was British, and they raised their boys in Putney. As a young child, Erskine was described as a chubby boy, who could often be found reading the Bible. But, his behavior became difficult to control and he subsequently ended up at a number of different schools for maladjusted children.

Erskine would attack his fellow students and his teachers violently, and he seemed to be living in some sort of fantasy world. During one school outing, the children were swimming and Erskine attempted to drown several of them. He also stabbed one of his teachers in the hand with a pair of scissors.

Before long, Erskine graduated to burglary. Because he wasn't very good at it, he was arrested and kept in jail on several occasions. Unable to deal with his behavior anymore, his family cut all contact with him. Erskine became a loner, drifting around flophouses. At one point, he lived on the streets.

When Erskine was later arrested for committing the murders, it was discovered that, although he was twenty-four years old, he had the mental age of an eleven-year-old. Throughout his subsequent interviews, he wasn't really mentally "present." This left the investigators with an enormous task as they tried to determine the level of Erskine's guilt and whether or not he even understood what was going on.

Murders

Erskine killed his first victim, Nancy Emms, on April 9, 1986. Initially, the doctor ruled her death as natural. But then a home healthcare worker noticed her television had been stolen. An autopsy was therefore conducted; it showed she had been raped and then strangled to death.

Janet Cockett was killed by Erskine on June 9, 1986, in her apartment. Her death was also considered natural at first, until her autopsy showed she had been strangled to death. It also revealed that she had not been sexually assaulted.

The next victims were killed on June 28, 1986, after Erskine broke into the home of Valentine Gleim and Zbigniew Strabawa. The two Polish men were sexually assaulted, then strangled to death. William Carmen was killed on July 8, 1986, in his apartment. He had been sexually molested and strangled, and robbed of cash.

William Downes was killed in a similar fashion on July 21, 1986, in a studio in Stockwell. The last victim of Erskine was Florence Tisdall. Her body was found by a caretaker on July 23, 1986, after she had been raped and strangled.

Timeline of known murders:

April 9, 1986 - Nancy Emms, seventy-eight

June 9, 1986 - Janet Crockett, sixty-seven

June 28, 1986 - Valentine Gleim, eighty-four

June 28, 1986 - Zbigniew Strabawa, ninety-four

July 8, 1986 - William Carmen, eighty-four

July 21, 1986 - William Downes, seventy-four

July 23, 1986 - Florence Tisdall, eighty-three

Arrest and Trial

Erskine had left an intact palm print at the scene of Crockett's murder. Because he had a long history of criminal activity, his fingerprints and palm prints were on file. He was arrested at a social security office on July 28, 1986. He was put into a lineup and positively identified by Fred Prentice, a survivor of one of Erskine's attacks.

In January of 1988, Erskine was found guilty of committing the seven murders.

Outcome

Erskine received a life sentence, with a minimum term of forty years before he would be eligible for parole. However, it was later discovered that he had a mental health disorder and he was transferred to Broadmoor Hospital, a maximum security mental health facility, in 2009. His convictions were reduced to manslaughter due to diminished responsibility. He will be eligible for parole in 2028.

Trivia

- In February of 1996, Erskine was again in the news, this time for preventing the possible murder of Peter Sutcliffe, the "Yorkshire Ripper," by raising the alarm as a fellow inmate, Paul Wilson, attempted to strangle Sutcliffe with the flex from a pair of stereo headphones.
- During his trial, Erskine masturbated and at times fell asleep.

DONALD LEROY EVANS

Date of birth: July 5, 1957
Aliases/Nicknames: Nil
Characteristics: Rape and murder
Number of victims: 3 - claimed over 70
Date of murders: 1975 - 1991
Date of arrest: August 5, 1991
Murder method: Strangulation
Known Victims: Ira Jean Smith, 38; Janet Movich, 38; Beatrice Louise Routh, 10
Crime location: Multiple states, USA
Status: Sentenced to death. Murdered in prison on January 5, 1999.

Background

By all accounts, Evans (who was born in Michigan) was a fairly ordinary child with a normal childhood until he reached his mid-teens. At sixteen years old, he tried to commit suicide using roach killer. It's not known why he tried to end his life, but he did undergo a lot of counselling for a year while he was attending high school.

When he was eighteen years old, Evan joined the Marines. But, he was discharged less than a year later. The reason cited was psychiatric issues. From then onwards, Evans became a bit of a drifter, and he developed an addiction to drugs.

In 1986, Evans was arrested in Texas for the rape of a woman in Galveston. Found guilty, he was sentenced to fifteen years in prison, but he only served five years. Paroled in 1991, he found a job at a motel working as a desk clerk. But he lost this job because parole officials deemed it inappropriate for a sex offender to be working in that setting.

Evans then found work on a fishing boat, but trouble still followed him. A former girlfriend lodged a complaint against him, claiming he had threatened her with violence. When Evans found out about the warrant to arrest him, he stole a car and fled to Mississippi. He thought he had evaded capture, but it wouldn't be long until he committed a crime that would bring his freedom to an end.

Murders

On August 1, 1991, Evans abducted Beatrice Louise Routh, ten, from a park in Gulfport. He sexually assaulted the young girl, then strangled her. Her body was found in a nearby rural area. The medical examiner later determined that she had been assaulted throughout the entire day of her abduction.

It wasn't until after he was arrested for this murder that Evans confessed to committing up to seventy others. One case that he was linked to, and later charged for, was the death of Ira Jean Smith in 1985.

Timeline of known murders:

1985 - Ira Jean Smith, thirty-eight

1985 - Janet Movich, thirty-eight

August 1, 1991 - Beatrice Louise Routh, ten

Arrest and Trial

Evans was arrested on August 5, 1991, for the murder of Beatrice Louise Routh. Initially, his elaborate confessions to dozens of other murders seemed unbelievable to the interviewing officers. But, he was later found to be responsible for the deaths of Ira Jean Smith and Janet Movich.

On August 16, 1993, Evans was convicted of the murder and sexual battery of Routh. He was sentenced to death three days later. In 1995, he went to trial for the murder of Smith and was again found guilty.

Outcome

On January 5, 1999, fellow inmate Jimmy Mack stabbed Evans to death while he was taking a shower. Evans was still a suspect in multiple unsolved murders at the time of his death.

Trivia

- He attempted suicide at age sixteen using roach poison and drugs.
- He confessed to killing victims at parks and rest areas across twenty states.
- He petitioned the court to refer to him as "Hi Hitler" instead of Donald Leroy Evans. He obviously didn't realize that the famous chant was "Heil Hitler."

GARY C. EVANS

Date of birth: October 7, 1954

Aliases/Nicknames: Nil

Characteristics: Robbery

Number of victims: 5

Date of murders: 1985 - 1997

Date of arrest: June 18, 1998

Murder method: Shooting

Known Victims: Michael Falco; Timothy Rysedorph; Damien Cuomo; Douglas J. Berry; Gregory Jouben

Crime location: New York

Status: Died jumping from a bridge after escaping from a police van on the way to trial.

Background

Evans had a troubled childhood in Troy, New York, as he was both emotionally and physically abused by his parents. They eventually divorced in 1968, and his mother later tried to commit suicide multiple times. At a young age, Evans began stealing, and it's believed his mother put him up to it. There are reports that, at the time, Evans was also abusing and killing pets in the neighborhood.

Not long after his parents divorced, Evans left his mother's home and spent a lot of time homeless. To survive, he would steal from the local drug dealers and commit burglaries. In 1970, he was arrested for breaking into a house. For this crime, he remained in jail for several months.

Evans moved into an apartment in the mid-1970s and shared it with Michael Falco and Timothy Rysedorph, whom he had known from his childhood. His stealing had moved up a notch, and he became more interested in the value of jewelry and antiques. He would visit different antique dealers under the pretense of being one himself. While talking to the dealer, he would case the store to work out how to break in and rob it.

Over the next couple of decades, Evans was arrested and convicted of fifteen felonies relating to the theft of antiques. In 1977, he was sent to the Clinton Correctional Facility for burglary. He was then transferred to the Great Meadow Correctional Facility, from which he was released in March 1980. But it wasn't long before he was jailed again.

On June 12, 1980, Evans was thrust into the limelight following a brazen prison escape, where he fled over the Rensselaer County Jail wall. He didn't get far—he was arrested at the local public library

128

while onlookers cheered. The prison authorities deemed him a high-risk, and he was caught trying to plan escapes on several occasions. Following his release in 1982, he was arrested for two more crimes and returned to jail. Finally, he was released again on March 31, 1984.

Evans and his partners continued with their jewelry and antique scams. Evans and Falco robbed a flea market in East Greenbush, New York, on February 16, 1985. Approximately a week later, Falco disappeared.

Murders

Evans' first known "partner in crime" to disappear was Michael Falco. The two men committed a burglary of a flea market in New York on February 16, 1985, and Falco went missing a week later. At the time, Evans had convinced everyone—including law enforcement and the local criminal element—that Falco had moved to California. The real story was that Evans shot Falco to death, put his body in a sleeping bag, and dumped it in a swamp in Lake Worth, Florida. His excuse was that he believed Falco had stolen from him and was possibly going to report him to the police for his burglaries.

On September 8, 1988, Evans and a new partner, Damien Cuomo, broke into a jewelry and coin store in Watertown, New York. The owner of the store, Douglas J. Berry, was sleeping in the back room, and when he woke, Evans shot him and killed him.

Cuomo was to meet a fate similar to Falco. He was last seen with Evans on December 27, 1989, as he left his apartment. Evans shot Cuomo and buried his body nearby, not long after they left the apartment that day. Evans later said killed Cuomo he thought Cuomo was stealing from him and was going to turn him in to the authorities.

Evans walked into a jewelry store owned by Gregory Jouben on October 17, 1991. He asked Jouben to give him a price on an item, then shot him. After running into some trouble with the law, Evans was released and got back into burglarizing with the help of Timothy Rysedorph. On October 4, 1997, Rysedorph phoned his wife. That was the last time anyone heard from him. Evans, thinking Rysedorph was stealing from him, waited until the man's back was turned, then shot him. He then used a chainsaw to dismember the body.

Timeline of known murders:

February 1985 - Michael Falco

September 8, 1988 - Douglas J. Berry, sixty-three

December 27, 1989 - Damien Cuomo

October 17, 1991 - Gregory Jouben, thirty-six

October 4, 1997 - Timothy Rysedorph

Arrest and Trial

Because Rysedorph had disappeared as soon as Evans jumped his probation, authorities became suspicious that Evans may be responsible. Authorities presumed Rysedorph was dead. They began hunting for Evans, and nearly eight months later, they found him. He was arrested in Vermont on May 27, 1998.

The murder case wasn't clear-cut, and while authorities were trying to bring charges of murder against Evans, he surprised them by suddenly confessing to killing Falco, Cuomo, and Rysedorph. He helped the police locate the bodies of the three men. He then confessed to killing Berry and Jouben.

Evans was charged with three counts of murder on August 12, 1998, in Rensselaer County, New York. The next day, he was charged with the murder of Jouben.

Outcome

Following his arraignment on August 12, 1998, Evans was being transported to the Albany Court when he put his escape plan into motion. Incredibly, he had managed to shove a handcuff key up his nose and into his sinus cavity, which he was able to retrieve and use to unlock his cuffs in the back of the police van. As the van made its way onto the Troy-Menands Bridge, Evans kicked out the side window and started running.

Quickly cornered by police officers, Evans jumped off the bridge. It was a sixty-foot drop to the Hudson River below, and he died on impact. When his body was retrieved from the frigid water, the handcuff key was found back up his nose and and a razor blade was taped to his ankle. Clearly, he had been determined to escape one way or another.

Trivia

- As a teen, he was physically abused by his brother-in-law after moving in with his older sister.
- He became friends with "Son of Sam" David Berkowitz while in jail for burglary.

LARRY EYLER

Date of birth: December 21, 1952

Aliases/Nicknames: The Highway Murderer, The Highway Killer, The Interstate Killer

Characteristics: Rape, mutilation, dismemberment, evisceration

Number of victims: 19 - 23

Date of murders: 1982 - 1984

Date of arrest: August 21, 1984

Murder method: Stabbing

Known Victims: Jay Reynolds, 26; Delvoyd Baker, 14; Steven Crockett, 19; Robert Foley; John Johnson, 25; John Roach, 21; Steven Agan, 23; Ralph Calise, 28; Richard Wayne; David Block, 22; Danny Bridges, 15; Edgar Underkofler, 27; Gustavo Herrera, 28; Ervin Gibson, 16; Jimmy T. Roberts, 18; Daniel McNeive, 21; Eric Hansen, 18; Derrick Hansen, 14; Michael Bauer, 22; John Bartlett, 19; others unidentified

Crime location: Indiana, Illinois, Ohio, Kentucky, Wisconsin

Status: Sentenced to death. Died of complications related to AIDS, March 6, 1994.

Background

Eyler was born in Crawfordsville, Indiana, in 1952. He had three older siblings, and when he was a young child, his parents divorced. Later, he dropped out of high school and worked a variety of odd jobs. He managed to get his GED while working, and he enrolled in college for the first time in 1974.

Over the next four years, Eyler would drop in and out of college. At the end of the four years, he had not put in enough work to earn a degree. He then decided to move to Chicago.

Unbeknownst to his closest friends or his family members, Eyler was fighting an internal battle. He had homosexual tendencies, and these both fascinated him and disgusted him at the same time. The thought of his family and friends finding out would have added to his stress, as there was much stigma associated with homosexuality at the time.

As many other serial killers, Eyler decided he would take sex wherever he could find it, using force. He would then have to eliminate all the evidence to prevent anyone from finding out. Likewise, he couldn't let those closest to him know his shame.

Murders

Jay Reynolds was murdered on March 22, 1982, near Lexington, Kentucky. He was Eyler's first victim and had been stabbed to death. On October 3 of the same year, the body of Delvoyd Baker was found on the side of the road north of Indianapolis; he had been strangled.

The next victim of Eyler was Steven Crockett, who was stabbed to death on October 23. Four of the stab wounds were to the head, and his body had been disposed of near Lowell, Indiana. Eyler moved to Illinois in November, and he left the body of Robert Foley in a field northwest of Joliet on November 6.

John Johnson was killed on Christmas Day, 1982, and his body was left in a field near Belshaw. On December 28, Eyler killed two men on the same day. Steven Agan was found near Newport and John Roach's body was discarded near Belleville.

As Eyler's murders progressed, so did his methods of murder and mutilation. Some of his later victims were disemboweled, and most were bound. Eyler had by now killed twelve men, including Edgar Underkofler on March 4, 1983, Gustavo Herrera on April 8, Ervin Gibson on April 15, Jimmy T. Roberts on May 9, and Daniel McNeive, also on May 9.

On August 31, the body of Ralph Calise was discovered in a field near Lake Forest, Illinois. His body had been bound and tied with surgical tape and clothesline. His pants were down around his ankles, and he had been stabbed seventeen times.

Derrick Hansen was found on October 4, 1983, near Kenosha, Wisconsin. His body had been dismembered. Then, on October 18, the bodies of four young men were found together at an abandoned farm in Newton County. All of the victims had their pants around their ankles and one had been decapitated. An unidentified male was found on December 5, near Effingham in Illinois. Two days later, the bodies of Richard Wayne and another unidentified male were discovered near Indianapolis.

On May 7, 1984, the body of David Block was found near Zion, Illinois; his body showed injuries similar to those seen on the other victims. Eyler's crime spree finally came undone on August 21, when a dog led his owner to Eyler's garbage, outside his home in Chicago. When police arrived on the scene, they found the dismembered body of Danny Bridges, packed in bags and ready for collection by the garbage truck.

Timeline of known murders:

March 22, 1982 - Jay Reynolds, twenty-six

October 3, 1982 - Delvoyd Baker, fourteen

October 23, 1982 - Steven Crockett, nineteen

November 6, 1982 - Robert Foley

December 25, 1982 - John Johnson, twenty-five

December 28, 1982 - John Roach, twenty-one

December 28, 1982 - Steven Argan, twenty-three

March 4, 1983 - Edgar Underkofler, twenty-seven

April 8, 1983 - Gustavo Herrera, twenty-eight

April 15, 1983 - Ervin Gibson, sixteen

May 9, 1983 - Jimmy T. Roberts, eighteen

May 9, 1983 - Daniel McNeive, twenty-one

August 31, 1983 - Ralph Calise, twenty-eight

September 27, 1983 - Eric Hansen, eighteen

October 4, 1983 - Derrick Hansen, fourteen

October 15, 1983 - John Doe

October 15, 1983 - Michael Bauer, twenty-two

October 15, 1983 - John Bartlett, nineteen

October 15, 1983 - two more victims discovered, unidentified

December 5, 1983 - John Doe

December 7, 1983 - Richard Wayne

December 7, 1983 - John Doe

May 7, 1984 - David Block, twenty-two

August 21, 1984 - Danny Bridges, fifteen

Arrest and Trial

Eyler was arrested and charged with the murder of Danny Bridges on August 21, 1984. Investigators noticed the similarities between the mutilations performed on Bridges and those of Derrick Hansen. Authorities now knew they had caught the serial killer they had been looking for.

Eyler went to trial for the murder of Bridges and was found guilty on July 9, 1986. He was sentenced to death. But by then, Eyler was already facing another death sentence from AIDS.

Eyler tried to save himself from execution by offering to help authorities in Indiana solve some of the murders he had committed. In November of 1990, he confessed that he had killed Steven Argan. But, he also claimed he had been helped by another man, Robert David Little, who happened to be the chairman of the Department of Library Science at the local university.

Eyler claimed Little had taken photos of Argan while he was being disemboweled, and masturbated as he watched. Eyler was convicted of the murder and received a sentence of sixty years. Little was charged, but Eyler's statement was the only evidence of his involvement, and he was subsequently acquitted.

Eyler then tried to make another deal with authorities. He would help them clear twenty murders, provided they had his death sentence commuted to life. The authorities declined the offer.

Outcome

On March 6, 1994, Eyler died from complications due to AIDS. Before his death, he confessed to committing twenty-one murders to his attorney. According to Eyler, four of these killings were committed with an accomplice, who has never been apprehended.

Trivia

- Larry Eyler lived with his male lover, his lover's wife, and their three kids.

PEDRO RODRIGUES FILHO

Date of birth: June 17, 1954

Aliases/Nicknames: Killer Petey

Characteristics: Vigilante murder, cannibalism, robbery

Number of victims: 71 - 100 +

Date of murders: 1968 - 2007

Date of arrest: May 24, 1973

Murder method: Stabbing

Known Victims: Unnamed criminals - vengeance killings

Crime location: Brazil

Status: Sentenced to 128 years in prison.

Background

Filho was born with a damaged skull, allegedly due to the physical abuse his father had inflicted on his mother during her pregnancy. The family lived on a farm in Santa Rita do Sapucai, in Brazil. Filho continued to suffer physical abused from his father throughout his childhood. He claimed that the first time he tried to kill was when he attempted to push his cousin into a sugar cane press, but failed.

When Filho was fourteen years old, his father, who had been working as a security guard at a high school, was fired for stealing food from the school's kitchen. Angered by what he perceived to be an injustice against his father, Filho picked up a shotgun and committed his first murder.

Murders

Filho's murderous spree lasted many years, and all of his victims were criminals. Whenever he heard of a crime being committed, he would find out who was responsible, track them down, and then execute them. A lot of his targets were gang members or drug dealers.

Filho's fiancée was murdered by gang members, which enraged him. Subsequently, Filho went to a wedding that had been organized by the leader of that gang and embarked on a murderous and violent rampage. Seven people were killed at the event and sixteen were injured. Several months later, he discovered his cousin had gotten pregnant and her boyfriend had refused to marry her, so he shot him to death.

When Filho discovered his father had stabbed his mother and butchered her with a machete, Filho paid him a visit while he was in prison. Face to face with his father, he stabbed him twenty-two times. Then he ripped out his father's heart and ate some of it.

Timeline of murders:

Unspecified date in **1967**:

An unnamed cousin

Unspecified dates in **1968**:

The unnamed vice-mayor of Alfenas

Unnamed school guard

Unspecified dates from **1969** to **1973**:

Unnamed man (a drug dealer)

Seven unnamed people (all gang members) - the wedding massacre

His unnamed father

The unnamed man who impregnated his cousin (shot)

At least eleven unnamed criminals

May 24, 1973:

Unnamed man (a rapist)

Unspecified dates from **1973** to **2003**:

Francisco de Assis Pereira (a serial killer and rapist)

João Acásio da Costa (a serial killer and robber)

Hosmany Ramos (a murderer and bank robber)

Unnamed inmate (a murderer)

Three unnamed inmates

At least 40 unnamed inmates

Arrest and Trial

Filho was arrested on May 24, 1973, and was taken to the police station in the back of a police car with another criminal who happened to be a rapist. When they arrived at their destination, officers discovered Filho had killed the rapist without them even realizing it was happening.

Filho was incarcerated until April 24, 2007, when he was released. But, on September 15, 2011, he was arrested again, and this time convicted of false imprisonment and rioting.

Outcome

Filho was finally given a sentence of one hundred twenty-eight years' imprisonment. During the numerous years of his previous incarceration, Filho had continued to kill fellow inmates, ending the lives of forty-seven criminals. Filho was despised by other inmates, and when a group tried to attack him, Filho ended up killing three of them. One of his prison victims was killed because of his snoring, but the majority were killed because of the crimes they were incarcerated for.

Trivia

- At the age of fourteen, he murdered the vice-mayor of Alfenas, Minas Gerais, because he had fired his father, a school guard, for stealing the school kitchen's food. Then he murdered another guard, supposedly the real thief.

ALBERT FISH

Date of birth: May 19, 1870

Aliases/Nicknames: The Werewolf of Wysteria, The Gray Man, Brooklyn Vampire, Moon Maniac, The Boogey Man

Characteristics: Cannibalism, pedophilia, coprophilia, urophilia, sadism

Number of victims: 3 +

Date of murders: 1924 - 1934

Date of arrest: December 13, 1934

Murder method: Strangulation, stabbing

Known Victims: Francis X. McDonnell, 8; Billy Gaffney, 8; Grace Budd, 10

Crime location: New York

Status: Executed by electric chair, January 16, 1936.

Background

Fish, whose full name was Hamilton Howard Fish, was the youngest of four children born to Randall and Ellen Fish. His father was forty-three years older than his mother, and he was seventy-five years old when Fish was born. When Randall died in 1875, Fish was sent to live in Saint John's Orphanage in Washington, where he regularly suffered abuse. After a while, he started to enjoy the pain he felt when he was beaten.

It was while he was at the orphanage, when the other children nicknamed his "Ham & Eggs," that he acquired the preference to be called "Albert,," the name of a deceased sibling. Fish later claimed that he not only experienced but also witnessed terrible "whippings" at the orphanage. And he saw things being done by young boys that they shouldn't have been doing.

His mother Ellen gained employment with the government in 1880, and was able to retrieve Fish from the orphanage. Two years later, at the age of twelve, Fish entered into a relationship with a telegraph boy. This boy allegedly introduced Fish to bizarre and perverted practices, such as eating feces and drinking urine. Fish started to visit the public baths so he could watch boys undress, and he would spend most of his spare time there.

Throughout his adulthood, Fish would write obscene letters to women he found advertising in matrimonial agencies and classified columns in papers and magazines. This fondness for shocking with the written word would take an even darker turn when his behavior truly entered into the realm of depravity.

Murders

Fish had convinced the parents of Grace Budd to allow the little girl to attend a party with him. He took the girl to an empty house. While she was outside picking flowers, Fish went inside and removed his clothing because he didn't want to get blood on them. He called out to Grace and hid in a closet until she came into the room. He strangled her to death and then cut her body into small pieces so he could carry it back to his home and eat it.

After Fish was arrested, his other murders were uncovered. Francis McDonell had been reported missing on July 14, 1924. The following day, his body was found hanging from a tree in the woods near his home. McDonell had been sexually assaulted and strangled to death. An autopsy revealed he had received severe lacerations to his abdomen and legs.

On February 11, 1927, Billy Gaffney was abducted and taken to the dump on Riker Avenue. Fish took him to a house nearby, gagged him, tied him up, and removed his clothes. His clothing was burned and his shoes tossed into the dump. Fish went home, and the next day he came back with tools. Gaffney was still alive, and Fish whipped him with a cat-o'-nine tails until blood was running down his legs. He cut the boy's mouth from ear to ear and cut off his nose and ears. By the time Gaffney's eyes were gouged out, he was dead. Fish stuck a knife in his belly and drank the blood.

Like Grace Budd, Gaffney's body was cut up into small pieces. The parts Fish wanted to eat were taken home, and the others were placed in sacks and weighted down before going into the river. In his confession, Fish gave graphic descriptions of how he cooked each part of the body he had kept and ate it.

Timeline of known murders:

July 15, 1924 - Francis X. McDonnell, eight

February 11, 1927 - Billy Gaffney, four

June 3, 1928 - Grace Budd, ten

Other suspected murders:

October 3, 1926 - Emma Richardson, five

1927 - Yetta Abramowitz, twelve

May 2, 1931 - Robin Jane Liu, six

February 15, 1932 - Mary Ellen O'Connor, sixteen

December 15, 1932 - Benjamin Collings, seventeen

Arrest and Trial

Fish sent a letter to Grace Budd's mother in November of 1934, which detailed the little girl's death and how Fish cannibalized her body. On the envelope was an emblem - N.Y.P.C.B.A. - which stood for the New York Private Chauffeur's Benevolent Association. When police investigated, a company janitor said he had taken some of the stationary home to use, but had left it behind when he moved out of a rooming house.

Further enquiries revealed Fish had checked out of that same room just a few days before the letter was sent. According to the landlady, Fish was expecting a check to come from his son and he had asked her to hold it for him, so the chief investigator waited outside the room until Fish came back. He asked Fish to come to the station with him for questioning. At first, Fish agreed. But then he pulled out a razor blade; the investigator quickly disarmed him.

When they arrived at the station, Fish didn't deny he had murdered Grace Budd. He even told the investigator that he had originally planned to kill her brother Edward. Fish's trial was set to begin on March 11, 1935, in New York. Fish pleaded insanity, saying God had told him to kill children. He was examined by several psychiatrists, who testified that Fish had many sexual fetishes. These included:

1. Sadism
2. Exhibitionism
3. Masochism
4. Cunnilingus
5. Anilingus
6. Flagellation
7. Voyeurism
8. Fellatio
9. Cannibalism
10. Pedophilia
11. Piquerism
12. Coprophilia
13. Infibulation
14. Urophilia

When one psychiatrist was asked if Fish was insane and if he knew right from wrong, he replied that Fish was insane. Though he knew what he had done was wrong, his thoughts were overrun by his opinions of religion, sin, and atonement. Fish had claimed that by killing a child he was atoning for his sins.

Although the members of the jury believed Fish was insane, they felt he should be executed anyway, so they declared him sane and found him guilty of murder. He was therefore convicted and sentenced to death.

Outcome

On January 16, 1936, Fish was strapped into the electric chair at Sing Sing prison. The execution began at 11:06 p.m., and he was declared dead just three minutes later. Like many other executed prisoners, Fish was buried in the prison cemetery. Reportedly, Fish even assisted the executioner with putting the electrodes in place on his body. The last words he spoke were supposedly, "I don't even know why I'm here."

Immediately after his execution, his lawyer James Dempsey told the awaiting press that he had Fish's final statement, but he would never show it to anyone because "it was the most filthy string of obscenities that I have ever read."

Trivia

- At the age of sixty-five, he was the oldest person ever to be put to death at Sing Sing prison.
- His family had a history of serious mental illness and his brother lived in a mental hospital.

Quotes from Fish:

- "What a thrill that will be if I have to die in the electric chair. It will be the supreme thrill. The only one I haven't tried."
- "I like children they are tasty."
- "I have no particular desire to live. I have no particular desire to be killed. It is a matter of indifference to me. I do not think I am altogether right."

Letter from Fish to Grace Budd's mother:

"My dear Mrs. Budd,

In 1894 a friend of mine shipped as a deck hand on the steamer Tacoma, Capt John Davis.

They sailed from San Francisco to Hong Kong China. On arriving there he and two others went ashore and got drunk. When they returned the boat was gone. At that time there was a famine in China. Meat of any kind was from $1 to 3 Dollars a pound. So great was the suffering among the very poor that all children under 12 were sold to the Butchers to be cut up and sold for food in order to keep others from starving. A boy or girl under 14 was not safe in the street. You could go in any shop and ask for steak – chops – or stew meat. Part of the naked body of a boy or girl would be brought out and just what you wanted cut from it. A boy or girls behind which is the sweetest part of the body and sold as veal cutlet brought the highest price. John staid there so long he acquired a taste for human flesh. On his return to N.Y. he stole two boys one 7 one 11. Took them to his home stripped them naked tied them in a closet then burned everything they had on. Several times every day and night he spanked them – tortured them – to make their meat good and tender. First he killed the 11 yr old boy, because he had the fattest ass and of course the most meat on it. Every part of his body was cooked and eaten except Head – bones and guts. He was roasted in the oven, (all of his ass) boiled, broiled, fried, stewed. The little boy was next, went the same way. At that time I was living at 409 E 100 St, rear – right side. He told me so often how good human flesh was I made up my mind to taste it. On Sunday June the 3 – 1928 I called on you at 406 W 15 St. Brought you pot cheese – strawberries. We had lunch. Grace sat in my lap and kissed me. I made up my mind to eat her, on the pretence of taking her to a party. You said Yes she could go. I took her to an empty house in Westchester I had already picked out. When we got there, I told her to remain outside. She picked wild flowers. I went upstairs and stripped all my clothes off. I knew if I did not I would get her blood on them. When all was ready I went to the window and called her. Then I hid in a closet until she was in the room. When she saw me all naked she began to cry and tried to run down stairs. I grabbed her and she said she would tell her mama. First I stripped her naked. How she did kick – bite and scratch. I choked her to death then cut her in small pieces so I could take my meat to my rooms, cook and eat it. How sweet and tender her little ass was roasted in the oven. It took me 9 days to eat her entire body. I did not fuck her, though, I could of had I wished. She died a virgin."

BOBBY JACK FOWLER

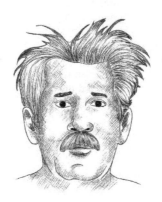

Date of birth: June 12, 1939
Aliases/Nicknames: Nil
Characteristics: Rape
Number of victims: 1 - 20 +
Date of murders: 1973 - 1995
Date of arrest: June 28, 1995
Murder method: Strangulation
Known Victims: Colleen MacMillen, 16; suspected of killing many others
Crime location: Oregon and British Columbia, Canada
Status: Sentenced to 16 years, but died of lung cancer, May 15, 2006.

Background

Little is known about Fowler's childhood or his younger years, but as an adult, he was known to live a transient lifestyle. He would travel throughout North America, getting work in construction or roofing as he went along. He would stay in cheap motels and travel around in old, beat-up cars, and he was fond of small-town bars.

An abuser of methamphetamine, amphetamine, and alcohol, Fowler found himself in trouble with the law on multiple occasions. He liked driving and he enjoyed picking up hitchhikers on his travels. Fowler was charged with the murders of a man and woman in Texas in 1969, but he was acquitted, convicted only of discharging a firearm within the city limits.

Fowler was also charged with attempted murder and sexual assault after he tied up a woman, beat her, and left her to die, covered in brush to hide her body. The woman survived, and Fowler was sent to prison in Tennessee. Fowler believed that women who drank in bars or hitchhiked actually wanted to be sexually assaulted, so he didn't see anything wrong with his actions. Before long, however, his assaults would take a deadly turn.

Murders

Fowler's DNA was found on the body of murder victim Colleen MacMillen. Authorities also suspected him of killing Pamela Darlington and Gale Weys in 1973. He was also considered a suspect in up to twenty murders that occurred along Highway 16, which was nicknamed the "Highway of Tears" because of the number of women who went missing along that stretch of road.

Other murders Fowler was a suspect in included Sheila Swanson, nineteen, and her friend Melissa Sanders, seventeen, who had last been seen at a pay phone near the park they were camping at, on May 3, 1992. On October 10, 1992, their bodies were discovered in woods near Eddyville, Oregon, by hunters.

Jennifer Esson, sixteen, and Kara Leas, sixteen, were last seen on January 28, 1995, as they walked toward Highway 101. Their bodies were found on February 15, 1995, hidden beneath brush in woods. Both girls had been strangled.

Arrest and Trial

Fowler was arrested on June 28, 1995, after a woman jumped out of a motel window in Newport, Oregon. She had a rope tied to her ankle and was able to tell police what had happened. Fowler had kidnapped and sexually abused her; he had also attempted to rape her.

On January 8, 1996, Fowler was found guilty on the counts of kidnapping, attempted rape, sexual abuse, assault, coercion, and menacing. He received a sentence of sixteen years and three months with the possibility of parole.

Fowler was never charged with any murders, even though his DNA was found on the body of Colleen MacMillen.

Outcome

Suffering with lung cancer, Fowler succumbed to his illness on May 15, 2006, and died while still incarcerated at the Oregon State Penitentiary.

Trivia

- "He was of the belief that women who hitchhiked and drank and went to bars desired to be violently sexually assaulted..."

LONNIE DAVID FRANKLIN, JR.

Date of birth: August 30, 1952

Aliases/Nicknames: The Grim Sleeper

Characteristics: Rape

Number of victims: 10 +

Date of murders: 1985 - 2007

Date of arrest: July 7, 2010

Murder method: Shooting, strangulation

Known Victims: Debra Jackson, 29; Henrietta Wright, 34; Barbara Ware, 23; Bernita Sparks, 26; Mary Lowe, 26; Lachrica Jefferson, 22; Alice "Monique" Alexander, 18; Princess Berthomieux, 15; Valerie McCorvey, 35; Janecia Peters, 25

Crime location: Los Angeles

Status: Sentenced to death, awaiting execution.

Background

Franklin seemed to be the epitome of a good, hardworking man who took care of his family. Sure, he was a small-time criminal, but as a member of the community, he was thought of as a kind and responsible family-oriented man. Everyone in the neighborhood knew that if you needed a part for your car, Franklin could probably help you out. He had a good supply of parts behind his house, and he would sell them in a "don't ask don't tell" agreement.

An outgoing neighbor, Franklin would often purchase birthday gifts for the elderly people in the neighborhood. He was even known to attend graduation ceremonies of the children in the neighborhood. His marriage wasn't perfect (it had a recurrent on-again, off-again pattern), but he still took care of his mother-in-law when she got ill.

Franklin doted on his two children. He enjoyed teaching them how to fix their cars when they broke down, and he even taught them how to drive. As far as anyone knew, Franklin was a good, friendly, and helpful man. But Franklin had been hiding a secret for a very long time, and he had urges he couldn't ignore.

Murders

Debra Jackson, twenty-nine, was found in Vermont-Slauson, having been shot three times in the chest, on August 10, 1985. A year later, the body of Henriette Wright, thirty-four, was found in Hyde Park on August 12, 1986. She had been shot in the chest twice.

On January 10, 1987, Barbara Ware, twenty-seven, was found in Central-Alameda after being shot once in the chest. On April 15, Bernita Sparks, twenty-six, was also shot once in the chest; she was found in Gramercy Park. Another body found in Gramercy Park on November 1 was that of Mary Lowe, twenty-six; she too had been shot just once in the chest.

The next victim, Lachrica Jefferson, twenty-two, was found on January 30, 1988, in Westmont. She had been shot in the chest twice, and the killer had placed a napkin over her face. Written on it was the word "AIDS."

Alice "Monique" Alexander, eighteen, was shot twice in the chest on September 11; she was found in Vermont Square. There was a break in the murder spree with the next killing occurring on March 19, 2002. Fifteen-year-old Princess Berthomieux was found strangled to death in Inglewood.

On July 11, 2003, the body of Valeria McCorvey, thirty-five, was found in Westmont. She had been strangled to death. Again, there was a significant break in the killings. On January 1, 2007, the body of Janecia Peters, twenty-seven, was found in Gramercy Park. She had been shot once in the back.

Timeline of known murders:

August 10, 1985 - Debra Jackson, twenty-nine

August 12, 1986 - Henrietta Wright, thirty-four

August 14, 1986 - Thomas Steele, thirty-six

January 10, 1987 - Barbara Ware, twenty-three

April 15, 1987 - Bernita Sparks, twenty-six

November 1, 1987 - Mary Lowe, twenty-six

January 30, 1988 - Lachrica Jefferson, twenty-two

September 11, 1988 - Alice "Monique" Alexander, eighteen

March 19, 2002 - Princess Berthomieux, fifteen

July 11, 2003 - Valerie McCorvey, thirty-five

January 1, 2007 - Janecia Peters   , twenty-five

Arrest and Trial

Franklin was arrested on July 7, 2010, and charged with ten counts of murder, along with one count of attempted murder. Because of the size of the case, there were several delays to the trial dates. Franklin finally went on trial on February 16, 2016. By May 4, the jury was in the process of deliberating, and they found him guilty on all counts the following day.

Sentencing began on June 6, 2016, with the jury recommending Franklin be given the death penalty. On August 10, he was sentenced to death.

Outcome

Franklin is also suspected of being responsible for five other murders, but he has yet to be formally charged in those cases. He remains on death row awaiting his execution date.

Trivia

–   Franklin had once worked as a garage attendant for the LAPD

FREEWAY PHANTOM

Date of birth: Unknown

Aliases/Nicknames: The Freeway Phantom

Characteristics: Rape, pedophilia, kidnapping

Number of victims: 6

Date of murders: April 25, 1971 - September 5, 1972

Date of arrest: Never apprehended

Murder method: Strangulation

Known Victims: Carol Spinks, 13; Darlenia Johnson, 16; Brenda Crockett, 10; Nenomoshia Yates, 12; Brenda Woodward, 18; Diane Williams, 17

Crime location: Washington

Status: Unidentified, not apprehended.

Background

Since 1971, investigators have been trying to solve the mystery of the Freeway Phantom. To date, nobody has been formally identified as being responsible for the six murders attributed to the Phantom, and there doesn't appear to be a firm suspect.

Despite receiving numerous tips via phone and mail alluding to potential suspects, the task force set up by the Metropolitan Police Department is no closer to solving this case. Some of the leads received were eliminated quickly, while others took substantial investigating. There have been some interesting suspects along the way, but so far, the Freeway Phantom remains just that - a phantom.

Murders

The first murder believed to be the work of the Freeway Phantom was that of Carol Spinks, a thirteen-year-old girl who had been sent to the grocery store. She was abducted while walking back home; Six days later, her body was found on an embankment next to the I-295 freeway.

On July 8, 1971, Darlenia Johnson was abducted while traveling to the recreation center where she worked over the summer. Her body was found eleven days after her disappearance, just fifteen feet away from where Spinks had been discovered.

Brenda Crockett, ten, was sent to the store by her mother on July 27, 1971. But she never came home. A phone call was placed by Brenda to her home three hours after she had gone to the store, and it was answered by her little sister who was seven at the time. Brenda, who was crying, said, "A white man picked me up, and I'm heading home in a cab." She told her sister she thought she was in Virginia. The call ended abruptly with Brenda saying "bye" and disconnecting the call.

Another call came through a little while later, this time answered by the boyfriend of Brenda's mother. This time Brenda repeated what she had said earlier, and the boyfriend told her to get the man to come to the phone. He heard heavy footsteps in the background and Brenda quickly said, "I'll see you," and hung up the phone. Brenda's body was found a few hours later by a hitchhiker on Route 50. She had been raped before being strangled with a scarf.

On October 1, 1971, Nenomoshia Yates was walking home from a store in Northeast Washington when she was kidnapped. Within hours, her body was found near Pennsylvania Avenue, raped and strangled.

Brenda Woodward, eighteen, got on a bus on November 15, 1971, heading for her home. Police found her body around six hours later, near the Route 202 access ramp. She had been stabbed and strangled, and a coat was laid across her chest. The pocket of the coat held a note from the killer. Written on the note was:

This is tantamount to my insensitivity [sic] to people especially women.

I will admit the others when you catch me if you can!

Free-way Phantom

It would be another year before the next murder victim was found. Diane Williams was last seen getting on a bus on September 5, 1972. Her body was found shortly afterwards, strangled and dumped beside the I-295 freeway.

Timeline of known murders:

April 21, 1971 - Carol Spinks, thirteen

July 8, 1971 - Darlenia Johnson, sixteen

July 27, 1971 - Brenda Crockett, ten

October 1, 1971 - Nenomoshia Yates, twelve

November 15, 1971 - Brenda Woodard, eighteen

September 5, 1972 - Diane Williams, seventeen

Suspects

Despite numerous tips being given to the Metropolitan Police, no clear suspect has ever been identified or apprehended. The investigation included team members from a number of law enforcement agencies, including the FBI.

A gang known as the "Green Vega Rapists" was thoroughly investigated as potentially being responsible for the murders. Each member of the gang was interrogated, including those that were incarcerated at the time. One such inmate claimed to have information about the killer, but he would only tell what he knew if his identity could be kept secret. Police agreed, and the inmate gave them the date and location of a murder, along with details considered a "signature" that the general public was unaware of.

Consideration was given as to whether or not the inmate was involved in the murder, but he was cleared due to his alibi. At that time, an election was being held in Maryland. During a press conference, one of the candidates announced that an inmate had provided information on the Freeway Phantom. Because this threatened his secret identity, the inmate refused to tell the investigators any more information. Subsequently, he denied having ever told them anything.

Outcome

At the time when these murders were being investigated, it was common practice for the case files at the Metropolitan Police Department to be kept within files maintained by detectives who were assigned to them. Many of the case files and notes on the Freeway Phantom have been lost. With many of the original investigators either retired or deceased, it would be difficult to track down the missing investigation.

The Freeway Phantom case is still open.

WILLIAM PATRICK FYFE

Date of birth: February 27, 1955

Aliases/Nicknames: The Killer Handyman

Characteristics: Rape

Number of victims: 9 - 25

Date of murders: 1979 - 1999

Date of arrest: December 22, 1999

Murder method: Stabbing

Known Victims: Hazel Scattolon, 52; Monique Gaudreau, 46; Anna Yarnold, 59; Teresa Shanahan, 55; Mary Glenn, 50; Suzanne-Marie Bernier, 62; Nicole Raymond, 26; Louise Poupart-Leblanc, 37; Pauline Laplante, 45

Crime location: Montreal, Quebec, Canada

Status: Sentenced to life - serving in a psychiatric hospital.

Background

Born in Canada in 1955, Fyfe would later be described by police as being an "ordinary man." The communities he lived in certainly thought he was a good person, and one who showed a lot of community spirit. Others described him as being very generous, although he did have an annoying habit of preaching to people about their health and weight.

Fyfe, who was addicted to drugs at one point, moved to Quebec to receive help and treatment for his addiction. He ended up staying there, and he spent time counseling others who also had addictions like his own while he worked as a handyman.

In the fall of 1999, Fyfe traveled from Barrie to Montreal (a distance of over four hundred miles) four times, committing his awful crimes—in a sort of frenzy—along the way. He managed to stay under the radar of the authorities for a while, but he was eventually brought down by a single fingerprint.

Murders

The first known victim was Suzanne-Marie Bernier, who was murdered on October 17, 1979, in Cartierville, Montreal. She had been sexually assaulted and stabbed to death. A month later, on November 14, Nicole Raymond, twenty-six, was sexually assaulted and stabbed in Pointe-Claire, Montreal.

Hazel Scattolon was found on March 21, 1981. She had been sexually assaulted and stabbed to death. The next murder didn't occur until September 26, 1987, when Louise Poupart-Leblanc was sexually assaulted and stabbed to death in Saint-Adele, Laurentides.

On June 9, 1989, Pauline Laplante was sexually assaulted and stabbed to death in Saint-Adele, Laurentides. The next murder was that of Monique Gaudreau, in October of 1999. She was discovered deceased in Sainte-Agathe-des-Monts, Quebec.

On the fifteenth of that same month, the body of fifty-nine-year-old Anna Yarnold was found in Senneville, Quebec. The next victim was Teresa Shanahan, a fifty-five-year-old woman. She was found stabbed to death in Laval, Quebec, in November. The body of Mary Glenn was found on December 15, in Baie-d'Urfe, Quebec. She had been beaten and then stabbed to death.

Timeline of known murders:

October 17, 1979 - Suzanne-Marie Bernier, sixty-two

November 14, 1979 - Nicole Raymond, twenty-six

March 21, 1981 - Hazel Scattolon, fifty-two

September 26, 1987 - Louise Poupart-Leblanc, thirty-seven

June 9, 1989 - Pauline Laplante, forty-five

October, 1999 - Monique Gaudreau, forty-six

October 15, 1999 - Anna Yarnold, fifty-nine

November, 1999 - Teresa Shanahan, fifty-five

December 15, 1999 - Mary Glenn, fifty

Arrest and Trial

A fingerprint found at the crime scene of one of the murders led police straight to Fyfe. After surveilling him for a while, he was finally arrested on December 22, 1999. At the time, he was returning to his truck after having a meal at a truck stop.

Through DNA testing it was established Fyfe was responsible for the murders. However, he only confessed to some of the crimes, so just how many women he killed is unknown. His trial started on November 6, 2000, and he was subsequently found guilty.

Outcome

Fyfe was sentenced to life imprisonment; he was sent to a psychiatric hospital in Saskatchewan to serve his sentence.

JOHN WAYNE GACY

Date of birth: March 17, 1942

Aliases/Nicknames: The Killer Clown

Characteristics: Rape, torture

Number of victims: 33

Date of murders: 1972 - 1978

Date of arrest: December 21, 1978

Murder method: Strangulation

Known Victims: Timothy McCoy, 18; John Butkovich, 17; Darrell Sampson, 18; Randall Reffett, 15; Sam Stapleton, 14; Michael Bonnin, 17; William Carroll, 16; Rick Johnston, 17; Kenneth Parker, 16; William Bundy, 19; Gregory Godzik, 17; John Szyc, 19; Jon Prestidge, 20; Matthew Bowman, 19; Robert Gilroy, 18; John Mowery, 19; Russell Nelson, 21; Robert Winch, 16; Tommy Boling, 20; David Talsma, 19; William Kindred, 19; Timothy O'Rourke, 20; Frank Landingin, 19; James Mazzara, 21; Robert Piest, 15; eight unidentified

Crime location: Chicago, Illinois

Status: Executed by lethal injection on May 10, 1994.

Background

John Wayne Gacy was born on March 17, 1942, to a dysfunctional household that would mark the beginnings of his twisted philosophies. Gacy later would claim that his father was an abusive alcoholic who regularly beat him and his mother because Gacy was a bit effeminate, and he couldn't meet his father's approval no matter what he did. In his senior year of high school Gacy dropped out. He moved out of the family home for a while and found work in a mortuary in Las Vegas. But, he eventually went back home to attend business college. For a while, he worked as a shoe salesman.

When Gacy was twenty-two, he married into a business family. His wife's father owned a chain of Kentucky Fried Chicken restaurants, and Gacy became the manager of the family business. He became active in the community, joining the Jaycees, where he received a number of honors and held key offices.

A darker side of Gacy began to emerge in 1968, when he was arrested and charged with molesting a teenager who had been employed in the restaurant Gacy managed. He pleaded guilty and received a prison sentence, of which he served eighteen months. His wife divorced him, and he worked as a cook for a while before starting his own construction business.

Gacy was in trouble again in 1971, after a teenager accused him of trying to force the youth to have sex. This time, the accuser failed to turn up at court, so the charges were dropped. Soon after, Gacy married again. But, early in to the marriage, he ceased having any form of sexual relations with his new wife. By now, Gacy had started performing at children's parties and hospital wards as Pogo (or sometimes "Patches") the clown.

To impress the local politicians, dignitaries, and his neighbors, Gacy would throw large parties at his home. By all accounts, he was a great host at these parties. But there came a time when his wife and visitors to the home would comment on a strange smell that was present. Gacy explained that the odor was due to dampness in the crawl space beneath the house. That wasn't entirely the truth.

Murders

Gacy would lure young men and boys to his home, claiming he wanted to hire them to do some work for his building company. He would then offer to show them his "handcuff trick." This resulted in his victims being incapacitated, and he was then free to do as he wished to them. Gacy used chloroform to sedate his victims, and then he would sodomize them.

After the sexual assault, he would throw a rope tied in a loop around the victim's neck, put a stick in the loop, then slowly twist it, strangulating his victim until he was dead. Often, he would recite Bible passages while he was killing them.

His house had a crawl space beneath it, and this is where the majority of his thirty-three victims were buried. He would cover the bodies with lime to hasten the decomposition. Gacy flew under the radar of the local authorities for a long time—until he made a major mistake in December of 1978.

Gacy was providing a building estimate at a local pharmacy when he decided to lure a teenage boy back to his home. The boy's mother had dropped him off so he could fill out a job application at the pharmacy. When his disappearance was reported, police discovered that Gacy had been in the store at the same time. On looking further into his background, they learned Gacy had previously been prosecuted for molestation.

They began to watch Gacy very closely and paid a visit to his home on December 21, 1978. One of the detectives asked if he could use Gacy's bathroom. He thought he could smell the distinctive odor of decomposition as soon as the furnace fan started. Suspecting the worst, they got a search warrant and searched the crawl space.

Beneath the house they found multiple decomposing corpses. Gacy was immediately arrested.

Timeline of known murders:

January 2, 1972 - Timothy McCoy, eighteen

July 31, 1975 - John Butkovich, seventeen

April 6, 1976 - Darrell Sampson, eighteen

May 14, 1976 - Randall Reffett, fifteen

May 14, 1976 - Samuel Stapleton, fourteen

June 3, 1976 - Michael Bonnin, seventeen

June 10, 1976 - William "Billy" Carroll, sixteen

August 6, 1976 - Rick Johnston, seventeen

October 24, 1976 - Kenneth Parker, sixteen

October 26, 1976 - William Bundy, nineteen

December 12, 1976 - Gregory Godzik, seventeen

January 20, 1977 - John Szyc, nineteen

March 15, 1977 - Jon Prestige, twenty

July 5, 1977 - Matthew Bowman, nineteen

September 15, 1977 - Robert Gilroy, eighteen

September 25, 1977 - John Mowery, nineteen

October 17, 1977 - Russell Nelson, twenty-one

November 11, 1977 - Robert Winch, sixteen

November 18, 1977 - Tommy Baling, twenty

December 9, 1977 - David Talsma, nineteen

February 16, 1978 - William Kindred, nineteen

June of 1978 - Timothy O'Rourke, twenty

November 3, 1978 - Frank Wayne "Dale" Landingin, nineteen

November 13, 1978 - James Mazzara, twenty-one

December 11, 1978 - Robert Piest, fifteen

Arrest and Trial

During the initial interrogation, Gacy began confessing to the terrible murders he had committed. He even drew a map to show where each victim was buried under his house. However, he refused to sign his statements. When he went to trial, he was found guilty of all the murders and sentenced to death.

Outcome

Gacy was transported from the Menard Correctional Center to the Statesville Correctional Center on the morning on May 9, 1994, for his execution. He was able to have a private picnic with his family on the prison grounds. Later that evening, he observed prayer with a Catholic priest prior to being taken to the execution chamber.

Before the lethal injection could be administered, the chemicals clogged the IV tube, and the curtains covering the observation windows were drawn while the problem was sorted out. Ten minutes later, the curtains were opened and the execution process began. From start to finish, the execution took eighteen minutes to complete. Allegedly, Gacy's last words before his death were "Kiss my ass."

His death was confirmed at 12:58 a.m. Gacy's brain was removed and given to Dr. Helen Morrison for the purposes of researching serial killers and trying to determine whether there is a biological reason for their need to kill.

Trivia

- Gacy's final meal was shrimp, Kentucky Fried Chicken, and French fries.
- The execution lasted for eighteen minutes because one of the IV lines clogged.
- Had an IQ of 118.
- Gacy dabbled in oil paintings while in prison. He would paint Disney characters like the Seven Dwarves, Michelangelo's *Pieta*, or even self-portraits such as "Pogo the Clown." After his execution, these paintings became trendy collectors' items. Film director John Waters and actor Johnny Depp are some celebrities who own his paintings. Gacy's art dealer was Rick Station of Grindhouse Graphics.

LUIS GARAVITO

Date of birth: January 25, 1957
Aliases/Nicknames: La Bestia (The Beast), Tribilin, El Cura, El Loco, Bonifacio Morera Lizcano
Characteristics: Rape, torture, dismemberment, mutilation
Number of victims: 138 - 300 +
Date of murders: 1992 - 1999
Date of arrest: April 22, 1999
Murder method: Stabbing
Known Victims: Unnamed male children aged 6 - 16 years
Crime location: Colombia, Ecuador
Status: Sentenced to 1,853 years, but due to the law, will only serve 22 years.

Background

Garavito was born in Génova, Colombia in 1957. He was the eldest of seven children, all boys. During his childhood, he suffered emotional and physical abuse at the hands of his father. He later claimed he was also sexually abused as a child.

He would become a controversial killer after his convictions, not just because of the sheer number of victims he raped and killed, but also because of the absurdity of the sentencing laws in Colombia.

Murders

The victims of Garavito were found on the streets, most coming from poor homes or no homes at all. They were generally between the ages of six and sixteen. To lure them away, Garavito offered them money or small gifts. Once they trusted him, he would take them for a walk until they got too tired. Then he would carry out his atrocious crimes.

The children were raped by Garavito, and their throats were cut. The bodies were usually dismembered; many of them displayed signs of torture.

Arrest and Trial

On April 22, 1999, Garavito was caught and arrested. He subsequently confessed to killing one hundred forty children, but he remained under suspicion for the murders of at least one hundred seventy-two. The murders spread across fifty-nine towns in Colombia.

When Garavito went to trial, he was found guilty of murder in one hundred thirty-eight of the one hundred seventy-two cases he was believed to be responsible for. Charges for the other murders were still pending, depending on the outcome of investigations. The total of his sentences was one thousand eight hundred fifty-three years and nine days, but there are restrictions in Colombia which meant he could only serve thirty years. To make things worse, because he helped the investigators locate the bodies, his sentence was further reduced to just twenty-two years.

Outcome

There has been public outcry regarding the length of Garavito's sentence, with many believing there should be a death penalty, or at least life imprisonment. The families of the victims and others opposed to his sentence called for a change in the Colombian laws so that harsher penalties could be handed down to criminals as vicious as Garavito.

An interview with Garavito took place in 2006, by TV host Pirry. During the interview, Garavito tried to play down the seriousness of his crimes, and said he wanted to go into politics so he could help children who were abused.

Trivia

- Would often pose as a monk or a priest.
- Garavito traveled widely during his killing spree, committing murders in at least eleven of Colombia's thirty-two departments.

DONALD HENRY GASKINS

Date of birth: March 13, 1933

Aliases/Nicknames: Pee Wee, Junior Parrott, Meanest Man in America, The Redneck Charles Manson

Characteristics: Rape, sodomy, torture, mutilation, cannibalism

Number of victims: 8 - 100 + (claimed)

Date of murders: 1969 - 1975, 1982

Date of arrest: December of 1975

Murder method: Stabbing

Known Victims: Unnamed young men and women - some he knew, others were hitchhikers

Crime location: South Carolina

Status: Executed by electric chair, September 6, 1991.

Background

Gaskins was born in South Carolina to Eulea Parrott, who gave birth to a number of illegitimate children. As a child, Gaskins was neglected quite extensively by his mother, who seldom supervised her brood. This was more evident, when at the age of one, Gaskins drank a bottle of kerosene. It's believed that this poisoning led Gaskins to have seizures until he was three years old.

His mother would have numerous boyfriends, and these so-called "stepfathers" would often beat Gaskins and the other children. Because he was so small in stature as a child, Gaskins was given the nickname "Pee Wee." Apparently, he didn't even know his name was Donald until his first court appearance following a crime spree he had embarked on with other school dropouts.

This group had gang-raped a sister of one of their friends, as well as committed multiple robberies. A hatchet was used to assault one victim, who survived and was able to give the police the identities of the culprits. Because of his age, Gaskins was sent to reform school.

Gaskins claimed he was raped regularly by the other inmates at the reform school. He eventually escaped from the school and got married, but he voluntarily returned to finish his sentence. He was released in 1951, when he was eighteen. He worked for a while on a tobacco plantation. But, he was arrested again in 1953, after attacking a teenage girl with a hammer. He was charged and convicted of attempted murder and sent to prison for six years.

While in prison, Gaskins was raped again. This time though, he fought back against his assailant, slicing the man's throat. This earned him an extra three years added to his sentence. This was a major

154

turning point for Gaskins, however. From then onward, he became the aggressor, not the victim. He managed to escape from prison in 1955. But, he was captured and finished his sentence, receiving parole in 1961.

Gaskins went back to committing robberies, but he also continued to attack females. He was arrested in 1963 for the rape of a twelve-year-old girl. But, once again, he managed to escape before he could be sentenced. Soon after, he was recaptured and sent to prison for eight years—but he only served five. In November of 1968, he was paroled. This time, when he committed his crimes, he would try not to leave any witnesses behind.

Murders

The majority of Gaskins' victims were hitchhikers he picked up, and he committed his first murder in September of 1969. He had picked up a female hitchhiker, tortured her, and then killed her and disposed of her body in a swamp. He later said that all he could think about was that he could do anything he wanted to her.

From then onwards, Gaskins drove along the coastal highways in the south, picking up male and female hitchhikers he would then murder. He referred to these murders as "coastal kills." He didn't care if the victim was male or female; he got the same pleasure out of it either way.

Gaskins generally went looking for a victim every six weeks, when his lust for killing would start to bother him too much to ignore. He would try to keep the victim alive as long as possible, getting great pleasure out of torturing them. He didn't stick to one way of killing, like most serial killers. His methods included suffocation and stabbing. In addition to mutilating them, some were also cannibalized.

The selection of his murder victims changed in November of 1970, when Gaskins began to kill people he knew. These murders were also unlike the others in the sense that these victims were killed for personal reasons. The first of these kills was his niece, fifteen-year-old Janice Kirby, and her friend Patricia Ann Alsbrook, seventeen. Once he had control over them, he tried to sexually assault them before beating them to death.

Sometimes the "personal" victim was someone who had laughed at him, owed him money, had stolen from him, or mocked him. In some cases, he claimed he was paid to kill them. These victims were generally shot to death, and not tortured or mutilated like the others. However, the rape and murder of his neighbor Doreen Dempsey and her infant daughter were particularly gruesome.

Although those who knew Gaskins did not suspect him of being a serial killer, there were some people who knew he was a killer for hire. Suzanne Kipper Owens hired Gaskins in February of 1975 to kill Silas Barnwell Yates, her boyfriend. After this murder, Gaskins claimed he had to kill another four times to cover it up.

In November of 1975, one of Gaskins' criminal associates reported to police that he had seen Gaskins kill two men - Dennis Bellamy and Johnny Knight. The associate, Walter Neeley, also confessed that Gaskins had told him he had committed several murders over the previous five years.

Arrest and Trial

The confessions of Walter Neeley convinced the police that Gaskins was the man responsible for the murders, and he was arrested on November 14, 1975. Gaskins ended up confessing, and on December 4, he accompanied the police to his property in Prospect and showed them where he had buried eight of his victims.

Gaskins went to trial on May 24, 1976, charged with eight counts of murder. The trial lasted only four days, and he was found guilty of all charges. Initially, he received the death sentence, but it was commuted to life imprisonment due to law changes in South Carolina. While in prison, however, Gaskins killed a fellow inmate on September 2, 1982.

The inmate, Rudolph Tyner, was also on death row. Gaskins was paid to kill Tyner by the son of one of his victims. He had tried to poison him to death several times without success and decided explosives would be more successful. To do this, he rigged up a radio and told Tyner they could communicate with each other through the radio. Little did Tyner know that the radio was rigged with a C-4 plastic explosive. He held the radio to his ear as he was told to do, and Gaskins detonated the bomb.

For the murder of Tyner, Gaskins was again sentenced to death, and this time he wasn't going to get it commuted.

Outcome

On September 6, 1991, Gaskins was executed by the electric chair. He was pronounced dead at 1:10 a.m. Just a few hours beforehand, he had tried to kill himself by slashing his wrists with a razor blade. He had swallowed the blade a week earlier and then coughed it up again. The last words he spoke were, "I'll let my lawyers talk for me. I'm ready to go."

Trivia

- He tried to commit suicide the night before his scheduled execution. Gaskins slashed his wrists and the crooks of his arms with a razor blade he had lodged in his throat and regurgitated. It took twenty stitches to save him for the electric chair at 1:10 a.m. on September 6, 1991.
- He plotted to kidnap the daughter of the man who sent him to death row.
- He was a small man, barely five feet five inches tall, with a one-hundred-thirty-pound frame.
- He drove a hearse as his personal vehicle.

ED GEIN

Date of birth: August 27, 1906

Aliases/Nicknames: The Butcher of Plainfield, The Mad Butcher, The Plainfield Ghoul

Characteristics: Necrophilia

Number of victims: 2 +

Date of murders: December 8, 1954, and November 16, 1957

Date of arrest: November 17th, 1957

Murder method: Shooting

Known Victims: Mary Hogan, 54; Bernice C. Worden, 58

Crime location: Plainfield, Wisconsin

Status: Found not guilty by reason of insanity and sentenced to life in a mental hospital. Died on July 26, 1984, due to lung cancer.

Background

Ed Gein was the real life "Psycho," an incredibly disturbed individual who was heavily influenced by his mother. Gein was born in La Crosse County, Wisconsin, to parents George and Augusta. Gein was the second child, the first being his one and only brother Henry. Their father was an alcoholic who was unable to hold onto a job; he worked in multiple areas such as insurance sales, carpentry, and tanning. At one point, George owned a grocery store, but he sold it and moved to Plainfield, Wisconsin. The parents wanted their family to live in isolation.

Whenever outsiders approached Gein and his brother, their mother would chase them off. The only times the boys were allowed to leave the property was to go to school. Their mother Augusta was a devout Lutheran who would preach to her children about the immorality of the world, including the evils of alcohol and the belief that women were instruments of the devil and, naturally, prostitutes. Every afternoon she would spend time repeating verses from the Bible, mainly focusing on those that mentioned murder, divine retribution, and death.

In 1940, Gein's father died from heart failure, likely caused by his alcoholism. To help support the family, Gein and his brother Henry would undertake a variety of odd jobs around town. As they grew older, Henry worried about how close Gein and his mother were. Whenever he spoke badly about their mother, Gein would respond with hurt and shock.

In May of 1944, Gein and Henry were busy burning off the marsh vegetation on the farm when the fire became uncontrolled. The fire department arrived, and after they had finished extinguishing the fire,

Gein claimed Henry was missing. It was almost dark, so, armed with lanterns, a search party was organized to look for Henry. His body was eventually found, lying face down on the ground. It seemed he had been dead for quite a while.

There were no overt signs of injury on Henry's body, so the cause of death was put down as asphyxiation, although a report later stated there had been bruises on his head. Had he been murdered? And was the murder committed by Gein, his own brother? Most who have questioned Gein later in life believe he did indeed kill his brother Henry.

Shortly after Henry's death, Gein's mother suffered a serious stroke, and Gein became her caregiver. She suffered a second stroke, and died in December of 1945. Gein was completely devastated at the loss of his mother, the one person who had been his only friend in life. He managed to keep the farm and would do odd jobs to help support himself. As a handyman, he was eligible for a farm subsidy from the government, and he started receiving this in 1951.

Gein sealed off the rooms his mother had used and left them completely pristine and untouched. However, the small areas of the house he lived in were nothing short of squalid. Alone all the time, Gein developed an interest in magazines, particularly those that dealt with death and cannibalism.

Murders

Bernice Worden, the owner of the Plainfield hardware store, went missing on November 16, 1957. Her son told the investigating officers that Gein had been in the store the night before she disappeared, saying that he was going to return the next day for antifreeze. The police were suspicious, and when they found a written receipt Worden had written for antifreeze the morning she disappeared, the officers decided to search Gein's property.

Upon searching a shed they found Worden's body, hung up like an animal. She had been decapitated, and she was hung using a crossbar at her ankles and ropes at her wrists. Witnesses said she was "dressed out like a deer." Her body had been mutilated after her death, which was caused by a gunshot from a .22 caliber rifle. They then searched the house for more evidence.

Items found during the search of his house:

Whole human bones and fragments

Wastebasket made of human skin

Human skin covering several chair seats

Skulls on his bedposts

Female skulls, some with the tops sawn off

Bowls made from human skulls

A corset made from a female torso skinned from shoulders to waist

Leggings made from human leg skin

Masks made from the skin of female heads

Mary Hogan's face mask in a paper bag

Mary Hogan's skull in a box

Bernice Worden's entire head in a burlap sack

Bernice Worden's heart in a plastic bag in front of Gein's potbellied stove

Nine vulvae in a shoe box

A young girl's dress and the vulvae of two females judged to have been about fifteen years old

A belt made from female human nipples

Four noses

158

A pair of lips on a window shade drawstring

A lampshade made from the skin of a human face

Fingernails from female fingers

Arrest and Trial

Gein was arrested on November 17, 1957, and taken in for questioning. Gein admitted he had made many nighttime visits to the local cemetery and had exhumed the bodies of those recently buried. Sometimes he left the cemetery without taking anything, but other times he would take the bodies of women who looked like his mother and transport them home. Once there, he would remove their skins and "tan" them so he could make up the various items found in his home.

Not long after his mother's death, Gein had begun making what he called a "woman suit," so, in his words, "he could become his mother - to literally crawl into her skin." He denied any allegations that he had slept with the corpses; he said they smelled bad.

While under interrogation, he also confessed to killing Mary Hogan, the owner of a bar who had disappeared in 1954. Her head was found in Gein's house, but he couldn't remember any details of her murder. Gein was also a suspect in several other unsolved murders in Wisconsin, including the disappearance of a babysitter in La Crosse, Evelyn Hartley, who went missing in 1953.

Gein's trial began on November 21, 1957. He was charged with first-degree murder, and he pleaded not guilty by reason of insanity. He was assessed and diagnosed with schizophrenia and mental incompetence, meaning he was unfit for trial. He was subsequently sent to a mental hospital for the criminally insane.

Gein was determined to be mentally fit in 1968, and his trial started again on November 7, 1968. It lasted only a week, and his defense team had requested there be no jury. Seven days later, on November 14, he was found guilty and sentenced to spend the rest of his life in a mental hospital. Although he had confessed to the murder of Mary Hogan, he was only charged with the death of Worden.

Outcome

Gein died from complications of lung cancer on July 26, 1984. He was interred within the Plainfield Cemetery. Over the course of many years, people would chip bits off his headstone as souvenirs. The entire headstone was stolen in 2000. It was later found in 2001 and stored at the Waushara County Sheriff's Department. No replacement stone has ever been placed on the grave.

Trivia

- Gein has served as the inspiration for many notable literary and cinematic villains, most notably Norman Bates, the character from the novel and movie *Psycho*.
- Leatherface, of *The Texas Chain Saw Massacre*, was also loosely based on Gein's human trophy collecting. Leatherface, the franchise's antagonist, wears a mask made of human flesh.
- Thomas Harris, the creator of the legendary movie character Hannibal Lecter, based Buffalo Bill, the main antagonist of his 1988 novel *The Silence of the Lambs*, on Gein.

LORENZO GILYARD

Date of birth: May 24, 1950

Aliases/Nicknames: The Kansas City Strangler

Characteristics: Rape

Number of victims: 12 +

Date of murders: 1977 - 1993

Date of arrest: April 19, 2004

Murder method: Strangulation

Known Victims: Catherine M. Barry, 34; Naomi Kelly, 23; Ann Barnes, 36; Kellie A. Ford, 20; Sheila Ingold, 36; Carmeline Hibbs, 30; Stacie L. Swofford, 17; Gwendolyn Kizine, 15; Margaret J. Miller, 17; Debbie Blevins, 32; Helga Kruger, 26; Connie Luther, 29; Angela M. Mayhew, 19

Crime location: Kansas City, Missouri

Status: Sentenced to life without parole.

Background

Gilyard was in and out of trouble during his youth, convicted of a variety of charges including sexual abuse, molestation, assault, and burglary. He married his first wife when he was just eighteen years old, and he would go on to father eleven children with multiple partners.

Gilyard's trouble with the law started with charges including disturbing the peace, a weapons violation, and lying to the police. But, these crimes usually resulted in brief jail times and small fines. His behavior became more violent in 1974, when he was charged with raping a twenty-five-year-old woman. Despite the victim identifying Gilyard, he was not convicted.

A few months later, he was arrested again, this time for raping and beating a thirteen-year-old girl. He tried to deny the allegation at first, saying the victim was lying. But, he eventually pleaded guilty to molestation. He was sentenced to nine months in jail.

In 1979, Gilyard was accused of kidnapping, and of holding a male at gunpoint while he raped the female he was with. The male victim identified Gilyard, and hair evidence was found at Gilyard's workplace. Remarkably, he was acquitted in 1980. Also in 1980, Gilyard was arrested, charged, and convicted of aggravated assault. He had threatened to shoot his ex-wife, and in January of 1981, she divorced him. A month later, he beat her twice, pistol-whipping her the first time. The second time, he broke her teeth and stabbed her with an ice pick in the arm. He received third-degree assault convictions for each incident.

Over the next few years, Gilyard was in and out of jail for a variety of charges, including making bomb threats. But, once he was released, he seemed to settle down. He started working for a trash collection company in 1986, and he stayed with this job until he was arrested for murder in 2004. The police had become suspicious of Gilyard when a DNA match was made between him and one of the twelve victims they were investigating.

Murders

Although Gilyard began killing in 1977, these murders were either undiscovered or not linked to him until years later. It wasn't until 2004, after the bodies of more than a dozen women had been found, that he came under the scrutiny of the local police. By then, DNA testing was well established, and authorities had fortunately had the forethought to keep a blood sample from one of the crime scenes.

In April of 2004, the DNA came back as belonging to Gilyard and the police began to track him. He was now linked to twelve murders. The victims were comprised of eleven prostitutes and a woman who was mentally unwell at the time of her death. All of the victims had been strangled, and eleven of them were assaulted sexually. The majority of the bodies were nude when they were discovered; they had also been posed by Gilyard.

Some of the bodies showed evidence of being bound at the wrists, and six of them still had shoestrings, clothing, or electrical cords tied around their necks. It seemed that the murderer used whatever was close at hand to carry out his crimes. Five of the dead women were also strangled, but there was nothing around their necks.

Timeline of known murders:

April 1977 - Stacie L. Swofford, seventeen

January 23, 1980 - Gwendolyn Kizine, fifteen

May 9, 1982 - Margaret J. Miller, seventeen

March 14, 1986 - Catherine M. Barry, thirty-four

August 16, 1986 - Naomi Kelly, twenty-three

November 27, 1986 - Debbie Blevins, thirty-two

April 17, 1987 - Ann Barnes, thirty-six

June 9, 1987 - Kellie A. Ford, twenty

September 12, 1987 - Angela M. Mayhew, nineteen

November 3, 1987 - Sheila Ingold, thirty-six

December 19, 1987 - Carmeline R. Hibbs, thirty

February 1989 - Helga Kruger, twenty-six

January 11, 1993 - Connie Luther, twenty-nine

Arrest and Trial

Once Gilyard was identified as the killer, police monitored his every move until they could finish tying up any loose ends that may affect his arrest or prosecution. Originally, they had planned to arrest him on April 19, but because officers were concerned Gilyard suspected he was being followed, they moved the arrest date forward. On April 16, while he was at a Denny's restaurant, police walked in and asked Gilyard to accompany them, which he calmly did.

Initially, he was charged with thirteen counts of murder, but six of those charges were dropped for a variety of reasons. He pleaded not guilty to the other seven charges. In exchange for dropping the death penalty, Gilyard's defense team agreed to a trial without jury.

On April 13, 2007, Gilyard was found guilty of six counts of first-degree murder, and he was acquitted on the seventh charge. He was sentenced to life imprisonment without the possibility of parole.

Outcome

Gilyard will spend the rest of his natural life incarcerated behind bars. Investigations are still ongoing to determine whether or not he could be involved in several other murders. The six cases that were dropped before trial could be reinstated at a later date, but the result would still be the same - life without parole.

Trivia

- His sister was a prostitute who was also convicted of murder.
- His probation records show that between 1969 and 1974 he was suspected of 4 rapes, but these rapes were never proven.
- Each victim was discovered without their shoes.

HARVEY GLATMAN

Date of birth: October 10, 1927

Aliases/Nicknames: The Lonely Hearts Killer, The Glamour Girl Slayer, Johnny Glenn, George Williams, Frank Johnson, Frank Wilson

Characteristics: Sadomasochistic rape

Number of victims: 3 +

Date of murders: August 1, 1957 - July 13, 1958

Date of arrest: October 27, 1958

Murder method: Strangulation by ligature

Known Victims: Judith Ann Dull, 19; Shirley Ann Bridgeford, 24; Ruth Mercado, 24

Crime location: Riverside and San Diego Counties, California

Status: Executed by gas chamber on September 18, 1959.

Background

From a very young age, Glatman's parents, Albert and Ophelia, knew something wasn't right with their child. His emotional behavior was strange, and when he was just three years old, his mother caught him in the midst of a sadomasochistic act and he was taken to see the physician. His parents were told not to be concerned, it was just a phase. Believing the physician's assertion that Glatman would grow out of these strange behaviors, his parents ignored or dismissed any further incidences.

When Glatman was twelve years old, he was subjected to a fair amount of bullying because of the way he looked, and he had a terrible fear of females. By this time, he was also committing numerous burglaries of homes owned by women. Before long, he started sexually assaulting women who were at home when he robbed their houses.

Finally, his actions led his parents to seek psychiatric help for the son. Needless to say, it didn't help. In May of 1945, Glatmanbroke into the home of a woman named Elma Hamum. Captured in the act, he was found to be carrying a .25 caliber pistol and a length of rope. Glatman was charged with first-degree robbery, and bail was posted by his parents.

The next month, Glatman abducted a woman named Noreen Laurel. Before he dropped her at home, he touched her. The authorities were notified right away and he was arrested. His parents couldn't afford the bail this time. While he was incarcerated, Glatman was examined by psychiatrists. He was diagnosed with "split personality disorder," which today is known as schizophrenia. Things were only going to get worse when he was released in November of 1945.

Murders

Glatman posed as a professional photographer and, in exchange for cash, would convince women to pose for him tied up in bondage-type situations. In August of 1957, he contacted Judith Ann Dull, a young woman in desperate need of money for a child custody battle with her ex-husband, and asked her if she would pose for him. He told her to wear a tight sweater and skirt, and she agreed.

When Dull arrived at Glatman's apartment, he tied her up, explaining that it was part of the photo shoot, and started taking photos of her. He then threatened her with a gun, forcing her to undress so he could take more explicit photos. Glatman then raped Dull, got her into his car, and drove her out past Thousand Palms. He strangled her and took further photos of her dead body before leaving it in the desert.

At the Lonely Hearts Club in March of 1958, Glatman, using the name George Williams, met Shirley Bridgeford. They agreed to have dinner together, and afterwards, he took her to the Vallecito Mountains. Once there, he pointed a gun at her and ordered her to take her clothes off. After raping her, he took more photos and then murdered her. He photographed her dead body before leaving it there and driving off.

His third victim, Ruth Mercado, had been offered money in exchange for some photographs. It was July of 1958, and he was using another alias, Frank Wilson. This time, he was actually working as a legitimate photographer for a modeling agency. Her murder was carried out in the same way as the others.

Timeline of known murders:

August 1957 - Judith Ann Dull, nineteen

March 1958 - Shirley Ann Bridgeford, twenty-four

July 1958 - Ruth Mercado, twenty-four

Arrest and Trial

While working for the Diane Studio modeling agency, Glatman was signed up to photograph one of the models, Lorraine Vigil. He abducted her, but she fought back and managed to escape. Fortuitously, she happened to run right into two policemen who arrested Glatman on the spot.

While he was being interrogated for the attack on Lorraine Vigil, Glatman broke and confessed to killing the three women. He told the police he had a toolbox which was filled with all the photos he had taken of his victims. They found the toolbox at his apartment, and took the photos to use as evidence.

When he went to trial, his own mother got up and apologized for his crimes, saying he was "sick." The defense attempted to claim Glatman was insane, but when he was examined, it was determined he wasn't psychotic. He was responsible for his actions.

Glatman was tried for the murder of Bridgeford and Mercado and found guilty. He received the death penalty.

Outcome

Glatman was sent to the gas chamber, nicknamed "the green room," on September 18, 1959. The cyanide gas was administered, and he was pronounced dead twelve minutes later.

Trivia

- His family physician told his mother he would grow out of his sadomasochistic sexual tendencies.
- When his mother inquired as to what caused the welts on his neck, he said that he had tied a rope around his neck and was hanging from it—that torturing himself like this gave him pleasure.
- His IQ, measured while he was in San Quentin, was 130.

Quote by Glatman:

- He wanted to die, saying, "It's better this way. I knew this was the way it would be."

BILLY GLAZE

Date of birth: July 13, 1944
Aliases/Nicknames: Jesse Sitting Crow, Jesse Coulter, Butcher Knife Billy
Characteristics: Rape
Number of victims: 3 +
Date of murders: 1986 - 1987
Date of arrest: August 31, 1987
Murder method: Stabbing
Known Victims: Kathleen Bullman; Angeline Whitebird Sweet; Angela Green
Crime location: Minneapolis, Minnesota
Status: Sentenced to three life sentences. Died in prison on December 22, 2015, from lung cancer.

Background

The story of Billy Glaze is full of controversy. Following a tip from the public, he was initially identified as a suspect in the murder of three Native American women. At the time, Glaze was a transient who was known to go by different names and use different dates of birth. He took on Native American names, despite being a Caucasian.

Glaze had a habit of making derogatory comments about Indian women, especially when he was in bars. He was considered a nuisance, and the bouncers at the bars warned him on several occasions to behave or leave.

Although Glaze seemed like a good suspect in the murders, he strongly denied any involvement, and they were unable to find a link between Glaze and the victims. He did admit that he didn't like Indian women, but he swore he hadn't killed anyone.

Needing to find a way to arrest Glaze for the murders, the authorities' prayers were answered when more people started to come forward with what seemed like tangible proof.

Murders

Glaze was eventually suspected in the murders of around fifty women. He had once boasted to police that he had killed more than twenty and then later recanted his admission. In the end, he was charged with the murders of three Native American women between 1986 and 1987.

Each of the victims was a mother of young children, and they were all seen by themselves at night on the streets. All were alcoholics who drank at the same type of bars. The cases were so similar that it didn't take police or the medical examiner long to work out they were the work of just one man.

All three women had been beaten around the face and head, and the mouths were a focal point of the bludgeoning. All had been violated with a stick inserted in their vagina, and they were left posed in degrading positions, mostly nude.

Timeline of murders convicted of:

July 27, 1986 - Kathleen Bullman

April 12, 1987 - Angeline Whitebird Sweet

April 29, 1987 - Angela Green

Arrest and Trial

A witness came forward and told police that Glaze was the man responsible for the three murders. The man's girlfriend told them where to look for Glaze in New Mexico, and on August 31, 1987, he was stopped and arrested for driving under the influence of alcohol. Glaze was on parole at the time, and because he had violated his parole, officers were able to search his vehicle. Inside they found a crowbar, nightstick, and a bloody shirt.

When Glaze went to trial, forensic evidence served as the main tool in securing his conviction of the three murders. On the crowbar in his car they found hair samples, and these were matched to the victims. He was sentenced to life imprisonment with parole after fifty-two years.

Outcome

On December 22, 2015, seventy-two-year-old Glaze died from lung cancer, which he had only recently been diagnosed with. He had been incarcerated for over twenty-five years for murders he possibly didn't commit.

Trivia

– This case was one of only two that were undetermined after a review of fourteen thousand murder and sexual assault cases throughout Minnesota undertaken by county attorneys and the Minnesota Innocence Project going back to 1981. The review used new DNA technology, not available when the crimes were committed, to determine if any wrongful convictions might have occurred. None were found.

BILLY GOHL

Date of birth: 1860

Aliases/Nicknames: Ghoul of Grays Harbor, Timber Town Killer

Characteristics: Robbery

Number of victims: 2 - 100 +

Date of murders: 1902 - 1910

Date of arrest: 1910

Murder method: Shooting

Known Victims: Unnamed male sailors

Crime location: Aberdeen, Washington

Status: Sentenced to life imprisonment and transferred to a mental asylum. Died in 1928 from complications of syphilis.

Background

Little is known about Gohl's early life, though at one point as an adult, he went to the Yukon chasing gold. He was unsuccessful, and on his return to Aberdeen he took on work as a bartender. During this time, it's believed he may have been responsible for numerous murders. The bodies of migrant workers were found after washing up on shore, and all seemed to have been robbed of any valuables or money they were known to be carrying.

Gohl then was employed at the Sailor's Union of the Pacific as a union official. He was a large man, and he used this to his advantage to intimidate potential strikers and to help recruit new members. As sailors arrived at Aberdeen port, they would normally go to the union building right after leaving their ship. If there was any mail for them they could collect it there, and some also made deposits there as a way of saving money.

The man they usually encountered at the union building was Gohl, who was by himself. First, he would ask each sailor about their families and friends, trying to find out if anyone in the area knew the sailor. If the sailor was just passing through, it would be a long time before he was missed by anybody. Somehow he would turn the conversation to valuables and money. Depending on the conversation and how the sailor answered, they would become a target for the greedy Gohl.

Murders

Most of Gohl's victims were shot to death in the union building where he worked. He would then rob them of any cash or valuables they had on them, and then discard the bodies in the Wishkah River, behind the building.

Apparently, there was a chute that ran from a trapdoor in the union building directly into the river, and he would push the bodies into the river using the chute. Many people suspected Gohl of being responsible for the numerous disappearances of sailors who disembarked there, but nobody did anything about it. He would have continued to get away with it, except that his accomplice, John Klingenberg, got arrested and ratted him out.

Arrest and Trial

According to Klingenberg, he had seen Gohl with Charles Hatberg (a sailor who had recently been found floating in the harbour) just before he disappeared. Gohl was arrested, charged with the murder of Hatberg, and convicted. He also was tried for the murder of John Hoffman, a man who had seen him murder Hatberg. Although Hoffman was killed by Klingenberg the next day, it was found by the court that Gohl was complicit and therefore guilty. He was sentenced to life imprisonment.

Outcome

Gohl died in 1927 from lobar pneumonia and erysipelas complicated by dementia paralytic caused by syphilis. He was considered the prime suspect in at least forty-one other murders.

STEPHEN GRIFFITHS

Date of birth: December 24, 1969

Aliases/Nicknames: The Crossbow Cannibal

Characteristics: Cannibalism, dismemberment

Number of victims: 3

Date of murders: June 22, 2009 – May 21, 2010

Date of arrest: May 24, 2010

Murder method: Crossbow, stabbing

Known Victims: Susan Rushworth, 43; Shelley Armitage, 31; Suzanne Blamires, 36

Crime location: Bradford, England

Status: Sentenced to life imprisonment without parole.

Background

Although quiet and a bit withdrawn as a child, Griffiths appeared to have a normal childhood, and nothing seemed to be amiss until he reached his late teens. Griffiths began shoplifting, and when the manager of a store tried to stop him, Griffiths attacked him with a knife. Since he was only seventeen years old, he received a sentence of three years in youth custody. While incarcerated, he informed his probation officer that he had fantasized about being a serial killer.

By the time he was eighteen years old, Griffiths had cut off all contact with his family, including his mother. In 1989, he was caught with an air pistol he had been using to kill birds so he could dissect them. He was charged and convicted of having an offensive weapon. The following year, he was arrested for an attack on a young girl; he had held a knife to her throat. This resulted in Griffiths receiving a two-year prison sentence. At that time, he wasn't showing any signs of suffering from a mental illness.

Griffiths' behavior deteriorated significantly from then onwards. He became terrified of insects crawling into his ear canals and started stuffing cotton wool in his ears at night. He didn't work, living off grants and benefits while he attained a degree in psychology. He then began studying for a PhD in criminology, and his thesis was on homicide in Bradford, where he lived.

Griffiths began a relationship in 1989 that would last for two years. His girlfriend would later describe how Griffiths had every surface in his apartment covered in plastic. She began to sense something wasn't right with Griffiths and ended the relationship. His next relationship with a woman was abusive; after they split, he continued to harass her relentlessly. A neighbor noticed he had two pet lizards that he would walk around the neighborhood on dog leashes. He invited her to his home see his pets one day and he was enthralled watching one of his lizards devour a live rat. Griffiths' mental status seemed to have deteriorated, and before long, he would act on those fantasies he had described many years before.

Murders

It was first discovered that Griffiths had committed a murder when detectives were reviewing CCTV footage which showed him outside his apartment building in Bradford with a woman. The woman, later identified as Suzanne Blamires, was seen walking into the building with Griffiths on May 21, 2010. Just minutes later, she ran out, and Griffiths chased after her carrying a crossbow. He knocked her down and fired a bolt into her head.

Blamires was dead, and Griffiths, who knew the camera was there, faced toward it and held the crossbow above his head, almost as though he was proud of what he had just done and was bragging. Then he dragged her body out of sight.

A while later, Griffiths was seen on camera carrying trash bags and a rucksack in and out of the building. The following day, female body parts were found in the River Aire in Shipley by a member of the public. They were identified as belonging to Blamires. A caretaker of the building where the murder took place discovered the CCTV footage and took it to the police, also identifying the man on tape as being Griffiths.

When police searched Griffiths' flat, they found disturbing video footage that indicated his role in the death of Shelly Armitage on April 26, 2010. The footage showed the dead body of Armitage naked and hog-tied in a bath. On her back, the words "My Sex Slave" had been spray-painted in black paint. Audio of the tape revealed Griffiths saying, "I am Ven Pariah, I am the Bloodbath Artist. Here's a model who is assisting me."

As authorities continued their search for more of Blamires' body parts in the River Aire, part of Armitage's spine was also found.

Timeline of known murders:

June 22, 2009 - Susan Rushworth, forty-three

April 26, 2010 - Shelley Armitage, thirty-one

May 21, 2010 - Suzanne Blamires, thirty-six

Arrest and Trial

Griffiths was arrested on May 24, 2010. During the interrogation, he admitted he was responsible for the deaths of Suzanne Blamires, Shelley Armitage, and Susan Rushworth. He claimed that he had cooked and eaten parts of two victims and had eaten part of the third victim raw. But, police were never able to find any evidence to confirm this as true. The remains of Susan Rushworth were never found, but despite this, Griffiths was charged with the murders of all three women.

At his first court appearance, when he was asked to state his name, Griffiths stated, "The Crossbow Cannibal." He was remanded in custody, and his next appearance on June 7 was via video link. His trial date was then set for November 16, 2010.

His trial came to an end on December 21, 2010. Griffiths pleaded guilty and was convicted of the three murders. He was sentenced to life in prison without the possibility of parole.

Outcome

Griffiths claimed to have killed "loads" of women, but no further cases have been identified that are linked to him. After studying criminology for so long it is remarkable that Griffiths wasn't clued up enough to get away with his crimes. Thankfully though, he wasn't that clever. Now no women will ever die at his hands again.

Trivia

- His idol was Yorkshire Ripper Peter Sutcliffe, who killed thirteen women, most of them prostitutes.

Quotes by Griffiths:

- "I am misanthropic. I don't have much time for the human race."
- He described himself as a "pseudo-human at best. A demon at worst."
- "I've killed a lot more than Suzanne Blamires - I've killed loads."
- He has attempted suicide four times while incarcerated.

ROBERT HANSEN

Date of birth: February 15, 1939

Aliases/Nicknames: The Butcher Baker

Characteristics: Rape, would make victims run through the wilderness while he hunted them

Number of victims: 17 +

Date of murders: 1973 - 1983

Date of arrest: October 27, 1983

Murder method: Shooting

Known Victims: Lisa Futrell, 41; Malai Larsen, 28; Sue Luna, 23; Tami Pederson, 20; Angela Feddern, 24; Teresa Watson; DeLynn "Sugar" Frey; Paula Goulding, 17; Andrea "Fish" Altiery; Sherry Morrow, 23; "Eklutna Annie," 16-25; Joanna Messina, 24; "Horseshoe Harriet"; Roxanne Easland, 24; Ceilia "Beth" Van Zanten, 17; Megan Emerick, 17; Mary Thill, 23

Crime location: Anchorage, Alaska

Status: Sentenced to life plus another 461 years. Died in prison on August 21, 2014, of natural causes.

Background

Hansen remains one of the coldest killers to date. Born in Iowa in 1939, he grew into a very shy, thin youth, who developed a terrible stutter and a severe case of acne. The acne and resultant scars led to him being bullied throughout school; needless to say, this didn't help his stuttering. The pretty girls at school ignored him, and he would fantasize about seeking revenge. Quiet and a loner, his relationship with his father was strained and somewhat dysfunctional, due to his father's domineering personality.

One hobby that Hansen could escape into, where nobody could tease or control him, was hunting. He enlisted in the Army Reserve in 1957, but was discharged after a year. He then worked at a police academy in Iowa as a drill instructor. While he was there, he met a younger woman and they later married in 1960.

Hansen was arrested in December of 1960 for burning down a school bus garage in Pocahontas County. He was sentenced to three years in prison, but only served twenty months before being released. However, his wife had filed for divorce while he was behind bars. He would end up being arrested numerous times for petty theft over the next few years.

By 1967, Hansen had remarried, and the couple and their two children moved to Anchorage, Alaska. Hansen was well-liked by the community, and he competed in local hunting competitions, setting several hunting records. When this mild-mannered, quiet family man and baker embarked on a terrifying killing spree, nobody suspected a thing.

Murders

From 1971 to 1984, Hansen killed prostitutes in Anchorage, Alaska. He would arrange for their services and then kidnap them before raping them. Sometimes he flew them in his plane to his cabin in Knik River Valley. Once there, he would often make them run naked through the woods while he hunted them, eventually killing them with his rifle or knife.

The first body found was that of an unidentified woman, later nicknamed Eklutna Annie because of the location of her shallow grave. She had been buried on Eklutna Lake Road, and her body was discovered by construction workers on July 21, 1980. Decomposition and animal damage was so severe, that identification proved impossible. A facial reconstruction was created and publicized widely, to no avail. Also in July of 1980, the body of topless dancer Joanne Messina was found in a gravel pit. She too was badly decomposed, so there was very little evidence that could be found or that was useful.

The body of Sherry Morrow was found on September 12, 1982, in a shallow grave along the Knik River. She had been missing since November 17, 1981. She was fully clothed in the grave. But despite being shot three times in the back, there were no bullet holes in her clothes. Clearly, she had been redressed after she was shot and killed.

Another body was found on the banks of the Knik River on September 2, 1983. The victim was Paula Goulding, a seventeen-year-old topless dancer, who had also been dressed after she had been shot to death. The next body wasn't found until April 24, 1984. This body belonged to Sue Luna, and it is unknown when she disappeared or when she was killed. Hansen had taken her to the river and made her strip before hunting her down and shooting her to death.

Hansen abducted another young woman on June 13, 1983, but this time the victim was able to escape. Cindy Paulson, seventeen, had been offered two hundred dollars to perform oral sex on Hansen, but when she agreed and got into his car, he pulled a gun on her. He drove her back to his house and kept her captive so he could torture, sexually assault, and rape her. She was chained to a post in the basement by a chain around her neck; at one point Hansen took a nap on the couch.

After he woke up, he put Paulson in his car, drove to the local airfield, and told her they were going to his cabin near Knik River. Paulson was handcuffed and crouching in the back seat, and while Hansen was busy getting the plane ready, she managed to escape through the driver's door. She ran to Sixth Avenue, with Hansen in hot pursuit, and flagged down a truck. Robert Yount was driving the truck; shocked by her appearance, he stopped and let her in.

Yount dropped Paulson off at the Mush Inn, a local motel, and she tried to get the clerk to contact her boyfriend. Meanwhile, Yount called the police to report the incident. Officers arrived at the Inn and discovered Paulson had taken a taxi to her boyfriend at Big Timber Motel. They found her there, still wearing the handcuffs. After she gave them her story at the police station, they brought Hansen in and questioned him. He passed it off as a disgruntled prostitute trying to get more money, and because of his meekness and the alibi from his friend, they let him go.

With three bodies being found, the authorities contacted the FBI and asked for help with a profile of the killer. The profiler determined the killer would be an experienced hunter, have a history of rejection by women, have low self-esteem, may stutter, and was likely to keep souvenirs from each murder, most likely jewelry. With this information, the head detective took another look at potential suspects and this time he decided Hansen fitted the profile.

Timeline of known murders or dates they were found:

December 22, 1971 - Ceilia "Beth" Van Zanten, seventeen

July 7, 1973 - Megan Emerick, seventeen

July 5, 1975 - Mary Kathleen Thill, twenty-three

June 28, 1980 - Roxanne Eastland, twenty-four

July of 1980 - Joanne Messina, twenty-four

July 21, 1980 - "Eklutna Annie," sixteen to twenty-five

September 6, 1980 - Lisa Futrell, forty-one

November 17, 1981 - Sherry Morrow, twenty-four

December 2, 1981 - Andrea "Fish" Altiery

May 26, 1982 - Sue Luna, twenty-three

April 25, 1983 - Paula Golding, seventeen

April 25, 1984 - DeLynn "Sugar" Frey

April 26, 1984 - Teresa Watson

April 26, 1984 - Angela Feddern, twenty-four

April 29, 1984 - Tamera "Tami" Pederson, nineteen

Other victims, killed between 1980 and 1983:

Malai Larsen, twenty-eight

Jane Doe

Arrest and Trial

Acting on the profile from the FBI and Paulson's original testimony about her abduction, the police requested a warrant to search Hansen's home, plane, and cars. During the search on October 27, 1983, a collection of jewelry was discovered, later identified as belonging to several victims. They also found a supply of firearms. Hidden behind the headboard in Hansen's bedroom, they found an aviation map marked with small "x" marks.

Hansen tried to deny responsibility for the murders for as long as possible, despite the evidence, but eventually he caved. At first he said it was the fault of the women, that he was justified in killing them. As each piece of evidence was placed in front of him, he finally admitted he had been killing women since 1971.

Ballistics evidence linked Hansen's rifle to the bullets found at the crime scenes. Faced with even more incriminating evidence, Hansen agreed to a plea bargain. In exchange for serving his sentence in a federal prison, he pleaded guilty to four murders, the ones authorities had clear evidence in, and agreed to provide information on the other victims. He also had to explain the marks on the map which were suspected to be burial locations.

As part of the deal, Hansen showed seventeen grave sites to the investigators. However, there were still three marks on the map he refused to divulge, and police suspected these might be the graves of Megan Emrick, Mary Thill, and a third unidentified victim. Hansen denied responsibility for the murders of both Emrick and Thill.

By pleading guilty to four murders, Hansen was convicted and sentenced to four hundred sixty-one years in prison, without the possibility of parole.

Outcome

Hansen died from an ongoing health condition on August 21, 2014. The nature of the illness leading to his death is undisclosed.

Trivia

- He was a local hunting champion in Anchorage, Alaska.
- In the spring of 1990, Robert Hansen was moved from the Lemon Creek Prison in Juneau to the maximum security facility at Spring Creek in Seward, about one hundred twenty miles southwest of Anchorage. It was discovered that Hansen was collecting materials - including aeronautical maps - that indicated he was planning to try to escape from Lemon Creek.
- John Cusack portrayed Hansen in the film "The Frozen Ground" (2013), opposite Nicolas Cage (portraying Sergeant Jack Halcombe, a character based on Glenn Flothe) and Vanessa Hudgens (as victim Cindy Paulson).

KEITH HUNTER JESPERSON

Date of birth: April 6, 1955

Aliases/Nicknames: The Happy Face Killer

Characteristics: Rape

Number of victims: 8 +

Date of murders: 1990 - 1995

Date of arrest: March 30, 1995

Murder method: Strangulation

Known Victims: Taunja Bennett, 23; Claudia; Cynthia Lynn Rose, 32; Laurie Ann Pentland, 26; Angela Surbrize, 21; Julie Ann Winningham, 41; others unidentified

Crime location: Nebraska, California, Florida, Washington, Oregon, Wyoming

Status: Sentenced to life imprisonment without parole.

Background

Like many other killers, Jesperson grew up with an alcoholic father who was domineering, as well as a violent grandfather. He was one of five children born to Leslie and Gladys Jesperson in Chilliwack, British Columbia. Jesperson was very big for his age and was teased a lot by other children, leading to him becoming a rather lonely young boy.

Like an outcast within his own family, Jesperson was treated differently than his siblings. After the family moved to Washington, the bullying continued; his brothers were often the ringleaders, nicknaming him "Ig" or "Igor" because he was so tall.

Jesperson was known to torture and kill animals, which should have indicated serious trouble ahead. He would later state that he enjoyed watching animals kill each other, and then he got satisfaction from killing them himself. He claimed he would fantasize what it would be like to do the same thing to a person. He often got into trouble as a youth, and twice he was stopped while trying to kill children whom he felt had crossed him.

One of these boys was his friend Martin, one of the few boys who associated with Jesperson. Martin would often do things that would be blamed on Jesperson, and he would get punished for things he hadn't done. He attacked Martin, beating him violently until he was stopped by his father. He claimed later that he had fully intended to kill Martin. About a year later, Jesperson tried to drown another boy while they were swimming. He tried to do it again later at a public pool until the lifeguard stopped him.

Despite these incidences, Jesperson managed to graduate from high school. He got a job driving trucks, and eventually he married and had three children. Fifteen years into his marriage, Jesperson and his wife divorced. He had also suffered an injury which prevented him from following his dream of becoming a Royal Canadian Mounted Policeman. By the time Jesperson was thirty-five years old, he stood six feet seven and a half inches tall and weighed around two hundred forty pounds. He returned to truck driving. Before long, he started to act on his fantasies and began killing.

Murders

Jesperson's first known victim was Taunja Bennett. He met her at a bar on January 23, 1990, in Portland, Oregon, and invited her back to his house. After participating in sexual activity, they had an argument; Jesperson beat and then strangled her. He created an alibi by going back out, having some drinks, and talking to people. Then he went back and disposed of Bennett's body.

There was a substantial gap between the first murder and the next. The body of an unidentified woman was found on August 30, 1992, near Blythe in California. The woman had been raped and then strangled to death. Although this victim has never been identified, Jesperson later stated her name was Claudia.

In September of 1992, the body of Cynthia Lyn Rose was found in Turlock. Jesperson claimed she was a prostitute who had entered his truck uninvited while he was asleep in it. The body of another prostitute was found in November of 1992. Laurie Ann Pentland, of Salem, had allegedly tried to double charge Jesperson for sexual services and when she threatened to report it to the police, he strangled her to death.

In June of 1993, more than six months later, the body of another unidentified woman was found in in Santa Nella, California. According to Jesperson, her name was either Cindy or Carla. In September of 1994, the body of yet another unidentified woman was found in Crestview, Florida, and Jesperson later claimed her name had been Susanne.

Jesperson was asked by Angela Surbrize in January of 1995 for a ride to Indiana from Spokane, Washington. He agreed. About a week into the journey, she started to nag Jesperson, telling him to speed up so she could see her boyfriend. Instead, Jesperson raped and then strangled her. Afterwards, he tied her to the undercarriage of his truck, facedown. He dragged her down the road to remove her face and destroy any fingerprints.

The only personal murder was that of his girlfriend, Julie Ann Winningham. Jesperson got it into his head that she only wanted him for his money. So, on March 10, 1995, he strangled her to death. This was the murder that alerted police to Jesperson because Winningham had been in a relationship with him before her death.

Timeline of known murders:

January 23, 1990 - Taunja Bennett, twenty-three

August 30, 1992 - Claudia (Jane Doe)

September of 1992 - Cynthia Lyn Rose, thirty-two

November of 1992 - Laurie Ann Pentland, twenty-six

June of 1993 – "Carla" or "Cindy" (Jane Doe)

September of 1994 – "Susanne" (Jane Doe)

January of 1995 - Angela Surbrize, twenty-one

March 10, 1995 - Julie Ann Winningham, forty-one

Arrest and Trial

Jesperson was brought in for questioning after Winningham's death, but he wouldn't answer any questions and authorities had no grounds to formally arrest him for the murder. He was released without being charged. Over the next several days, Jesperson felt certain he was going to be arrested in a matter of time.

Jesperson decided to turn himself in to the police with the hope that it would help when it came to sentencing. He was arrested on March 30, 1995. During his interviews, Jesperson began to talk about the details of not only Winningham's murder, but also of several others he claimed to have committed. Later, he changed his story and said he was innocent. In a letter he had written his brother, however, he admitted killing eight people.

Despite eventually claiming to have killed around one hundred sixty women, investigators were only able to link him to eight. A number of trials commenced. The murders had been committed in several states, so each case was filed in the relevant location.

Just before Jesperson was about to go on trial for the murder on Winningham, he pleaded guilty in October of 1995. He was subsequently sentenced to life imprisonment. He was then transferred to Oregon, and on November 2, 1995, he entered a no contest plea for the murder of Taunja Bennett. Again he was sentenced to life imprisonment, this time with a minimum period of thirty years before he could apply for parole.

While in prison in Oregon, a case was being put together for the murder of Laurie Ann Pentland. Once investigators discovered Jesperson was the "Happy Face Killer," they were able to link him to the death of Pentland. Letters had been written by Jesperson after the murder of Pentland claiming responsibility for the killing, and they were signed the Happy Face Killer. He was convicted of the murder and sentenced to life again with a thirty-year minimum period.

An extradition order was secured by the state of Wyoming to put Jesperson on trial for the murder of Angela Surbrize. Jesperson frustrated the authorities by threatening to change his story about where he had actually killed her—if she hadn't been murdered in Wyoming, the costly court process would be invalid. Eventually a deal was made, and he pleaded guilty to Surbrize's murder with the agreement that prosecutors in Laramie County would not seek the death penalty.

On June 3, 1998, Jesperson received a life sentence for the murder of Surbrize. It is still possible for other charges and trials to take place regarding the many other murders he is yet to be tried for.

Outcome

One important outcome of Jesperson being convicted of the murder of Taunja Bennett was the release of two people who had previously been convicted of the crime. Laverne Pavlinac was tired of being in the longlasting abusive relationship she had been in with John Sosnovske. Thinking it would be a good way to get rid of him, she went to the detectives and claimed Sosnovske had forced her to help him with the rape and murder of Bennett.

This tactic backfired on Pavlinac; both she and Sosnovske were charged and convicted in February of 1991. In an effort to avoid being found guilty and receiving the death penalty, Sosnovske plead guilty. He was sentenced to life imprisonment, and Pavlinac received ten years. Although she was quick to admit she had made the whole story up, nobody paid her any attention.

Four years later, on November 27, 1995, both Pavlinac and Sosnovske were released after Jesperson and his attorney provided his confession. To prove they were innocent, Jesperson informed the detectives of where they could find Bennett's purse - information only the killer would know.

Trivia

Quotes by Jesperson:

- "It was their fate to die by my hands, like a car accident or illness."
- "Look over your shoulder. I'm closer than you think."

DELFINA AND MARÍA DE JESÚS GONZÁLEZ

Date of birth: Delfina - 1912; Maria - unknown

Aliases/Nicknames: Las Poquianchis

Characteristics: Ran a brothel in Mexico

Number of victims: 91 +

Date of murders: 1950s - 1963

Date of arrest: January 14, 1964

Murder method: Unknown

Known Victims: Unnamed prostitutes, fetuses, male clients

Crime location: San Francisco del Rincón, Guanajuato, Mexico

Status: Both sentenced to 40 years. Delfina died in prison from an accident, and Maria was later released, date unknown.

Background

Sisters Delfina, Maria de Jesus, Maria Luisa, and Carmen were all born into poverty in El Salto do Juanacatlan, Jalisco. Their father was an authoritative and abusive beast, who was also a member of the Rural Police. His job was to ride through town and make sure nothing was amiss. He liked to abuse his power, and during an argument he once shot and killed a man. If his daughters did anything he didn't approve of, such as wear makeup, he would lock them in the jail to teach them a lesson.

By shooting the man, their father gained a lot of enemies, so his wife and daughters moved to San Francisco del Rincon, otherwise known as San Pancho. The sisters grew up fearful of poverty, so as they became young adults, they opened up a few businesses. They opened a saloon which provided food for the table if nothing else.

They soon decided they could make more money out of prostitution, and they would bribe the local officials to turn a blind eye. Before long they had opened up a string of brothels in San Francisco del Rincon, Leon, Purisima del Rincon, San Juan de los Lagos, El Salto, San Juan del Rio, and Jalisco.

Sisters Delfina, Maria de Jesus, and Carmen operated the brothels in Jalisco and Guanajuato, while Maria Luisa ran the brothel near the border of Mexico. Between them, they also bought a bar in Lagos, Jalisco; through the previous owner they inherited the nickname "Las Poquianchis" which they despised.

Pretty young girls were sought out throughout the countryside and they would be told the sisters could provide them with jobs such as maids or waitresses. The young girls, dreaming of a better life in the bigger cities, would eagerly accept, not knowing what they were really getting in to. They would be put to work immediately as prostitutes, except for those who were virgins - they were saved for the wealthiest clients. Aside from the debauchery, there was much more going on behind the walls of these brothels. By the time the truth came out, there would be an estimated ninety-one or more skeletons in the ground, some of which belonged to the unborn fetuses of girls who got pregnant.

Murders

The sisters inflicted horrific abuse, brutality, and murder on the multitudes of young girls they were forcing to work for them as prostitutes. If a girl became sick, she was often starved or the other girls would be forced to beat her to death with objects like heavy logs and sticks. The bodies would either be buried in a mass grave or burnt until they were ashes.

Many of the prostitution clients, who were wealthy, were also murdered so they could be robbed. Their bodies often ended up in the same mass graves, along with the dead prostitutes and their aborted babies.

After the police shot Delfina's son Ramon Torres (El Tepo), to death in 1963, she ordered them to be killed. Hermenegildo Zuniga was the hitman and he did what he was told, killing the officers who had been involved in Ramon's death.

Arrest and Trial

One of the prostitutes at Loma del Angel managed to escape in January of 1964, and she fled to the police. Fortunately, the officers she talked to were not the corrupt men on the sisters' payroll. A search warrant was obtained and the sisters were arrested on January 14, 1964, during a raid at the Loma del Angel ranch.

The sisters, all dressed in mourning black, were paraded through the ranch while people outside called for them to be lynched. A dozen women were found at the ranch in an emaciated and filthy state, and they didn't hesitate to point out areas in the ground where bodies were buried.

The decomposed bodies and skeletal remains of at least ninety-one men, women, and fetuses were found buried in mass graves. Because the public were adamant the sisters needed to be hanged, they were sent to another jail further away. Sister Maria Luisa turned herself in a week later, terrified the people were going to lynch her. She thought she would at least be protected in jail. She was subsequently arrested.

The trial was described as chaotic, with insults being shouted back and forth across the courtroom. Details of the sisters forcing their working prostitutes to engage in sexual acts with animals, to torture other girls and clients, and to kill when instructed, enraged and disgusted those in the room. They were also charged with corruption for bribing the authorities. The trial was over quite quickly, and the three sisters were each sentenced to serve forty years in prison.

Outcome

The youngest sister, Maria de Jesus Gonzalez Valenzuela, was the only sibling to be released from prison. The date of her release is unknown, but rumors were rife that she met a sixty-four-year-old man while in prison and they married following their release from prison. They allegedly died of old age sometime during the 1990s.

Trivia

- Their father, Isidro Torres, was abusive and expected his children to follow a rigid set of rules; ironically, he was also part of the local grassroots police force that patrolled the remote area of Mexico on horseback.
- He often locked the sisters in jail as punishment for wearing sexy clothing or makeup.

JACK THE RIPPER

Date of birth: Unknown

Aliases/Nicknames: The Whitechapel Murderer, Leather Apron

Characteristics: Vivisection, mutilation

Number of victims: 5 +

Date of murders: 1888 - 1891

Date of arrest: Never identified, never apprehended

Murder method: Strangulation, slashing

Known Victims: Mary Ann Nichols; Annie Chapman; Elizabeth Stride; Catherine Eddowes; Mary Jane Kelly

Crime location: Whitechapel, London, England

Status: Never identified

Background

Perhaps the most famous murder mystery of all time, Jack the Ripper wrought terror on the Whitechapel district of London in the late 1800s. This area of London was more or less a red-light district, where prostitutes were commonly seen walking the streets at night, along with other undesirables, such as gangsters, criminals, and drug addicts.

It was a time when poverty was rife, and people would do anything for a crust of bread or a pint of beer. At its lowest point, it was estimated there were up to twelve hundred prostitutes actively selling their bodies, and in some respects their souls, on the cobbled streets of Whitechapel. They were easy targets for depraved assailants, but none were as horrific as Jack the Ripper.

Murders

When Mary Ann "Polly" Nichols was found on August 31, 1888, her body showed multiple injuries and mutilations. Her throat had been slashed twice; her abdomen had received several cuts and was partially ripped open.

Annie Chapman was killed on September 8, 1888. Her throat had been slashed twice, and she had been disemboweled. Her intestines were thrown over her shoulder. Her uterus, parts of her bladder, and vagina, were all removed and taken away from the scene by the killer.

The night of September 30, 1888, saw two women savagely killed. One of the victims, Elizabeth Stride, had her throat slashed once. However, the other victim, Catherine Eddowes, suffered a more horrific postmortem attack. Her throat had been slashed along with her abdomen, and she was missing a kidney and an earlobe.

Mary Jane Kelly was murdered on November 9, 1888. Her throat had been slashed so severely that it was cut down to her spine. Her body was so horribly mutilated that it was difficult to identify who she was. Her heart had been taken out of her body and removed from the scene by the killer.

There were a number of similar murders that took place between 1888 and 1891. Though they are widely believed to be the work of the Ripper, they have yet to be categorically proven to be his victims. The first of these murders took place on April 2, 1888, when the body of Emma Elizabeth Smith was found. She had been sexually assaulted with a blunt instrument and robbed of her personal effects. She wasn't killed right away; she fell into a coma and died two days later.

Martha Tabram was found in the George Yard Buildings on August 6, 1888. She had been stabbed thirty-nine times in the neck and body. Then, on December 20, 1888, Rose Mylett was found having been strangled to death.

The year of 1889 was quiet until July 17, when the body of Alice McKenzie was found with her throat slashed and her abdomen cut. On September 10, a torso was found in Pinchin Street. Because no other body parts were found, the identity remained unknown. Finally, Frances Coles was killed on February 13, 1891, in Swallow Gardens. Her throat had been slashed twice.

Timeline of murders:

August 31, 1888 - Mary Ann "Polly" Nichols, forty-two - Buck's Row

September 8, 1888 - Annie Chapman, forty-seven - 29 Hanbury Street, Spitalfields

September 30, 1888 - Elizabeth Stride, forty-four - Dutfield's Yard

September 30, 1888 - Catherine Eddowes, forty-six - Mitre Square, London

November 9, 1888 - Mary Jane Kelly, twenty-four - 13 Miller's Court, Dorset Street

Other suspected murders:

April 2, 1888 - Emma Elizabeth Smith, forty-five - Osborn Street

August 6, 1888 - Martha Tabram, thirty-nine - George Yard Buildings, George Yard

December 20, 1888 - Rose Mylett, twenty-nine - Clarke's Yard

July 17, 1889 - Alice McKenzie - Castle Alley

September 10, 1889 - "The Pinchin Street torso" - Pinchin Street

February 13, 1891 - Frances Coles - Swallow Gardens

Suspects

George Chapman:

Real name was Seweryn Klosowski
Barber
Had fatally poisoned three women

David Cohen:

A Jewish cobbler

Aaron Kosminski:

A Polish Jewish butcher

Was put in an insane asylum in 1891, after the killings ended
Was supposedly linked to the Ripper crimes in September 2014 through DNA evidence extracted from a shawl found near Catherine Eddowes

Montague John Druitt:

A schoolmaster and barrister
Committed suicide after the death of Mary Jane Kelly

Prince Edward Albert Victor, Duke of Clarence and Avondale:

The grandson of Queen Victoria
Heir to the throne

Walter Sickert:

A German-born painter
Believed to be the Ripper due to his painting of the "Ripper's Room"

John Pizer:

A Jewish cobbler

James Maybrick:

Alleged he was the author of the "Diary of Jack the Ripper"

Unnamed female, a.k.a. "Jill the Ripper":

A widely speculated theory
The lead inspector on the Ripper case, Frederick Abberline, was the first of the investigating officers to suggest that Jack may in fact be a Jill

Mary Pearcey:

Believed to be "Jill the Ripper" by many
Convicted of the murder of her husband's former lover and baby
Was hanged in 1889

Doctor William Gull:

Physician to Queen Victoria and the British royal family

Carl Feigenbaum:

German merchant sailor
Was convicted of an unrelated murder and executed in New York in 1894

Lewis Carroll:

Author of Alice in Wonderland
Has been proposed as a suspect based on possible anagrams in his work
The theory is not taken seriously

Other:

An unidentified American serial killer (dubbed the Servant Girl Annihilator) has been suggested by some as a being connected to the Ripper

Trivia

From a letter sent by Jack the Ripper:

> "I am down on whores and I shant quit ripping them till I do get buckled."

- Derek Brown, a rapist who had an obsession with serial killers, attempted to copy the MO of the Ripper in the same Whitechapel area of the historic murders. He killed two women and butchered them and became known as the Jack the Ripper Killer.

MILTON JOHNSON

Date of birth: May 15, 1950

Aliases/Nicknames: The Weekend Murderer

Characteristics: Rape, random killings

Number of victims: 10 +

Date of murders: June - August 1983

Date of arrest: March 9, 1984

Murder method: Stabbing, shooting

Known Victims: Anthony Hackett, 19; Marilyn Baers, 45; Barbara Dunbar, 38; Pamela Ryan, 29; Agnes Ryan, 75; George Kiehl, 24; Cathleen Norwood, 25; Richard Paulin, 32; Officer Denis Foley, 50; Officer Steven Mayer, 22

Crime location: Cook and Will Counties, Illinois

Status: Sentenced to death, awaiting execution.

Background

If there was ever a case where early parole was granted and it shouldn't have been, it is with serial killer Milton Johnson. When Johnson was nineteen, he was charged and convicted of the brutal rape and torture of a woman in Joliet. During the rape, Johnson had burned his victim with a cigarette lighter; for this crime, he received a sentence of twenty-five to thirty-five years in prison. He was also convicted of burglary, and another term of five to ten years was added on, to be served consecutively.

However, Johnson was released early, far earlier than he should have been, on March 10, 1983. Even with good behavior, he still should have been incarcerated until at least 1986. Authorities would later regret their decision to release Johnson, as he went on to commit at least ten murders.

Murders

On July 16, 1983, Johnson committed his first known murders. Officers Foley and Mayer had stopped to help what they thought was a driver in need of assistance. Johnson's pickup truck was blocking part of the road, and the front bumper was against another parked car. As the officers drove close to the scene, Johnsoncalled out that they needed a jump-start.

As they got out of their vehicle to help, both officers were shot. Mayer died almost right away, and Foley had a serious wound to his throat. As another car came around the corner and slowed down, Johnson fired at them as well, killing the driver and hitting the passenger six times. The car rolled down the road and stopped, and the passenger got out and went looking for assistance.

Meanwhile, other police officers were desperately trying to find the two missing officers. It wasn't until a farmer called the police to report a lot of noise behind his buildings, including a siren, that they were able to locate them. In addition to the two police officers who had been shot, the bodies of Richard Paulin and Cathleen Norwood were found in the car in front of the pickup.

In the early hours of July 17, Anthony Hackett and his girlfriend Patricia Payne were sleeping in Hackett's car after traveling a long distance. A tap on the window woke them up, and they were instantly fired upon multiple times. Hackett was killed, and Johnson ordered Payne to get in his truck. As they were driving down the road, Johnson sexually assaulted Payne; then he raped her after stopping the truck. They started moving again. Ten minutes later, he pulled over, stabbed Payne in the chest, and pushed her out of the truck.

On August 20, Johnson entered a store owned by Marilyn Baers and went on a rampage, shooting and stabbing the four people inside. Along with Marilyn, customers Agnes Ryan, Pamela Ryan, and Barbara Dunbar were killed. Johnson had stolen their purses and they were dumped nearby, the money inside them. It's unclear as to why Johnson took them if he wasn't going to keep the money.

Timeline of known murders:

July 16, 1983 - Officer Denis Foley, fifty

July 16, 1983 - Officer Steven Mayer, twenty-two

July 16, 1983 - Cathleen Norwood, twenty-five

July 16, 1983 - Richard Paulin, thirty-two

July 16, 1983 - George Kiehl, twenty-four

July 17, 1983 - Anthony Hackett, nineteen

August 20, 1983 - Marilyn Baers, forty-five

August 20, 1983 - Barbara Dunbar, thirty-eight

August 20, 1983 - Pamela Ryan, twenty-nine

August 20, 1983 - Agnes Ryan, seventy-five

Arrest and Trial

A piece of eyewitness evidence that was reported to the Will County sheriff's office in August of 1983 was not handed over to the State Police until February of 1984. Ann Shoemaker had reported a pickup truck playing a game of "cat and mouse" with her while she was driving in July of 1983, and she was able to get the license plate number. The state police received the number on March 6, 1984, and they traced it to Sam Myers, the stepfather of Johnson.

The police made contact with Myers and he agreed to sign a consent form giving them permission to search the truck. They found hair, a steak knife, bloodstains, fibers, and a receipt for a stuffed toy - the same toy Hackett had bought the day he died. A search warrant was then obtained to search Myer's home, where Johnson also lived. Inside they found cartridges from a .357 Magnum.

The same day the police were searching the house, Payne had been brought in to look at mug shots to see if she could identify the man who had shot her and Hackett. She looked at five photographs and picked out Johnson, but her identification wasn't strong. So, she was brought in again on March 9 for a lineup. This time, the people in the lineup were instructed to say the commands the killer had given her on that night. She positively, without hesitation, identified Johnson this time.

The trial was eventually set for July 26, 1984. Johnson was found guilty of murdering Hackett, and he was convicted of the attempted murder, rape, sexual assault, and kidnapping of Payne. He was sentenced to death for the murder of Hackett and forty years for the attack on Payne.

Outcome

Johnson and his legal team filed a petition alleging he had received ineffective counsel assistance. The court held that Johnson's claims of ineffective assistance had been properly dismissed. In other words, his sentence remained as initially imposed. Johnson currently sits on death row awaiting his execution date.

Trivia

–   Johnson became pen pals with an elderly woman who used to visit him in prison once a month until her age made it impossible.

JOHN JOUBERT

Date of birth: July 2, 1963
Aliases/Nicknames: The Nebraska Boy Snatcher, the Woolford Slasher
Characteristics: Kidnapping, sadism, biting
Number of victims: 3 +
Date of murders: August 22, 1982 - December 2, 1983
Date of arrest: January 12, 1984
Murder method: Stabbing
Known Victims: Richard Stetson, 11; Danny Joe Eberle, 13; Christopher Walden, 12
Crime location: Maine, Nebraska
Status: Executed by electric chair, July 17, 1996.

Background

Born in Massachusetts in 1963, Joubert was considered an intelligent child, one who began reading at just three years old. By five years of age, he was already borrowing books from the local library. He lived with his mother after his parents divorced when he was six. He grew to resent his mother later in life, whom he considered controlling; she would not allow him to have contact with his father.

Joubert was small. He suffered at the hands of bullies because of his size, up until he attended high school. Little did his peers know that Joubert had been experiencing sadistic and violent fantasies since he was six. One of these fantasies involved his babysitter; he would imagine killing her and indulging in cannibalism. He later told a psychiatrist that he had no bad feelings toward the babysitter; she was just someone he could murder.

When Joubert was twelve years old, he confessed that he was having homosexual thoughts, and this led to even more bullying. At thirteen, he took a pencil and stabbed a young girl with it, and when she cried out in pain, he found it sexually stimulating. The following day, he slashed at a girl with a razor blade as he rode past her on his bike.

From then onwards, Joubert continued to attack children his own age (and those younger) for the thrill of it. When he was sixteen, he attacked an eight-year-old boy, throttling him almost to death. The violence he exhibited was getting stronger and stronger each time he attacked, but so far he had managed to avoid getting caught. It was no surprise that Joubert would become a killer, it was just a matter of when.

Murders

Richard Stetson went for a run on August 22, 1982, along the Back Cove Trail in Portland, Maine. His body was discovered the following day alongside the freeway. He had been stabbed and strangled, and there were bite marks on his body. Although a suspect was initially arrested for killing the young boy, his teeth didn't match the bite marks; he was eventually released without being charged.

On September 18, 1983, Danny Joe Eberle went missing while delivering newspapers in Bellevue, Nebraska. His body was found three days later, four miles away from where his bicycle had been left. He was dressed only in his underwear, and his hands and feet were bound. Surgical tape had been used to tape his mouth, and he had been stabbed nine times.

Joubert's third victim disappeared in Papillion, Nebraska, on December 2, 1983. Christopher Walden had been walking when Joubert ordered him into his vehicle with the threat of a knife. He instructed Walden to take off his clothes, which he did, leaving his underwear on. Walden refused to lie down which angered Joubert. During a struggle, he stabbed the boy. He cut Walden's throat so deeply that his head was almost removed from his body. Two days later, his body was found five miles away from town.

Timeline of known murders:

August 22, 1982 - Richard Stetson, eleven

September 18, 1983 - Danny Joe Eberle, thirteen

December 2, 1983 - Christopher Walden, twelve

Arrest and Trial

A teacher reported to police on January 11, 1984, that she had seen a man driving around suspiciously, and when the driver saw her write down his license plate, he stopped and threatened her before driving off. Police checked the license plate and found the vehicle was a rental and was in the possession of Joubert. His personal car, which matched witness reports from the abductions, was in the shop for repairs.

The police obtained a search warrant for his home. During the search, they found the same type of rope that had been used to bind two of the victims. Joubert was brought in for questioning. He confessed to being responsible for killing Eberle and Walden and was therefore charged for the murders.

Initially Joubert plead not guilty, but then he changed his plea to guilty. He was assessed on several occasions by psychiatrists, one of whom diagnosed him as having an obsessive-compulsive disorder, sadistic tendencies, and a schizoid personality disorder. But, he had not been psychotic when he committed the crimes.

Joubert was found guilty of the two murders and sentenced to death. Later, he was also convicted of killing Stetson in Maine and he received a sentence of life imprisonment for that murder.

Outcome

Joubert was executed by the electric chair on July 17, 1996, in Nebraska. Because of the state of Joubert's body afterwards, his execution led to an appeal to the Nebraska Supreme Court to have the electric chair abolished as a "cruel and unusual" punishment method. Joubert had received a brain blister four inches in size on the top of his head, as well as blisters on both sides of his scalp above his ears.

Trivia

- Final statement before execution: "I do not know if my death will change anything or if it will bring anyone any peace."

Quote by Joubert:

- "It was the power and the domination and seeing the fear. That was more exciting than actually causing the harm."

THEODORE KACZYNSKI

Date of birth: May 22, 1942
Aliases/Nicknames: The Unabomber
Characteristics: Domestic terrorism, mail bombs
Number of victims: 3
Date of murders: 1985, 1994, 1995
Date of arrest: April 3, 1996
Murder method: Explosive devices - bombs
Known Victims: Hugh Scrutton, 38; Thomas J. Mosser, 50; Gilbert P. Murray
Crime location: California, New Jersey
Status: Sentenced to life imprisonment without parole.

Background

Some may disagree that Ted Kaczynski was a true serial killer because his attacks were driven by political thoughts rather than homicidal ones. Nevertheless, he does meet the definition of a serial killer because of the number of his victims, and the manner in which the killings were carried out over a period of time.

Kaczynski was exceptionally good at mathematics at a very young age and was considered a child prodigy in the subject. He went from fifth grade to seventh, skipping the sixth grade altogether because of his high level of intelligence; testing determined he had an IQ of 167. But, because he was advanced a grade, the older children bullied him and he didn't really fit in.

Harvard University accepted Kaczynski when he was just sixteen years old, and he graduated in 1962. He then went on to gain a PhD in mathematics at the University of Michigan. He began teaching at the University of California, but he wasn't comfortable in front of the students. In 1969, he resigned from his position.

He moved back with his parents in 1971, and built a cabin for himself in Montana. With financial help from his family, and by undertaking odd jobs, Kaczynski was able to support himself. He began studying survival skills, including the identification of edible plants in the wild and how to track animals. But, over a period of time, he came to realize that modern urbanization would prevent him from continuing in this way of life. It's believed that Kaczynski decided to fight back when one of his favorite wilderness places had been destroyed to make a new road.

Murders

In 1985, Hugh Scrutton was at his computer store in Sacramento when a nail and splinter bomb exploded in the car park outside. He was killed in the blast. A similar bomb was detonated at another computer store on February 20, 1987. Despite horrific injuries, there were no deaths in that blast.

The next attack occurred in 1993. A bomb was mailed to David Gelernter, who was working as a computer science professor at Yale. Gelernter was seriously injured, but he survived. Charles Epstein, who worked at the University of California, received a bomb in the mail the same weekend. He lost several fingers when it exploded.

Thomas J. Mosser was killed in 1994, after a bomb arrived in the mail at his home in New Jersey. In 1995, Gilbert Brent Murray was killed by a bomb mailed to his office at the California Forestry Association. The bomb was actually addressed to William Dennison, whom Murray had replaced when he retired.

Kaczynski was responsible for the building and distribution of sixteen bombs. Fortunately, despite that number of explosive devices, only three were killed and twenty-three injured.

Arrest and Trial

After a thorough investigation into the bombings, the FBI identified and arrested Kaczynski on April 3, 1996. When they searched his cabin, they discovered a lot of components used in the construction of the bombs. They also found a journal with thousands of pages describing the bombings, the bombs, and experiments in bomb making Kaczynski had undertaken. Additionally, they found a live bomb that was ready to be sent out in the mail.

When Kaczynski went on trial for the three murders, he was found guilty and convicted. He received a life sentence without parole.

Outcome

Kaczynski was at one point considered a possible suspect for the Zodiac Killer crimes. He had been living in the San Francisco Bay area during the period that the killings occurred. And, like Kaczynski, the Zodiac Killer also had an interest in bombs and codes. Both had also written letters to newspapers making demands and threatening more acts of violence. However, it was decided there was not enough convincing evidence of Kaczynski being the Zodiac Killer and he was not pursued any further.

Trivia

- While incarcerated at the maximum security facility in Florence, Colorado, Kaczynski developed a friendship with two other notorious bombers - Timothy McVeigh, the Oklahoma bomber, and Ramzi Yousef, who bombed the World Trade Center in 1993.

PATRICK KEARNEY

Date of birth: September 24, 1939

Aliases/Nicknames: The Freeway Killer, The Trash Bag Killer

Characteristics: Rape, mutilation, homosexual victims, children, necrophilia

Number of victims: 35 +

Date of murders: 1965 - 1977

Date of arrest: July 1, 1977

Murder method: Shooting, asphyxiation

Known Victims: Mike, 18; George; John Demchik, 13; James Barwick, 17; Ronald Smith Jr., 5; Albert Rivera, 21; Larry Walters, 20; Kenneth Buchanan, 17; Oliver Molitor, 13; Larry Armedariz, 15; Michael McGhee, 13; John Woods, 23; Larry Epsy, 17; Wilfred Faherty, 20; Randall Moore; Robert Benniefiel, 17; David Allen, 27; Mark Orach, 20; Timothy Ingham, 19; Nicholas Hernandez-Jimenez, 28; Arturo Marquez, 24; John LaMay, 17; Merle Chance, 8; others unidentified

Crime location: California

Status: Sentenced to life imprisonment without parole.

Background

Kearney enjoyed a normal, stable childhood with his family in California, but he was subjected to bullying when he was young. By the time he was a teenager, he was already fantasizing about committing murders. As an adult, he lived in Texas for a while before moving back to California. An aircraft engineer, Kearney was also prolific at picking up gay men, often using his fluent Spanish skills to facilitate the pickup.

When he moved to Redondo Beach, he met David Hill and they began a relationship. The men would have fights and arguments, after which Kearney would go out for a long drive. But he wasn't doing this to calm down the fighting; he was actually picking up other men from bars or the side of the road as they hitchhiked.

Murders

The first murder attributed to Kearney was that of an unidentified man in 1962. Kearney had taken him on the back of his motorcycle to a secluded spot and shot him in the head. He then performed acts of necrophilia with the corpse. Over the next several years, he continued to kill.

Most of Kearney's victims were either picked up from gay bars or had been hitchhikers. They were almost always shot in the temple with a .22 caliber pistol, and they were often distracted or asleep when they were killed. After engaging in necrophilia, the bodies would be taken back to Kearney's home where they would be sodomized with a craft knife.

Kearney used a hacksaw to dismember the bodies, sometimes taking out the bullets lodged in their heads. Then he would put the body parts in trash bags and dump them in landfills, canyons, or beside the freeways. Sometimes Kearney drained the blood from his victims to remove the odor of decomposition and death; he even washed the body parts to remove any potential fingerprints.

Timeline of known murders:

Spring, 1962 - Unnamed man, nineteen

1962 - Unnamed man, sixteen

1962 - Mike, eighteen (surname not revealed)

1965- Unnamed man

December of 1967 - George (surname not revealed)

June 21, 1971 - John Demchik, thirteen

September 22, 1973 - James Barwick, seventeen

August 24, 1974 - Ronald Dean Smith Jr., five

April 13, 1975 - Albert Rivera, twenty-one

November 10, 1975 - Larry Gene Walters, twenty

March 3, 1976 - Kenneth Eugene Buchanan, seventeen

March 21, 1976 - Oliver Peter Molitor, thirteen

April 19, 1976 - Larry Armedariz, fifteen

June 16, 1976 - Michael Craig McGhee, thirteen

June 20, 1976 - John Woods, twenty-three

August 23, 1976 - Larry Epsy, seventeen

August 28, 1976 - Wilfred Lawrence Faherty, twenty

August of 1976 - Randall Lawrence Moore

Fall of 1976 - Robert Benniefiel, seventeen

Fall of 1976 - David Allen, twenty-seven

October of 1976 - Mark Andrew Orach, twenty

November 15-24, 1976 - Timothy B. Ingham, nineteen

January 23, 1977 - Nicholas "Nicky" Hernandez-Jimenez, twenty-eight

February of 1977 - Arturo Romos Marquez, twenty-four

March 13, 1977 - John Otis LaMay, seventeen

April 6, 1977 - Merle Chance, eight

Arrest and Trial

One of the victims had last been seen with Kearney and Hill, and when the men became aware of the police's interest in them, they fled to El Paso, Texas. But, they ended up turning themselves in at the urging of their families. They were both arrested on July 1, 1977, but Hill was quickly released when investigators worked out he hadn't been involved in the murders.

During his interrogation, Kearney confessed to killing thirty-eight victims, but police were only able to charge him with twenty-one counts of murder. At trial, Kearney pleaded guilty to all charges which prevented him from receiving the death penalty. Instead, he was sentenced to life without parole.

Outcome

Investigators believe that not only is Kearney most likely responsible for the thirty-eight murders he confessed to, but he could also be responsible for even more. In the meantime, Kearney is incarcerated at California State Prison where he will live out the rest of his days.

EDMUND KEMPER

Date of birth: December 18, 1948

Aliases/Nicknames: The Co-ed Killer, The Co-ed Butcher

Characteristics: Necrophilia, irrumatio, dismemberment

Number of victims: 10

Date of murders: 1964, 1972 - 1973

Date of arrest: April 24, 1973

Murder method: Shooting, striking with a hammer, strangulation

Known Victims: Edmund Kemper Sr., 72 (grandfather); Maude Kemper, 66 (grandmother); Mary Pesce, 18; Anita Luchessa, 18; Aiko Koo, 15; Cindy Schall, 19; Rosalind Thorpe, 24; Allison Liu, 23; Clarnell Strandberg, 52 (mother); Sara Hallett, 59

Crime location: California

Status: Sentenced to life imprisonment without the possibility of parole.

Background

Kemper was the middle child between two sisters. His parents Edmund Jr. and Clarnell later separated in 1957; this had a deep impact on Kemper as he was especially close to his father. His mother took the children and moved to Helena, Montana, far away from their father. Kemper was very bright and intelligent and was later determined to have an IQ of 145. However, he showed sociopathic traits at a very young age.

Kemper would play with his sisters' dolls, but not in the way most young boys play with dolls. He would use them to enact murderous acts and sexual rituals that were bizarre, and he took great delight in pulling off the heads of the dolls. At the same time, he also showed signs of pyromania.

Before long, Kemper shifted his focus from the inanimate dolls to small animals in his neighborhood, especially cats. He would torture them before killing them, and sometimes he would bury them alive. One such incident involved digging the buried cat up again, cutting off its head, and then placing the head on top of a pole. Another favorite game of his was to pretend he was being electrocuted by an electric chair.

Kemper's mother, described as emotionally abusive, started locking the prepubescent Kemper in the basement; she seemed convinced he might rape his youngest sister. When he was thirteen, Kemper ran away and made his way to California to see his father. However, his father had remarried and seemed devoted to his new stepson. Kemper was returned to his mother, heartbroken.

By the time Kemper was fourteen, he already stood six feet four inches tall. Because his mother struggled to manage him, he was sent to live with his grandparents. Edmund Sr. and Maude Kemper lived on a ranch in North Fork, California, and it was thought that this would be a good environment for Kemper. But they were very wrong. Kemper and his grandmother didn't get along very well, and he was continuously bullied at school, despite his huge build. Everything came to a head on August 27, 1964.

On that August afternoon, Kemper took the rifle he had been given the previous Christmas and shot and killed his grandmother. Upon his grandfather's arrival home from the store, Kemper also shot and killed him, supposedly to prevent him from having to see his wife's dead body. Then Kemper picked up the telephone and called his mother to tell her what he had done. Afterwards, he called the local police to report his actions. When the police arrived, Kemper was sitting on the porch waiting for them.

Following his arrest, Kemper was assessed by psychiatrists and diagnosed with paranoid schizophrenia. He was admitted to the Atascadero State Hospital for the Criminally Insane and behaved so well, he eventually became an assistant to his psychiatrist. Kemper was subsequently released on his twenty-first birthday in 1969, despite the protests of several of the hospital's psychiatrists. To make matters worse, he was put back into the care of his mother, who by now was living in Santa Cruz.

Murders

Many of the murders occurred after Kemper and his mother argued. He would cruise along the Pacific coast looking for suitable victims; most often they were hitchhikers. The first two women he murdered were Mary Anne Pesce and Anita Luchessa on May 7, 1972.

They were on their way to Stanford University when Kemper offered them a ride. Kemper then drove down a dirt road and murdered both girls in the car. He wrapped them up in blankets and took them home. He decapitated both girls and held on to them for a while before disposing of them in a ravine. The body of Pesce was later found, but no remains of Luchessa were ever located.

On September 14, 1972, Kemper picked up fifteen-year-old Aiko Koo. He put tape over her mouth and suffocated her until she passed out. Then he removed her from the car and raped her before using a scarf to asphyxiate her. He took her body back to his home and dismembered it. Ironically, when he went for a meeting with court psychiatrists (who were very pleased with the progress he had made), Koo's head was sitting in his car.

The next murder occurred on January 8, 1973. Cindy Schall was picked up by Kemper and taken into the hills. He forced her to get into the trunk of the car and then shot her. Again, he took the body back to his residence. The following morning, he had sexual intercourse with the corpse. When he dismembered the body, he removed the bullets from her head before burying it in his mother's backyard.

Rosalind Thorpe and Alice Liu were both killed by Kemper on February 5, 1973. Then, on April 20, Kemper killed his last two victims - his own mother and her friend Sara Hallett. He waited until his mother had fallen asleep and then struck her in the head with a hammer before slitting her throat. After cutting off her head, he raped his mother's corpse. He cut out her tongue and tried to destroy it in the garbage disposal unit.

He then called his mother's friend Hallett and invited her over. When she arrived, he killed her and cut off her head. Then, once the mess was cleaned up, he went to bed.

Timeline of known murders:

August 27, 1964 - Edmund Kemper Sr., seventy-two

August 27, 1964 - Maude Kemper, sixty-six

May 7, 1972 - Mary Anne Pesce, eighteen

May 7, 1972 - Anita Luchessa, eighteen

September 14, 1972 - Aiko Koo, fifteen

January 8, 1973 - Cindy Schall, nineteen

February 5, 1973 - Rosalind Thorpe, twenty-four

February 5, 1973 - Alice Liu, twenty-one

April 20, 1973 - Clarnell Strandberg, fifty-two

April 20, 1973 - Sara Hallett, fifty-nine

Arrest and Trial

After the murders of his mother and Hallett, Kemper decided to flee. As he was driving, he listened for news reports on the radio about the murders. Four days later, there had been nothing on the radio about the deaths, so he decided to call the police. At a phone booth he placed a call to officers at the Santa Cruz police department and claimed he had killed eight women.

The authorities didn't take him seriously at first because they knew Kemper well. But after they made a few calls, they realized his confession carried weight. Kemper sat in his car and waited for the police to come. He was arrested on April 24. During the interview at the station, he confessed to all of the murders he had committed.

When Kemper went on trial, he initially tried to plead insanity, but this defense failed. Instead he asked for the death penalty; he wanted to die in the electric chair, just as he had fantasized. But capital punishment had been suspended at the time. Instead, he received a life sentence without the possibility of parole.

Outcome

At the time Kemper was actively murdering women, the FBI behavioral sciences unit had come up with an idea to interview serial killers. They believed this would help them to gain a better understanding of the type of people they are and what makes them kill. Kemper was one of the first to be interviewed; he was eventually interviewed by Robert Ressler three times. During the last interview, Kemper made death threats against Ressler, but when the guards came he said he had just been joking around with him.

One of the other FBI interviewers was John Douglas, a renowned forensic profiler who, along with Ressler, was one of the first professional profilers for the FBI. He later said that he liked Kemper and found him open, sensitive, and friendly. Kemper is still serving his life sentence.

Trivia

- Kemper's IQ was measured at 145.

Quote by Kemper:

- "When I see a pretty girl walking down the street, I think two things. One part of me wants to take her out, talk to her, be real nice and sweet and treat her right ... and the other part of me wonders what her head would look like on a stick."
- "If I killed them, you know, they couldn't reject me as a man. It was more or less making a doll out of a human being... and carrying out my fantasies with a doll, a living human doll."

ROGER KIBBE

Date of birth: 1941

Aliases/Nicknames: The I-5 Strangler

Characteristics: Rape, kidnapping

Number of victims: 7 +

Date of murders: 1977, 1986 - 1987

Date of arrest: 1987

Murder method: Strangulation

Known Victims: Lou Ellen Burleigh, 21; Lora Heedrick, 20; Barbara Ann Scott, 29; Stephanie Brown, 19; Charmaine Sabrah, 26; Katherine Kelly Quinones, 25; Darcie Frackenpohl, 17

Crime location: California

Status: Sentenced to six terms of life without parole.

Background

Kibbe grew up with a domineering mother who would beat him frequently. In his eyes, she acted as though she didn't even like him. Kibbe was a known bed-wetter as a youngster, and he suffered a terrible stutter, leading to constant ridicule and bullying at school. Because of this he became a loner, preferring his own company. He was an established liar who had a habit of stealing. When he was fifteen, he was arrested for theft.

Kibbe had been seen riding his bike through a local park carrying a cardboard box and a shovel. The witness informed the police, and when they arrived at the scene, they dug up the box Kibbe had buried. Contained inside were women's clothing, including two bathing suits and a dress, which had been reported stolen from a neighborhood clothes line. Also stolen were several pairs of nylon stockings, but these weren't in the box.

Suspecting a fetishist, the police interviewed numerous witnesses until they discovered Kibbe was the culprit. He was subsequently charged with prowling and petty theft. There had been several other similar thefts over the past year, and although he initially denied being responsible, he eventually admitted to the crimes. Kibbe had disposed of most of the items he had stolen, but he kept some. When he handed them over to the police, they noticed the garments had been cut up with scissors.

But there was much more going on in Kibbe's mind than just theft of women's clothing. He had an active sexual fantasy life which included tying himself up with women's underwear. His behaviors and actions would today be considered warning signs of psychopathy, but at the time, children who showed antisocial tendencies were not studied or diagnosed.

Kibbe did attend sessions with a psychiatrist for a while, but this accomplished nothing. Kibbe found the sessions a nuisance, and he came up with other ways to continue his disturbing behaviors so that they wouldn't be detected. He became very secretive.

As an adult, Kibbe somehow managed to marry a woman who was very much like his mother. His wife Harriet was mean and domineering, traits his mother had also displayed when Kibbe was a child. Harriet ruled the roost and kept Kibbe in line; it was later speculated that his wife's treatment of him most likely increased his anger toward women.

Murders

Kibbe would troll the south Sacramento freeways late at night looking for broken down cars with young women needing help. After offering his assistance, he would then kidnap the women, take them to remote areas, and strangle them.

His first known murder took place on September 11, 1977. The victim, Lou Ellen Burleigh, had left home and was on her way to a job interview when she disappeared. She was kidnapped by Kibbe, tied up, and taken to Lake Berryessa where he raped and killed her.

Lora Heedrick was last seen alive on April 20, 1986, in an area where drug addicts and prostitutes were known to frequent. That night, she had agreed with her boyfriend James Driggers that she would prostitute herself so they could get money for drugs. He claimed they had gotten into a car being driven by a man in his fifties. After they dropped Driggers off at a motel, they drove off to get some drugs. But Heedrick never returned.

On July 3, 1986, Kibbe abducted Barbara Ann Scott in Pittsburg. She was raped before being killed, and her body was left at a golf course in Contra Costa County. She was Kibbe's oldest victim. Just two weeks later, on July 15, Kibbe came across a young woman, Stephanie Brown, who was broken down on the side of the freeway. He raped and killed her and then cut off her hair, which investigators later surmised was a fetish or a trophy.

Charmaine Sabrah and her mother broke down on Peltier Road and I-5 on August 17, 1986. A man stopped to offer assistance, and when the women said they wanted to get to a phone, he said he only had room in his car for one. Sabrah went with him but was unable to contact anyone. They returned to the car and the man, later identified as Kibbe, said he would take them home. Because Sabrah had a baby at home, she went first, but the driver never came back for her mother.

When her mother finally was able to get help from the police to get home, Sabrah wasn't there. Her body was found almost three months later at the base of the Sierra Mountains. On examination, it was clear that she had been strangled with a ligature—it was still present around her neck. Parts of her clothing had been cut out, and clumps of hair had been yanked out and twisted in the waistband of her underwear.

Katherine Kelly Quinones was abducted in Sacramento on November 5, 1986. Like the others, she was raped before being killed, and her body was disposed of at Lake Berryessa. Kibbe's final known murder was that of Darcie Frackenpohl toward the end of 1986. A runaway, she was last seen alive in an area of Sacramento popular with prostitutes. She had been strangled with a garrote, and her pantyhose had been stuffed into her mouth. Her clothing showed the same cutting that was typical with the other victims.

Timeline of known murders:

September 11, 1977 - Lou Ellen Burleigh, twenty-one

April 21, 1986. - Lora Heedrick, twenty

July 3, 1986 - Barbara Ann Scott, twenty-nine

July 15, 1986 - Stephanie Brown, nineteen

August 17, 1986 - Charmaine Sabrah, twenty-six

November 5, 1986 - Katherine Kelly Quinones, twenty-five

1986 - Darcie Frackenpohl, seventeen

Arrest and Trial

Kibbe was initially arrested after assaulting a prostitute. He had picked her up and driven around for a while before parking. Then he became violent, and she struggled against him as he tried to handcuff her. She screamed as loud as she could and an officer, who was on patrol nearby, came to her aid and chased after Kibbe.

While investigators were processing the assault charge, the body of Kibbe's fifth victim was found. When Kibbe's car was searched, they found rubber hair bands, scissors, a wooden dowel, a vibrator, and handcuffs. They also found some cord, and the detectives realized it was the same as the cord and dowel found in the garrote used on Quinones.

Kibbe was given bail, and investigators continued to work on the items to see if they could be matched with the victims, all the while having him under surveillance. Finally, they found the evidence they needed, and Kibbe was arrested again and charged with first-degree murder. On May 10, 1991, he was found guilty of the murder of Frackenpohl and received twenty-five years to life.

On November 5, 2009, Kibbe was charged with a further six counts of murder. He agreed to a plea bargain to avoid the death penalty and received six life sentences instead.

Outcome

In 2003, Kibbe accompanied detectives and prosecutors to the dry creek he believed he had disposed of Burleigh's body in, but her remains were not found. The area was searched again in 2007, with no results. Kibbe went back to the site in 2009 with detectives, and they still couldn't find the remains.

A detective went back to the creek bed in 2011, and this time he discovered a bone. It was sent for DNA testing, and it came back as belonging to Burleigh.

SCOTT LEE KIMBALL

Date of birth: September 21, 1966

Aliases/Nicknames: Hannibal, Joe Snitch

Characteristics: Fraud, self-professed hitman

Number of victims: 4 +

Date of murders: January of 2003 - August of 2004

Date of arrest: March 14, 2006

Murder method: Shooting

Known Victims: Kaysi McLeod, 19; Jennifer Marcum, 25; LeAnn Emry, 24; Terry Kimball, 60 (his uncle)

Crime location: Boulder County, Colorado

Status: Sentenced to 70 years' imprisonment.

Background

Kimball was one of those criminals who just couldn't keep his mouth shut. He had spent quite a bit of time in prison for fraud and somehow managed to become an informant for the FBI on his release. Kimball was an experienced and successful conman who had lived a life of deceit and treachery, and his biggest con of all was convincing the FBI to get him released from prison in 2002 so he could be an informant for them.

While Kimball was incarcerated in Alaska for check fraud, he notified the FBI that he had information regarding a plot to murder a federal judge, and he convinced them that if he was released he could provide important information on the alleged hitman. Despite his extensive criminal history, including an escape from a Montana prison and a recommendation from a presiding judge that he could not be supervised successfully in the community, the FBI decided the information he could provide superseded the risk of Kimball committing further crimes.

As a prison inmate, Kimball had bragged to whoever would listen that he was, in fact, a hitman. He even gave himself the nickname "Hannibal," after the famous character in the novels written by Thomas Harris. He claimed he had committed numerous murders for financial gain as a "killer for hire." When news of this reached the FBI, an investigation into their informant was undertaken, and it was discovered that, for once, Kimball may have been telling the truth.

Murders

Between January of 2003 and August of 2004, Kimball was responsible for the deaths of at least four people. He was still working as an informant for the FBI at the time, and he later claimed to have committed many other murders. But, they have not been proven.

One of his victims, Kaysi McLeod, went missing while on her way to work. At the time, Kimball was dating her mother, and he was supposed to be giving her a ride to work. But he said he didn't, insisting he had gone hunting instead. Her body wasn't found until 2007.

Kimball killed Jennifer Marcum in February of 2003, in a canyon in Utah. He claimed that, apart from facilitating her death, he wasn't the one who pulled the trigger. He did say though that he had given her a "hot shot" of heroin to overdose her. To date, her remains have not been found.

LeAnn Emry was shot and killed in January of 2003. At first, Kimball claimed she was shot by someone else in a canyon in Utah. But he had told others that he had shot her twice in the back of her neck when she tried to get away. Emry was the girlfriend of a former cellmate of Kimball's.

Timeline of known murders:

January 29, 2003 - LeAnn Emry, twenty-four

February 17, 2003 - Jennifer Marcum, twenty-five

August 23, 2003 - Kaysi McLeod, nineteen

September 1, 2004 - Terry Kimball, sixty

Arrest and Trial

Kimball was already in jail (for check fraud and a variety of other crimes) when he was charged with committing the four murders. This made it easier for investigators to question him about the murders. They discovered Kimball had written a letter, consisting of one hundred forty-seven pages, to his family where he admitted he was the man responsible for the deaths, including that of his uncle Terry.

The investigation showed that there was a link between Kimball and each of the victims. Further evidence was gleaned from his computer and from previous cellmates whom he had boasted to about the murders. When he went on trial in October of 2009, he pleaded guilty to two counts of second-degree murder, as per the plea deal he had agreed to. In exchange, he was to draw maps showing where the undiscovered bodies were buried.

Kimball received a sentence of seventy years for the two murders he was charged with.

Outcome

The FBI is still investigating the possibility that Kimball killed far more people than the four victims they know about. Kimball himself had openly bragged about committing a lot more murders. His cousin, Ed Coet, claims Kimball is expecting to be interviewed about further cases as time goes on.

ANTHONY KIRKLAND

Date of birth: September 13, 1968

Aliases/Nicknames: Nil

Characteristics: Set victims on fire to hide evidence

Number of victims: 5

Date of murders: 1987, 2006 - 2009

Date of arrest: March 8, 2009

Murder method: Strangulation

Known Victims: Leola Douglas, 27 (his girlfriend); Casonya Crawford, 15; Mary Jo Newton, 45; Kimya Rolison, 14; Esme Kenny, 13

Crime location: Hamilton County, Ohio

Status: Sentenced to death, awaiting execution.

Background

Nothing is really known about Kirkland's early years and childhood, until he came under the police spotlight at the age of 18 in 1987. His first known violent crime took place at this time—the murder of his girlfriend Leola Douglas. He beat and strangled her, then set her on fire, and an autopsy later showed she had still been alive when she started to burn. The murder had taken place on his own doorstep, so police were quickly led to Kirkland as the main suspect.

He was convicted of the murder and sentenced to sixteen years in prison, which he served in full. Kirkland was released in 2003, and his parole period ended in 2004. Just a few months later, he was arrested on suspicion of raping a woman at knifepoint, but he was subsequently acquitted of this crime in October of 2005.

By May of 2006, Kirkland's anger and hatred of women reached an all new level, but his deeds would not be uncovered for a few more years. In 2007, he spent more time in prison after threatening to kill his son, who was only eighteen months old at the time. He served one hundred fifteen days, but would soon be in trouble with the law again. Later that year, he was arrested and charged with trying to solicit sex from a thirteen-year-old girl, the daughter of his girlfriend. Kirkland was sentenced to a year in prison but was released just seven months later because of overcrowding.

After being sent to live in a halfway house, Kirkland embarked on a downward spiral, leading to the deaths of four more victims.

Murders

The first known murder committed by Kirkland was that of Leola Douglas on May 20, 1987. She was his girlfriend at the time, and on the night she died he had taken her to a house, knocked her out, and set her on fire. He was sent to prison for this murder and served sixteen years for manslaughter after pleading guilty to the lesser charge.

On May 11, 2006, the body of Casonya Crawford was found near Blair Avenue in Avondale. She had been killed and her body set on fire. This was becoming a pattern of Kirkland's. The next victim, Mary Jo Newton, met the same fate sometime in April or May of 2006. Her body had also been set on fire and was found behind a vacant building.

The body of Kimya Rolison, fourteen, was discovered stabbed to death and burnt, just like the other victims, in December of 2006. Kirkland's final victim was Esme Kenny, whom he abducted on March 7, 2009. Her body was found by police in woods not far from her home. She had been strangled to death and the lower half of her body had been set on fire. Sleeping nearby, up against a tree, was Kirkland.

Timeline of known murders:

May 20, 1987 - Leola Douglas, twenty-seven

March, 2006 - Casonya Crawford, fifteen

April or May, 2006 - Mary Jo Newton, forty-five

December 22, 2006 - Kimya Rolison, fourteen

March 7, 2009 - Esme Kenny, thirteen

Timeline of other violent crimes during the killing spree:

October 25, 2004 - Released from parole.

January 25, 2005 - Accused of raping a female neighbor in Evanston at knifepoint. A jury acquits him in October of 2005.

May 14, 2007 - Kirkland threatens to kill his eighteen-month-old son during a SWAT standoff at Kirkland's house. He is convicted of two counts of unlawful restraint three months later and sentenced to one hundred fifteen days in jail.

September 17, 2007 - The Rev. Walter Bledsoe seeks a restraining order against Kirkland on behalf of the Bledsoe family. Court records do not say why he applied for the order, but it was granted by a judge in December of 2007.

September 26, 2007 - Kirkland solicits sex from the thirteen-year-old daughter of his girlfriend. In March of 2008, he is convicted of importuning and sentenced to one year in prison. Kirkland is designated a sex offender, and he has to register his address with the sheriff's office.

October 20, 2008 - He is released from prison and ordered to spend five years on parole. He enters the Pogue Rehabilitation Center, a halfway house in Over-the-Rhine run by Volunteers of America.

February 27, 2009 - Kirkland gets into a fight with another resident at the halfway house. Police are called, but Kirkland is not arrested because the other man refuses to press charges. Kirkland is thrown out of the residence by the managers (for breaking the no fighting rule), but they don't notify his parole officer until two days later. Kirkland doesn't immediately register a new address with the sheriff as required by law.

March 1, 2009 - Kirkland is accused of breaking into a home, hiding in the bathroom, and attacking Frederick Hughes with scissors. Hughes suffers at least ten stab wounds but survives. Kirkland flees the scene, and a warrant is issued for his arrest on charges of aggravated burglary and felonious assault.

March 2, 2009 - Kirkland's parole officer is notified of his release from the halfway house and begins looking for him.

March 4, 2009 - A second warrant is issued for Kirkland's arrest because he failed to register his address with the sheriff after his release from the halfway house.

March 5, 2009 - Kirkland is accused of threatening Roberta Baldwin, his child's mother, with a knife. He flees and another warrant is filed against him on charges of domestic violence, aggravated menacing, and violation of a protection order.

Arrest and Trial

When police approached Kirkland near the body of his last victim, they searched him and discovered in his possession some items belonging to the young girl. He was immediately arrested and taken to the police station for questioning. He was formally charged with the murder of Kenney.

While investigating, authorities were able to connect Kirkland to the murders of Newton and Rolison as well, and he was charged with those murders as well as abuse of a corpse. When he went to trial, Kirkland entered a guilty plea to all charges. Subsequently, the jury found him guilty of all counts on March 12, 2010.

Kirkland was sentenced to death for the murders of Kenney and Crawford, and he received seventy years to life for the murders of Rolison and Newton.

Outcome

At this point in time, Kirkland remains on death row awaiting his execution. Though his legal team filed a number of appeals, a Hamilton County judge agreed with the jury's decision. On August 28, 2018, the judge upheld the ruling to sentence Kirkland to death..

Appeals:

May 13, 2014 - The Supreme Court of Ohio upheld Kirkland's conviction and death sentence.

October 16, 2014 - The Supreme Court of Ohio granted a motion by Kirkland for a stay of execution.

April 6, 2015 - The U.S. Supreme Court refused to hear Kirkland's appeal.

May 2016 - The Supreme Court of Ohio granted a motion for a new sentencing hearing for Kirkland.

PAUL JOHN KNOWLES

Date of birth: April 14, 1946

Aliases/Nicknames: The Casanova Killer, Lester Daryl Gates, Daryl Golden

Characteristics: Rape, robbery

Number of victims: 18 - 35

Date of murders: July - November of 1974

Date of arrest: December 17, 1974

Murder method: Shooting, strangulation

Known Victims: Alice Curtis, 65; Lillian Anderson, 11; Mylette Anderson, 7; Marjorie Howe; Kathy Pierce; William Bates; Emmett Johnson; Lois Johnson; Ann Dawson; Doris Hovey, 53; Carswell Carr; Carswell's daughter, 15; Edward Hilliard; Debbie Griffin; Trooper Charles Campbell; James Meyer; Ima Sanders, 13; Charlynn Hicks; Karen Wine; Dawn Wine, 16

Crime location: Across many states

Status: Killed by law enforcement while trying to escape, December 18, 1974.

Background

Knowles had a difficult start in life, spending most of his childhood in foster care or reformatories. His father had been convicted of a fairly minor crime, but gave his son up anyway. Knowles was nineteen years old when he was first arrested and incarcerated for criminal activity. From then onwards, he was in and out of prison for numerous crimes, until things took a change for the better in 1974.

Knowles had been corresponding with a woman in San Francisco, Angela Covic. At one point, she traveled to Florida to visit Knowles in prison, and he immediately proposed marriage to her. She accepted and worked hard to get him released from prison, using her own finances to pay for his legal counsel.

As soon as Knowles was released, he flew to San Francisco to be with Covic. However, she had received a warning from a psychic that a dangerous man was entering her life, so she ended the engagement and the relationship. Knowles suffered the rejection terribly, and he returned to Jacksonville, Florida. He claimed that the night the relationship ended, he killed three people in San Francisco.

Not long after his return to Florida, Knowles was involved in a bar fight and was arrested for stabbing a bartender. On July 26, he picked the lock on his cell and made his escape.

Murders

On the night he escaped from prison, Knowles attacked his first victim. Alice Curtis, sixty-five, was gagged and bound by Knowles after he broke into her home on July 26 to rob her of any valuables and money. Although he didn't kill Curtis outright, she did choke on her dentures and die; it is unknown whether Knowles was still there when it happened.

He had stolen her car and, realizing the police would be looking for it, he decided to ditch it on a street. It was August 1, 1974. As he parked the car, he noticed sisters Lilian and Mylette Anderson, who were acquainted with his family. Worried they might identify him, he abducted both girls and strangled them to death before burying their corpses in a swamp.

Ima Jean Sanders disappeared in Georgia on August 1, 1974, after running away from her home in Beaumont, Texas. She had been hitchhiking when Knowles abducted her. She remained unidentified until 2011.

The following day, August 2, Knowles killed Marjorie Howie in her apartment in Florida. It is unclear whether she had invited him in or he had forced his way in. He used a nylon stocking to strangle her, and then he stole her television.

In late August, Knowles forced his way into Kathie Sue Pierce's home in Musella, Georgia. She was strangled to death with a telephone cord, but her child was left unharmed. Then on September 3, Knowles came across William Bates in a bar in Ohio. They left the bar together, and Bates' wife reported him missing the next day. His body was found in October, strangled and naked.

Knowles drove to Nevada in the car he had stolen from Bates. He came across Emmett and Lois Johnson on September 18; he shot them to death after he tying them up. He stole their credit cards and used them for a while, but nobody suspected him as being the culprit until his confession after he was arrested.

Charlynn Hicks was stranded on the side of the road after her motorcycle broke down when she was abducted by Knowles. He raped Hicks and then used her pantyhose to strangle her. He dragged her body though a barbed wire fence and disposed of it; the body was discovered four days later, on September 25.

On September 23, Knowles met Ann Dawson in Birmingham, Alabama. They traveled together for almost a week, until Knowles murdered her on September 29. Her body was thrown into the Mississippi River, but it has never been found.

The next murders occurred on October 16, in Connecticut. Knowles broke into the home where Karen Wine and her daughter Dawn lived, bound them, then raped them. Both were strangled with a nylon stocking.

Doris Hovey was shot and killed in her home in Woodford, Virginia, on October 18. Knowles had used a rifle belonging to Hovey's husband who wasn't home at the time. He wiped off his prints and left the rifle next to Hovey's body. No robbery took place on this occasion, so there was no known motive for this murder.

On November 2, Knowles killed hitchhikers Edward Hilliard and Debbie Griffin. The body of Griffin has never been found. Knowles was still driving Bates' car when he met Carswell Carr in Georgia on November 6. Carr invited Knowles back to his house for drinks and was repaid for his kindness by being strangled. His young daughter was home at the time, and Knowles strangled her to death as well. He did attempt to have sexual intercourse with her corpse, but he was unable to carry out the deed.

Knowles had stolen another car, and on November 17, it was recognized by Trooper Charles Campbell as being a stolen vehicle. Trooper Campbell attempted to arrest Knowles, but Knowles managed to get hold of the officer's pistol. He then drove off in the patrol car with Trooper Campbell as his hostage. Feeling conspicuous in the cop car, he used the lights and siren to pull over James Meyer. He then had two hostages, and they continued driving in Meyer's car.

They drove to an area of woods in Pulaski County, Georgia, where Knowles handcuffed both men to a tree. He then shot them in the head at close range. Not long afterwards, a police roadblock had been set up in Henry County, Georgia. Knowles attempted to drive through it, but he lost control of the car and crashed into a tree. Firing at the officers chasing him, he took off on foot.

Despite being chased by numerous officers, police dogs, helicopters, and other law enforcement agencies, Knowles managed to travel several miles from the main search area. Until he came across a civilian carrying a shotgun.

Timeline of known murders:

July 26, 1974 - Alice Curtis, sixty-five

August 1, 1974 - Lilian Anderson, eleven

August 1, 1974 - Mylette Anderson, seven

August 1, 1974 - Ima Jean Sanders, thirteen

August 2, 1974 - Marjorie Howie, forty-nine

August of 1974 - Kathy Sue Pierce

September 3, 1974 - William Bates, thirty-two

September 18, 1974 - Emmett Johnson

September 18, 1974 - Lois Johnson

September 21, 1974 - Charlynn Hicks

September 29, 1974 - Ann Dawson

October 16, 1974 - Karen Wine

October 16, 1974 - Dawn Wine, sixteen

October 18, 1974 - Doris Hovey, fifty-three

November 2, 1974 - Edward Hilliard

November 2, 1974 - Debbie Griffin

November 6, 1974 - Carswell Carr

November 6, 1974 - Carswell's daughter, fifteen

November 17, 1974 - Trooper Charles Campbell

November 17, 1974 - James Meyer

Arrest and Trial

Knowles was escorted to a house by the civilian armed with a shotgun and the police were called. They arrived on the scene and arrested him. When he was being questioned at the police station, he claimed he was responsible for committing thirty-five murders. But, the investigations only linked him to twenty.

Outcome

On December 18, 1974, Knowles was being transported to Henry County, Georgia, where he had claimed to have dumped a gun used in the murder of State Trooper Charles Eugene Campbell. He was accompanied by Sheriff Earl Lee and Agent Ronnie Angel of the Georgia Bureau of Investigation. At some point in the journey, Knowles managed to grab Lee's gun, which discharged, and while the two men were struggling to gain control of the gun, Agent Angel shot Knowles three times in the chest. He died instantly.

VASILI KOMAROFF

Date of birth: 1871

Aliases/Nicknames: The Wolf of Moscow, The Shabolovka Street Killer, Vasili Terentevich Petrov

Characteristics: Murdered his customers

Number of victims: 33

Date of murders: 1921 - 1923

Date of arrest: March 18, 1923

Murder method: Strangulation, striking with a hammer

Known Victims: Unnamed men - horse traders

Crime location: Moscow, Russia

Status: Executed by firing squad on June 18, 1923.

Background

Early family life for Komaroff was one of poverty and alcoholism. Born into a large family in Russia in 1871, many of his immediate family members were alcoholics, and Komaroff himself began drinking when he was fifteen. Army conscription was compulsory, and he spent four years serving in the Russian Army. He married when he was twenty-eight years old, and he traveled to the Far East with the Army during the Russo-Japanese War in 1904. While there, he was able to make a substantial amount of money, but it didn't last long.

At one point, Komaroff was arrested and sentenced to a year in prison for robbing a warehouse belonging to the military. While he was incarcerated, his wife contracted cholera and passed away. Following his release from prison, he moved to Riga where he met and married Sophia, a Polish widow. They went on to have two children, but Komaroff was still drinking heavily and would often beat both his children and his wife.

Komaroff took his family and moved to the Volga region of Russia in 1915, as the Germans began to enter the Baltic region during World War I. By 1917, the Russian Empire was facing collapse, so Komaroff joined the Red Army, moving his way up to platoon commander by learning to read and write. At one point, he was captured by the White Army but was able to escape. Fearful of the Military Revolutionary Tribunal, he changed his surname from Petrov to Komaroff.

In 1920, Komaroff and his family moved and settled in Moscow at 26 Shablovka Street. He started working as a horse trader and carriage driver, but he continued to steal wherever possible. By 1921, the New Economic Policy was declared in Russian by then-leader Vladimir Lenin, and Komaroff embarked on a murderous spree that would span two years and leave at least thirty-three dead.

Murders

All of the murders committed by Komaroff were carried out in the same manner. Each victim had wanted to buy a horse, and Komaroff would invite them back to his home. They would be served some vodka before either having their head smashed in with a hammer or their throat cut. The corpse would then be hidden around the house in a bag or dumped in the Moscow River. Some bodies were buried in the ground.

In 1922, Komaroff's wife found out he had committed multiple murders. Unfazed, she started helping Komaroff with the killings. The police began investigating the possibility of a serial killer after twenty-one bodies had been discovered after a number of Thursday/Saturday trash pickups. People who attended the horse market also started to wonder about Komaroff when they noticed he was always at the market on Wednesdays and Fridays, hardly ever had a horse with him, and always left with a horse buyer.

Arrest and Trial

Police had their suspicions about Komaroff. Early in 1921, they executed a search warrant at his home. The warrant was meant to be regarding illegal alcohol, but when they searched the stable, they found a man's body hidden beneath some hay. Komaroff made a run for it, escaping out the window. On March 18, he was found in Moscow Oblast and arrested.

During his interrogation, he confessed to the murders of thirty-three men and said that each one had wanted to buy a horse. He claimed he killed them so he could rob them, but he never gained a lot of money from it. After his confession, he showed the police where he had buried the bodies. Not all of them were found, however.

At the end of his trial, Komaroff was found guilty of the murders, as was his wife Sophia. Both were sentenced to death.

Outcome

While in prison awaiting his execution, Komaroff attempted suicide three times.

Komaroff was executed by firing squad on June 18, 1923, along with his wife, in Moscow.

RANDY STEVEN KRAFT

Date of birth: March 19, 1945

Aliases/Nicknames: The Scorecard Killer, The Freeway Killer, Southern California Strangler

Characteristics: Rape, mutilation, torture, dismemberment, sodomy

Number of victims: 16 - 67

Date of murders: September 20, 1971–May 13, 1983

Date of arrest: May 14, 1983

Murder method: Strangulation, drugs and alcohol

Known Victims: Edward Moore, 20; Kevin Bailey, 17; Ronnie Wiebe, 20; Keith Crotwell, 18; Mark Hall, 22; Scott Hughes, 18; Roland Young, 23; Richard Keith, 20; Keith Klingbeil, 23; Michael Inderbieten, 21; Donald Crisel, 20; Robert Loggins, 19; Eric Church, 21; Rodger DeVaul, 20; Geoffrey Nelson, 18; Terry Gambrel, 25

Crime location: California, Oregon, Michigan

Status: Sentenced to death, awaiting execution.

Background

Kraft was born in California in 1945, the only male child in a family of daughters. He was terribly accident-prone as a young child, having broken his collarbone when he was just twelve months old, after falling down stairs. A year later, he had another clumsy accident that knocked him unconscious.

When he was three, the family moved to Westminster, Orange County. There, Kraft had a normal childhood. In high school he got along well with his peers, and he was a member of the school band, playing the saxophone. In 1963, he graduated from high school. Along with his friends, he moved so that he could attend Claremont College in Pomona, California.

Kraft had an interest in politics, and was a member of the ROTC while at college. He also took part in demonstrations in favor of America entering the Vietnam War. He campaigned fervently for the right-wing presidential candidate in 1964, but just a year later, his political beliefs shifted to the left. At this time, he started working as a part-time bartender at a gay bar.

In his junior year at college, rumors were drifting around the campus that Kraft was fond of bondage. His roommate later recalled how Kraft would disappear for periods of time a few times a week and always return at odd hours of the night. Suffering from migraines and stomach pains, Kraft would take valium regularly, even in between classes.

In 1966, he moved away from the campus and shared an apartment with a friend. He was spending the majority of his free time in gay bars, and he was arrested for lewd conduct that same year for propositioning an undercover police officer. He was let go with a warning. When the rest of his class graduated in 1967, Kraft had made to repeat a class. He earned his bachelor's degree in economics several months later.

Following the assassination of Robert Kennedy, whom Kraft had campaigned for, he enlisted with the Air Force. He was sent to the Edwards Air Force Base to supervise the painting of test planes. In 1969, Kraft finally admitted that he was gay which came as a huge surprise to his family. After his admission, he was discharged from the Air Force on "medical grounds" and went back to bartending.

From then onwards, Kraft's openly gay lifestyle revolved around gay bars, alcohol, and drugs. His friends from his earlier days were shocked—even more so fourteen years later, when the truth about Kraft's actions Kraft would finally become known.

Murders

Kraft actively committed murder for more than ten years, between 1972 and 1983. He killed only males, most of them homosexual. Sometimes he mutilated and tortured his victims while they were still alive. When police were investigating the multiple murders, they found evidence of a second person's involvement. But, Kraft has never admitted this or identified an accomplice.

Timeline of known murders:

December 23, 1972 - Edward Daniel Moore, twenty

April 9, 1973 - Kevin Clark Bailey, eighteen

July 28, 1973 - Ronnie Gene Wiebe, twenty

January 17, 1975 - Keith Daven Crotwell, nineteen

January 3, 1976 - Mark Howard Hall, twenty-two

February 12, 1978 - Geoffrey Alan Nelson, eighteen

February 12, 1978 - Roger James DeVaul, twenty

April 16, 1978 - Scott Michael Hughes, eighteen

June 11, 1978 - Roland Gerald Young, twenty-three

June 19, 1978 - Richard Allen Keith, twenty

July 6, 1978 - Keith Arthur Klingbeil, twenty-three

November 18, 1978 - Michael Joseph Inderbieten, twenty

June 16, 1979 - Donnie Harold Crisel, twenty

September 3, 1980 - Robert Wyatt Loggins, nineteen

January 27, 1983 - Eric Herbert Church, twenty-one

May 14, 1983 - Terry Lee Gambrel, twenty-five

Suspected victims:

September 24, 1971 - Wayne Joseph Dukette, thirty

February 6, 1973 – "Wilmington" (unidentified male)

April 22, 1973 – "Hawth off Head" (unidentified male - from Kraft's scorecard)

December 23, 1973 - Vincent Cruz Mestas, twenty-three

June 2, 1974 - Malcolm Eugene Little, twenty

June 22, 1974 - Roger E. Dickerson, eighteen

August 3, 1974 - Thomas Paxton Lee, twenty-five

August 12, 1974 - Gary Wayne Cordova, twenty-three

November 27, 1974 - James Dale Reeves, nineteen

January 4, 1975 - John William Leras, seventeen

January 17, 1975 - Craig Jonaites, twenty-four

December 12, 1976 - Paul Joseph Fuchs, nineteen

September 30, 1978 - Richard A. Crosby, twenty

August 29, 1979 - "76" (unidentified male)

September 14, 1979 - Gregory Wallace Jolley, twenty

November 24, 1979 - Jeffrey Bryan Sayre, fifteen

February 18, 1980 - Mark Alan Marsh, twenty

April 10, 1980 - Michael Duane Cluck, eighteen

July 17, 1980 - Michael Shawn O'Fallon, seventeen

July 18, 1980 - "Portland Eck" (unidentified male)

August 20, 1981 - Christopher Williams, seventeen

January 19, 1982 - Arne Mikael Laine, twenty-four

July 29, 1982 - Robert Avila, sixteen

July 29, 1982 - Raymond Davis, thirteen

November 28, 1982 - Brian Witcher, twenty-six

December 9, 1982 - Lance Trenton Taggs, nineteen

December 9, 1982 - Dennis Alt, twenty

December 9, 1982 - Christopher Schoenborn, twenty

December 18, 1982 - Anthony Silveira, twenty-nine

Arrest and Trial

On the morning of May 14, 1983, Kraft was pulled over for driving in a weaving manner. As soon as he was stopped, he got out of his car and walked over to the patrol car. Officers suspected he was hiding something, so they walked him back to his car. In the passenger's seat was the dead body of Terry Gambrel, who had been strangled. Kraft was immediately arrested.

When police search Kraft's house, they found photographs of three men and realized they were unsolved murder cases from Southern California. One was Robert Loggins, who was killed in September of 1980, and the others were Geoffrey Nelson and Roger De Vaul, both of whom were last seen alive in February of 1983.

The rug in Kraft's garage had fibers that matched those found on Scott Hughes' body. There were also items that had once belonged to a victim who was found near Grand Rapids, Michigan. Investigators found a notebook with handwritten notes inside that were written in some sort of code. Kraft had kept a record of every murder, and he became known as a "score-card" killer.

By September of 1983, Kraft had received sixteen murder charges, nine counts of sexual mutilation, eleven counts of sodomy, and three counts of robbery. January of the following year, the prosecution added twenty-one additional murders to the charges. With the forensic evidence the police had found, Kraft was found guilty of all charges and sentenced to death.

Outcome

There was a lot of suspicion that an accomplice participated in at least some of the murders, but nothing has ever come of this. Some of this speculation was based on the theory that it would have been too difficult for Kraft to move the dead bodies around on his own.

Kraft hasn't really said anything about the murders he committed or the possibility of someone helping him, so the mystery may never be solved. Currently, he is still on death row awaiting his execution.

Trivia

- Despite Kraft getting multiple photographs of dead victims processed, no photo developer ever reported the disturbing images to the police.

JOACHIM KROLL

Date of birth: April 17, 1933

Aliases/Nicknames: Ruhr Cannibal, Ruhr Hunter, Duisburg Man-Eater

Characteristics: Cannibalism, mutilation, rape, pedophilia

Number of victims: 14

Date of murders: February 8, 1955 –July 3, 1976

Date of arrest: July 3, 1976

Murder method: Strangulation, stabbing, drowning

Known Victims: Irmgard Strehl, 19; Erika Schuletter, 12; Klara Tesmer, 24; Manuela Knodt, 16; Petra Giese, 13; Monika Tafel, 12; Barbara Bruder, 12; Hermann Schmitz; Ursula Rohling; Ilona Harke, 5; Maria Hettgen, 61; Jutta Rahn, 13; Karin Toepfer, 10; Marion Ketter, 4

Crime location: North Rhine-Westphalia, Germany

Status: Sentenced to life imprisonment. Died of a heart attack, July 1, 1991.

Background

Kroll was one of eight sons born into a mining family in Hindenburg (now part of Poland), Germany. He was a weak child who was known to be a bed-wetter which was most likely the reason behind his poor self-esteem. His father was taken prisoner and subsequently killed during World War II, and after the end of the war, the family moved to North Rhine-Westphalia, Germany.

Struggling financially as a single parent during the post-war economic crisis, his mother and her eight children moved into a small two-bedroom home. Kroll was sent to school, but he barely completed five years before he had to leave and work on the family farm. This prevented Kroll from maturing as a normal adult; he was incapable of forming regular relationships with people his own age.

By today's standards, Kroll was mentally retarded and was later found to have an IQ of just 76. He was a full-grown man with the intelligence of a young boy, and he continued living with his mother until her death, when he was twenty-two years old. Following her death, he moved to Duisburg and gained employment as a lavatory assistant. He was considered by most to be the town idiot, and he preferred to spend his time with children.

Kroll was popular among the local children because he always had plenty of toys and dolls to play with and candy to share. The building he lived in prohibited children, yet he happily invited them up to his home so they could play. The children knew him as "Uncle Joachim," and to them he seemed to be a harmless, generous man, who could relate to them on the same mental level. But what the children

218

didn't know, or didn't see, was the collection of sex dolls he kept hidden in his apartment. He would later say that he would practice strangling the dolls while masturbating.

As a remarkable show of how low his intelligence was, Kroll was eventually arrested for horrible crimes against children because of a statement he made to a neighbor. He told the neighbor not to use the shared toilet on the top floor of the building because it was "full of guts." The neighbor thought it was remains from meat butchering and summoned a plumber.

As the plumber looked down inside the toilet bowl, what he saw was truly incomprehensible. Blocking the toilet were the internal organs of a child.

Murders

After Kroll's mother died in 1955, he began committing murders. Kroll seemed to have some control over his murderous tendencies, as he was very particular about where and when he killed. He liked to kill in the same place, but always years apart and only on a few occasions. At the time, there were a number of murderers in the same area, so police were not close to capturing him.

Kroll would take his victims by surprise and immediately strangle them. Then he would take off all their clothing and have sexual intercourse with the body. Next, he would masturbate over the corpse before mutilating it. He cut off certain pieces of the body so he could eat them later. As soon as he returned home after a murder, he would have sex with a rubber doll.

Timeline of murders:

February 8, 1955 – Irmgard Strehl, nineteen

1956 – Erika Schuletter, twelve

June 16, 1959 – Klara Frieda Tesmer, twenty-four

July 26, 1959 – Manuela Knodt, sixteen

April 23, 1962 – Petra Giese, thirteen

June 4, 1962 – Monika Tafel, twelve

September 3, 1962 – Barbara Bruder, twelve

August 22, 1965 – Hermann Schmitz

September 13, 1966 – Ursula Rohling

December 22, 1966 – Ilona Harke, five

July 12, 1969 – Maria Hettgen, sixty-one

May 21, 1970 – Jutta Rahn, thirteen

May 8, 1976 – Karin Toepfer, ten

July 3, 1976 – Marion Ketter, four

Arrest and Trial

Kroll was arrested on July 3, 1976, after the murder of Marion Ketter. When police entered his apartment, they found parts of the little girl in the refrigerator; her hand was being cooked in a pot and the entrails were caught in the waste pipe. Under questioning he admitted killing Ketter as well as thirteen other victims over a twenty-year period. He admitted cannibalizing the bodies to keep his grocery bills down. While he was being held in jail, Kroll thought they were going to give him a minor operation to make him stop killing, and that he would be sent back home.

Kroll was charged with eight murders and one attempted murder. His trial, which lasted one hundred fifty-one days, ended in April of 1982. He was found guilty on all counts and sentenced to life imprisonment.

Outcome

On July 1, 1991, Kroll suffered a heart attack and died while incarcerated at Rheinbach.

RICHARD KUKLINSKI

Date of birth: April 11, 1935
Aliases/Nicknames: The Iceman
Characteristics: Contract killer
Number of victims: 6 - 100 +
Date of murders: 1949 - 1986
Date of arrest: December 17, 1986
Murder method: Shooting, stabbing, poisoning, beating
Known Victims: Charley Chase; Daniel E. Deppner; Gary T. Smith; George Malliband; Louis Masgay; Detective Peter Calabro; Paul Hoffman
Crime location: New York, New Jersey
Status: Sentenced to life imprisonment. Died of natural causes, March 6, 2006.

Background

Kuklinski was born in New Jersey to parents Stanley and Anna, the second of four children. His father, a brakeman at the railroad, was a violent alcoholic who would beat Anna and the children on a regular basis. Anna, a devout Catholic, was a very strict parent, and she too would beat the children if she deemed it necessary.

Tragedy struck the family when Kuklinski was five years old, after his older brother Florian was beaten to death by their father. Their mother told the emergency services that the boy had fallen down the stairs, and Stanley was never charged. He left the family home not long afterwards, and Kuklinski was left to take care of himself without a father figure.

The very first murder committed by Kuklinski took place in 1949 when he was only thirteen years old. At that time, there was a gang of teenagers called "The Project Boys" in the neighborhood, and they took great delight in bullying and beating Kuklinski. After one such beating, Kuklinski decided to take revenge on one of the gang members, Charley Chase. He attacked him with a piece of wood, beating him until he did not wake up. He then chopped off the boy's fingertips and removed his teeth before dumping him over a bridge.

Following the murder, Kuklinski sought out the other gang members and attacked them all with a metal pole. They were nearly beaten to death. According to Kuklinski later on in life, it was the murder of Charley Chase that taught him it was better to give than receive. From then onwards, whenever someone made him feel "bad," he hurt them.

As an adult, Kuklinski became associated with the Gambino crime family through an associate, Roy DeMeo. Initially, Kuklinski was tasked with the job of performing robberies and a variety of other jobs including pirating pornography. By now, Kuklinski had grown into a very imposing figure, standing six feet five inches and weighing around three hundred pounds. It was decided Kuklinski would be tested to determine whether he would make a good hitman for the family.

Murders

George Malliband met with Kuklinski on January 31, 1980, to sell some videos. His body was discovered in a fifty-five-gallon drum several days later. On the day he was killed, he was carrying a large sum of money with him—around twenty-seven thousand dollars.

On March 14, 1980, Kuklinski fired a shotgun at the head of Detective Calabro as he was carefully driving his car through a snowstorm. In July of 1981, Louis Masgay had a meeting with Kuklinski to discuss a videotape deal and disappeared. He had ninety-five thousand dollars hidden inside the door panel of his vehicle. His body wasn't found until fifteen months later. He had been shot in the head and then stored in a freezer, wrapped in multiple plastic bags.

Another victim who was last seen just before a scheduled meeting with Kuklinski was Paul Hoffman. He had twenty-two thousand dollars with him and was planning on buying prescription drugs from Kuklinski on April 29, 1982. To date, his body has not been located.

The last two victims, Gary Smith and Daniel Deppner, were roommates. Smith was killed on December 27, 1982, and his body was found beneath a bed in a motel. Daniel Deppner was killed by Kuklinski on May 14, 1983.

Kuklinski used a variety of methods to commit the murders including guns, knives, poison, and strangulation. Bodies were often dismembered and buried, though some were placed in the trunk of a car and then crushed at a junkyard. Kuklinski also said that on some occasions he simply left the body on a park bench.

Sometimes Kuklinski used an ice cream truck to store the bodies for a period of time before disposing of them. This interfered with the medical examiners' ability to determine the time and date of death. At one point, he was friends with Robert Pronge, known as Mister Softee. Kuklinksi claimed it was Pronge that gave him the information on how to use poisons to kill. Pronge was found shot to death in his truck in 1984, and many believe it was Kuklinski who pulled the trigger.

Timeline of known murders:

1949 - Charley Chase

January 31, 1980 - George Malliband, forty-two

March 14, 1980 - Detective Peter Calabro,

July of 1981 - Louis Masgay, fifty

April 29, 1982 - Paul Hoffman, fifty-one

December 27, 1982 - Gary Smith, forty-two

May 14, 1983 - Daniel Deppner, forty-six

Arrest and Trial

Kuklinski was arrested on December 17, 1986, based on an undercover agent's testimony. The investigation had taken six years; it was a joint operation that involved the Attorney General's Office, the New Jersey State Police, and the Bureau of Alcohol, Tobacco, and Firearms. To perform the arrest, multiple officers were deployed and the whole street was blocked off.

The trial took place in 1988 in New Jersey, and Kuklinski was convicted of committing five murders. He was sentenced to five life sentences and wouldn't be eligible for parole until he was over one hundred years old.

A second trial took place in 2003, for the murder of Detective Peter Calabro. Kuklinski was again convicted and had another thirty years added on to his sentence. While he was incarcerated, Kuklinski agreed to numerous interviews with criminologists, psychiatrists, writers, prosecutors, and television producers.

During these interviews, Kuklinski provided greater insight into the type of man and killer he was. He stated he would never harm or kill children or women. Some of his murder techniques were extremely sadistic, including leaving a victim tied up in a cave so rats could eat them alive. These particular murders were filmed so the client could have proof that the victim suffered terribly before dying.

Outcome

During an interview with Philip Carlo prior to his death, Kuklinski stated he had been involved with the kidnapping and murder of Jimmy Hoffa, the well-known union boss who had disappeared without a trace. In a previous interview though, he claimed he didn't know anything about what had happened to Hoffa—apart from rumors that he had been murdered and placed in a barrel that was then put into a Japanese car that was compacted and shipped overseas. To date, there has been no evidence to support this story.

Kuklinski was transferred to the St. Francis Medical Center in Trenton, New Jersey, and died at 1:15 a.m. on March 5, 2006. Although he was seventy years of age, his death was considered by many to be suspicious, as he had been due to testify against Sammy Gravano, the Gambino crime family underboss. Kuklinsky was going to testify that Gravano had ordered him to kill Detective Peter Calabro. Within a few days of Kuklinski's death, all charges against Gravano were dropped as they were not confident of getting a conviction without his testimony.

Before his death, Kuklinski had commented to family members that he thought he was being poisoned by the Gambino crime ring while he was in prison to prevent him from testifying. After he died, a renowned forensic pathologist was asked to examine the autopsy results to determine if there had in fact been any poisoning. He concluded there was no evidence of poisoning and Kuklinski had died from natural causes.

Trivia

- In April of 2006, news reports surfaced that Kuklinski had confessed to author Philip Carlo that he was part of a group who had kidnapped and murdered famed union boss Jimmy Hoffa.
- However, during an earlier HBO interview he denied any knowledge of Hoffa's fate. Kuklinski claimed that he had only heard rumors, specifically, that Hoffa had been killed, put in a barrel, placed into a Japanese car which was compacted with other cars, and then shipped overseas.

LEONARD LAKE AND CHARLES NG

Date of birth: October 29, 1945; December 24, 1960

Aliases/Nicknames: Lake - Leonard J. Hill, Alan Drey, Randy Jacobsen, Robin Stapley, Leonard Hill, Charles Gunnar, Paul Cosner

Characteristics: Rape, torture, robbery

Number of victims: 11 -25

Date of murders: 1983 - 1985

Date of arrest: June 2, 1985; July 6, 1986

Murder method: Shooting

Known Victims: Harvey Dubs, his wife Deborah, and infant son, Sean; Lonnie Bond Sr., his wife, Brenda O'Connor, and his infant son, Lonnie Bond Jr; Clifford Peranteau; Jeffrey Gerald; Michael Carroll; Kathleen Allen; Robin Scott Stapley; Randy Jacobson

Crime location: Calaveras County, California

Status: Lake - committed suicide by cyanide shortly after his arrest. Ng - sentenced to death and awaiting execution

Background

Leonard Lake

Lake was born in San Francisco. Following his parents' divorce when he was six years old, he was sent with his siblings to live with their grandparents. He was described as a bright child, but at a young age he had an unhealthy fondness for pornography. Apparently, his grandmother would encourage him to take naked photos of his sisters, and later it was alleged Lake would also extort his sisters for sexual favors.

At nineteen, Lake joined the Marine Corps and became a radio operator. He served two tours of duty in the Vietnam War before he was diagnosed with a schizoid personality disorder in 1971. He was medically discharged from the Marines and was given psychotherapy. He enrolled at college in San Jose but only attended for one semester before dropping out and moving into a hippie commune.

Lake married in 1975. But, the marriage didn't last long once his wife discovered he was making amateur pornographic films. He was a main character in the films, and in each one, sadomasochism and bondage were prevalent. Lake went on to marry Claralyn Balasz in 1981, after he was released from prison for car theft. This marriage also didn't last, as Claralyn couldn't tolerate his increasingly erratic behavior. Lake also tried to push her into starring in the pornographic films which was the final straw for Claralyn.

In 1982, Lake was picked up by police and arrested for a firearms violation, but he skipped bail. He moved to his ex-wife's ranch in a remote area in Wilseyville and met Charles Ng the same year. The two men became friends and lived together at the ranch. Discovering they had the same tendencies, they had the perfect location for carrying out their abhorrent deeds.

Charles Ng

Born in Hong Kong, Ng's father was a wealthy Chinese executive, and according to Ng, a harsh disciplinarian who dished out abuse. Ng was a loner as a teenager and got into trouble a lot, resulting in him being expelled from a number of good schools. At fifteen years of age, he was caught shoplifting, and his father decided to send him to a boarding school in England. However, Ng continued to steal and was expelled soon after he arrived at the school. He was then sent back to Hong Kong.

In 1978, Ng moved to America on a student visa and attended Notre Dame College in California. However, he dropped out after only completing one semester. He was involved in a hit-and-run motor vehicle accident soon after. In an attempt to try to escape prosecution, he enlisted in the Marine Corps.

To become a Marine, you have to be a United States citizen, which Ng was not. But, he was able to bluff his way in using false documentation in 1979. A year after he joined, he was arrested for stealing automatic weapons while stationed in Hawaii. Fearing the result of a court martial, he fled, becoming a deserter. He managed to find his way back to California and he subsequently moved in with Lake.

The mobile home they shared was raided by federal authorities in 1982, and both men were arrested following the discovery of a huge stash of explosives and weapons. Ng was sent back into the custody of the Marines, and he subsequently orchestrated a plea deal, receiving an eighteen-month sentence in the military stockade. Lake had been set free on bail; he then absconded, drifting around under numerous aliases until he caught up with Ng again.

Murders

The meeting of Lake and Ng would have a tragic effect on those who crossed paths with them, particularly between the years of 1983 and 1985. The two men went on a murderous spree, killing neighbors, associates, and strangers they met, regardless of whether they were men, women, or children.

Their strategy was to kill the men and children first, then kidnap the women and keep them in a structure Lake had built next to his cabin which he called the "dungeon." There, the women would be repeatedly raped, tortured, and subjected to psychological abuse—all while being videotaped. The women were called their "sex slaves" and would only be killed when they tired of them.

It was later discovered in Lake's journal that he anticipated a nuclear war. This was why he had built the "bunker" or dungeon; he planned on rebuilding the human race after the war was over using his female slaves. He referred to this plan as "Operation Miranda," the name of a character in "The Collector," a book by John Fowles.

Timeline of known murders:

July 25, 1984 - Harvey Dubs, thirty

July 25, 1984 - Deborah Dubs, thirty-three

July 25, 1984 - Sean Dubs, one

October of 1984 - Randy Jacobson, thirty-four

April of 1985 - Kathleen Allen, eighteen

April of 1985 - Michael Carroll, twenty-three

May of 1985 - Lonnie Bond, twenty-seven

May of 1985 - Brenda O'Connor

May of 1985 - Lonnie Bond Jr., two

May of 1985 - Robin Scott Stapley, twenty-six

Unspecified dates in 1983:

Charles Gunnar

Donald Lake (Lake's younger brother; disappeared and was presumed to have been killed by Lake and Ng)

Suspected:

November of 1984 - Paul Cosner, thirty-nine

July of 1984 - Donald Giuletti, thirty-six

Arrest and Trial

Ng was seen shoplifting from a store in South San Francisco on June 2, 1985. He had fled the scene before the police arrived, but Lake, who was in his own car at the scene, was arrested when a pistol was discovered in his car. He told police his name was Robin Stapley and produced a driver's license in Stapley's name. But, Stapley was only twenty-six, and police could tell Lake was much older than that. He was taken back to the station to be questioned.

While searching Lake's cabin in Wilseyville, they discovered Lake's collection of weapons and other items suggesting he was a survivalist. They proceeded to search the ranch thoroughly. Investigators found a burial site close to the dungeon. Through a long and difficult process, they found approximately forty pounds of crushed and burned bone fragments. In all, the number of bone pieces they found added up to at least eleven bodies.

A map was found that led investigators to a spot where two five-gallon buckets were buried. They contained envelopes with names on them and IDs belonging to the victims which lead to an estimated twenty-five victims in total. One of the buckets contained journals Lake had written in during 1983 and 1984, as well as two videotapes. One tape showed the torture of Brenda O'Connor. The other was a film of the severe assault against Deborah Dubs; it was so extreme, there was no way she could have survived.

On the run, Ng fled to Canada, but his shoplifting problem soon got him into trouble. He was arrested on July 6, 1985, in Alberta, following the shooting of a security guard who had tried to restrain Ng after he'd shoplifted. Ng was subsequently convicted of assault with a weapon, shoplifting, and possession of a concealed weapon. He was sentenced to four and a half years. When he had finished the sentence, he was retained in prison due to the extradition request for the murders in California.

Ng attempted to fight against the extradition because California had the death penalty and Canada did not. The Canadian Supreme Court denied his request and he was extradited to California in 1991. There he was charged with twelve counts of first-degree murder, and so began one of longest trials in American legal history.

A total of ten attorneys worked for Ng, some of whom Ng sued for malpractice before he even went to trial. Eventually he decided to represent himself, which further delayed his trial by a whole year. Six years passed between the time he was extradited to the start of his trial; he finally appeared in court in October of 1998.

The trial ended in February of 1999, and Ng was found guilty of eleven of the twelve murders. He received the death penalty. A motion was put forward requesting the sentence to be reduced, but the presiding judge refused, and the original sentence remained. By the time it was all over, it was estimated that the prosecution of Ng had cost California around twenty million dollars.

Outcome

The day Lake was arrested, he was placed in a jail cell to await questioning by the investigating officers. He asked for a glass of water which he received. He then proceeded to swallow cyanide pills that he had sewn into his shirt collar. Lake was taken to the hospital. Four days later, on June 6, his life support was turned off and he quickly died.

Ng remains on death row, awaiting his date with the executioner.

Trivia

Quotes:

-   "Give my baby back to me: I'll do anything you want." Victim Brenda O'Connor. "You're going to do anything we want anyway." Leonard Lake
-   "God meant women for cooking, cleaning house and sex. And when they are not in use they should be locked up." Leonard Lake
-   Donald Lake, the younger brother of Leonard, disappeared in 1983. He is presumed dead, but no remains have been found.
-   Charles Gunnar was a friend of Lake's from when they were in the military together. His remains were discovered at the ranch in September of 1992.
-   "The Ballad of Leonard and Charles" is a song written about the two killers by Exodus, a thrash metal band.

DERRICK TODD LEE

Date of birth: November 5, 1968

Aliases/Nicknames: The Baton Rouge Serial Killer

Characteristics: Rape

Number of victims: 7 +

Date of murders: August 23, 1992 – March 3, 2003

Date of arrest: May 27, 2003

Murder method: Stabbing

Known Victims: Randi Mebruer, 28; Gina Wilson Green, 41; Geralyn Barr DeSoto, 21; Charlotte Murray Pace, 21; Pamela Kinamore, 44; Trinesha Dene Colomb, 23; Carrie Lynn Yoder, 26

Crime location: Baton Rouge, Lafayette, Louisiana

Status: Sentenced to death. Died of heart disease, on January 21, 2016.

Background

Lee was born in 1968 in St. Francisville, Louisiana, to parents Samuel Roth and Florence Lee. His father left soon after Lee was born, which his mother thought was for the best given Samuel's mental illness. Samuel was later confined to a mental institution after attempting to murder his ex-wife. Florence went on to marry Coleman Barrow, who took care of the children as if they were his own flesh and blood.

By the time he was eleven years old, Lee was peeping in the windows at girls in the neighborhood. Later, he also claimed he liked torturing small animals. When he was thirteen, he was caught committing a minor burglary but received no punishment. The police were already well aware of his propensity for peeping in windows, but he hadn't displayed any violent tendencies at that time. This changed when he was sixteen, however, when he pulled out a knife during a fight with another boy. At seventeen, he was arrested for peeping but still managed to avoid being sent to juvenile detention.

Lee's obsession with peeping continued as an adult, even after he married Jaqueline Denise Sims in 1988. They had two children together, Derrick Jr and Dorris. Early on in the marriage, Lee was arrested and charged with entering an inhabited dwelling without authorization. In the years that followed, Lee seemed to be living two different lives. On the one hand he was a good father who worked hard to support his family; on the other hand, he dressed himself up and frequented bars to pick up women.

The couple inherited a large amount of money following the accidental death of Jacqueline's father, and Lee couldn't have been happier. Now he could dress even better, spend money on women, and have flashy cars. He ended up with a regular mistress, Casandra Green, who gave birth to their son in 1999. By now the money had all been spent, and Lee was back to working and living off wages.

In 2000, Lee was stressed with financial difficulties, and he and Casandra were fighting a lot. This eventually escalated to violence, and she sought a protective order against him. However, he found her three days later in the parking lot of a bar and beat her. Arrested and charged, Lee spent the next year in prison. Upon his parole, he was ordered to wear monitoring equipment and remain under house arrest. Though he violated this order, he wasn't returned to prison.

Murders

Lee came across two teenagers "making out" in a parked car in 1993, and attacked them, using a harvesting tool that was six feet long. He hacked ferociously at the young couple until he was startled by an approaching car and fled. Miraculously, the couple survived and would identify Lee six years later. Over the next ten years, Lee's attacks became even more violent, leading to a number of murders that would eventually be solved using DNA.

The first known victim of Lee was Randi Mebruer who disappeared from her home in Zachary, Louisiana on April 18, 1998. There was blood throughout the house. Although it was certain she was murdered, her body was never found.

Gina Wilson Green was murdered in her home in Baton Rouge on September 23, 2001. Her body was found the following day when she hadn't turned up at work and a colleague came by to check on her. The medical examiner determined she had been raped and strangled to death.

In Addis, Louisiana, Geralyn Barr DeSoto was killed on January 14, 2002. She had been killed at her home on Stanford Avenue. She was stabbed so severely she was almost decapitated. Her body was discovered when her husband came home from work later that day.

On May 31, 2002, Charlotte Murray Pace was raped before being stabbed to death in her home in Baton Rouge. She had moved to Sharlo Avenue from Stanford Avenue after Gina Wilson Green was killed. A screwdriver had been used to stab Pace eighty-three times.

Pamela Piglia Kinamore went missing from her home in Baton Rouge on July 12, 2002. Four days later, her body was discovered underneath the Whiskey Bay Bridge. Her throat had been slit so severely that her head was almost removed; she had been raped.

Trinesha Dene Colomb had been visiting her mother's grave on November 21, 2002, in Grand Coteau, Louisiana, when she disappeared. Three days later, her raped and beaten body was found by a hunter in the woods in Scott, Louisiana.

The final known victim was Carrie Lynn Yoder. She disappeared from her home in Baton Rouge on March 3, 2003. Ten days later, her body was found underneath the Whiskey Bay Bridge. Like the other victims she had been raped and badly beaten before she was strangled to death.

Timeline of murders:

April 18, 1998 - Randi Mebruer, twenty-eight

September 24, 2001 - Gina Wilson Green, forty-one

January 14, 2002 - Geralyn DeSoto, twenty-one

May 31, 2002 - Charlotte Murray Pace, twenty-one

July 9, 2002 - Diane Alexander

July 12, 2002 - Pamela Kinamore, forty-four

November 21, 2002 - Trinesha Dene Colomb, twenty-three

March 3, 2003 - Carrie Lynn Yoder

Other possible victims:

August 23, 1992 - Connie Warner

June 13, 1997 - Eugenie Boisfontaine

Arrest and Trial

In May of 2003, an identikit sketch of the alleged serial killer was released by a Multi-Agency Taskforce of the Baton Rouge police. At the same time, authorities were visiting the local parishes and collecting DNA samples from all the males they came across to try to find a suspect. One of those men was Lee; the investigators were interested in him right away because of his likeness to the sketch and his criminal history.

A few weeks later, the DNA testing came back as a positive match to samples found on the bodies of Green, Yoder, Kinamore, Pace, and Colomb. The same day Lee had submitted his sample, he took his family and left Louisiana. He was caught and arrested in Atlanta on May 27, 2003, and taken back to Louisiana.

His first trial, for the murder of Geralyn DeSoto, took place in August of 2004. He was found guilty and sentenced to life imprisonment without the possibility of parole. Just a few months later, in October, he went on trial for the rape and murder of Charlotte Murray Pace. Again he was found guilty, and he received the death penalty.

Outcome

Lee was transported to a hospital for medical treatment and died on January 21, 2016, from heart disease.

He is still a suspect in multiple murders, but these are unlikely to be solved due to his death.

CODY LEGEBOKOFF

Date of birth: January 21, 1990

Aliases/Nicknames: Nil

Characteristics: Rape, sexual assault

Number of victims: 4

Date of murders: October 2009 - November 2010

Date of arrest: November 28, 2010

Murder method: Blunt force trauma

Known Victims: Jill Stacey Stuchenko, 35; Cynthia Frances Maas, 35; Natasha Lynn Montgomery, 23; Loren Donn Leslie, 15

Crime location: Prince George, Vanderhoof, Canada

Status: Sentenced to life imprisonment with parole after twenty-five years.

Background

Tall, blond, and attractive, those who knew Legebokoff would never in a million years have thought him capable of murder. He came from a good and loving family and had what could only be described as a great childhood. He was popular with his peers all through school, and he competed in ice hockey, downhill skiing, and other sports. He had gotten into minor trouble from time to time with the local police, but never for anything that warranted concern.

When Legebokoff moved from Fort St. James to Prince George, he moved into an apartment with three female friends. He was working as a mechanic, and he liked to spend time on social media. He hadn't displayed any violent tendencies; all who knew him found him to be "normal," just an everyday guy that got along with most people.

That would all change in 2010, following a routine traffic stop by the Royal Canadian Mounted Police. What followed would leave his family and friends completely shocked and bewildered. The young man they knew had another side that nobody ever expected.

Murders

On October 9, 2009, Jill Stacey Stuchenko disappeared; her body was found in gravel in British Columbia four days later. The next known victim was Natasha Lynn Montgomery who disappeared around August 31, 2010. Although her remains have not been found, her DNA was discovered in the apartment Legebokoff was living in.

Cynthia Frances Maas went missing on September 10, 2010. Her body was found a month later in a park, and she had suffered numerous injuries. Her jaw and cheekbone had been fractured, her neck showed evidence of being stomped on, there was a penetrating wound in her shoulder blade, and she'd received multiple blunt-force trauma injuries to her head.

The last known victim was teenager Loren Leslie, who was killed on November 27, 2010. Legally blind, Leslie was believed to have met Legebokoff online through a website.

Timeline of murders:

October 9, 2009 - Jill Stacey Stuchenko, thirty-five

August 31, 2010 - Natasha Lynn Montgomery, twenty-three

September 10, 2010 - Cynthia Frances Maas, thirty-five

November 27, 2010 - Loren Leslie, fifteen

Arrest and Trial

Legebokoff was seen speeding in his truck on Highway 27 in British Columbia on November 27, 2010; he was subsequently pulled over by a police officer. At first, the officer thought Legebokoff must have been out poaching, because it was unusual to see anyone on the highway at that time of night in the frigid November temperatures.

Another officer arrived on the scene. As they approached Legebokoff in his truck they noticed he had blood smeared on his chin, face, and legs, and there was more blood on the mat beneath his feet. As they searched the truck they found a wrench and a multi-tool also covered in blood. A wallet in a monkey backpack carried an ID card belonging to Loren Leslie. When questioned about the blood, Legebokoff said it was from a deer he had poached.

Although there was no deer in the truck, they arrested him and called a conservation officer to the scene to look for the deer. As he started tracking Legebokoff's footprints in the snow, he came across the body of Leslie instead.

After his arrest, Legebokoff's DNA samples linked him to the murders of Maas, Montgomery, and Stuchenko. He was charged with four counts of murder, and his trial eventually took place in June of 2014. He pleaded not guilty, saying he had been involved with three of the murders but that he wasn't the person who had taken the victims' lives.

Despite his attempts to throw the blame on unidentified others, he was found guilty of the four murders. He received four life sentences with the possibility of parole after twenty-five years.

Outcome

Legebokoff filed an appeal in February of 2015 due to issues with his legal representation throughout the trial and decisions made by the court to change the venue for the trial. The Court of Appeal in British Columbia dismissed his appeal in September of 2016, and the original conviction and sentencing was kept.

BOBBIE JOE LONG

Date of birth: October 14, 1953

Aliases/Nicknames: Robert Joseph Long, The Adman Rapist, The Classified Ad Rapist, Joseph Long

Characteristics: Rape

Number of victims: 10 +

Date of murders: March 28 - November 11, 1984

Date of arrest: November 16, 1984

Murder method: Strangulation, shooting, cutting of throat

Known Victims: Ngeun Thi Long, 20; Michelle Denise Simms, 22; Elizabeth B. Loudenback, 22; Chanel Devon Williams, 18; Karen Beth Dinsfriend, 28; Kimberly Kyle Hopps, 22; Virginia Lee Johnson, 18; Kim Marie Swann, 21; Vicki Elliott; an unidentified woman; Artis Wick

Crime location: Tampa Bay Area, Florida

Status: Sentenced to death, awaiting execution.

Background

Long was born with a genetic mutation giving him an extra X chromosome, and during puberty he developed breasts like a female. This resulted in severe teasing by other children, and after his parents separated, Long slept in his mother's bed until he was a teenager. The relationship between Long and his mother was dysfunctional, largely because she went through a series of boyfriends who only ever lasted a brief period. He also suffered a number of head injuries as a child, but it is not clear what these were or how they occurred.

In 1974, Long and his high school girlfriend got married, and they went on to have two children. The marriage was short-lived, and she filed for divorce in 1980. A year later, Long would embark on a long and violent period of raping women. He would go through advertisements for appliances, and if the advertiser was a woman who was alone, he would rape her. He was arrested for rape in 1981 and convicted. But, he requested a new trial and the charges were eventually dropped.

Long moved to the Tampa Bay area in 1983. At that time, the region experienced an average of thirty to thirty-five murders per year. A year after Long's arrival, this rate escalated dramatically, and murdered women were being found every other week. Was this a coincidence? It wouldn't take too long to find out.

Murders

In 1984, Long began an eight-month-long period of murder, with an average of one murder each week between March and November. He would drive around looking for suitable victims, often picking up prostitutes and women who were hanging out in seedy bars. He always made sure they were alone, and he later claimed that the women always approached him.

The women would agree to get into his car and he would take them back to an apartment. He would then tie them up with ligature collars and rope. After raping his victim, he would then kill them by strangulation, bludgeoning, or slitting their throat.

When Long disposed of the bodies, he would pose them in bizarre and degrading positions, usually with their legs spread apart. The bodies were often found in the woods or near a rural roadside. Of the victims, two were exotic dancers, five were prostitutes, and one was a student; the occupation of the other victim was unknown.

Timeline of known murders:

March 27, 1984 - Artis Wick

May 4, 1984 - Ngeun Thi Long, twenty

May 27, 1984 - Michelle Simms, twenty-two

June 8, 1984 - Elizabeth Loudenback, twenty-two

September 7, 1984 - Vicky Elliott, twenty-one

September 30, 1984 - Chanel Devon Williams, eighteen

October 7, 1984 - Kimberly Hopps, twenty-two

October 13, 1984 - Karen Beth Dinsfriend

November 6, 1984 - Virginia Johnson, eighteen

November 10, 1984 - Kimberly Swann, twenty-one

November 16, 1984 - Vicky M. Elliot, twenty-one

Arrest and Trial

A large amount of forensic evidence had been collected from the crime scenes including carpet fibers, ligature marks, semen, and rope knots. These led to three warrants being issued for Long's arrest on suspicion of sexual battery and the kidnapping of Lisa McVey. He was arrested and charged on November 16, 1984.

Long confessed to the attack on McVey. But, when the detectives began asking him about the unsolved murder cases he didn't want to answer their questions. They produced photos of the victims and, at this point, Long said he needed an attorney. An attorney was never called, and he went on to confess to committing eight murders.

A plea bargain was reached and on September 24, 1985, he pleaded guilty to all charges. Another trial for the murder of Michelle Simms took place in July of 1986. This trial only lasted a week, and Long was found guilty and sentenced to death.

Outcome

In total, Long received the following sentences:

- – One five-year sentence
- – Four ninety-nine-year sentences
- – Twenty-eight life sentences
- – One death sentence

Long is still on death row awaiting his turn in the electric chair.

LONG ISLAND SERIAL KILLER

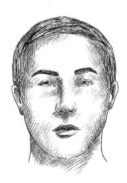

Date of birth: Unknown

Aliases/Nicknames: The Gilgo Killer, The Gilgo Beach Killer, The Seashore Serial Killer, The Craigslist Ripper

Characteristics: Prostitutes, escorts

Number of victims: 10 - 16

Date of murders: Possibly 1996 - 2016

Date of arrest: Never identified

Murder method: Strangulation

Known Victims: Maureen Brainard-Barnes, 25; Melissa Barthelemy, 24; Megan Waterman, 22; Amber Lynn Costello, 27; Jessica Taylor, 20; others unidentified

Crime location: New York

Status: Not identified or apprehended.

Background

The Long Island Serial Killer was known by many names, but his true identity has never been uncovered. It is believed he was responsible for up to sixteen murders over a twenty-year period, and his victims typically were involved in prostitution. After the murders were committed, the bodies would be tossed along the Ocean Parkway near Gilgo Beach, Oak Beach, and Jones Beach State Park.

There is little more terrifying than knowing a rampant serial killer had been committing numerous murders without being caught. There isn't even a good suspect at the top of the list. It's believed the Long Island Serial Killer could have still been operating as recently as 2016, leaving the authorities scrambling and calling on all possible resources to try to identify and capture the murderer before he kills again.

Murders

It is believed the Long Island Serial Killer may be responsible for between ten to sixteen people over the course of two decades, most of whom were involved in the prostitution trade. Their bodies were usually dumped along the Ocean Parkway, an area near Long Island. In total, there have been ten sets of remains (some of which were only partial) found, and many of the victims remain unidentified.

Maureen Brainard-Barnes went missing from Long Island on July 9, 2007. An escort, she found her clients by advertising her services online, which was a common practice in the business. Her body was found in December of 2010.

On July 10, 2009, Melissa Barthelemy disappeared from the Bronx. She also advertised online as an escort. On the night she disappeared, she had been with a client who paid nine hundred dollars directly into her bank account for her services. She tried to call her ex-boyfriend but couldn't get through.

Another escort who advertised on Craigslist was Megan Waterman of Maine. She disappeared on June 6, 2010. At the time, she had told her boyfriend she was going out. She never returned, and her remains were discovered in December of 2010.

Prostitute and heroin addict Amber Lynn Costello was killed on September 2, 2010, in North Babylon, New York. A stranger had apparently offered her fifteen hundred dollars for sexual services. She disappeared after leaving to meet the man.

Twenty-year-old Jessica Taylor went missing in July of 2003. Her torso was found on July 26, east of Gilgo Beach, the hands and head missing. She was identified using DNA. Further remains of Taylor were found in May of 2011. Taylor had been working as a prostitute at the time of her murder.

Timeline of murders:

June 28, 1997 - "Peaches"

November 19, 2000 - Jane Doe VI

July of 2003 - Jessica Taylor, twenty

July 9, 2007 - Maureen Brainard-Barnes, twenty-five

June 6, 2010 - Megan Waterman, twenty-two

July 10, 2009 - Melissa Barthelemy, twenty-four

September 2, 2010 - Amber Lynn Costello, twenty-seven

April 4, 2011- John Doe

April 4, 2011 - Baby Doe

April 11, 2011 - Jane Doe III

April 11, 2011 - Jane Doe VII

Possible victims:

March 3, 2007 - "Cherries"

May 17, 2011 - Tanya Rush, thirty-nine

May 1, 2010 - Shannan Maria Gilbert

March 16, 2013 - Natasha Jugo, thirty-one

Suspects
Profile:

- White male
- Aged twenties to forties
- Access to burlap sacks
- May have law enforcement knowledge
- May have ties to law enforcement

Joel Rifkin

An active serial killer in the area at the time, many have speculated that Joel Rifkin may have been the Long Island Killer. However, although he has confessed to his other crimes, he denies being responsible for any of the Long Island murders.

Former Police Chief James Burke

Shannan Gilbert's family raised the possibility that Burke may have been responsible for the murders. He was convicted in November of 2016 for trying to conceal that he had beaten a man who had stolen a bag from Burke's vehicle which happened to be full of pornography and sex toys. There has been no other evidence to suggest Burke may be responsible—or capable—of committing these atrocious murders.

PEDRO LÓPEZ

Date of birth: October 8, 1948
Aliases/Nicknames: The Monster of the Andes
Characteristics: Rape, pedophilia
Number of victims: 53 - 300 +
Date of murders: 1969 - 1980, possibly 2002
Date of arrest: March 9, 1980
Murder method: Strangulation
Known Victims: Unnamed young girls aged 9 - 12 years
Crime location: Colombia, Peru, Ecuador
Status: Absconded from authorities in 1998 - unknown status or whereabouts.

Background

According to his own statements, López had a terrible start in life as one of thirteen children born to a prostitute. At the age of eight, his mother caught him inappropriately fondling his little sister and she threw him out of the house. A man picked the boy up and took him to an empty house where he proceeded to sodomize young López repeatedly. Thus, he had been brutalized sexually, admonished and abandoned by his mother, and ostracized from his family.

When López was twelve, an American family took him in, and he was enrolled in a school that was primarily for orphans. According to López, he was molested by one of the male teachers, so he ran away. He ended up spending some time in prison when he was eighteen, at which point he claimed to have been gang-raped. He claimed he sought revenge on his attackers while still incarcerated, killing three of them. But this has not been proven.

With so much of his childhood and youth consisting of sexual assault and rape, it is no surprise that following his release from prison López became exactly the person his own assailants had been. But, he took it one step further, later confessing to the murders of over three hundred girls.

Murders

After his release from prison, López went on an astonishing murder spree in Colombia and Ecuador, averaging three murders each week. With over three hundred young girls missing, the authorities initially thought they were being sold into sexual slavery and prostitution. They didn't suspect a serial killer was at work until López was arrested for a failed abduction.

Arrest and Trial

On March 9, 1980, López tried to kidnap a young girl. But, he was disturbed by market traders and trapped until police arrived. During an interview at the police station, he confessed to the multitude of murders. Police initially didn't believe him. Then a flash flood unearthed a mass grave, and they were convinced he was telling the truth.

Outcome

In 1998, López was released from the psychiatric wing of a hospital on a fifty-dollar bail to await his murder trial. However, he absconded and has not been seen or heard from since. To date, it is not known if he is still alive or if he is dead.

PETER LUNDIN

Date of birth: February 15, 1972

Aliases/Nicknames: Bjarne Skounborg

Characteristics: Parricide, dismemberment

Number of victims: 4

Date of murders: April of 1991 and June of 2000

Date of arrest: July 5, 2000

Murder method: Broken neck, strangulation

Known Victims: His mother; Marianne Pedersen and her two sons

Crime location: North Carolina and Denmark

Status: Sentenced to life imprisonment.

Background

Lundin was born in Denmark to parents Ole and Anna. When he was seven years old, the family migrated to the United States, settling in Maggie Valley, North Carolina. His childhood is described as unremarkable, with no apparent indications of violence. Although, he did later say that he and his father would abuse his mother regularly.

In 1991, an argument allegedly took place between Lundin and his mother over a haircut, and Lundin proceeded to strangle his mother to death. His father, Ole, then helped him hide the body by burying her on a beach at nearby Cape Hatteras. It would take eight months for her remains to be found, and Lundin and his father were quickly arrested.

Lundin, nineteen years old at the time, was sentenced to serve fifteen years in prison; his father received two years for being an accomplice after the fact. While in prison, Lundin was the subject of a Danish television interview, during which he was filmed with half his face painted black. This interview was later shown to Professor Sten Levander, a Swedish psychiatrist, who gave Lundin a score of 39 out of 40 on the Psychopathy Checklist.

In 1999, prisons were overloaded, so Lundin was released and deported back to Denmark. Upon his return, he married a woman who later kicked him out of the home for being violent toward her. It was then that he met Marianne Pedersen and her two children—a meeting that would lead to tragedy for the young woman and her boys.

Murders

When Lundin met Pedersen, she was working in a brothel in Rødovre, Copenhagen. When Pedersen and her two children were reported missing on July 3, 2000, Lundin told authorities that they had gone on vacation and he was there to paint her house. When police searched the house, they found traces of blood in the basement and in Pedersen's car.

The bodies of Pedersen and her two boys have never been found, though small amounts of human tissue was discovered in the house. Forensic evidence also revealed markings on the floor that indicated an axe and an angle grinder had been used. Police then assumed the victims had been dismembered and disposed of.

Timeline of known murders:

April 1991 - Anna Lundin

June 16, 2000 - Marianne Pedersen and her two sons

Arrest and Trial

Lundin was arrested on July 5, 2000 and charged with the murders. He made a statement three weeks later claiming he had discovered Pedersen unconscious from drugs; he then hit her, resulting in her death. He said he had dismembered the bodies. Lundin said he withheld this at first because he didn't think the police would believe that he didn't intend to kill Pedersen due to his history.

Lundin changed his statement again on October 10, 2000. This time he admitted he was responsible for the murders; he had killed Pedersen because he heard her talking sweetly to another man on the phone. He had broken her neck and then the necks of the two young boys.

At the end of his trial in 2001, Lundin was found guilty of the three murders. He was sentenced to life imprisonment.

Outcome

While incarcerated, Lundin has filed a number of lawsuits against journalists and politicians. The first was filed against a journalist who made the statement: "We are, basically, not clinical psychopaths in the Peter Lundin category." This sentence appeared in an editorial that wasn't even about Lundin. The case went to court where it was settled, and the journalist was cleared of any wrongdoing.

Another lawsuit was filed in November of 2008 against Pia Kjærsgaard, the leader of the Danish People's Party. During a program on television, Lundin was described as "callous" which prompted he to file the lawsuit. He demanded compensation of one hundred thousand kroner but lost the case.

Lundin decided to change his name while in prison, and he is now known as Bjarne Skounborg.

Trivia

- Lundin was married three times while he was incarcerated, including his first stint in prison for murdering his mother.

KENNETH MCDUFF

Date of birth: March 21, 1946

Aliases/Nicknames: The Broomstick Killer, The Broomstick Murderer, Richard Fowler

Characteristics: Kidnapping, rape, torture, robbery

Number of victims: 9 - 14 +

Date of murders: August 6, 1966 - March 1, 1992

Date of arrest: May 4, 1992

Murder method: Strangulation

Known Victims: Robert Brand, 17; Edna (Louise) Sullivan, 16; Marcus Dunman, 15; Sarafia Parker, 31; Brenda Thompson; Regenia Moore, 17; Cynthia Gonzalez, 23; Colleen Reed; Valencia Joshua; Melissa Northrup, 22

Crime location: Texas

Status: Executed by lethal injection on November 17, 1998.

Background

McDuff was born in Rosebud, Texas, in 1946. His father John had a concreting business that was successful during the construction boom of the area during the 1960s. His mother Addie indulged McDuff as a child, and she was once nicknamed "pistol packing momma" after threating a school bus driver with a gun after McDuff's older brother was kicked off the bus. McDuff became known as a bully; he would often pick on those who were smaller, weaker, and younger than himself. At one point he picked a fight with the wrong boy though and was beaten. He left school and started working for his father.

In 1964, when he was eighteen, he was charged and convicted of committing twelve counts of burglary and attempted burglary spanning three counties in Texas. He received twelve sentences of four years each that were meant to be served concurrently, but he was paroled in 1965. He would later end up back in prison following a fight, but he didn't remain there for long. By 1966, he had made friends with an eighteeen-year-old young man named Roy Dale Green who would end up serving as McDuff's partner in the crimes that followed.

Murders

McDuff and his friend Roy Dale Green were driving around on August 6, 1966, when they came across three teenagers standing next to a car on a baseball field in Everman Texas. It was 10:00 p.m.

McDuff noticed Louise Sullivan, whom he thought was pretty, and parked a short distance away. Producing a gun, he approached the teens and forced Sullivan, along with Marcus Dunman and Robert Brand, into the trunk of their car.

McDuff drove off and Green followed behind driving McDuff's car. They drove into a field off the highway. After they stopped the cars, McDuff made Sullivan get out of the trunk and get into the trunk of his own car. He then fired six times into the trunk, killing Brand and Dunman. Green wiped any fingerprints off the car, and they drove to another location in McDuff's car.

Sullivan was raped by McDuff, and then by Green, who did so somewhat under duress. The men raped her repeatedly. Then McDuff got a piece of broomstick out of the car and used it to choke Sullivan to death. Her body was dumped in the bushes nearby.

A couple of days later, Green ended up confessing what they had done to the parents of an acquaintance, and they told his mother. Green was urged to turn himself in, which lead to McDuff also being arrested. Green served eleven years in prison. Although McDuff received three death penalties, his sentence was later commuted to life. Remarkably, he was released on parole in 1989.

On October 10, 1991, drug addicted prostitute Brenda Thompson was picked up by McDuff in Waco, Texas. After tying her up, he was driving along when he saw a police roadblock. He stopped about fifty feet before reaching the patrol cars. As an officer walked toward the truck, Thompson started kicking out the windshield, so McDuff took off, driving straight through the roadblock. When he reached a wooded area, he tortured Thompson and killed her.

Witnesses saw McDuff and prostitute Regenia Moore engaged in an argument at a motel in Waco on October 15, 1991. McDuff and Moore drove off. After reaching a remote area, he tied Moore up and killed her. His next victim was Colleen Reed, and this time he had an accomplice, Alva Hank Worley. They kidnapped Reed on December 29, 1991, tortured her, and raped her before ending her life.

Prostitute Valencia Johnson was last seen on February 24, 1992, knocking on McDuff's door. She was strangled and dumped at a golf course. Just five days later, McDuff kidnapped pregnant Melissa Northrup from a store she was working in. Her body was found by a fisherman on April 26.

Timeline of known murders:

August 6, 1966 - Marcus Dunman, fifteen

August 6, 1966 - Robert Brand, seventeen

August 6, 1966 - Louise Sullivan, sixteen

October 10, 1991 - Brenda Thompson

October 15, 1991 - Regenia Moore, seventeen

December 29, 1991 - Colleen Reed

February 24, 1992 - Valencia Joshua

February 29, 1992 - Melissa Northrup, twenty-two

Arrest and Trial

Authorities found out that McDuff was selling drugs and that he had an illegal gun, so a warrant was issued on March 6, 1992. In April, Worley (who was a known associate of McDuff) had been brought in for questioning, and Worley confessed his involvement in the abduction of Reed. This was a major breakthrough for the police, and they held Worley in custody while they looked for McDuff.

On May 1, 1992, a co-worker of McDuff's noticed his similarity to a man featured on *America's Most Wanted*. McDuff was going by the name of Richard Fowler at this stage, and after the co-worker notified the police, it was found that Fowler was in the system for soliciting prostitutes. Fingerprint comparisons were done and authorities discovered that Fowler and McDuff were the same person. On May 4, McDuff was arrested.

McDuff was indicted for the murder of Melissa Northrup on June 26, 1992, and found guilty. The jury sentenced him to death. Following the appeal process, the execution date was set for November 17, 1998. Two weeks before his execution, McDuff told authorities where he had buried Colleen Reed's body.

Outcome

McDuff was taken to the execution chamber on November 17, 1998. He was declared dead at 6:26 p.m.; the execution lasted for eight minutes. He was buried in the Captain Joe Byrd Cemetery, commonly called "Peckerwood Hill," in Texas. If a family does not want the remains, they are buried in this cemetery. The only thing written on his headstone is the date of his death, his death row number (999055) and an X which symbolizes death by execution.

Trivia

– Final statement before execution - "I'm ready to be released. Release me."
– His execution took eight minutes.
– McDuff is buried in the Captain Joe Byrd Cemetery, also called "Peckerwood Hill."
– He requested a steak for his final meal but instead received hamburger shaped into a steak.

MICHAEL WAYNE MCGRAY

Date of birth: July 11, 1965

Aliases/Nicknames: Nil

Characteristics: Requested psychiatric treatment for "demons"

Number of victims: 7 - 18 +

Date of murders: 1984 - 1998

Date of arrest: February 29, 1998

Murder method: Stabbing, strangulation

Known Victims: Elizabeth Gale Tucker, 17; Mark Daniel Gibbons (cab driver); Joan Hicks, 48, and her daughter Nina, 11; Robert Assaly, 59; Gaetan Ethier, 45; Jeremy Phillips, 33

Crime location: Canada

Status: Sentenced to life imprisonment without the possibility of parole.

Background

Like so many other serial killers, McGray claimed to have had a terrible childhood at the hands of his alcoholic father who beat him often; he was also victimized by sexual predators at the group homes and reform homes he grew up in. According to McGray, he enjoyed torturing and killing animals as a child. As an adult, he had an unquenchable thirst to commit murder.

He claimed he was controlled by "demons" that made him kill, and after his arrest he requested psychiatric treatment. He was assessed by psychiatrists. One found he had a severe form of Tourette's syndrome that prevented him from stopping himself from killing.

McGray committed numerous murders before he was caught, and he continued his murderous ways once he was incarcerated. He had said that nothing was going to stop him from killing people, and it seems that so far, he was right.

Murders

McGray picked up hitchhiker Elizabeth Tucker on May 1, 1985, and brutally murdered her. Then, in 1987, he murdered Mark Gibbons, who had allegedly been his accomplice in a robbery that took place in Saint John.

On February 29, 1998, McGray was arrested for the murders of Joan Hicks and her daughter Nina in

Moncton, New Brunswick. While in custody, he confessed to killing Robert Assaly and Gaetan Ethier after meeting them in a gay bar in Montreal. At the time, he had been on a three-day pass from prison.

Timeline of known murders:

May 1, 1985 - Elizabeth Tucker, seventeen

1987 - Mark Gibbons

1991 - Robert Assaly, fifty-nine

1991 - Gaetan Ethier, forty-five

February 28, 1998 - Joan Hicks, forty-eight

February 28, 1998 - Nina Hicks, eleven

November 2010 - Jeremy Phillips, thirty-three

Arrest and Trial

McGray eventually confessed to killing at least eleven people in numerous locations, namely Saint John, Halifax, Toronto, Ottawa, Vancouver, Seattle, and Calgary. He offered to give details on these murders if the authorities met his demands.

On March 20, 2000, McGray pleaded guilty to killing Joan Hicks. Then in May of 2001, he was charged with the death of Elizabeth Tucker. He was eventually sentenced to life imprisonment with the possibility of parole after serving twenty-five years for both cases.

Outcome

Following his murder of fellow inmate Jeremy Phillips in 2010, the coroner's inquest recommended that serial killers should be kept in single cells rather than shared rooms. McGray was moved to the Ste-Anne-des-Plaines Institution which has the highest security rating in Canada. He is serving his life sentences concurrently, without the possibility of parole.

PETER MANUEL

Date of birth: March 13, 1927

Aliases/Nicknames: The Beast of Birkenshaw

Characteristics: Rape, robbery

Number of victims: 9 - 12

Date of murders: January 2, 1956–January 1, 1958

Date of arrest: January 13, 1958

Murder method: Shooting, strangulation, bludgeoning

Known Victims: Anna Knielands, 17; Marion Watt, 45, her daughter Vivienne, 16, and Marion's sister Margaret, 41; Sydney Dunn (taxi driver); Isabelle Cooke, 17; Peter Smart, 45, his wife Doris, and their son Michael, 10

Crime location: Scotland, England

Status: Executed by hanging on July 11, 1958.

Background

Manuel was born in New York in 1927, to Scottish parents, and in 1932 the family moved back to the United Kingdom, settling in Birkenshaw, North Lanarkshire. Throughout his childhood, he was bullied, and he developed a habit of stealing. By the time he was ten years old, the local police already knew of Manuel as a petty thief.

Manuel's crimes turned more violent in his teens, and at the age of fifteen, he attacked a young woman in her own home. He broke into the house, woke her up, and used a hammer to batter her after he pulled her underwear down. He went on to attack a number of other women until he was caught at the age of sixteen. This time he was arrested and convicted, sentenced to serve sixteen years in Peterhead Prison.

Manuel ended up serving more sentences for attacks against women, including rape. In 1953, he decided to move to Glasgow, Scotland, where the rest of his family had moved to. Manuel had learned by now that if he left witnesses, he was likely to be caught. So, from then onwards his attacks moved from sexual assault and rape to murder.

Murders

On January 2, 1956, Manuel attacked Anne Knielands on a golf course in East Kilbride. He raped her and then used a length of iron to bludgeon her to death. Police questioned him about the murder, but his father gave him an alibi and he was let go.

On September 17, 1956, Manuel entered the home of Marion Watt, Vivienne Watt, and Margaret Brown, and shot the three women to death. At the time, he was out on bail for a burglary. Police considered him a suspect in the murders, but they instead arrested William Watt, the husband of Marion. Watt was eventually released two months later.

Manuel's next victim was Sydney Dunn, a taxi driver, who was killed on December 8, 1957. He was shot to death and dumped on the moorlands in Northumbria. By the time his body was found Manuel had gone to Lanarkshire.

Isabelle Cooke disappeared on her way to a dance at the local grammar school on December 28, 1957. Manuel abducted the young girl, raped her, and then strangled her to death. He buried her body in a field nearby.

Peter, Doris, and Michael Smart were shot and killed on January 1, 1958, in their home in Uddingston. Following the murders, Manuel lived in their house for almost a week. He even fed their pet cat. When he left the property, he took the Smart's car and, ironically, picked up a policeman who needed a ride. He told the officer that they were looking in the wrong places.

Timeline of murders:

January 2, 1956 - Anne Knielands, seventeen

September 17, 1956 - Marion Watt, forty-five

September 17, 1956 - Vivienne Watt, sixteen

September 17, 1956 - Margaret Brown, forty-one

December 8, 1957 - Sydney Dunn, thirty-six

December 28, 1957 - Isabelle Cooke, seventeen

January 1, 1958 - Peter Smart, forty-five

January 1, 1958 - Doris Smart., forty-two

January 1, 1958 - Michael Smart, ten

Arrest and Trial

Manuel was arrested on January 13, 1958, after using the new banknotes he had stolen from the Smart's at a bar. Police were notified by the bartender who thought it was suspicious he had the notes. After interviewing Manuel, he was charged with seven counts of murder.

His trial took place at Glasgow High Court, and in May of 1958 he was found guilty. He had represented himself in court and tried to plead insanity, but his plan failed. He was sentenced to death.

Outcome

Manuel was led from his cell to the execution chamber at 8:00 a.m. on July 11, 1958. He stood on the platform and had a hood placed over his head, his arms behind his back and legs strapped together, before the noose was placed around his neck. Only twenty-four seconds passed from the time the trapdoor dropped until he was pronounced dead. By 8:35 a.m., Manuel's body had been put into a coffin and a short service was conducted by the chaplain.

Manuel was then buried in the prison cemetery which was customary at that time. By 9:30 a.m., senior officers of the prison provided evidence at the public enquiry regarding Manuel's execution and death. Manuel left behind just nine personal belongings: a ballpoint pen, a pair of armbands, a shirt, three handkerchiefs, a broken comb, and two ties, along with £10.79 in cash which was collected by his father on July 19.

Trivia

Poem Manuel wrote during his trial:

I'm Peter Anthony Manuel,
In Barlinnie Jail, I lie,
Awaiting on a High Court jury,
To sentence me to die.
I know the Jury's verdict,
Will sentence me to death,
For I'm Peter Anthony Manuel,
The foulest beast on earth.
I know you read your papers,
And shall read about my crime,
I have not caused the death of one,
But have caused the death of nine.
I'm looking for not sympathy,
For don't you realise,
I'm Peter Anthony Manuel,
A reptile in disguise.
I murdered Isabella (sic) Cook,
And young Anne Knielands too,
Shot the Watts and shot the Smarts,
And Sidney (sic) Dunn I slew.
I did these deeds without a doubt,
My guilt was found by law,
I'm Peter Anthony Manuel,
The Rat of Birkenshaw.
I wonder who the hangman is,
Since Pierrepoint's gone away,
But I know that I shall meet him,
On that ill fated day.
That day I'll get breakfast,
I know I'll get no lunch,
For the law must have its pound of flesh,
And they can hang me only once.
And when I'm dead they'll bury me
In a pit of burning lime
But my name will live for evermore,
In the story book of crime.
And when they write my epitaph
These words, they shall be seen.
Here lies Peter Anthony Manuel
Scotland's Frankenstein.

RICHARD LAURENCE MARQUETTE

Date of birth: December 12, 1934

Aliases/Nicknames: Nil

Characteristics: Rape, dismemberment

Number of victims: 3

Date of murders: 1961 - 1975

Date of arrest: June 30, 1975

Murder method: Strangulation

Known Victims: Joan Rae Caudle, 23; Betty Wilson, 37; unidentified woman

Crime location: Portland and Salem, Oregon

Status: Sentenced to life imprisonment without parole.

Background

Marquette was born in Portland, Oregon in 1934. Little is known of his early life and childhood. He first came into contact with law enforcement in 1956, at the age of twenty-two. He had been arrested for attempted rape, but his victim dropped the charges, so he was released without conviction. Only a few months afterwards, he was picked up by police again for disorderly conduct.

In 1957, armed with a number of wrenches to use as weapons, Marquette attempted to rob a service station in Portland but was thwarted. This time, he was convicted and sentenced to serve eighteen months in prison. However, he was released early due to good behavior after serving only twelve months.

It would be another four years before Marquette would once again be in the line of sight of the local police. This time, he would be brought down by a dog that happened to return home to its owner carrying a human foot.

Murders

Joan Caudle was reported missing by her husband on June 8, 1961. She was last seen leaving a bar with an unidentified man, later identified as Marquette. He claimed they went back to his house for sex, and he got too drunk and strangled her. He had no car to use to dispose of her body, so he dismembered it in the bathroom. Parts of her body were found wrapped up like butchered meat in his refrigerator.

The mutilated body of Betty Wilson was found in a shallow waterway in Marion County by a fisherman in April of 1975. Marquette later told the authorities that he had met her at a nightclub and taken her back to his place for sex. When she refused to have sex with him, he strangled her and cut up her body.

An unidentified woman had met the same fate in 1974. She too had been picked up by Marquette in a bar and had agreed to go back to his home. He choked her to death and dismembered her body before burying the remains.

Timeline of murders and discoveries:

June 8, 1961 - Joan Caudle, twenty-three

1974 - Jane Doe

April of 1975 - Betty Wilson, thirty-seven

Arrest and Trial

Investigations into the murder of Caudle had led detectives to Marquette. But by the time they got to his house, he had already gone on the run. They issued a warrant for his arrest and the FBI was asked for assistance.

The day after Marquette was placed on the FBI's Most Wanted list, he was arrested and charged with Caudle's murder. He was found guilty and sentenced to life in prison. He served eleven years before being released in 1973.

On June 30, 1975, Marquette was arrested for the murder of Betty Wilson. At trial, he pleaded guilty due to the overwhelming evidence; he was sentenced to life imprisonment without parole.

Outcome

Following assessments by criminal psychiatrists, it was found that Marquette was a normal, socially adjusted man, but he would go into a murderous rage when women refused his advances.

After Marquette confessed to the murder of the unidentified woman, he took investigators to the burial site. They located most of her remains in two shallow graves, but her head was never found. Because there was no evidence with the body, and Marquette had no idea of what her name was, she was never identified.

Trivia

- He was the first person ever to be added as an eleventh name on the FBI Ten Most Wanted List.

DAVID MAUST

Date of birth: April 5, 1954

Aliases/Nicknames: Crazy Dave

Characteristics: Rape

Number of victims: 5

Date of murders: 1974 - 2003

Date of arrest: December 9, 2003

Murder method: Stabbing, strangulation, drowning

Known Victims: James McClister, 13; Donald Jones, 15; Michael Dennis, 13; James Raganyi, 16; Nicholas James, 19

Crime location: Germany, Illinois, Indiana

Status: Sentenced to life imprisonment. Committed suicide in his cell by hanging, January 20, 2006.

Background

From a very young age, Maust was rejected, abandoned, and generally disliked by his own mother. His parents divorced when he was seven years old, and he was left to live with his mother. Mentally unwell, she was once described as psychotic, disturbed, narcissistic, and marginally functioning by a social worker.

Maust's mother would leave him in the care of mental institutions from the time he was nine years old, claiming he was dangerous, and alleging he once set his brother's bed on fire. She also claimed Maust had tried to drown his brother, but social workers came to realize that really she was dropping him off at the hospital because she just didn't want him at home with her.

At one point, Maust was placed in a children's home following his discharge from the mental hospital when he was thirteen. Although he had behaved very well while in the hospital, he was greatly upset by his mother's lack of care or her unwillingness to visit him regularly. According to Maust and his brother, he was sexually molested by another boy while he was in the home. This would have a lasting impact on Maust.

As a young adult, Maust worked for his uncle in construction. Although he was a good worker, he crashed the company truck and was fired. He went back to his mother when he was eighteen, hoping to live with her. But she refused to have him and instead took him to an Army recruitment office. He enlisted, and after his basic training, he was stationed in Frankfurt, Germany, where he worked as a cook. It was while he was there that he committed his first murder.

Murders

Maust was stationed in Germany with the Army in 1974 when he killed James McClister. He was court-martialed for the crime and claimed that a moped accident had killed the young boy. He was found guilty of manslaughter and larceny and sentenced to four years' imprisonment in Fort Leavenworth. He was released in 1977, despite his requests to stay in prison.

The death of Donald Jones in 1981 was a case of being in the wrong place at the wrong time. Maust had actually been looking for the boy who had molested him when he came across Jones. He decided to murder him anyway, and he was drowned at a quarry.

On September 10, 2003, Maust committed three murders, killing James Raganyi, Michael Dennis and Nicholas James. All three had been wrapped in plastic and encased in concrete. The body of Raganyi was later found in the basement of Maust's home in Indiana.

Timeline of known murders:

1974 - James McClister, thirteen

1981 - Donald Jones, fifteen

September 10, 2003 - James Raganyi, sixteen

September 10, 2003 - Michael Dennis, thirteen

September 10, 2003 - Nicholas James, nineteen

Arrest and Trial

Maust was extradited to Illinois for the murder of Donald Jones in 1982, and he was found to be unfit to stand trial. He was sent to a mental facility instead. He eventually went on trial in 1994 and pleaded guilty. He was sentenced to thirty-five years. But, because he had been waiting for his trial for ten years, they credited him for the time served. He was released in 1999, and he then went on to commit the other murders.

Maust was arrested and charged with the murders of the three teenage boys, and he pleaded guilty at his trial in November of 2005. For these murders, he was sentenced to three terms of life imprisonment.

Outcome

On Thursday, January 19, 2006, Maust was told that he was going to be transferred to a state prison. Around ten minutes later, guards found Maust hanging in his cell; he had used a bed sheet he had braided into a rope. He was taken to a local hospital but died the following morning, Friday, January 20. He had left a seven-page note, part of which said: "Maybe with my death the families and the people can go on with their lives and not waste energy wondering why I was still alive."

IVAN MILAT

Date of birth: December 27, 1944

Aliases/Nicknames: The Backpacker Murderer, The Backpacker Killer

Characteristics: Rape

Number of victims: 7 +

Date of murders: 1989 - 1993

Date of arrest: May 22, 1994

Murder method: Shooting, stabbing

Known Victims: James Gibson, 19; Deborah Everist, 19; Simone Schmidl, 21; Gabor Neugebauer, 21; Anja Habschied, 20; Caroline Clarke, 21; Joanne Walters, 22

Crime location: New South Wales, Australia

Status: Sentenced to life imprisonment without parole.

Background

Milat was one of fourteen children born to a Croatian immigrant and an Australian mother. They lived in rural Australia, and the family tended to keep to themselves. In his youth, he was fond of hunting and fascinated with guns. One brother later claimed Milat showed psychopathic traits from a young age, though this is disputed by other family members.

The parents were very strict, most likely necessary given the large size of the family, but it was hard for them to keep track of what every child was up to. They were hardworking parents, so the children were often left to their own devices. Milat was described as an athletic, attractive boy who would take care to ensure he always looked good.

Because the children were running a little wild while the parents worked, the family became well-known to the local police. Milat was constantly in trouble from the time he was seventeen years old, charged with offences like armed robbery, burglary, and car theft. But it wasn't until 1971 that he first exhibited violent tendencies.

Two women who had been hitchhiking claimed Milat had raped them at knifepoint, and Milat was quickly identified and arrested. When the case went to trial, however, he was acquitted due to lack of evidence. Twenty years later, bodies started to turn up in the area, and Milat once again became the focus of attention of the local and federal police.

Murders

The bodies of Caroline Clarke and Joanne Walters were discovered on September 19, 1992, after two people running in Belanglo State Forest reported they had found a decomposed body. The two women had gone missing in April of 1992 from Kings Cross in Sydney. Walters had been stabbed a total of fourteen times, with one wound in the neck, nine in the back, and four wounds to her chest. The wound to her neck would have paralyzed her instantly. Clarke, however, was shot in the head ten times.

In October of 1993, some bones were found in the same forest and police discovered two more bodies. They belonged to James Gibson and Deborah Everist, who had disappeared in 1989. Gibbons had a similar wound to his neck and would have been instantly paralyzed. He had also been stabbed in the chest and back. Gibson had numerous wounds and had clearly been savagely beaten. Her skull was fractured in two places and her jaw was fractured. She had knife wounds to her forehead and had been stabbed in the back.

A skull was found in the forest on November 1, 1993; it was later identified as belonging to missing German hitchhiker Simone Schmidl. When they found her skeleton, they discovered wounds to her spine and body totalling at least eight altogether. Clothing was found nearby, but it wasn't hers - they belonged to Anja Habschied, another missing backpacker, who had disappeared along with her boyfriend Gabor Neugebauer in 1991.

The bodies of Habschied and Neugebauer were found buried in shallow graves on November 3, 1993. Habschied had been decapitated, but her head wasn't with the rest of her remains and has never been found. Neugebauer had been shot six times in the head.

Timeline of known murders:

1989 - Deborah Everist, nineteen

1989 - James Gibson, nineteen

January 20, 1991 - Simone Schmidl, twenty-one

Late 1991 - Gabor Neugebauer, twenty-one

Late 1991 - Anja Habschied, twenty

April of 1992 - Joanne Walters, twenty-two

April of 1992 - Caroline Clarke, twenty-one

Arrest and Trial

A report placed by Paul Onions, a survivor of an attack by Milat, was found by a detective on April 13, 1994. He had hitched a ride with a man called "Bill" and was held at gunpoint before escaping. As "Bill" fired at him, Onions was able to jump into a vehicle driven by Joanne Berry. There had also been a tip from the girlfriend of Milat's co-worker that Milat should be questioned about the murders.

Milat had a history of serving time for abducting women and raping them, so he was quickly considered a prime suspect. Onions, who was living in England, came back to Australia. When shown a picture of Milat, he identified him as "Bill," the man who had attacked him.

Milat was arrested at his home on May 22, 1994. At his first court appearance, he didn't enter a plea. On May 30, he was charged with the seven murders as well as the crimes against Onions. The trial began in March of 1996. Fifteen weeks later, he was found guilty of all charges. He received a total of eighteen years in prison for the charges related to the attack on Onions, and for each of the murders he received a life sentence, to be served consecutively with no possibility of parole.

Outcome

Milat is suspected of committing many more murders but has yet to be charged due to lack of evidence. There are at least seven cases where Milat is considered to be the perpetrator, but these haven't been proven yet. His brother, Boris, stated in 2015 that Milat had admitted killing taxi driver Neville Knight in 1962. Boris and the man convicted of the murder, Allan Dillon, were both given polygraph tests which showed that neither man was lying. Nothing has come of the accusations as yet.

Trivia

- Milat had a habit of self-mutilating himself while incarcerated. On January 26, 2009, he used a plastic knife to cut off his little finger. His intention was to post it to the High Court, but instead he was taken to the hospital where medical staff was determined it was unable to be reattached.
- In 2001, he deliberately swallowed a number of items including staples, razor blades, and any other metal objects he could find. He also went on a hunger strike in 2011 because he wanted a PlayStation. He lost 25 kg during the strike but never received the gaming system.
- Matthew Milat, his great-nephew, was found guilty of murder in 2012 after killing a man with an axe in 2010. He was sentenced to forty-three years in prison. During the murder, his friend Cohen Klein recorded the whole thing on his mobile phone. For his part in the murder, he received a sentence of thirty-two years.
- John Marsden, a lawyer who had initially represented Milat but was fired before the trial, made a shocking statement on his deathbed on July 18, 2005. He claimed Milat's sister had helped him in the murders of the British backpackers.

JOHN ALLEN MUHAMMAD
AND LEE BOYD MALVO

Date of birth: December 31, 1960; February 18, 1985

Aliases/Nicknames: The Beltway Sniper, The D.C. Sniper

Characteristics: Sniper attacks

Number of victims: 10 +

Date of murders: February 2002 - October 2002

Date of arrest: Both arrested on October 24, 2002

Murder method: Shooting

Known Victims: James Martin, 55; James Buchanan, 39; Premkumar Walekar, 54; Sarah Ramos, 34; Lori A. Lewis-Rivera, 25; Pascal Charlot, 72; Dean Harold Meyers, 53; Kenneth Bridges, 53; Linda Franklin, 47; Conrad Johnson, 35; Keenya Nicole Cook, 23; Jerry Ray Taylor, 60; Billy Gene Dillon, 37; Million Waldemariam, 41; Claudine Parker, 52; Hong Im Ballenger, 45

Crime location: Washington, Maryland, Virginia

Status: Muhammad - Death sentence, executed by lethal injection on November 10, 2009. Malvo was sentenced to life imprisonment without parole.

Background

John Allen Muhammad

Muhammad was born John Allen Williams. After his mother died when he was four, an aunt raised him in Baton Rouge, Louisiana. He married after high school, and the couple had a son they called Lindbergh. Muhammad joined the Louisiana Army National Guard, and it seemed as though he had a promising career in the military. But, he started getting into trouble in the early 1980s, once for striking an officer and another time for failing to report for duty.

In 1985, Muhammad and his first wife separated, and he enlisted in the US Army. By now he had converted to Islam. While he was stationed in Washington State, he met Mildred Green, whom he would later marry. The marriage produced three children, and Muhammad was doing well in the

Army. He learned to be a skilled marksman, and he served duties in Germany, as well as in the Middle East during the Gulf War.

In 1994, Muhammad decided to leave the Army. He made two attempts to start his own business but failed both times. His marriage was failing, and in 1999, Mildred filed for divorce. Muhammad proceeded to make threats towards her, and she was able to obtain a restraining order. Soon after, Muhammad took their children and fled to Antigua. It is here that he met Lee Boyd Malvo.

Lee Boyd Malvo

Malvo was born to Lesley Malvo and Una James, and he spent his early years living in Kingston, Jamaica. The relationship between his parents was volatile, and his father left the home when Malvo was five or six. Lesley's departure followed a violent argument where he had punched Una and she in turn tried to attack him with a machete. Una was a very domineering, strong woman, and Lesley couldn't tolerate her anymore.

From then onwards, as his mother chased an income, young Malvo was passed from family member to friend to family member. His mother would regularly drop him off at someone's house while she went away to work, and this devastated the young boy. He would shift from home to home, and sometimes he would end up in shelters or boys' homes. Despite all of this, Malvo was an intelligent child, and he continued to go to school even though his home life was so unsettled.

Each time Una came back into town, she would uproot Malvo from wherever he was staying. They moved around the area multiple times. Just when he would settle into a place and a school they would move again. As Malvo became a teenager, he started to seek out his father. But, their relationship was never really mended, and Lesley stayed out of his life so he could keep Una out of his.

By the time Malvo crossed paths with John Allen Muhammad he was in desperate need, not only of a father figure, but also of an adult that wasn't going to make him move all the time. They developed a mutual friendship and rapport, and their relationship would lead them into a future filled with violence. Muhammad was successful in brainwashing Malvo into believing every word he said, and it was easy for Muhammad to convince Malvo to follow him to America.

Murders

The first victim of the snipers was Keenya Nicole Cook on February 16, 2002. Cook was shot in the face and killed in Tacoma, Washington. Sometime in February or March, an unidentified man was shot and killed during a robbery. His identity has never been publicly announced. Jerry Ray Taylor was shot in the back on March 19 in Tucson, Arizona. This murder was linked after Muhammad confessed to it. The last victim killed in the first half of the year was Billy Gene Dillon who was killed on May 27.

On September 21, Million Waldemariam was shot in the head in Atlanta, Georgia. Although Muhammad never confessed to this shooting, the case was attributed to him because of the nature and similarities of the murder to his other crimes.

Muhammad shot Claudine Lee Parker in the back on September 21, while he was robbing the liquor store where she worked. Then, on September 23, Hong Im Ballenger was shot in the head in Baton Rouge, Louisiana. On October 2, James Martin was outside a food warehouse in Silver Spring, Maryland, when he was shot and killed.

On October 3, the shootings escalated. James Buchanan was shot in the chest in Rockville, Maryland, and Premkumar Walekar was shot in the chest and arm in Aspen Hill. In Norbeck, Sarah Ramos died after being shot in the head. Lori A Lewis-Rivera was killed in Kensington by a gunshot to the back. In Washington, Pascal Charlot died after a shot to the chest.

Dean Harold Meyers was at a gas station in Manassas, Virginia, on October 9, when he was killed by a gunshot to the head. Kenneth Bridges was shot and killed on October 11 in Fredericksburg while pumping gas at a station.

The last two known victims were Linda Franklin and Conrad Johnson. On October 14, Franklin was shot in the head as she helped her husband put packages in their car at a Home Depot store in Falls Church. On October 22, Johnson was shot in the abdomen while the bus he drove was parked on the street. He later died in the hospital.

Timeline of known murders:

February 16, 2002 - Keenya Nicole Cook, twenty-one

February or March of 2002 - Unidentified male

March 19, 2002 - Jerry Ray Taylor, sixty

May 27, 2002 - Billy Gene Dillon, thirty-seven

September 21, 2002 - Million Waldemariam, forty-one

September 21, 2002- Claudine Lee Parker, fifty-two

September 23, 2002 - Hong Im Ballenger, forty-five

October 2, 2002 - James Martin, fifty-five

October 3, 2002 - James Buchanan, thirty-nine

October 3, 2002 - Premkumar Walekar, fifty-four

October 3, 2002 - Sarah Ramos, thirty-four

October 3, 2002 - Lori A. Lewis-Rivera, twenty-five

October 3, 2002 - Pascal Charlot, seventy-two

October 9, 2002 - Dean Harold Meyers, fifty-three

October 11, 2002 - Kenneth Bridges, fifty-three

October 14, 2002 - Linda Franklin, forty-seven

October 22, 2002 - Conrad Johnson, thirty-five

Arrest and Trial

At one of the murder scenes, a note had been left by either Malvo or Muhammad telling police to look at a liquor store robbery where a murder had taken place in Montgomery, Alabama. Investigators located the scene and found a magazine with fingerprints on it. They were identified as belonging to Malvo. Because it was known that Malvo was associated with Muhammad, he was also investigated.

Police discovered Muhammad had owned a blue Chevrolet Caprice, a former police vehicle, in 2002. The information was broadcast to the public, and it was soon located at a rest stop in Myersville, Maryland. He was subsequently arrested.

In Virginia, the trial for the murder of Meyers started in October of 2003, and Muhammad was found guilty the next month. He was sentenced to death for the capital murder and was then extradited to Maryland to face murder charges there. There, he was convicted of six counts of first-degree murder on May 30, 2006. One of the most crucial pieces of evidence was the testimony of Malvo.

Muhammad never went on trial for the other murders, largely because he had already received the harshest penalty possible. His legal team made appeals regarding the Meyers murder conviction and subsequent sentence, but these were all denied.

Malvo went to trial in December of 2003, and on December 18, he was found guilty of capital murder, terrorism, and the use of a firearm during the commission of a murder for the death of Linda Franklin. On March 10, 2004, he was sentenced to life imprisonment without the possibility of parole.

Malvo entered a plea deal for the murder of Kenneth Bridges and the wounding of Caroline Seawell, and he received another life sentence, on October 26, 2004. In 2006, Malvo confessed to murdering Jerry Taylor in 2002. In November of 2006, he received further life sentences for the murders of six victims in Maryland. During an interview with William Shatner in July of 2010, Malvo claimed he was responsible or involved with more than forty murders. These claims have not been proven by the police.

Malvo appealed the Maryland federal courts in June of 2013 to have his life sentences vacated. But the appeal was denied a year later. A further appeal was filed in July of 2014. This time, two of the life sentences were overturned. Malvo remains in prison to this day, waiting to be resentenced.

Outcome

On November 10, 2009, Muhammed was led to the execution chamber at the Greensville Correctional Center. He had been given the choice of lethal injection or electrocution, but he declined to choose, so the lethal injection was chosen for him. The execution process started at 9:00 p.m., with the lethal chemicals being released at 9:06 p.m. He was declared deceased at 9:11 p.m. After his body was cremated, the ashes were given to his son.

Trivia

Muhammad:

- His last meal consisted of chicken and red sauce and "some cakes."
- Muhammed declined to make a final statement.

JOSEPH NASO

Date of birth: January 7, 1934

Aliases/Nicknames: Crazy Joe, The Double Initial Killer

Characteristics: Rape

Number of victims: 6 - 10

Date of murders: 1977 - 1994

Date of arrest: April 11, 2011

Murder method: Strangulation

Known Victims: Roxene Roggasch, 18; Carmen Colon, 22; Pamela Parsons, 38; Tracy Tafoya, 31; Sharileea Patton, 56; Sarah Dylan

Crime location: California

Status: Sentenced to death, awaiting execution.

Background

Naso served with the US Air Force in the 1950s, and he was married to Judith for eighteen years until they divorced. He still carried on visiting her in the Bay Area after they had split. Their son Charles developed schizophrenia, and Naso took care of him later on. Naso enrolled in a variety of classes at different colleges in the 1970s, and he was living in San Francisco in the 1980s.

When he was arrested in 2011, Naso was living in Reno, Nevada, where he had been working as a freelance photographer. Although he had a history of committing crimes which continued even as he reached his mid-seventies, they were largely confined to petty crimes like shoplifting. It's because of this behavior that his friends had given him the nickname "Crazy Joe." They had no idea just how bad Naso's behavior had been in the past, but soon they would find out.

Murders

The body of Roxene Roggasch was found on January 10, 1977, near Fairfax, California. Naso had strangled her to death. On August 13, 1978, the nude body of Carmen Colon was found beside a highway just thirty miles from the site of the previously discovered body.

Sharileea Patton's body washed up on the beach in 1981 near the Naval Net Depot in Tiburon, California. At the time of her disappearance, Naso was the manager of the residence she lived in. Initially, he was considered a suspect in Patton's disappearance, but police couldn't charge him at the time and he was let free.

Sarah Dylan was a big fan of musician Bob Dylan and was originally named Renee Sharpiro. She disappeared in May of 1992 while on her way to a Dylan concert in San Francisco. It's believed she was killed near Nevada County in California.

The body of Pamela Parsons was found in 1993 in Yuba County, California. She was working as a waitress at the time near Cooper Avenue where Naso lived. The last known victim was Tracy Tafoya. Her body was found in 1994 in Yuba County. She had been drugged, then raped and strangled.

Timeline of murders:

January 10, 1977 - Roxene Roggasch, eighteen

August 13, 1978 - Carmen Colon, twenty-two

1981 - Sharileea Patton, fifty-six

May of 1992 - Sarah Dylan

1993 - Pamela Parsons, thirty-eight

1994 - Tracy Tafoya, thirty-one

Arrest and Trial

Naso was arrested by the probation and parole authorities on April 11, 2010. When they searched his home, they found a diary containing a list of ten women and locations. A number of photographs were also discovered, and the subjects were identified as the murder victims. He was subsequently charged with the murders of Roggasch, Colon, Parsons, and Tafoya.

Although the other women listed in the diary were unidentified at first, investigators were able to confirm that two of them were Patton and Dylan. Naso went on trial and on August 20, 2013; he was convicted and sentenced to death.

Outcome

Naso was considered a "person of interest" in the Alphabet murders that took place in Rochester between 1971 and 1973. The link was made because four of Naso's victims also had double initials, and Naso had lived in Rochester for a long time. However, he was later ruled out through DNA evidence.

Trivia

- Naso's DNA was found on the pantyhose Roggasch was wearing when her body was found. The pantyhose around Roggasch's neck also had DNA from Naso's ex-wife on them.

DONALD NEILSON

Date of birth: August 1, 1936
Aliases/Nicknames: The Black Panther
Characteristics: Kidnapping, robbery
Number of victims: 5
Date of murders: 1974 - 1975
Date of arrest: December 11, 1975
Murder method: Shooting
Known Victims: Donald Skepper; Derek Astin; Sidney Grayland; Lesley Whittle 17; Gerald Smith
Crime location: England
Status: Sentenced to life imprisonment without parole. Died of natural causes, December 18, 2011.

Background

Neilson was actually born Donald Nappey in 1936. When he was ten years old, his mother succumbed to breast cancer at the young age of thirty-three. He was an unhappy child and started getting into trouble by breaking into shops when he was just twelve years old. But he was always given a stern warning by the police because he had lost his mother at such a young age.

When Neilson was eighteen, he married Irene Tate, who was twenty. He had been enlisted in the Army at the time, serving in the King's Own Yorkshire Light Infantry, but Irene managed to talk him into leaving. Five years later, their daughter Kathryn was born. The decision was made four years after that to change their surname to Neilson, so the young girl wouldn't suffer the teasing and bullying her father had as a youngster.

When Neilson's taxi business failed, he became a builder in Bradford, West Yorkshire, and it was then that he started down the spiral of committing crimes. In the early days of his criminal behavior, it is estimated he burglarized over four hundred homes without being caught. To dupe the police, Neilson would change his MO each week, so they couldn't establish a pattern that would lead them to him.

Before long, Neilson started committing armed robberies, and he is believed to have done eighteen of these between 1971 and 1974. Still, he hadn't been caught. His crimes started becoming more violent, however, as victims started to fight back. One such incident occurred when Neilson broke into a post office and threatened the postmaster with a rifle. When Neilson stated the gun was loaded, the postmaster challenged him by pulling the trigger himself. This resulted in the gun going off and blowing holes in the ceiling. A struggle ensued and the postmaster received several broken toes and a knee to the groin. Despite getting a good look at Neilson and giving a description, the police were still none the wiser.

The postmaster wasn't to know just how lucky he was that night to escape with his life, because it was very soon afterwards that Neilson's actions turned to murder.

Murders

While robbing post offices, Neilson shot and killed three people. Donald Skepper was killed on February 15, 1974, in Harrogate. Then Derek Astin was killed on September 6, 1974, in Baxenden. The third victim was Sidney Grayland, killed on November 11, 1974, in Langley, West Midlands.

Lesley Whittle was kidnapped from her home on January 17, 1975, as part of Neilson's plan to ask her family for a ransom. He left a note behind at her home in Highley, Shropshire, asking for fifty thousand pounds. The family was prepared to pay the ransom, but a number of mistakes and other issues meant the money was not delivered on time.

Her body was found hanging by wire in a drainage shaft in Bathpool Park, Staffordshire, on March 7. Initially, it was thought she had died from strangulation. But the pathologist determined she had died from vagal inhibition, caused by the shock of the fall, which made her heart stop. There was later some debate over whether Neilson had pushed her down the shaft or she had fallen.

The final known victim was Gerald Smith, who was killed in March of 1976. Smith was a security guard. During the hunt for Neilson for the murder of Whittle, Neilson shot him. Smith survived, but he died a year later due to complications of his injuries.

Timeline of known murders:

February 15, 1974 - Donald Skepper

September 6, 1974 - Derek Astin

November 11, 1974 - Sidney Grayland

January 17, 1975 - Lesley Whittle, 17

March 1976 - Gerald Smith

Arrest and Trial

On December 11, 1975, Neilson approached two police officers in their parked car on the main road out of Mansfield, North Nottinghamshire. As he walked past he turned his face away. This seemed suspicious to Officer Mackenzie. Nielson was called back to the car by the officers, at which time he pulled a sawn-off shotgun out of the bag he was carrying.

Neilson ordered the officers back into their car and sat himself in the passenger seat with the gun pressing into Mackenzie's armpit. He told him to drive to Rainworth and ordered the officers not to look at him. At one point, they came to a junction in the road. As Mackenzie asked which way to go, he swerved the steering wheel violently one way and then the other.

This made Neilson look straight ahead; his concentration shifted from the gun enough for it to lower and Mackenzie saw his opportunity to end the situation. He brought the car to a halt at the same time as he pushed the gun forward. Although the gun went off, it only grazed the hand of White. Mackenzie fell out of the car and ran to a shop for help. Two customers, Roy Morris and Keith Wood, ran to help and assisted them in overpowering Neilson. He was arrested successfully after receiving a bit of a beating from the civilians who came to help the officers.

During interviews at the police station, it was discovered that Neilson's fingerprints matched those left at the drain shaft where Whittle's body was found. Neilson confessed to the kidnapping of Whittle, and he provided a long statement of the crime to the police.

Following his trial in July of 1976, Neilson was convicted of kidnapping and murdering Whittle; he a sentence of life imprisonment. A few weeks later, he was convicted of the other murders and received another five life sentences. He was also given another twenty-one years for kidnapping Whittle, ten years for blackmailing Whittle's mother, and a total of thirty years for the burglary charges and gun possession. The judge recommended he serve a whole life sentence, meaning he would never get parole.

Outcome

In the early hours of December 17, 2011, Neilson was transported to the Norfolk and Norwich University Hospital due to having difficulties breathing. He died the next day.

Trivia

- **Ransom note left for the Whittle family:**

   NO POLICE £50000 RANSOM TO BE READY TO DELIVER WAIT FOR TELEPHONE CALL AT SWAN SHOPPING CENTRE TELEPHONE BOX 6 PM TO 1 PM IF NO CALL RETURN FOLLOWING EVENING WHEN YOU ANSWER GIVE NAME ONLY AND LISTEN YOU MUST FOLLOW INSTRUCTIONS WITHOUT ARGUMENT FROM TIME YOU ANSWER YOU ARE ON A TIME LIMIT IF POLICE OR TRICKS DEATH

   SWAN SHOPPING CENTRE KIDDERMINSTER DELIVER £50000 IN A WHITE VAN

   £50000 IN ALL OLD NOTES £25000 IN £1 NOTES AND £25000 IN £5 THERE WILL BE NO EXCHANGE ONLY AFTER £50000 HAS BEEN CLEARED WILL VICTIM BE RELEASED

- The nickname "The Black Panther" was given to Neilson after Astin's murder. His wife had described the killer as being quick like a panther, and he had been wearing dark clothing. A journalist therefore called him the Black Panther and the nickname stayed.
- **Film:** *The Black Panther* (1977) - a film about Neilson's life and the crimes he committed.

DENNIS NILSEN

Date of birth: November 23, 1945

Aliases/Nicknames: The Muswell Hill Murderer, The Kindly Killer

Characteristics: Rape, necrophilia, dismemberment

Number of victims: 12 - 15

Date of murders: December 30, 1978–January 26, 1983

Date of arrest: February 9, 1983

Murder method: Strangulation by ligature, drowning

Known Victims: Stephen Holmes, 14; Kenneth Ockenden, 23; Martyn Duffey, 16; William Sutherland, 26; Malcolm Barlow, 23; John Howlett, 23; Archibald Graham Allen, 27; Stephen Sinclair, 20; others unidentified

Crime location: London, England

Status: Sentenced to life imprisonment without parole.

Background

Nilsen's father Olav had been a Norwegian soldier, and when the Nazi's conquered Norway during World War II, he was sent to Scotland for safety. There, he met Elizabeth Whyte, the daughter of a fisherman. They married, and had three children - Olav Jr., Dennis, and Sylvia. Olav Sr. was not happy in his paternal role, and the couple divorced in 1948, at which time Elizabeth's father stepped in to fulfil the fatherly role.

Nilsen was close to his grandfather until he died in 1951, just before Nilsen turned six. He had suffered a fatal heart attack while at sea, and when his body was brought back to land, Nilsen's mother encouraged the young boy to look at his dead grandfather, telling him he was "sleeping." From then onwards, Nilsen's personality changed. He became more subdued, and he pushed away any adults who tried to show him affection.

A few years later, Nilsen had a near-death experience when he almost drowned in the sea. Following the initial panic, he became calm, and he was convinced his grandfather was coming to save him. Instead, he was rescued by other young people nearby. His mother remarried not long afterwards, and they moved further inland, away from the sea.

As Nilsen entered puberty, he came to realize that he wasn't heterosexual. But he also wasn't sure if he was bisexual or gay, and he noticed that the boys he found attractive looked similar to his own sister. To try to figure out how he felt, Nilsen fondled both his brother and sister while they were asleep, but his brother woke up. From then on, he bullied Nilsen about it.

At fourteen, Nilsen joined the Army Cadet Force, and he subsequently enlisted in the British Army when he finished high school. He was deployed to West Germany, and he discovered that by drinking large amounts of alcohol he was able to socialize more comfortably. An incident occurred where he awoke on the floor of a friend's apartment after a heavy night of drinking. Nothing sexual had taken place, but the event became the background for the fantasy Nilsen would come to enjoy, one where he would have sex with an immobile or unconscious partner.

Nilsen was deployed to South Yemen in 1967, where violent ambushes and abductions were taking place, and several of his companions were subsequently kidnapped and murdered. Nilsen almost met the same fate when he was abducted, but he was able to fight back and escape. From there, he was sent to serve in Cyprus and Britain before being sent back to Germany. In 1972, Nilsen retired from the Army and decided to become a police officer. It was at this time that his brother outed him to his mother as being homosexual.

During his year of service with the Metropolitan Police, Nilsen frequented the local gay bars. Following his resignation from the police force, he became a security guard for a short period. Then he settled into work at a job center. He embarked on several romantic relationships but all ended quickly, and he came to believe he was incapable of having a normal relationship. Now, he could act out those fantasies that had been on his mind for a long time.

Murders

Stephen Holmes met Nilsen at a pub on December 29, 1978. The young teenager had tried, without success, to buy some alcohol. Nilsen, having consumed quite a bit of alcohol, invited him back to his house for drinks. Nilsen thought the boy was older. They drank until they fell asleep. When Nilsen woke the next morning, he looked at Holmes sleeping and was scared the boy would leave and Nilsen would have to spend New Year's Eve by himself. So, using a necktie, he strangled Holmes until he was unconscious then drowned him in a bucket of water.

After he had killed Holmes, he twice masturbated over the body and then placed it under his floorboards. About eight months later, Nilsen constructed a pyre, like many cultures build to burn their dead, and incinerated Holmes in his backyard.

Nilsen met Kenneth Ockenden on December 3, 1979, in a pub in London. He offered to give the young Canadian a tour of London, and when they were finished, he invited him back to his apartment. While they were listening to music, he strangled Ockenden to death. The next morning, Nilsen posed the body in a variety of positions and took photographs. He watched television for a while, then wrapped the body in plastic and put it under the floorboards. Over a two-week period, Nilsen dug up and reburied Ockenden's body four times. In between each reburial, he would put the body in a chair near him while he drank alcohol and watched television.

Martyn Duffey was hitchhiking when he crossed paths with Nilsen. He was invited back to Nilsen's apartment, then strangled into unconsciousness and drowned in the sink in the kitchen. He washed the body, and over the next two days, he masturbated over the corpse and kissed it. He eventually placed the body under the floorboards when it started to bloat.

By August of 1980, Nilsen had tried a number of methods to eliminate the decomposition odors and maggot infestations. He finally removed the bodies from beneath the floorboards, dismembered them, and burned them behind his home. His landlord told him he was going to renovate in October, so Nilsen disposed of Ockenden's body and shifted to a flat in Muswell Hill. This place was much smaller, with no garden access and no room under the floorboards, so it was going to be harder to dispose of any bodies.

Nilsen was followed home by William Sutherland in August of 1980. Sutherland was soliciting for money by offering sex, which Nilsen initially declined. Back at his apartment, Nilsen woke up the next morning and found the strangled corpse of Sutherland. But he couldn't remember actually doing the deed.

In March of 1982, John Howlett was invited back to Nilsen's apartment for a drink. After Howlett fell asleep, Nilsen watched him for a while and then tried to strangle him. Howlett woke and struggled against Nilsen as hard as he could, but Nilsen managed to strangle him unconscious again. After three unsuccessful attempts to strangle him to death, he eventually drowned Howlett in the bath. Howlett's body was dismembered, and the organs and flesh were flushed down the toilet. The bones were put out with the trash, without detection.

Archibald Graham Allen was killed sometime in late 1982, after being invited to Nilsen's apartment for a meal. While Allen was eating the omelette Nilsen prepared for him, he was strangled. His body was put into the bath, and it stayed there for the next three days, at which point Nilsen requested a day off work so that he could dismember the body.

The last known victim was Stephen Sinclair, who was killed on January 26, 1983. The two men had consumed alcohol and drugs, and while Sinclair was in a stupor in the chair, Nilsen strangled him. Afterwards, he removed bandages from Sinclair's wrists and discovered the young man had tried to kill himself just days before. He washed the body and applied talcum powder to it before laying it on his bed. He placed different mirrors around the bed, then undressed himself and lay beside Sinclair's corpse. He even slept beside it for the night. He them dismembered the body and disposed of it in trash bags.

Timeline of known murders:

December 29, 1978 - Stephen Dean Holmes, fourteen

December 3, 1979 - Kenneth Ockenden, twenty-three

May of 1980 - Martyn Duffey, sixteen

August of 1980 - William Sutherland, twenty-six

November of 1980 - May of 1981 - Seven unidentified victims

September 18, 1981 - Malcolm Barlow, twenty-three

March of 1982 - John Howlett, twenty-three

Late 1982 - Archibald Graham Allen, twenty-seven

January 26, 1983 - Stephen Sinclair, twenty

Arrest and Trial

Strangely, Nilsen made a complaint on February 4, 1983, that the drains were blocked. A plumber investigated the problem and reported to Nilsen that he had found it blocked with small bones and a fleshy substance. Nilsen joked that someone must have flushed their Kentucky Fried Chicken down the toilet.

The plumber and his supervisor came back the next day to finish clearing out the drain, but they discovered someone had already done it. This seemed suspicious, so they further investigated the pipes and found more flesh and bones. They immediately notified the police who had the flesh and bones examined and identified as being human remains.

On February 9, Police waited at Nilsen's door for him to come home. While there, they noticed the familiar decomposition odor wafting out from under the door. When Nilsen arrived, they told him there were human remains in the drain and he pretended to be shocked. The officers asked him where the rest of the body was, and Nilsen took them inside and showed them the body parts in his closet.

When the officers asked if there were more victims, Nilsen stated that he would tell the long story at the station. On the drive to the station, one of the officers asked if the remains belonged to one person or two, to which Nilsen replied, "Fifteen or sixteen, since 1978." At the station he made a full confession and showed police where remains had been destroyed at his former place on Melrose Avenue.

For his trial, Nilsen was assessed by two psychiatrists to determine whether or not he was sane. They found he had difficulty with his emotions, and the only one he could express was anger. One of the psychiatrists diagnosed him with borderline pseudo-normal narcissistic personality disorder. He also suffered from occasional schizoid outbreaks.

At his trial, Nilsen stated he never had a premeditated plan to kill his victims; rather it was something that suddenly occurred moments before the act. He was found guilty of six murders on November 4, 1983. He was sentenced to life imprisonment with the possibility of parole after twenty-five years.

Outcome

Home Secretary Michael Howard changed Nilsen's sentence to whole life sentence, removing the possibility of parole. Nilsen responded that he was happy with it, and that he didn't want to be free again anyway.

Trivia

- In the years following his incarceration, Nilsen has composed an unpublished, four-hundred-page autobiography, entitled The History of a Drowning Boy.
- "When I was with people, I was in the 'real' world, and in my private life, I snapped instantly into my fantasy life. I could oscillate between the two with instant ease."
- Several items confiscated from Nilsen's Cranley Gardens address — some of which had been introduced as evidence at Nilsen's trial — now remain on display at New Scotland Yard's Black Museum. These exhibits include the stove upon which Nilsen had boiled the heads of his final three victims, the knives he had used to dissect several of his victims' bodies, the headphones Nilsen had used to strangle Kenneth Ockenden, the ligature he had fashioned to strangle his last victim, and the bath from his Cranley Gardens address in which he had drowned John Howlett and retained the body of Graham Allen prior to dissection.

GORDON STEWART NORTHCOTT

Date of birth: November 9, 1906

Aliases/Nicknames: Nil

Characteristics: Kidnapping, sadism, dismemberment

Number of victims: 3 - 20

Date of murders: 1926 - 1928

Date of arrest: September 19, 1928

Murder method: Shooting, bludgeoning with an axe

Known Victims: unidentified Mexican boy; Lewis Winslow, 12; Nelson Winslow, 10; Walter Collins, 9

Crime location: Riverside, California

Status: Executed by hanging on October 2, 1930.

Background

Northcott's childhood is largely unknown, though he did claim that his father had sexually abused him when he was ten years old. His father ended up in a mental asylum and committed suicide later in life. Northcott's paternal uncle was imprisoned for murder and died while serving a life sentence.

In 1926, Northcott, his mother Sarah Louise, and his thirteen-year-old nephew Sanford Clark, settled on a chicken ranch in Wineville, near California. Following their arrest, Clark claimed Northcott had repeatedly raped and beaten him and forced him to do things to the boys they abducted, including murder. Just how much Northcott's mother Sarah and young Clark were responsible for is unclear, but a number of boys disappeared at the chicken ranch, and all three were eventually caught and charged.

Murders

Brothers Lewis and Nelson Winslow went missing in Pomona on May 16, 1928. Northcott later claimed that he had killed Lewis, but Sanford had killed Nelson. He said he felt sorry later, because Lewis had been so distressed at the time.

Walter Collins vanished from his home on March 10, 1928. Northcott's mother was convicted of murdering the boy, but evidence suggested her son had ordered her to do it. The disappearance of Collins became a major incident, especially after another little boy appeared and tried to convince Mrs. Collins that he was Walter. She knew he wasn't, and she notified the authorities who put her into a mental institution. Eventually she was released, and the young boy, later identified as Arthur Hutchins Jr., confessed that he was an imposter.

After kidnapping the boys, Northcott would get tired of them after a while and kill them either with an axe or by gunshot. The bodies were covered with quicklime to dissolve the flesh and the bones were buried in the desert. Only one body, belonging to a Mexican teenaged boy, was ever found. But the head was missing and the victim was never identified.

Arrest and Trial

In the summer of 1928, Northcott filed a complaint with the district attorney's office about his neighbor, claiming his behavior was violent and profane and upsetting his nephew. When this was discussed with the neighbor, he claimed he had seen Northcott occasionally beating Clark; he urged the investigators to see what was going on at the Northcott ranch.

Meanwhile, Sanford's parents contacted immigration about wanting their son back, so immigration officials went out to the ranch and took Sanford into custody. Once he was away from Northcott, Sanford informed authorities about what exactly had been going on at the ranch. He went back to the ranch with investigators and showed them grave sites. When these were dug up, fingers and ankle bones were discovered.

Also found at the ranch were a hatchet and axe, stained with blood. Northcott had taken off to Canada, but he was caught and sent back to face the murder charges. His mother was also arrested and charged with the murder of Walter Collins.

Northcott's trial lasted for twenty-seven days, finally ending on February 8, 1929. He was found guilty of the murders of the Mexican victim and the Winslow brothers and was sentenced to death. His mother went on trial for the death of Collins. After being found guilty, she was sentenced to life imprisonment on December 31, 1928. The only reason she didn't get the death penalty was because she was female.

Outcome

On October 2, 1930, Northcott was led to the execution room screaming. His whole body trembled as he begged the guards not to walk so fast. It was thirteen steps up to the gallows and the guards had to drag him almost the entire way. He asked the guards if the hanging would hurt and requested a blindfold so he wouldn't have to see the gallows. Northcott moaned, screamed, and cried out all the way to the top. Just before the trapdoor was released, he screamed out, "A prayer--please, say a prayer for me." The trapdoor sprung, and he was hanged.

Trivia

- **Film:** *The Changeling* (2008) - A film based on the Wineville murders, and the search by Christine Collins to find her missing son, starring Angelina Jolie.

ANATOLY ONOPRIENKO

Date of birth: July 25, 1959

Aliases/Nicknames: The Beast of Ukraine, Terminator, Citizen O

Characteristics: Robbery

Number of victims: 52

Date of murders: 1989 - 1996

Date of arrest: April 16, 1996

Murder method: Shooting, striking with an axe

Known Victims: Men, women, children, including whole families

Crime location: Ukraine

Status: Death sentence later commuted to life imprisonment. Died from natural causes on August 27, 2013.

Background

Onoprienko's father was a decorated soldier who had served during World War II and received medals for bravery. His mother died when he was four years old, and Onoprienko was raised by his grandparents for a short while before being sent to an orphanage. His brother was thirteen years older, so was spared from being sent away.

Onoprienko later claimed that it was the orphanage and his experiences there that set him on the violent path he eventually took. By the time he was caught by the authorities at the age of thirty-seven, he had (by his own accounts) committed fifty-two murders. Onoprienko spared no one, killing every member of a household, including the children.

Murders

Onoprienko always looked for a house that was isolated. He would then create some sort of commotion outside to get the attention of the occupants. First, he would kill the adult male of the house, followed by the wife and then the children. To try to cover his tracks, he would set the house on fire, hoping that by burning it down no evidence would be found. He also killed any potential witnesses who happened to cross his path at the scenes.

The first victims, in 1989, were a large family of ten. He had been in the middle of robbing their house when they interrupted him. He later claimed another man had been with him that night, Sergei Rogozin. Within the same year, Onoprienko killed five people who had been sleeping in their car. He then set fire to the bodies.

On December 24, 1995, he killed the Zaichenko family while robbing their home. The family of four was shot with a sawed-off double-barrelled shotgun. He then set the house on fire. Another family of four was shot dead on January 2, 1996. Immediately after, Onoprienko killed a man who had walked by at the time.

Four more people were killed on January 6, 1996, but this time they weren't a family in their home. Onoprienko stopped cars on the highway, then killed the drivers. Eleven days later, he murdered the Pilat family in their home and set it on fire. Two other people were killed outside the home, as Onoprienko was worried about witnesses.

On January 30, 1996, a woman and her two sons were killed, as well as their visitor. Another family, the Dubchaks, was killed on February 19, 1996. The father was shot along with the son, but the mother and daughter were mauled to death with a hammer. He tried to demand money from the daughter but she refused, so he killed her.

The Bodnarchuk family was brutally killed on February 27, 1996. The parents were shot to death and the young daughters, just seven and eight, were hacked to death with an axe. About an hour after killing the family, Onoprienko noticed a neighbor wandering around the property, so he shot him and hacked his body with the axe.

The last of the known victims were the Novosad family of four. They were shot and killed on March 22, 1996, and their house was set on fire.

Timeline of murders:

1989 - A family of ten

1989 - Five victims sleeping in a car

December 24, 1995 - Four members of the Zaichenko family

January 2, 1996 - Family of four

January 6, 1996 - Four people in separate killings

January 17, 1996 - Five members of the Pilat family, and two witnesses

January 30, 1996 - Marusina, her two children, and a visitor

February 19, 1996 -Four members of the Dubchak family

February 27, 1996 - Four members of the Bodnarchuk family and another man

March 22, 1996 - Four members of the Novosad family

Arrest and Trial

In April of 1996, Onoprienko had moved in with a relative and they noticed he had a collection of weapons. The relative kicked him out of the home, and the police were notified. He was arrested on April 16, 1996, at which time police discovered over one hundred items that could be linked to the multiple murders.

He initially confessed to killing eight people between 1989 and 1995. But, later he admitted being responsible for a total of fifty-two murders. He told the authorities that he had been hearing voices that instructed him to kill.

His trial was delayed for a number of reasons, the main one being that under Ukraine law, the defendant has to read all of the evidence against them before the trial can start. Considering there were more than ninety-nine volumes of information on the case, that was going to take a while. Also, under the law, the court must pay for accommodation and travel costs for witnesses, and in this trial, there were going to be four hundred witnesses called. The court was unable to finance it, so they made an appeal on television and the government agreed to carry the costs.

Once the trial started in November of 1998, the defense lawyer initially tried to convince the court that Onoprienko was insane, but psychiatrists examined him and found him fit to stand trial. When Onoprienko was brought into the court, he was put into a metal cage, most likely for his own protection from an enraged public.

His accomplice in the first murders, Rogozin, was charged at the same time and was convicted of being an accomplice for the first nine murders. He was sentenced to thirteen years in prison. For Onoprienko, the jury deliberated for just three hours before reaching their verdict of guilty. Onoprienko received the death penalty which was to be carried out by firing squad.

Fortunately for Onoprienko, the Ukraine was hoping to join the Council of Europe. For this reason, they abolished capital punishment. Although many politicians and the general public felt that this case was so abhorrent, he should still die, his sentence was commuted to life imprisonment.

Outcome

On August 27, 2013, Onoprienko died of heart failure while incarcerated at Zhytomyr prison. He was fifty-four years old at the time of his death.

CLIFFORD OLSON

Date of birth: January 1, 1940

Aliases/Nicknames: The Beast of British Columbia

Characteristics: Paedophilia, rape, mutilation

Number of victims: 11 +

Date of murders: 1980 - 1981

Date of arrest: August 12, 1981

Murder method: Strangulation, stabbing, bludgeoning with a hammer

Known Victims: Christine Weller, 12; Colleen Daignault, 13; Daryn Johnsrude, 16; Sandra Lynn Wolfsteiner, 16; Ada Anita Court, 13; Simon Patrick James Partington, 9; July Kozma, 14; Raymond Lawrence King Jr., 15; Sigrun Charlotte Elisabeth Arnd, 18; Terry Lyn Carson, 15; Louise Simonne Marie Evelyn Chartrand, 17

Crime location: British Columbia, Canada

Status: Sentenced to life imprisonment. Died from cancer on September 30, 2011.

Background

Olson had been a problem right from the start; even as a young boy, he constantly got into trouble. Quite short but very stocky, he regularly got into fights and often lost. He told his father he was going to learn how to box, and after he started training, he went round and sought revenge on every boy that had ever beaten him up.

Schooling was unsuccessful, with Olson dodging classes from the age of ten. He left school after completing eighth grade and embarked on a life of committing crime. As a teenager, he was a loner, and he failed at everything he attempted. The first time he went to jail was in 1957, when he was seventeen. Over the next twenty-four years, he was convicted of almost one hundred crimes, including forgery, fraud, theft, armed robbery, escape, gross indecency, buggery, possession of firearms, and numerous others.

Olsen managed to flee from jail on seven occasions, at one point feigning illness and escaping on his way to the hospital, despite being escorted by three guards. He was on the run for a week before getting caught with the help of a police dog. This wasn't the first time he had been found by a police dog - he had experienced the same situation a year earlier while on the run.

In 1980, Olson met Joan Hale, a woman who had recently divorced her violent and abusive husband. A year later, their son Stephen was born, and they married a month after the birth. What Joan didn't know was that her new husband had already murdered someone by the time they married, and he had no intention of stopping.

Murders

Christine Weller, the first known victim, was abducted on November 7, 1980, from Surrey in British Columbia. Her body wasn't discovered until Christmas Day; she had been stabbed multiple times until she was dead.

Olsen kidnapped Colleen Daignault on April 16, 1981, and her body was found five months later. The next victim was Daryn Johnsrude, who was killed on April 22. Two weeks after his death, his body was found. On May 19, Sandra Wolfsteiner was abducted and killed by Olsen, followed by Ada Court in June.

Olsen's murderous acts were escalating, and in July of 1981, there were six victims. Nine-year-old Simon Partington was abducted on June 2, raped, and then strangled. The next was Judy Kozma on July 9; she abducted from New Westminster and also raped and strangled. Her body was found near Weaver Lake on July 25. Raymond King was abducted, raped, and bludgeoned to death on July 23. Then, German tourist Sigrun Arnd was raped and bludgeoned to death on July 25.

The last two victims were Terri Lyn Carson and Louise Chartrand. Carson was raped and strangled to death on July 27, and Chartrand was killed on July 30.

Timeline of known murders:

November 17, 1980 - Christine Weller, twelve

April 16, 1981 - Colleen Daignault, thirteen

April 22, 1981 - Daryn Johnsrude, fifteen

May 19, 1981 - Sandra Wolfsteiner, sixteen

June 21, 1981 - Ada Court, thirteen

July 2, 1981 - Simon Partington, nine

July 9, 1981 - Judy Kozma, fourteen

July 23, 1981 - Raymond King, fifteen

July 25, 1981 - Sigrun Arnd, fourteen

July 27, 1981 - Terri Lyn Carson, fifteen

July 30, 1981 - Louise Chartrand, seventeen

Arrest and Trial

Olsen was arrested on August 12, 1981, under suspicion of trying to abduct two girls. He was then charged with the murder of Judy Kozma on August 25. At this time, he reached an agreement with the authorities. In exchange for confessing to eleven murders and showing them where the bodies were, he would receive ten thousand dollars per victim to be paid to his wife.

His wife and son received one hundred thousand dollars thanks to the deal Olsen made with the authorities, which made a lot of people angry. He then pleaded guilty to the eleven murders in January of 1982. He received eleven life sentences to be served concurrently.

Outcome

It was reported by the media in September of 2011 that Olsen had terminal cancer, and he had been taken to a hospital for treatment. Olson died on September 30, 2011. He was seventy-one years old.

Trivia

- Olson scored 38/40 on the Psychopathy Checklist.
- Escaped from prison seven times.
- Sent crude and vulgar cards to the parents of the murdered children.
- Sent pornographic letters to members of parliament.

CARL PANZRAM

Date of birth: June 28, 1891

Aliases/Nicknames: Carl Baldwin, Jeff Davis, Jefferson Davis, Jefferson Rhodes, Jeff Rhodes, Jack Allen, Jefferson Baldwin, John King, John O'Leary, Cooper John, Teddy Bedard

Characteristics: Sodomy, robbery

Number of victims: 22

Date of murders: 1920 - 1929

Date of arrest: August 16, 1928

Murder method: Strangulation, shooting, bludgeoning

Known Victims: Men and boys - most unnamed or unidentified

Crime location: New York, Massachusetts, Connecticut, Maryland, Pennsylvania, Kansas, USA; Luanda, Angola

Status: Executed by hanging on September 5, 1930.

Background

Panzram was raised on the family farm along with his five brothers and sisters. At the age of twelve, he stole food and a gun from a neighbor. Not long afterwards, he was sent to the Minnesota State Training School to straighten him out. According to Panzram, he received numerous beatings and torture by staff. These took place in "The Painting House." The other children there had named it this because those who went into the room came out "painted" - in other words, they were covered in colorful bruises and blood. Full of hatred, Panzram burnt the "Painting House" down, but he was never suspected.

By the time he was into his mid-teens, Panzram was already an alcoholic. He committed multiple burglaries and thefts and was in constant trouble with the law. He had run away from home when he was fourteen, and was allegedly gang-raped by a group of men on a train car. When he was fifteen, he enlisted in the Army, but he was convicted of larceny within a year. He was sent to Fort Leavenworth's United States Disciplinary Barracks and served a two-year sentence until he was released in 1910.

As an adult, Panzram continued to commit burglaries, and he was incarcerated numerous times. Even in prison he was in constant trouble for attacks against the guards and failure to follow orders. As a result, the guards would sometimes beat Panzram or dole out other similar punishments. Panzram was a very strong man; later, this strength would enable him to overpower his victims.

Murders

For eight years, Panzram terrorized people in many counties, robbing and killing as he traveled. His motive was almost always robbery, and if there happened to be someone present, they were killed. At one point, he bought a yacht; he would lure sailors from bars in New York, get them drunk, and then rape them before shooting them. He would dump the bodies in Long Island Sound, near Execution Rocks Light.

After his yacht sank, Panzram traveled to Africa. According to Panzram, he killed a young boy, and another time he hired a rowing boat and shot the six rowers before tossing them overboard to the crocodiles. He returned to America, and he beat one small boy to death on July 18, 1922, in Salem. Later that year, he strangled another young boy to death near New Haven.

According to Panzram, he shot and killed a man in June of 1923 when he attempted to rob Panzram. He claimed he had killed someone while burglarizing a home, and he had killed two more young boys in Philadelphia - one in 1921 and the other in 1928. He later claimed that he was considering putting arsenic into the city's water supply so he could kill masses.

Arrest and Trial

On August 16, 1928, Panzram was arrested for committing a burglary in Washington. While he was being interrogated about the burglary, he confessed to killing two boys. He was tried and convicted and sentenced to twenty-five years to life imprisonment. He told the warden he would kill the first person that bothered him, and this later came true.

On June 20, 1929, Panzram killed Robert Warnke, the prison laundry foreman. He bashed him to death with an iron bar. This time, when he went on trial he was given the death sentence. He refused all efforts to appeal his sentence and when human rights activists tried to help on his behalf, he sent them death threats.

Outcome

On September 5, 1930, Panzram's scheduled execution took place. He didn't go quietly though; he reportedly spat in the face of the executioner as he placed the hood over his head. After he was hanged, he was buried at the Leavenworth Penitentiary Cemetery. The only thing on his headstone is his prison number.

Trivia

- The best friend Panzram ever had was a prison guard, Henry Lesser, who eventually wrote out Panzram's life story.
- He boasted of committing over one thousand acts of sodomy.
- His final words were, "Hurry it up, I could hang a dozen men while you're fooling around."
- "I don't believe in man, God nor Devil. I hate the whole damned human race, including myself... I preyed upon the weak, the harmless and the unsuspecting. This lesson I was taught by others: Might makes right."

Poem written by Panzram:

I sat down to think things over a bit.
While I was sitting there,
a little kid about eleven or twelve years old came bumming around.
He was looking for something. He found it, too.
I took him out to a gravel pit about one-quarter mile away.
I left him there,
but first I committed sodomy on him and then killed him.
His brains were coming out of his ears when I left him,
and he will never be any deader.

GERALD PARKER

Date of birth: 1955

Aliases/Nicknames: The Bedroom Basher, The Bludgeon Killer

Characteristics: Rape, home invasion

Number of victims: 5 +

Date of murders: 1978 - 1979

Date of arrest: Was already in prison for a parole violation when DNA matched him to the killings.

Murder method: Bludgeoning with blunt objects

Known Victims: Sandra Kay Fry, 17; Kimberly Gaye Rawlins, 21; Marolyn Kay Carleton, 31; Debora Kennedy, 24; Debra Lynn Senior, 17; an unborn child (Chantel Marie Green)

Crime location: Orange County, California

Status: Sentenced to death, awaiting execution.

Background

Parker was a former US Marine who had a fairly clean criminal record until 1980. He had spent a period of time in juvenile detention in the 1960s after being caught sniffing glue, but he had stayed out of trouble from then onwards.

In 1980, he was stationed at the Marine Air Station in El Toro California. During this time, he raped a four-year-old girl and was quickly apprehended. He received a six-year prison sentence for the crime, and a DNA sample was stored as was protocol. As time passed, and technology advanced, it was this sample that would crack open a murder case. And further revelations from Parker himself would lead to the release of a man who had previously been wrongly convicted of a murder he'd never committed.

Murders

Parker was nicknamed the "Bedroom Basher" because of the ferocity of the sex attacks and murders he committed in the 1970s in Orange County. Between 1978 and 1979, five women were raped and murdered by Parker. Another woman, Dianna D' Aiello (formerly Green) was pregnant when she was attacked; though she survived, her unborn child did not.

Timeline of known murders:

December 2, 1978 - Sandra Kay Fry, seventeen

April 1, 1979 - Kimberly Rawlins, twenty-one

September 14, 1979 - Marolyn Carleton, thirty-one

September 30, 1979 - Unborn child (Chantel Marie Green)

October 7, 1979 - Debora Kennedy, twenty-four

October 21, 1979 - Debra Lynn Senior, seventeen

Arrest and Trial

When Parker was linked to the murders through DNA technology, he was already in prison for other convictions. When investigators showed him the evidence, he confessed to being the Bedroom Basher. He went to trial and in October of 1998, he was convicted of six counts of first-degree murder, one count of attempted murder, and six counts of first-degree rape.

Parker was sentenced to death in January of 1999; he also received life plus sixty-four years.

Outcome

The father of the unborn baby that was killed, Kevin Green, was initially arrested and charged with the attack on his wife that resulted in the loss of the baby. Because the baby was full-term, Kevin Green was charged and convicted of the murder and was sent to prison for seventeen years before it was discovered that Parker was actually the attacker.

THIERRY PAULIN

Date of birth: November 28, 1963

Aliases/Nicknames: The Monster of Montmartre, The Grim Reaper of Paris, The Beast of Montmartre, The Old Lady Killer

Characteristics: Robbery

Number of victims: 18 - 21

Date of murders: 1984 - 1987

Date of arrest: December 1, 1987

Murder method: Strangulation, asphyxiation, stabbing, beating

Known Victims: Anna Barbier-Ponthus, 83; Rachel Cohen, 79; Genevieve Germont; Suzanne Foucault, 89; Ioana Seigaresco, 71; Alice Benaim, 84; Marie Choy, 80; Maria Mico-Diaz, 75; others unnamed

Crime location: Paris, France

Status: Died from complications of AIDS while awaiting trial.

Background

Paulin was born in Fort-de-France, Martinique in 1963. Shortly after his birth, his father took off, leaving Paulin's teenaged mother to care for the baby. Unable to cope, Paulin's paternal grandmother took him in, but she didn't show him a lot of attention or affection. Paulin moved back in with his mother when he was ten, but she had married and he had to learn where he fit in with stepbrothers and sisters. His behavior toward the other children was violent, so his mother contacted his father and asked if he could live with him in France.

Paulin struggled at school both academically and socially, and he was often teased or shunned because he was of mixed race. He failed his exams and decided to enlist in military service at seventeen. He joined the parachutists, but his homosexuality and race brought him much disdain from his fellow soldiers. While he was in the Army, he was arrested after robbing an old woman at knifepoint, and although he received a two-year sentence, it was suspended and he was able to remain in the Army.

Two years later, in 1984, Paulin left the Army and went to live with his mother once again in Nanterre, Paris. Paulin began working in a nightclub called the Paradis Latin which put on transvestite shows. He then began working as a drag artist, imitating Eartha Kitt. It was while he was at the Paradis Latin that he met Jean-Thierry Mathurin. They became lovers and both were drug addicts; however, Mathurin's addiction was far worse than Paulin's. They needed money to pay for their habits, and selling drugs wasn't providing enough for them, so Paulin embarked on a robbery spree that would result in multiple murders.

Murders

Anna Barbier-Ponthus and her friend Germaine Petitot were attacked on October 5, 1984. Petitot survived, but Barbier-Ponthus died after being beaten and asphyxiated. Petitot was so traumatized by the incident that she was unable to give any details or descriptions to the police.

Eight other victims were killed between October and November of 1984, most of whom lived in the 18th arrondissement in Paris. The methods used to commit the murders varied - some victims were suffocated with plastic bags, one was made to drink drain cleaner, and others were beaten to death. The only things that linked all of the murders together were the ages of the victims and the fact they had all been robbed.

A further eight murders were committed between December of 1985 and June of 1986. There was little evidence, but police were able to compare fingerprints found with those at the previous crime scenes and concluded they were from the same person.

Rachel Cohen was murdered by Paulin on November 25, 1987. He attacked another elderly woman the same day who survived, Berthe Finalteri. He killed Genevieve Germont two days later by strangulation.

After recovering from the attack, Madame Finalteri was able to give the police a good description of the man who had attacked her. This led to the arrest of Paulin on December 1, who was recognized from the description by a police inspector as he walked along the road.

Timeline of known murders:

October 5, 1984 - Anna Barbier-Ponthus, eighty-three

October 9, 1984 - Suzanne Foucault, eighty-nine

November 5, 1984 - Ioana Seigaresco, seventy-one

November 7, 1984 - Alice Benaim, eighty-four

November 8, 1984 - Marie Choy, eighty

November 9, 1984 - Maria Mico-Diaz, seventy-five

November 25, 1987 - Rachel Cohen, seventy-nine

November 27, 1987 - Genevieve Germont

NB: Eight more victims were killed between December of 1985 and June of 1986.

Arrest and Trial

Once he was in custody, Paulin confessed to the crimes, admitting to twenty-one murders. He was charged with eighteen, as the others had not yet been fully investigated. He was sent to jail to await his trial.

Outcome

In the early months of 1988, Paulin's body was becoming more ravaged by AIDS. Within the next year, he was almost paralyzed and was sent to the hospital with meningitis and tuberculosis. Paulin died on April 16, 1989. He was still awaiting his trial, and so he was never convicted of the crimes he had confessed to. Mathurin, however, was tried and convicted; he received a life sentence plus eighteen years without parole.

LOUISE PEETE

Date of birth: September 20, 1880
Aliases/Nicknames: Louise M. Gould, Anna Lee
Characteristics: Murder for financial gain
Number of victims: 3 +
Date of murders: 1912, 1920, 1944
Date of arrest: December 20, 1944
Murder method: Shooting
Known Victims: Joe Appel; Jacob Charles Denton; Margaret Logan
Crime location: Texas, California
Status: Executed by gas chamber, April 11, 1947.

Background

Born Lofie Louise Preslar, Peete was born into a wealthy family in Louisiana in 1880. Her parents paid a lot of money for her to receive the best possible education, but she was expelled from the school due to behavior that was deemed inappropriate.

In 1903, Peete met and married Henry Bosley, a traveling salesman. However, when Bosley caught Peete in bed with another man he committed suicide. Peete ended up living in Boston for a while working as a "high-class" prostitute. She was known to steal from her clients as well.

Her next marriage was to Joe Appel who was a wealthy oil baron in Waco, Texas. He was later murdered and his jewellery went missing; Peete was accused of killing him. Appel wasn't to be the only husband of Peete's that met an untimely end, and Peete's actions would eventually get her sent to the gas chamber.

Murders

When Peete was accused of killing Appel, she told the grand jury he had tried to rape her and she killed him in self-defense. She was therefore released from custody and the charges were dropped.

She married Harry Faurote, a hotel clerk, in 1913; he allegedly found her having an affair and committed suicide. Then she married Richard Peete in Denver in 1915. After their daughter was born, Peete left to go to Los Angeles. There, she met Jacob C. Denton who was an oil magnate. He disappeared in 1920, and by the time police arrived to search the house, Peete had already gone. She returned to her husband, but when Denton's body was found, she was tracked down, arrested, and charged.

Found guilty of Denton's murder, she was sentenced to life but only served eighteen years. While she had been incarcerated, her husband Richard committed suicide. Peete started working for Jessie Marcy as her housekeeper, but Marcy died soon after. Another co-worker died in what was considered suspicious circumstances.

Peete moved on to work for Emily Dwight Latham, and she also died. Her next job was as a housekeeper for Arthur C. Logan and his wife Margaret. Peete also married again, this time to Lee Borden Judson. Margaret Logan went missing, and because Peete tried to pass checks with her forged signature, she was instantly the main suspect.

Arrest and Trial

Peete was arrested on December 20, 1944. At her trial she was convicted of murder and was sentenced to die in the gas chamber. Her husband Judson was acquitted of any crimes, but the day after he was questioned by the police, he committed suicide.

Outcome

Peete entered the gas chamber at 10:03 a.m. on April 11, 1947. She was pronounced dead ten minutes later, at 10:13 a.m. She had appeared calm and was smiling as she walked into the chamber, but there was a trembling in her hands. She nodded and smiled at the warden whom she had come to know well, and she thanked a guard when he touched her on the shoulder and told her to "take it easy."

Trivia

Peete was the second woman executed in California.

CHRISTOPHER PETERSON

Date of birth: January 20, 1969

Aliases/Nicknames: Obadayah Ben-Yisrayl, Shotgun Killer

Characteristics: Robbery

Number of victims: 7

Date of murders: October - December 1990

Date of arrest: January 29, 1991

Murder method: Shooting

Known Victims: Lawrence Mills, 43; Rhonda L. Hammersley, 25; Harchand Singh Dhaliwal, 54; Marie Meitzler, 48; Ora L. Wildermuth, 54; Eli Balovski 60; George Balovski, 66

Crime location: Indiana

Status: Death sentence commuted to life imprisonment.

Background

There is little information available on Peterson leading up to his arrest for murder. What is known is that he was a Marine until he deserted. He then lived with his mother and sister in Gary, Indiana. His arrest and subsequent convictions for murder were highly controversial, and there are still those who believe he is innocent.

The controversy stemmed from initial police reports which claimed the perpetrator was a white man with long brown hair. Peterson is a black man who had short hair at the time of the shootings. This opened up allegations of racial prejudice, improper collection of evidence, and wrongful convictions. However, Peterson confessed to the murders when he was arrested. It wasn't until the trials started that he recanted.

Murders

Seven people were shot and killed by Peterson between October 30, 1990, and December 18, 1990, in northern Indiana. A witness was able to give police a description of the killer that would later prove controversial. The killer was described as a slender white man, clean-shaven, with long brown hair.

On October 30, 1990, Lawrence Mill was sitting in his car outside the American Legion Post 66 in Griffith when he was shot and killed. The same day, just hours later, Rhonda Hammersley was shot and killed in the parking lot of a gas station in Cedar Lake.

285

Harchand Singh Dhaliwal was killed while working at a gas station on December 13; money had been taken from the cash register. The next victim was Marie Meitzler who was shot and killed on December 15, while working behind the reception desk at a motel. Money had been stolen during the murder as well. Just six minutes after Meitzler was killed, Peterson shot Ora L. Wildermuth who was standing by an automated teller machine.

The last known victims were brothers George and Eli Balovski. They were shot on December 18, 1990, in a building next to their tailor shop.

Timeline of known murders:

October 30, 1990 - Lawrence Mills, forty-three

October 30, 1990 - Rhonda Hammersley, twenty-five

December 13, 1990 - Harchand Singh Dhaliwal, fifty-four

December 15, 1990 - Marie Meitzler, forty-eight

December 15, 1990 - Ora L. Wildermuth, fifty-four

December 18, 1990 - George Balovski, sixty-six

December 18, 1990 - Eli Balovski, sixty

Arrest and Trial

On January 29, 1991, Peterson was arrested with Antwion McGee after they had committed a robbery and attempted to kill the restaurant manager at a mall near Merrillville. While he was being interviewed, McGee told investigators that another man, Ronald J. Harris, had been with Peterson on two occasions when victims were killed. He also claimed Peterson had admitted to killing them.

Peterson's first trial—for the murders of Lawrence Mills and Rhonda Hammersley—began in September. Remarkably, despite the evidence and confession, Peterson was acquitted of these murders. It certainly didn't help that the original witness description was completely off - Peterson wasn't white, skinny, or long-haired.

He then went on trial in January for the murder of Wildermuth and the attempted murder of a man who had survived an attack. Once again, Peterson was acquitted! The next trial was for the murders of Dhaliwal and Meitzler. At first, a mistrial was called. But, the process started again, and evidence was put forward. This time, Peterson was convicted.

In April of 1992, Peterson went on trial for the Balovski murders. He was convicted. Despite the jury not recommending the death penalty, the judge sentenced Peterson to death.

Of his alleged accomplices, Harris was convicted of murdering Dhaliwal and Hammersley. Toward the end of 1991, McGee was tried for the attempted murder of the restaurant manager and the robbery. The prosecution for Peterson's cases needed McGee to testify, so a plea deal was reached where McGee would only be prosecuted for a lesser offense and receive a sentence of eight years.

Outcome

On December 12, 2004, Peterson was re-sentenced and received one hundred twenty years' imprisonment instead of the death penalty.

ALEXANDER PICHUSHKIN

Date of birth: April 9, 1974

Aliases/Nicknames: The Chessboard Killer, The Bitsa Park Maniac

Characteristics: Most victims were homeless

Number of victims: 49 - 63

Date of murders: 1992 - 2006

Date of arrest: June 14, 2006

Murder method: Bludgeoning with a hammer

Known Victims: Unnamed men, women, and children

Crime location: Moscow, Russia

Status: Sentenced to life imprisonment, with first 15 years in solitary confinement.

Background

Pichushkin was considered to be a normal, sociable, and a happy child until an incident involving a swing resulted in a head injury. Almost overnight, his behavior became more impulsive and aggressive; he was also taunted and physically bullied at school for being a "retard." Subsequently, his mother removed him from the mainstream school and enrolled him in a school for children with learning disabilities.

As a young teen, his grandfather recognized that Pichushkin was actually very intelligent. Believing the school wasn't encouraging him to achieve anything, he took Pichushkin to live in his home so he could encourage him to become involved in intellectual pursuits. Pichushkin had a strong interest in, and talent for, playing chess. Because he had been put back into mainstream schooling, the teasing and bullying by other children continued; it worsened when Pichushkin's grandfather died and he was forced to move back with his mother.

Around this time, Pichushkin began consuming alcohol, and he would join the older men he played chess with at Bitsa Park in drinking vodka. He quickly discovered that the alcohol didn't have the same effects on him as it did his older chess partners. He also developed a dark hobby where he would film himself threatening young children, then watch the videos over and over, admiring the strength and power he had over his victims. But soon this hobby wasn't enough to satisfy him. In 1992, he committed his first murder.

Murders

Pichushkin began killing in 1992. By 2001, his murderous spree had escalated. He targeted elderly men who were homeless and would lure them in by offering them vodka. He would drink with them for a while, then smash in their head with a hammer. Then, he would push the vodka bottle into the wound.

Later he expanded his victim choices, killing younger men, women, and children. His method was to attack his victim from behind to surprise them. This also helped him to avoid getting blood all over his clothes. Sometimes he threw his victims down the sewers beneath Bitsa Park, but this wasn't as successful as one of the victims survived.

The last murder committed by Pichushkin was in the spring of 2006. Thirty-six-year-old Marina Moskalyova's body was discovered in Bitsa Park with the same type of injuries the other victims had suffered. She also had a metro train ticket in her possession that led the police to check surveillance tapes from the station. There they saw her walking with Pichushkin along the platform.

Arrest and Trial

Pichushkin was arrested on June 16, 2006. He was quick to confess to his crimes and went on trial the following year. On October 24, 2007, he was found guilty of forty-nine murders and three counts of attempted murder. Throughout his trial he was kept in a special glass box to protect him from the public.

It took over an hour for the full verdict to be read out in court due to the vast number of charges he was convicted of. He was sentenced to life imprisonment, with the first fifteen years to be spent in solitary confinement.

Outcome

Pichushkin had planned to kill sixty-four people—to match the number of squares on a chessboard—but he was caught before he could reach his target. During his trial, he asked the judge to add another eleven victims to the total to bring it up to sixty, partly because he wanted to be better than his "idol" Andrei Chikatilo.

Trivia

Quote by Pichushkin:

-   "Life without murder is like a life for you without food."

ROBERT PICKTON

Date of birth: October 26, 1949

Aliases/Nicknames: The Pig Farmer Killer, The Pigheaded Killer, Pork Chop Rob, Willie

Characteristics: Rape, dismemberment

Number of victims: 6 - 49

Date of murders: 1995 - 2001

Date of arrest: February 2, 2002

Murder method: Shooting, strangulation with ligature

Known Victims: Sereena Abotsway, 29; Mona Lee Wilson, 26; Andrea Joesbury, 22; Brenda Ann Wolfe, 32; Marnie Lee Frey, 25; Georgina Faith Papin, 35; Jacqueline McDonell,23; Dianne Rock, 34; Heather Bottomley, 25; Jennifer Furminger; Helen Hallmark; Patricia Johnson; Heather Chinnook, 30; Tanya Holyk, 23; Sherry Irving, 24; Inga Hall, 46; Tiffany Drew; Sarah de Vries; Cynthia Feliks; Angela Jardine; Diana Melnick; Debra Jones; Wendy Crawford; Kerry Koski; Andrea Borhaven; Cara Ellis, 25

Crime location: Port Coquitlam, British Columbia, Canada

Status: Sentenced to life imprisonment with possibility of parole after 25 years.

Background

Pickton and his brother David owned a farm in Port Coquitlam, British Columbia in 1992. Although it was meant to be a pig farm, there weren't actually many pigs on the property. There was, however, a very large boar that would roam the property with the dogs, chasing people and trying to bite at them. Pickton was described as fairly quiet and difficult to have a conversation with.

The brothers began neglecting the farm and came up with another way to make money from it. They formed a nonprofit charity called the Piggy Palace Good Times Society and registered it with the Canadian government in 1996. The purpose of the charity was for organizing and operating special events, functions, shows, and dances. However, it mainly involved wild parties with plenty of prostitutes in attendance. The parties were held in a slaughterhouse on the farm that had been converted for such events, and at times up to two thousand people attended. It even became a regular haunt for the local Hells Angels gang.

In March of 1997, an altercation between Pickton and a prostitute called Wendy Lynn Eistetter took place at the farm. Eistetter claimed Pickton had handcuffed her and had cut her several times with a knife before she was able to escape by stabbing him in return. In January of 1998, the charges against Pickton were dismissed. Following this, the authorities banned the Picktons from throwing any more organized parties on the property and their nonprofit charity status was cancelled.

Women who visited the property over the next three years started going missing, and it wasn't until police searched the farm for illegal firearms that the true nature of what was going on at the farm became clear.

Murders

The exact details of each murder, including how they were killed and disposed of, are yet to be discovered. What is known is that Pickton would bring prostitutes to his farm and handcuff them before raping them. After strangling them to death, it is alleged he sometimes bled the body, removed the gut, and put the body through a woodchipper. The remains were then fed to his pigs. Another allegation is that the victims' bodies were ground up and mixed in with mincemeat to create sausages. These were then given to his family and friends.

It's believed Pickton lured the prostitutes back to the farm with the pretense of wanting to pay for sexual services. Sometimes, while engaged in sexual intercourse, Pickton would suddenly accuse the woman of doing something, like stealing from him, and this would cause his rage to build up to the point where he would kill them.

Timeline of known victims:

August of 2001 - Sereena Abotsway, twenty-nine

November 30, 2001 - Mona Lee Wilson, twenty-six

June of 2001 - Andrea Joesbury, twenty-two

April 25, 2000 - Brenda Ann Wolfe, thirty-two

Alleged victims:

August of 1991 - Mary Ann Clark (Nancy Greek), twenty-five

December of 1995 - Diana Melnick

1996 - Cara Louise Ellis (Nicky Trimble), twenty-five

October 1996 - Tanya Holyk, twenty-three

1997 - Sherry Irving, twenty-four

March of 1997 - Andrea Fay Borhaven

August of 1997 - Helen Mae Hallmark

December of 1997 - Cynthia Feliks

January of 1998 - Kerry Koski

February of 1998 - Inga Monique Hall, forty-six

April of 1998 - Sarah de Vries

November 20, 1998 - Angela Rebecca Jardine

January of 1999 - Jacqueline Michelle McDonell, twenty-three

December of 1999 - Wendy Crawford

December of 1999 - Tiffany Drew

1999 - Jennifer Lynn Furminger

December of 2000 - Debra Lynne Jones

December of 2000 - Dawn Teresa Crey

October 19, 2001 - Dianne Rosemary Rock, thirty-four

April 17, 2001 - Heather Kathleen Bottomley, twenty-five

March of 2001 - Patricia Rose Johnson

April of 2001 - Heather Chinnook, thirty

March 16, 2001 - Yvonne Marie Boen, thirty-four

Arrest and Trial

A search warrant was issued to search the property for illegal firearms on February 6, 2002. The Pickton brothers were arrested and taken to the police station, and investigators requested another warrant so they could search for evidence related to the many missing women cases. It was granted. During the search they found a few items belonging to one of the missing women.

The following day, Pickton was charged with numerous firearm offenses. Since there wasn't enough information to charge him with murder, he was released from custody. Police did keep him under surveillance, however. By the end of February, they had enough evidence and Pickton was arrested again on February 22. This time, he was charged with first-degree murder for the deaths of Mona Wilson and Sereena Abotsway.

Three more murder charges were added on April 2, regarding the deaths of Heather Bottomley, Jacqueline McDonell, and Diane Rock. That same month he was also charged with murdering Andrea Joesbury and Brenda Wolfe. On September 20, he received charges of murder for the deaths of Georgina Papin, Helen Hallmark, Patricia Johnson and Jennifer Furminger. Four more charges—for the murders of Tanya Holyk, Heather Chinnook, Inga Hall, and Sherry Irving—were added on October 3.

Now charged with a total of fifteen murders, Pickton was considered one of the worst serial killers in Canadian history. But it wasn't over yet. On May 26, 2005, he was charged with an additional twelve murders for the deaths of Andrea Borhaven, Cara Ellis, Debra Jones, Tiffany Drew, Marnie Frey, Sarah de Vries, Kerry Koski, Angela Jardine, Cynthia Feliks, Diana Melnick, Wendy Crawford, and a Jane Doe. The total murder charges equalled twenty-seven.

Pickton's initial trial began in Westminster on January 30, 2006, where he pleaded not guilty. It took almost a year to determine which evidence could be presented in court. The judge dismissed the charge for the Jane Doe on March 2 due to lack of evidence.

The judge decided to split the charges (due to the nature and size of the case) into two groups - one with six murder charges and the other with the remaining twenty. After a delay, the trial began on January 22, 2007. On December 9, 2007, the jury found Pickton not guilty of the first-degree murder charges. But, they found him guilty of second-degree murder for each of the six victims. Pickton was sentenced to life imprisonment with the possibility of parole after twenty-five years.

Outcome

On August 4, 2010, the rest of the pending murder charges against Pickton were stayed by the Crown prosecutors. This meant Pickton would never go to trial for the other twenty murder charges.

Trivia

A book that had apparently been written by Pickton about his life went on sale in 2016. It was called *Pickton: In His Own Words*, and the controversy surrounding it went as high as the government. The public didn't agree with Pickton getting any financial gain from sales of the book.

NORBERT POEHLKE

Date of birth: September 15, 1951

Aliases/Nicknames: The Hammer-Killer

Characteristics: Parricide, filicide, bank robbery

Number of victims: 6

Date of murders: 1984 - 1985

Date of arrest: Died before arrest

Murder method: Shooting

Known Victims: Siegfried Pfitzer, 47; Eugene Wethey, 37; Wilfried Scheider, 26; his wife Ingeborg Poehlke and his sons Adrian and Gabriel

Crime location: Germany, Italy

Status: Committed suicide before apprehension.

Background

Poehlke was considered an upstanding member of society, a German police officer whose job it was to uphold the law. But Poehlke was secretly spending a lot of his time on the wrong side of the law. As the authorities began investigating him, everything took a tragic turn for the worse.

Murders

Poehlke's first victim, Siegfried Pfitzer, was found on May 3, 1984, at a rest stop in Marback West Germany. He had been shot in the head. His car was later found a quarter of a mile away after it had been used in a bank robbery.

On December 21, Eugene Wethey was found dead at a rest stop near Nuremburg. He had been shot, and his car was missing. The car was used a week later by Poehlke to commit a bank robbery. Wilfried Scheider was found shot to death on July 22, 1985, in a parking lot in Beilstein-Schmidhausen. The weapon used was identified as a police officer issued pistol. The car had also been used in the commission of a bank robbery.

Timeline of known murders:

May 3, 1984 - Siegfried Pfitzer, forty-seven

December 21, 1984 - Eugene Wethey, thirty-seven

July 22, 1985 - Wilfried Scheider, twenty-six

October 20, 1985 - Ingeborg Poehlke

October 20, 1985 - Adrian Poehlke

October 23, 1985 - Gabriel Poehlke

Arrest and Trial

On September 29, 1985, a police uniform was found in a locker in a railway station by anti-terrorist officers who were checking the station for bombs. The uniform was traced back to Poehlke, and he said he had left it there after changing in a hurry to get to a funeral. But, when police looked into it, there hadn't been any deaths in Poehlke's family. They did discover, however, that he was about four hundred thousand dollars in debt, largely due to costly medical treatments for his daughter who had succumbed to cancer in 1984.

Poehlke requested sick leave on October 14, which was granted. Police went to his home several days later to question him about the robberies and the murders, but nobody answered the door. The police officers assumed Poehlke had fled, so they entered the house. In the bathroom they found the dead body of Poehlke's wife, who had been shot in the head twice. Their son Adrian was found in a bedroom, also shot to death.

On October 23, Poehlke's car was found near Brindisi, Italy. Inside were the bodies of Poehlke and his son Gabriel. Both had been shot in what was obviously a murder-suicide. The case was considered closed.

Outcome

Following Poehlke's suicide, ballistics confirmed that his gun was the murder weapon used in the first three murders.

HARRY POWERS

Date of birth: 1893

Aliases/Nicknames: Cornelius O. Pierson, A.R. Weaver, Mail-order Bluebeard, The West Virginia Bluebeard

Characteristics: Murder for financial gain

Number of victims: 5 +

Date of murders: 1931

Date of arrest: August of 1931

Murder method: Hanging, bludgeoning with a hammer

Known Victims: Aster Eicher, 50, and her children Greta, 14, Harry, 12, and Anabel, 9; Dorothy Lemke, 50

Crime location: Quiet Dell, West Virginia

Status: Executed by hanging on March 18, 1932.

Background

Powers was born Herman Drenth in the Netherlands in 1893. In 1910, he immigrated with his family to the United States, first settling in Iowa before moving to West Virginia in 1926. His father was a farmer, and Powers had no intention of being like him. He wanted a better and more highly esteemed way of life, and he came up with numerous ways to make money.

Powers married Luella Strother in 1927. Luella had placed an advertisement in the Lonely Hearts Magazine. In it, she stated she owned a grocery store and a farm, so naturally Powers was attracted to her right away. Despite now having a wife, Powers started putting his own advertisements in the magazine and he received many letters in response—up to twenty a day. Of course, he didn't use his own name; he created aliases so nobody would know his real identity.

Powers decided to build a basement and garage at his home. He believed he had come up with the perfect way to increase his finances, and now he had a place where he could carry out his plans without detection.

Murders

Powers had been writing letters to Asta Eicher using the alias Cornelius O. Pierson. Eicher was a widow with three children who lived in Park Ridge, Illinois. On June 23, 1931, Powers visited them. Leaving the children in the hands of Elizabeth Abernathy, Eicher went away with Powers.

Abernathy received a letter saying Powers was coming to collect the children. When he had, he got one of the children to try to withdraw money from Eicher's account at the bank. But, the bank refused to hand over any money due to the forged signature on the check. Powers gathered up the children and they quickly left, telling the neighbors they were going on a trip to Europe.

Powers' next victim was another lonely heart, Dorothy Lemke, who lived in Northboro, Massachusetts. After sending letters back and forth, Powers convinced her to come to Iowa to marry him. He managed to persuade her to withdraw a large amount from her account, to the value of four thousand dollars. She disappeared just as Eicher and her children had.

Arrest and Trial

On August 26, 1931, police started to investigate the disappearances of Eicher and her three children. Looking at her last known contacts, they came across the name Cornelius O. Pierson. They quickly established that there was no such person by that name, but the description was a match for Powers.

After Powers was arrested, police searched his home and stumbled across a horrific scene. There were four rooms in the basement, and bloody evidence was found in all of them. Hair, bloodstained clothes, a footprint of a child, and a burned bankbook were among the first items found. A ditch outside the house appeared to have been filled in recently, so the police began to dig it up. Buried in the dirt were the bodies of all the murder victims.

All of the female victims had been strangled, but Eicher's son had been bashed in the head with a hammer. The officers discovered a large number of love letters in the trunk of Powers' car, and it looked as though he was already planning his next murder and robbery.

Powers' trial began on December 7, 1931; it lasted only five days. He was convicted of all crimes and, on December 12, he was sentenced to die by hanging.

Outcome

Powers was taken to the gallows at the Moundsville State Penitentiary on March 18, 1932. He declined to make a final statement. After the hood was put over his head, the trapdoor was released, and Powers was hanged. He was pronounced deceased eleven minutes later.

Trivia

–   For an annual fee ($4.95 for men, $1.95 for women), members got a listing of available matches, mostly widows and widowers, with a description of their most attractive features - whether real or not. Among American Friendship's clients in 1931 was a man who, based upon his profile, should have had no trouble attracting the ladies.

–   "Wealthy widower," the ad read, "worth $150,000. Has income from $400 to $2,000 a month." His profession was listed as "civil engineer. Own a beautiful 10-room brick home, completely furnished with everything that would make a good woman happy. My wife would have her own car and plenty of spending money. Would have nothing to do but enjoy herself."

CRAIG PRICE

Date of birth: October 11, 1973

Aliases/Nicknames: The Warwick Slasher

Characteristics: Juvenile Murderer

Number of victims: 4

Date of murders: 1987, 1989

Date of arrest: September of 1989

Murder method: Stabbing

Known Victims: Rebecca Spencer, 27; Joan Heaton, 39, and her daughters, Jennifer 10, and Melissa 8

Crime location: Warwick, Rhode Island

Status: Sentenced to a total of 29 years due to bad behavior while incarcerated.

Background

Price is one of the youngest serial killers ever discovered in America. He came from a working-class family in Rhode Island. And, by the time he was fifteen years old, he already had an extensive history of criminal offenses. These included peeping, theft, drugs, and burglary. But, what authorities didn't know, was that two years earlier he had committed one of his worst crimes ever. At the age of just thirteen, Price had committed his first violent murder.

Price had a violent temper, often getting into fights at home with family members; the police had visited the home numerous times to break up disputes. At one point, Price and a group of other young delinquents joined together to commit multiple burglaries, breaking into homes to steal whatever they could to make money.

This violent and troubled youth would eventually come under suspicion for a murder that had taken place in his neighborhood. During his interview with police, he calmly confessed to committing four murders.

Murders

Price's first victim, Rebecca Spencer, was killed when he was just thirteen years old. The victim was a white woman living in the neighborhood whom Price would often watch through the windows. On the day she died, he had broken into her house and stabbed her to death with a knife he found in the kitchen. Price was never considered a suspect, most likely because of his age.

Two years later, at fifteen, he killed Joan Heaton and her two daughters, Jennifer and Melissa. Like Spencer, they had also been stabbed to death. It wasn't until a detective happened to notice a large cut on Price's hand that he became the number one suspect.

Arrest and Trial

Price was arrested in September of 1989. Without any form of persuasion, he openly confessed to the murders. This made him the youngest serial killer in American history. Price was tried as a minor because of his age, which meant that even though he was convicted, he could only be incarcerated until he was twenty-one.

Price was charged with numerous offenses while imprisoned, including criminal contempt, extortion, and violation of probation for fighting while incarcerated. He received a further sentence of ten to twenty-five years for these infractions.

Outcome

Price and another inmate engaged in a fight on July 29, 2009. While correctional officers were breaking up the fight, one of them was stabbed in the finger by a shank held by Price. As a result, Price was moved to another prison.

CLEOPHUS PRINCE JR.

Date of birth: July 24, 1967

Aliases/Nicknames: The Clairemont Killer

Characteristics: Rape, robbery

Number of victims: 6

Date of murders: January 12, 1990 –September 13, 1990

Date of arrest: February 4, 1991

Murder method: Stabbing

Known Victims: Tiffany Schultz, 20; Janene Weinhold, 21; Holly Tarr, 18; Elissa Keller, 38; Pamela Clark, 42, and her daughter Amber, 18

Crime location: San Diego County, California

Status: Sentenced to death, awaiting execution.

Background

Prince was born and raised in Birmingham to parents Cleophus Sr. and Dorothy. Before he had turned two years old, his father was arrested and convicted of murder following an incident outside a grocery store. According to Cleophus Sr., he was confronted by several men armed with knives, so he shot a man to death to defend himself. He was sentenced to forty years. But he only served just over eleven years in prison.

While his father was in prison, Prince's mother struggled to take care of him and his sister, so the children spent a lot of their time living with their grandparents. The children enjoyed the carefree lifestyle they experienced with their grandparents; living with their parents was stressful.

Prince was not keen on school and failed to stay in jobs. So, in 1987, he enlisted in the Navy. His parents were pleased with this and fully supported him. Prince completed his training at the Great Lakes Naval Training Center located near Chicago. He was then sent to the Miramar Naval Air Station in San Diego where he worked as a mechanic.

In 1989, Prince was charged with larceny. Following his court-martial, he was sentenced to twenty-seven days in the brig. He was subsequently discharged from the Navy. Moving to Buena Vista Gardens, he got an apartment. The following year, Prince's behavior took a deadly turn.

Murders

With each murder Prince committed, he entered the victim's home through an unlocked window or door during the day and waited for them to return home. He would surprise them—either just after or during bathing—and stab them to death with the victim's own kitchen knives. He bragged about the murders to a friend and kept jewelry items from the victims. One woman's wedding ring was worn around his neck and another ring was given to his girlfriend.

A witness had seen Prince running from the Buena Vista Garden Apartment complex after the murder of Holly Tarr. He gave the police a description and a composite drawing was distributed.

Timeline of known murders:

January 12, 1990 - Tiffany Schultz, twenty-one

February 16, 1990 - Janene Weinhold, twenty-one

April 3, 1990 - Holly Tarr, eighteen

May 20, 1990 - Elissa Keller, thirty-eight

September 13, 1990 - Pamela Clark, forty-two

September 13, 1990 - Amber Clark, eighteen

Arrest and Trial

In February of 1991, a woman heard someone outside her front door just as she was getting ready to shower, and she ran from the house. She asked a neighbor for help, and they confronted Prince. He tried to make up an excuse but then just rushed off. A witness noted his license plate number and identified him from photographs shown by the police.

Prince was arrested on February 4, 1991. When asked to provide saliva and blood samples for DNA analysis, he agreed. The test results proved a link to Janene Weinhold's murder. Due to the pattern and similarities between that case and the others, police were able to link Prince to all of the crimes.

Prince was put on trial in March of 1992. Despite arguments from the defense, Prince was found guilty of six counts of first-degree murder, as well as twenty-one felony charges, on July 15, 1993. On November 5, 1993, he was sentenced to death.

Outcome

Prince lodged an appeal against his sentence, claiming the media coverage had created a "presumption of guilt" with the jury. The California Supreme Court denied his appeal.

Prince is still on death row awaiting his execution.

DENNIS RADER

Date of birth: March 9, 1945

Aliases/Nicknames: The BTK Killer, The BTK Strangler

Characteristics: Fetishist, sadist

Number of victims: 10

Date of murders: 1974 - 1991

Date of arrest: February 25, 2005

Murder method: Strangulation with ligature, hanging, stabbing

Known Victims: Joseph Otero, 38, his wife Julie, 34, and two of their children: Joseph II, 9, and Josephine, 11; Kathryn Bright, 21; Shirley Vian Relford, 24; Nancy Fox, 25; Marine Hedge, 53; Vicki Wegerle, 28; Dolores E. Davis, 62

Crime location: Sedgwick County, Kansas

Status: Sentenced to life imprisonment with the possibility of parole after 175 years.

Background

Rader displayed disturbing behaviors from a very young age, though nobody seemed to take them too seriously. He was known to torture small animals while he was still a young child which is a known indicator of budding serial killers. Rader also developed a sexual fetish involving women's underwear; he would often wear them himself, especially if they had belonged to one of his victims.

From 1966 to 1970, Rader served in the United States Air Force. After he left the service, he worked in the meat department of a supermarket. In 1971, he married Paula Dietz, and they went on to have two children. Rader decided to further his education. He attended community college to gain an associate's degree in electronics, graduating in 1973. He then enrolled with Wichita State University and attained a bachelor's degree in administration of justice in 1979.

Despite his degrees, Rader went on to have a number of jobs over the years, including security work, outdoor supplies assembly, and dogcatcher. Ironically, he would be employed to install security alarms for people who were terrified of the BTK killer. Little did they know, the man they feared so much was in their homes! While working as a dogcatcher, many people reported his behavior with the animals as being overly strict, and he was also accused of euthanizing a dog for no legitimate reason.

Rader avoided suspicion for a long time because he was considered to be a fine member of society. He was a family man who worked hard, and he was a Cub Scout leader. He also attended church each week and was a member of the church council. Nobody had a clue that this man had brutally tortured and killed ten people, including children, over a period of nearly twenty years.

Murders

On January 15, 1974, Rader broke into the home of the Otero family and massacred them all. Joseph and his wife Julie were strangled to death. Their daughter Josephine was found bound and hanging in the basement. And their son Joseph was asphyxiated with a bag over his head. Their stolen car was later found in a parking lot outside a store.

Kathryn Bright was attacked by Rader in her home on April 4, 1974. She was stabbed to death; her brother was shot, but he survived his injuries. The next victim was Shirley Vian Relford, who was found bound and strangled in her home on March 17, 1977.

Rader next killed Nancy Fox on December 8, 1977. He had entered her home and strangled her to death. This time he placed a call to the emergency services to report the murder, and his voice was recorded for the first time.

On April 27, 1985, Marine Hedge disappeared from her home which was on the same block as Rader's. Her body was found on May 5. Vicki Wegerle was strangled in her home on September 16, 1985. Her car was stolen and later located two blocks away. The last known victim was Dolores Davis. She was abducted from her home on January 19, 1991, and was later found on February 1, 1991.

Timeline of known murders:

January 15, 1974 - Joseph Otero, thirty-eight

January 15, 1974 - Julie Otero, thirty-three

January 15, 1974 - Joseph Otero II, nine

January 15, 1974 - Josephine Otero, eleven

April 4, 1974 - Kathryn Bright, twenty-one

March 17, 1977 - Shirley Vian Relford, twenty-four

December 8, 1977 - Nancy Fox, twenty-five

April 27, 1985 - Marine Hedge, fifty-three

September 16, 1986 - Vicki Wegerle, twenty-eight

January 19, 1991 - Dolores E. Davis, sixty-two

Arrest and Trial

Time went on and the police didn't seem any closer to solving the cases. In 2004, Rader started sending letters to the local media. Some of the letters had crime scene photographs or a copy of a driver's license enclosed to prove the letters were written by the killer. The return address was "Bill Thomas Killman," although that was not how he got his nickname. He got it from letters he would write and deliver at the police stations, and sign them BTK for Bind, Torture, Kill. He wrote that under the initials on the first letter he wrote to the police.

More letters followed containing graphic details about the murders; even a chapter list for a proposed book *The BTK Story* was sent. Some of the items sent to the media and the police were chillingly bizarre, including a doll that was bound at the wrists and feet with a bag over its head.

In one of his letters, Rader actually asked the police if they could trace him if he put the letters on a floppy disk. The police placed an ad in the local paper saying it was safe to use disks, and Rader fell for the lie. Technicians found metadata embedded in a document Rader had deleted which contained the words "Christ Lutheran Church." The modifier of the document was "Dennis."

Rader was arrested on February 25, 2005. The arresting officer asked him if he knew why he was being arrested and Rader replied that he had his suspicions. A number of agencies joined in the search of Rader's home and vehicle, the church, and the library where some of the letters had been mailed from.

On February 28, 2005, Rader was charged with ten counts of first-degree murder. Soon after, the press ran an article claiming he had confessed to other murders, but this was false information. Rader's first court appearance was by video on March 1. His bail was set at ten million dollars and he was appointed a public defender.

Rader entered not guilty pleas on all counts on May 3. Then he changed his plea on June 27 to guilty on all ten counts of murder. He went on to graphically describe the murders; he showed no remorse or emotion, and he made no apologies. Sentencing took place on August 18, 2005. Rader was sentenced to ten consecutive life sentences and would be eligible for parole in the year 2180.

Outcome

Despite showing no emotion throughout his trial, apparently, while being transferred to El Dorado after his sentencing, he began to cry when the radio broadcast the statements from the families of the victims. Rader is held in a special management unit, also known as solitary confinement, for his own protection. He is likely to spend the rest of his days in there.

Trivia

Quotes by Rader:

- "When this monster entered my brain, I will never know, but it is here to stay. How does one cure himself? I can't stop it, the monster goes on, and hurts me as well as society. Maybe you can stop him. I can't."
- "I actually think I may be possessed with demons, I was dropped on my head as a kid."

RICHARD RAMIREZ

Date of birth: February 29, 1960

Aliases/Nicknames: The Night Stalker, The Walk-In Killer, The Valley Intruder

Characteristics: Robbery, rape, mutilation

Number of victims: 13 - 16 +

Date of murders: April 10, 1984 - August 24, 1985

Date of arrest: August 31, 1985

Murder method: Stabbing, shooting, bludgeoning

Known Victims: Jennie Vincow, 79; Dayle Okazaki, 34; Tsai "Veronica" Lan Yu, 30; Vincent Zazzara, 64, and his wife Maxine, 44; William "Bill" Doi, 66; Mable "Ma Bell" Keller, 83; Mary Louise Cannon, 75; Joyce Lucille Nelson, 61; Max Kneiding 68; Lela Kneiding, 66; Chainarong Khovananth,32; Elyas Abowath, 35

Crime location: Los Angeles, California

Status: Sentenced to death. Died due to complications of B-cell lymphoma, June 7, 2013.

Background

Ramirez was one of five children born to Julian and Mercedes Ramirez. His father had been a former police officer in Juarez, Mexico, but ended up working on the Santa Fe railroad after relocating to Texas. Although he was a hard-working man, he was prone to bursts of anger and would often physically abuse his wife and children.

When Ramirez was two years old, he was struck by a falling piece of furniture and sustained a large laceration on his forehead. Then, when he was five, he was struck in the head by a swing and knocked unconscious. As a result, he suffered frequently from seizures until his early teens.

From the age of twelve, Ramirez spent a lot of time with his cousin Miguel Ramirez. Miguel was much older and had been an Army Green Beret combat veteran who served in the Vietnam War. He would tell young Ramirez about the atrocities he witnessed and the violent rapes he committed while stationed in Vietnam. There was even a photo of him posing with a severed head belonging to a woman he had brutalized.

Ramirez had been smoking cannabis from a young age, and he would smoke with Miguel while listening to his gruesome war exploits. Miguel taught Ramirez some skills he learned in the military, including stealth tactics and how to kill. On May 4, 1973, Ramirez was with Miguel at his home when

Miguel shot his wife in the face during an argument. Miguel was found not guilty by reason of insanity, and he spent the next four years incarcerated in the state mental hospital.

For a while after the shooting, Ramirez lived with his sister and her husband Roberto, and he withdrew from friends and family. Roberto was a peeping tom, and he would take Ramirez along with him at night to peep through windows. It was at this time that Ramirez developed an interest in Satanism and started using harder drugs, namely LSD.

As a teenager, Ramirez began associating his sexual fantasies with violence. While he was still at school he worked part-time at a Holiday Inn, which he used to his advantage. He would use his passkey to enter the rooms and rob the guests. One night, however, a guest returned to his room to find Ramirez trying to rape his wife; the man proceeded to beat him. Ramirez was arrested, but the charges were dropped when the couple refused to testify. Nevertheless, he lost his job at the Holiday Inn.

Ramirez moved from Texas to California when he was twenty-two years old, and he decided to settle there. Within a few years, he would embark on a killing spree that would make him one of the most famous serial killers in America.

Murders

The body of Jennie Vincow was found on June 28, 1984, in her apartment. She had been stabbed multiple times while sleeping in her bed, and her throat had been cut so deep that she was almost decapitated. Ramirez had gained access to her apartment through a mesh screen covering an open window.

On March 17, 1985, Maria Hernandez was shot in the face outside her apartment, but she survived. Her roommate, Dayle Okazaki, heard the gunshot and hid behind a counter in the kitchen. As she raised her head to see where Ramirez was, he shot her in the forehead, killing her. Shortly afterward, he came across Tsai-Lan Yu in her car in Monterey Park. He pulled her out of her car and shot her twice.

Ramirez broke into a home in Whittier on March 27, 1985, and killed Vincent Zazzara in his bed. When his wife Maxine woke, Ramirez beat and bound her, and he demanded to know where their valuables were kept. While he searched the room, Maxine managed to get herself free, and she pulled a shotgun out from under the bed. Unfortunately, it wasn't loaded. Ramirez, now enraged, shot her three times and then mutilated her body with multiple stab wounds. He also gouged out her eyes and put them in a jewelry box he took with him.

Bill Doi and his wife Lillian were surprised by Ramirez in their home on May 14, 1985. He shot Bill in the face and then beat him until he was unconscious. He then bound Lillian and raped her before searching the house for valuables. Bill lived long enough to get to the hospital but eventually succumbed to his injuries.

Ramirez, driving a stolen vehicle, entered the home of Mabel "Ma" Bell and her sister Florence "Nettie" Lang on the night of May 29. Using a hammer he found in their kitchen, he bound Land and bludgeoned her. He then bound and bludgeoned Bell and gave her electric shocks using an electrical cord. Ramirez raped Lang and drew a pentagram on her thigh and on the bedroom walls with lipstick. The women weren't found for two days. Although both were alive, Bell later died from her injuries.

On July 2, 1985, Ramirez quietly entered the home of Mary Louise Cannon. She was asleep in her bed when he bludgeoned her with a lamp until she fell unconscious. Then he stabbed her using one of her own kitchen knives.

Five days later, Joyce Lucille Nelson was beaten to death in her home while sleeping on the living room couch. Kicking her in the head, he left a clear shoe print from his sneaker on her face.

Ramirez bought a machete on July 20, 1985, and drove a stolen car to Glendale. Entering the home of Lela and Maxson Kneiding, he burst into their bedroom. He hacked at both of them with the machete before he shot each of them in the head. After they died, he inflicted further wounds to their bodies with the machete.

Hours later, he killed Chainarong Khovananth in his home by shooting him in the head. Ramirez raped his wife Somkid multiple times, sodomized her, and beat her. Their young son was bound as Ramirez dragged Somkid around and told her to show him where the valuables were kept. As he attacked her, he forced her to "swear to Satan."

The next victims were Elyas Abowath and his wife Sakina. On August 8, 1985, Ramirez entered their home and made his way to the bedroom. He shot Elyas in the head, killing him instantly. Sakina was handcuffed, beaten, and forced to show him where the jewelry was stored before Ramirez sodomized and raped her. She too was forced to "swear to Satan." Her young son entered the room, so Ramirez tied him up. As soon as Ramirez left, Sakina untied her son and went to the neighbors for help.

The last known murder committed by Ramirez occurred on August 18. He broke into the home of Peter and Barbara Pan. Peter was shot in the head right away. Barbara was sexually violated and beaten before Ramirez shot her in the head. Remarkably, Barbara survived. Ramirez drew a pentagram on the bedroom wall in lipstick and wrote "Jack the Knife."

Timeline of known murders:

June 28, 1984 - Jennie Vincow, seventy-nine

March 17, 1985 - Dayle Okazaki, thirty-four

March 17, 1985 - Tsai Lan Yu, thirty

March 27, 1985 - Vincent Zazzara, sixty-four

March 27, 1985 - Maxine Zazzara, forty-four

April 14, 1985 - William Doi, sixty-six

June 1, 1985 - Mable Keller, eighty-three

July 2, 1985 - Mary Louise Cannon, seventy-five

July 7, 1985 - Joyce Lucille Nelson, sixty-one

July 20, 1985 - Max Kneiding, sixty-eight

July 20, 1985 - Leila Kneiding, sixty-six

July 20, 1985 - Chainarong Khovananth, thirty-two

August 9, 1985 - Elyas Abowath, thirty-five

Arrest and Trial

On August 24, Ramirez broke into the apartment of Bill Carns and Inez Erickson. Carns was shot in the head, and Ramirez raped Erickson. He tied her up before he left, but she was able to get to the window and see the vehicle he was driving. She gave a description of both the car and Ramirez to the police, and the information was broadcast on news reports. The car was identified by a teenager who managed to write down part of the license plate number.

On August 28, the car was located, and a fingerprint was found on the mirror. Authorities now knew their suspect was Ramirez. His mugshots were shown on national television and splashed across the cover of every major newspaper throughout California. The following day, a group of people saw Ramirez, surrounded him, and beat him as he tried to steal another car. When police arrived, the angry mob was still beating Ramirez. Police had to intervene before they killed him.

The trial took place in 1989 and ended on September 20 with a guilty verdict on multiple charges. These included thirteen counts of murder, five attempted murders, fourteen burglaries and eleven sexual assaults. On November 7, 1989, he was sentenced to death.

Outcome

While awaiting his execution date, Ramirez became unwell from B-cell lymphoma, a chronic hepatitis C infection, and a history of chronic substance abuse. His health deteriorated further, and he was transferred to Marin General Hospital in Greenbrae, California, where he died on June 7, 2013, as a result of the lymphoma. He was fifty-three years old at his time of death and had been sitting on death row for twenty-three years.

Trivia

This questionnaire with Richard appeared in Answer Me! Issue 4:

- Favorite Sports: Rugby, Football, Boxing
- Favorite Music: Heavy Metal
- Favorite Actress: Samantha Strong
- Favorite Vacation Spot: URANUS
- Favorite Food: Women's feet
- Favorite Color: Red
- Pastimes / Hobbies: Traveling and measuring coffins
- Biggest Like: Cocaine
- Biggest Dislike: Hypocrites, Authority
- Make a Wish: To have my finger on a nuclear trigger device
- What do you look for in a girl: Nice Ass, Good Legs
- Perfect way to spend a date: Moonlit night drinking rum at a cemetery
- Describe Yourself: Asshole - and proud of it
- Motto: Live each day as if it's your last.
- If you like a girl, how do you get a girl to notice you? I pull out my gun
- What's one thing you'd change about yourself? Not a damn thing, except where I'm at.
- How has your life changed as a result of your success? Privacy is a thing of the past.

- What's your message to your fans? Keep your spirit strong.

DAVID PARKER RAY

Date of birth: November 6, 1939

Aliases/Nicknames: The Toy-Box Killer

Characteristics: Built a torture chamber

Number of victims: Suspected of 60 Murders

Date of murders: 1960s - 1999

Date of arrest: March 12, 1999

Murder method: Unknown

Known Victims: Unidentified and unnamed women

Crime location: Truth or Consequences, New Mexico

Status: Not convicted of murder. Received a sentence of 224 years imprisonment for other crimes. Died of a heart attack on May 28, 2002.

Background

As a child, Ray lived with his grandfather, but his abusive father would visit from time to time. In addition to the physical abuse he suffered at the hands of his father, Ray was also bullied at school, largely because he displayed extreme shyness around girls. By the time he was a teenager, he had started using drugs and alcohol regularly and was having violent sexual fantasies.

Ray fantasized about torture, rape, and murder, and he collected photos of women in bondage. He also made a number of drawings, described as sadomasochistic, which were discovered by his sister. After he finished school, he worked as a mechanic. Then he enlisted with the Army. Ray continued to work as a mechanic while he served in the Army, and he received an honorable discharge when he left.

Ray eventually lived in Elephant Butte, New Mexico, where he planned and designed the perfect torture chamber so he could carry out his horrendous fantasies. Known as the "Toy Box," Ray fitted out a mobile home with every piece of equipment, tool, and torture device he could think of, including wall charts on how to inflict the most amount of pain.

In such an isolated location, Ray could get away with just about anything without detection—until one of his abductees fought her way out of the Toy Box and made a run for it.

Murders

Ray was accused by many people—including his accomplices—of committing multiple murders, though no bodies have ever been found. The police think the number of murders could be as high as sixty. Ray would abduct women and take them back to the Toy Box where he could do whatever he wanted to them, including brutal rape, sodomy, and torture.

He had set the Toy Box up with multiple tools and devices, mostly for inflicting pain and torture. These included clamps, pulleys, whips, chains, leg spreader bars, straps, saws, and surgical blades. There was also an abundance of sex toys and diagrams showing different ways to inflict pain on a person. A mirror on the ceiling meant the victim could see what was being done to them.

On March 19, 1999, Ray pretended to be an undercover police officer and convinced Cynthia Vigil that she was being arrested for prostitution. He handcuffed her and took her to the Toy Box. Three days later, she managed to escape, during which she was involved in a fight with Ray's partner Cindy Hendy. Vigil stabbed Hendy in the neck with an ice pick and ran out the door, naked, with an iron slave collar around her neck and padlocked chains.

Arrest and Trial

After Vigil contacted the police, they came and arrested Ray. At the time, they thought Ray was only involved in the attack on Vigil; they were unaware of the possibility that he might be a serial killer. Another victim came forward after details of the arrest were made public. Angelica Montano told the police she had endured the same vile treatment in the Toy Box; she had reported it at the time, but nobody had followed up on it.

A third victim was identified by a video Ray had recorded as he tortured her. Kelli Garrett was abducted and terrorized by Ray in July of 1996. He drugged her over a two-day period while he raped and tortured her. When he had had enough, he slashed her throat and dumped her on the side of the road. But, he didn't realize she was actually still alive.

It was decided that Ray would have three trials: one for each victim. The first trial ended up a mistrial and required a retrial. Ray was found guilty of all twelve counts attributed to his attack on Cynthia Vigil. The second trial was meant to be for Angelica Montano's case, but she died before it started, so the trial was dropped. For the third trial, he agreed to a plea bargain and was sentenced to two hundred twenty-four years in prison.

Outcome

Ray was on the way to Lea County Correctional Facility in New Mexico to be questioned by the state police when he collapsed and died on May 28, 2002. Ray had suffered a fatal heart attack.

MELVIN REES

Date of birth: 1928

Aliases/Nicknames: The Sex Beast

Characteristics: Rape

Number of victims: 5 - 9

Date of murders: June 26, 1957; January 11, 1959

Date of arrest: June 24, 1960

Murder method: Shooting, strangulation, asphyxiation, bludgeoning

Known Victims: Margaret Harold; Carroll Jackson, his wife Mildred, and their two daughters, Susan, 4, and Janet, 18 months

Crime location: Maryland, Virginia

Status: Sentenced to life imprisonment. Died in 1995, due to heart failure.

Background

Rees' childhood is a bit of a mystery, with little known about him until he attended college. In the early 1950s he enrolled with the University of Maryland, near Washington. His fellow classmates later stated he had a lot of musical talent and could play the piano, saxophone, and clarinet very well. He eventually dropped out of college with the hopes of becoming a successful musician.

Rees' criminal record began following an assault against a woman in 1955. Rees had apparently tried to force the woman into his car, but she was able to get away. The woman refused to press charges though, and the case was dropped. At the time, friends of Rees ignored this incident, not realizing that it was a serious sign of things to come.

Murders

Margaret Harold and her boyfriend were driving down the road in Maryland on June 26, 1957, when Rees forced them off the road. He got out of his car and pointed a gun at them as he gestured for them to roll down the window. He demanded money and cigarettes, but the young couple refused to give him anything. As a result, Harold was shot in the face and killed. Her boyfriend managed to get away and raised the alarm at a nearby farmhouse. When police arrived on the scene, Harold's clothing had been removed and Rees had sexually assaulted her.

While searching the crime scene area, officers found an abandoned building constructed from cinder blocks. The window of the basement was smashed. Inside the building, they found a large collection of violent pornographic pictures and autopsy photos taped to the walls. But nothing was found to implicate Rees.

The Jackson family disappeared on January 11, 1959, after visiting relatives. Their car was found abandoned on the side of a road, and it was reported to the police. Around two months later, the body of Carroll Jackson was found in brush near Fredericksburg. He had been tied up and shot in the back of the head. Beneath him they found Janet. It was determined she had been alive when put in the ditch and had suffocated from the weight of her father's body. The bodies of Susan and Mildred were found in a forest near Annapolis on March 21. Postmortem examinations showed both had been sexually assaulted and tortured before they were killed.

Timeline of known murders:

June 26, 1957 - Margaret Harold

January 11, 1959 - Carroll Jackson

January 11, 1959 - Mildred Jackson

January 11, 1959 - Janet Jackson, eighteen months

January 11, 1959 - Susan Jackson, four

Arrest and Trial

The police received a letter suggesting they investigate Rees for the murders. The letter was anonymous, but the writer was later identified as Glenn Moser. He told authorities that he and Rees often had deep philosophical conversations, including whether murder was acceptable. At one time, Rees confided he would consider committing a murder as part of the "human experience." This particular conversation took place on the day before the disappearance of the Jackson family murders.

Rees was arrested on June 24, 1960 in West Memphis, Arkansas. While searching his home, officers found notes written about the murders of the Jackson family. Later, a man who witnessed Margaret Harold's murder identified Rees as the man responsible.

Rees went on trial for the murder of Harold and was convicted, receiving a life sentence. He was then tried for the murders of the Jacksons and found guilty. Initially he was given the death penalty, but it was changed to life imprisonment in 1972.

Outcome

It's believed Rees was responsible for other murders in the area surrounding the University of Maryland, including the deaths of Mary Shomette, Mary Fellers, Ann Ryan, and Shelby Venable. He was never charged with these murders though. Rees died from heart failure in 1995.

MARTHA RENDELL

Date of birth: August 10, 1871

Aliases/Nicknames: Nil

Characteristics: Sadism, child killer

Number of victims: 3

Date of murders: July 28, 1907; October 6, 1907; October 6, 1908

Date of arrest: July of 1909

Murder method: Poisoning with hydrochloric acid

Known Victims: Annie Morris, 7; Olive Morris, 5; Arthur Morris, 14

Crime location: Perth, Australia

Status: Executed by hanging, October 6, 1909.

Background

Born in Adelaide, Southern Australia, Rendell would grow to become a young woman who didn't follow the rules and conventions of contemporary society. She moved out of the family home when she was just six years old and quickly gave birth to three illegitimate babies. This made her an outsider to society, as promiscuity was perceived as a terrible sin. She then became involved with a married man, Thomas Nicholls Morris.

Thomas, who had nine children with his wife, started his affair with Rendell in the mid-1890s. In 1900, Thomas had to go where the work was, and he moved his family to Perth, Western Australia. They also left because rumors were spreading around the small town of his affair with Rendell. Rendell, not willing to give up her affair with Thomas, left her own children behind and followed Thomas and his wife to Perth.

At that period in time, divorce was not a possibility, so there was no way Thomas could divorce his wife to be with Rendell. It was considered a sin to divorce as Christian marriage was the "foundation of the state and of the welfare of its citizens and their happiness and prosperity." A federal divorce bill had been proposed, but was quickly voted against.

Rendell and Thomas, however, continued their affair until Thomas finally left his wife in 1906. Although they couldn't divorce, they could separate. Thomas took the five youngest children with him and set up a house with Rendell. By now their affair had been going on for more than ten years, and it seemed Rendell finally had what she had always wanted. But, it wasn't all wonderful as she had thought it would be.

They moved to East Perth, to a neighborhood where few would ask questions, and Rendell posed as Thomas' wife. Although they were together at last, they were living in dire poverty, and Rendell spent all her time cleaning and taking care of the children. The children were resentful toward Rendell, most likely because they missed their mother who had been refused contact with them. The children were either too young or too busy to help out around the home, and Rendell was alone most of the time, with no family or friends. Unhappy with her lot in life, and fed up with the challenges brought on by the children, Rendell took matters into her own hands to try to get the life she wanted.

Murders

Little seven-year-old Annie was the first of the children to die at the hands of their stepmother. First, Rendell put something into Annie's food to make her throat sore. Then, she would swab what she called "medicine" at the back of her throat. The "medicine" was actually hydrochloric acid, which made the throat so inflamed the child was unable to eat. Annie essentially starved to death on July 28, 1907. When the doctor filled out the death certificate, he listed diphtheria as the cause of death.

A few months later, on October 6, 1907, Olive died in the same manner. Once again, the cause of death was determined to be diphtheria. Rendell then waited for a period of time before taking care of the youngest child, Arthur. He was fourteen at the time, and it took longer for Rendell's "treatment" to work. After his death on October 6, 1908, the doctor asked for an autopsy to be performed. Rendell agreed, but only if she could witness the process. The doctors didn't find anything incriminating.

Rendell waited until April of 1909 before she decided to end the life of another child, George. She gave him a cup of tea, and almost immediately he complained of having a sore throat. Rendell swabbed the acid on the back of his throat; this scared George so much he ran off to his mother's home.

Timeline of known murders:

July 28, 1907 - Annie Morris, 7

October 6, 1907 - Olive Morris, 5

October 6, 1908 - Arthur Morris, 14

Arrest and Trial

When George was reported missing, neighbors contacted the police, worried about the circumstances of the children's deaths and now the disappearance of George. Police investigators looked for George and found him at his mother's house. He told the police that Rendell had killed his siblings and that she had also tried to kill him with "spirits of salts," which is hydrochloric acid.

Because a fairly long period of time had elapsed since the last child died, the only way to check to see if they were murdered was to exhume the bodies. This was done on July 3, 1909, and the autopsies showed the children had been poisoned. But, there was still no proof of Rendell swabbing their throats. So, they experimented with guinea pigs and rabbits, and the results were the same as was seen on the children's autopsies.

Rendell was arrested along with her husband Thomas, and both were initially charged with the murders of the children. Thomas was eventually acquitted. But, Rendell was found guilty and sentenced to death.

Outcome

On October 6, 1909, Rendell was taken to the gallows at Fremantle Prison and hanged at 8:00 a.m. She never showed any guilt or remorse for the crimes she had committed. She was buried in Fremantle Cemetery.

Trivia

- Martha Rendell was the last woman executed in the state of Western Australia.
- An illusion appears on one of the prison windows which can only be seen on the outside of the window; when inside the prison's church looking out, the glass is smooth and even, with no unusual shape or texture. An urban legend has it that this illusion is the portrait of Rendell, who watches over the prison.
- Serial killer Eric Edgar Cooke was later buried in the same grave as Rendell following his execution.

ROBERT BEN RHOADES

Date of birth: November 22, 1945

Aliases/Nicknames: The Truck Stop Killer

Characteristics: Torture, rape

Number of victims: 3 - 50 +

Date of murders: 1975 - 1990

Date of arrest: April 1, 1990

Murder method: Strangulation by ligature, shooting

Known Victims: Regina Kay Walters, 14; Douglas Scott Zyskowski, 25; Patricia Candace Walsh, 24; Ricky Lee Jones

Crime location: Texas, Illinois

Status: Sentenced to life imprisonment without parole.

Background

For most of his early childhood, Rhoades was raised only by his mother. But his father returned from overseas while he was at school. His teen years were fairly unremarkable, until he was arrested at eighteen for interfering with a vehicle. He graduated high school in 1964 and promptly enlisted in the Marines. Also in 1964, Rhoades' father was arrested for allegedly molesting a twelve-year-old girl. Before he could be tried, he committed suicide.

Rhoades was dishonorably discharged from the Marines in 1966, but the reason for this is not common knowledge. The following year he got into trouble with the law again and was arrested for stealing. As an adult, Rhoades married three women and had one child. To support himself and his family he became a truck driver; this gave him the freedom he desired to commit multiple murders over a fifteen-year period.

There is no history of Rhoades being involved in violent crimes as a young man. Nor is there any record of him displaying any overtly disturbing behavior. Certainly there were no clues of the violence and torture he would later inflict on more than fifty women.

Murders

The first known victims of Rhoades were Douglas Zyskowski and his wife Candace Walsh. They were hitchhiking in January of 1990 when they were offered a ride by Rhoades in his truck. Zyskowski was killed right away, and his body was left on the roadside in Sutton County, Texas. Rhoades kept Walsh captive for a week, inflicting torture on her and raping her repeatedly. When she was dead, he disposed of her body in Millard County, Utah. She had been shot multiple times.

Ricky Lee Jones and his girlfriend Regina Kay Walters were believed to be the next victims of Rhoades. The youngsters disappeared after they had run away from home in Houston in February of 1990. Rhoades picked them up while they were hitchhiking; most likely, he killed Jones immediately. Walters was held captive by Rhoades for so long that her body (when it was found) had longer hair.

Early in the morning of April 1, 1990, Rhoades' truck was found parked on the side of the highway with its hazard lights on. When the officer from the highway patrol looked inside, he saw a naked and handcuffed woman who was screaming. Rhoades tried to talk his way out of the situation, but he failed and was arrested.

Arrest and Trial

Rhoades was later charged with sexual assault, aggravated assault, and unlawful imprisonment. When detectives investigated further, they found a connection between Rhoades and the murders in Houston. A search warrant was obtained for his house; inside, police found multiple photographs of a naked teenager and another woman. They were identified as Walters and Walsh.

Rhoades went on trial in 1994 and was subsequently convicted of the first-degree murder of Walters. He received a sentence of life imprisonment without parole.

Outcome

In 2005, he was then extradited to Utah for the murders of Walsh and Zyskowski. However, in 2006 the charges in Utah were dropped. Following this, he was extradited to Texas for the murder counts of Walsh and Zyskowski. He agreed to a deal with the DA and received another life sentence.

Trivia

–   A well-known photo Rhoades took of his victim Regina Kay Walters chillingly shows her just minutes before she was murdered in an abandoned barn.

GARY RIDGWAY

Date of birth: February 18, 1949

Aliases/Nicknames: The Green River Killer

Characteristics: Rape, necrophilia

Number of victims: 49 +

Date of murders: 1982 - 1998

Date of arrest: November 30th, 2001

Murder method: Strangulation

Known Victims: Wendy Lee Coffield, 16; Gisele Ann Lovvorn, 19; Debra Lynn Bonner, 23; Marcia Fay Chapman, 31; Opal Charmaine Mills, 16; Terry Rene Milligan, 16; Mary Bridget Meehan, 18; Debra Lorraine Estes, 15; Linda Jane Rule, 16; Denise Darcel Bush, 23; Shawnda Leea Summers, 16; Shirley Marie Sherrill, 18; Colleen Renee Brockman, 15; Alma Ann Smith, 18; Delores LaVerne Williams, 17; Gail Lynn Mathews, 23; Andrea M. Childers, 19; Sandra Kay Gabbert, 17; Kimi-Kai Pitsor, 16; Marie M. Malvar, 18; Carol Ann Christensen, 21; Martina Theresa Authorlee, 18; Cheryl Lee Wims, 18; Yvonne Shelly Antosh, 19; Carrie A. Rois, 15; Constance Elizabeth Naon, 19; Kelly Marie Ware, 22; Tina Marie Thompson, 21; April Dawn Buttram, 16; Debbie May Abernathy, 26; Tracy Ann Winston, 19; Maureen Sue Feeney, 19; Mary Sue Bello, 25; Pammy Avent, 15; Delise Louise Plager, 22; Kimberly L. Nelson, 21; Lisa Yates, 19; Mary Exzetta West, 16; Cindy Anne Smith, 17; Patricia Michelle Barczak , 19; Roberta Joseph Hayes, 21; Marta Reeves, 36; Patricia Yellowrobe, 38; Rebecca Marrero, 20; Unidentified White Female (12-17); Unidentified White Female (17-19); Unidentified Black Female (18-27); Unidentified White Female (14-18)

Crime location: Washington

Status: Sentenced to life imprisonment without parole.

Background

Ridgway was described by those who knew him as being a little strange but friendly. He had difficulty remaining loyal to his wives, and his first two marriages came to an end because both parties had been unfaithful. Marcia Winslow, his second wife, later stated that Ridgway had once put her in a choke hold, but no charges were ever made.

During his second marriage, Ridgway discovered religion, and he would go door-to-door to spread the word of God. He was often heard at work reading the Bible out loud, and he would do the same at home. He also instructed his wife to follow the church pastor's teachings. Sometimes Ridgway would cry after listening to sermons at church or even after reading passages in the Bible.

Throughout his marriages, Ridgway would pay for the services of numerous prostitutes. He asked his wives to engage in sexual activity with him in public places, or other areas where it would be inappropriate. According to his ex-wives and girlfriends, Ridgway had a very high sex drive. Occasionally, he would demand sex several times in one day, and he was particularly fond of having sex in the woods.

Although Ridgway admitted to regularly hiring prostitutes, he seemed to constantly be torn between his religious beliefs and his lust which at times was uncontrollable. He would regularly complain about the prostitutes being present in the neighborhood and how much it brought down the area. But then would pay for their services that same night.

It is perhaps this contradictory relationship he had with the prostitutes, and with himself, that led to him embarking on a long and prolific killing spree of the very women he loved to hate.

Murders

The number of murders committed by Ridgway is believed to be as high as seventy-one—possibly more. For a decade, he targeted prostitutes and runaways who were on the street at night. Most of the murders occurred in a two-year period, between 1982 and 1984. Ridgway himself isn't sure how many victims he killed because there had been so many he just couldn't remember.

After killing his victims, Ridgway disposed of most of the bodies around the Green River, hence his nickname. Sometimes there were clusters of bodies dumped, all nude, and often posed for impact. Occasionally Ridgway would go back and have intercourse with the corpses.

Ridgway's modus operandi was to gain the prostitute's trust by showing them a photo of his son. Once the prostitute agreed to go with him, he would rape them and then strangle them to death. Because of the way the victims struggled and left marks on him when he manually strangled them, Ridgway began using a ligature instead.

The crime scenes included his truck, his home, and some secluded areas where he could kill without being seen. During their hunt for Ridgway, investigators sometimes interviewed Ted Bundy to get his insight into the man they were looking for and the murders he committed. One tip Bundy gave them was that the killer was most likely going back to the bodies to have sex with them, which turned out to be right. He suggested that if they found a fresh grave, they should wait by it for him to return.

Because Ridgway had previous charges related to prostitution, he was considered a suspect in 1984; he was subjected to a polygraph test which he passed. Authorities interviewed Ridgway again in April of 1987, this time taking saliva and hair samples from him. The analysis of the DNA testing confirmed that Ridgway was the Green River killer.

Timeline of known murders:

July 8, 1982 - Wendy Lee Coffield, sixteen

July 17, 1982 - Gisele Ann Lovvorn, seventeen

July 25, 1982 - Debra Lynn Bonner, twenty-three

August 1, 1982 - Marcia Fay Chapman, thirty-one

August 11, 1982 - Cynthia Jean Hinds, seventeen

August 12, 1982 - Opal Charmaine Mills, sixteen

August 29, 1982 - Terry Rene Milligan, sixteen

September 15, 1982 - Mary Bridget Meehan, eighteen

September 20, 1982 - Debra Lorraine Estes, fifteen

September 26, 1982 - Linda Jane Rule, sixteen

October 8, 1982 - Denise Darcel Bush, twenty-three

October 9, 1982 - Shawnda Leea Summers, sixteen

October 20, 1982 - Shirley Marie Sherrill, eighteen

December 3, 1982 - Rebecca Marrero, twenty

December 24, 1982 - Sandra Denise Major, twenty

March 3, 1983 - Alma Ann Smith, eighteen

March 8, 1983 - Delores LaVerne Williams, seventeen

April 10, 1983 - Gail Lynn Mathews, twenty-three

April 14, 1983 - Andrea M. Childers, nineteen

April 17, 1983 - Sandra Kay Gabbert, seventeen

April 17, 1983 - Kimi-Kai Pitsor, sixteen

April 30, 1983 - Marie M. Malvar, eighteen

May 3, 1983 - Carol Ann Christensen, twenty-one

May 22, 1983 - Martine Theresa Authorlee, eighteen

May 23, 1983 - Cheryl Lee Wims, eighteen

May 31, 1983 - Yvonne "Shelly" Antosh, nineteen

May 31, 1983 - Carrie Ann Rois, fifteen

June 8, 1983 - Constance Elizabeth Naon, nineteen

July 18, 1983 - Kelly Marie Ware, twenty-two

July 25, 1983 - Tina Marie Thompson, twenty-one

August 18, 1983 - April Dawn Buttram, sixteen

September 5, 1983 - Debbie May Abernathy, twenty-six

September 12, 1983 - Trace Ann Winston, nineteen

September 28, 1983 - Maureen Sue Feeney, nineteen

October 11, 1983 - Mary Sue Bello, twenty-five

October 26, 1983 - Pammy Annette Avent, fifteen

October 30, 1983 - Delise Louise Plager, twenty-two

November 1, 1983 - Kimberly L. Nelson, twenty-one

December 23, 1983 - Lisa Yates, nineteen

February 6, 1984 - Mary Exzetta West, sixteen

March 21, 1984 - Cindy Anne Smith, seventeen

October 17, 1986 - Patricia Michelle Barczak, nineteen

February 7, 1987 - Roberta Joseph Hayes, twenty-one

March 5, 1990 - Marta Reeves, thirty-six

January 1998 - Patricia Yellowrobe, thirty-eight

Arrest and Trial

Ridgway was working at a truck factory on November 30, 2001, when officers arrived and arrested him. Initially, he was arrested under suspicion of murdering four women twenty years earlier. In August of 2003, Ridgway reportedly made a deal that if he pleaded guilty to the murders and confessed to the others, he wouldn't receive the death penalty.

At his trial on November 5, 2003, Ridgway pleaded guilty to forty-eight counts of aggravated first-degree murder. The statement he made to the court was that he had killed all of the victims in King

County, Washington, and had dumped them near Portland just to confuse the police. Sentencing occurred on December 18, 2003, and Ridgway received forty-eight life sentences with no possibility of parole. He also was sentenced to another life sentence, this one to be served consecutively. A further ten years per victim was added, totalling four hundred eighty, for tampering with evidence in each murder.

Outcome

Ridgway was kept in solitary confinement at the Washington State Penitentiary until he pleaded with the Federal government in 2005 to be moved to the minimum-medium security section of Airway Heights. He remained there until May of 2015, at which time he was transferred to a high-security federal prison in Colorado. In September that year, however, he was flown back to Washington via a chartered plane so he could be more "accessible" to investigators working on open murder cases.

Trivia

Quotes:

- In a later statement, Ridgway said that murdering young women was his "career."
- "I would talk to her... and get her mind off of the, sex, anything she was nervous about. And think, you know, she thinks, 'Oh, this guy cares'... which I didn't. I just want to, uh, get her in the vehicle and eventually kill her."

JOEL RIFKIN

Date of birth: January 20, 1959

Aliases/Nicknames: Joel the Ripper

Characteristics: Dismemberment

Number of victims: 9 - 17 +

Date of murders: 1989 - 1993

Date of arrest: June 28, 1993

Murder method: Strangulation

Known Victims: Heidi Balch ("Susie"), 25; Julie Blackbird (remains never found); Barbara Jacobs, 31; Mary Ellen DeLuca, 22; Yun Lee, 31; "Number six" unidentified, never found; Lorraine Orvieto, 28; Mary Ann Holloman, 39; "Number nine" unidentified; Iris Sanchez, 25; Anna Lopez, 33; Violet O'Neill, 21; Mary Catherine Williams, 31; Jenny Soto, 23; Leah Evens, 28; Lauren Marquez, 28; Tiffany Bresciani, 22

Crime location: New York

Status: Sentenced to 203 years to life.

Background

Rifkin was the result of an unwanted pregnancy, his biological parents both being young college students. He was put up for adoption within three weeks of his birth. His adoptive parents were from Long Island and considered upper-middle-class. His adoptive mother was of Spanish descent and his adoptive father was of Russian-Jewish descent; his mother converted to Judaism when they married.

The family moved to East Meadow in 1965, and Rifkin would spend most of his life there. He was keen on photography and craft hobbies. But, although he was a bright child, he didn't fit in with the other kids. Despite having a high IQ, he didn't do well at school, most likely because he was constantly teased and bullied due to the way he stood and walked. His nickname was "the Turtle" because he moved slowly with a slouching posture. Despite all of this, he did manage to graduate from high school. But, although he made an effort at college, he was unable to graduate, dropping out numerous times.

Rifkin spent most of his time living ngat home. Even as a young adult, he seemed unable to hold down a steady job. He was involved in a relationship with a girl at one point. She described him as being sweet but prone to suffering from depression. Rifkin's adoptive father was stricken with cancer; in February of 1987, he committed suicide to end his own suffering. Rifkin was tasked with delivering the eulogy at his funeral, and his behavior began to deteriorate from then onwards.

Rifkin was arrested for soliciting a prostitute in August, just six months after his father died. He was able to keep the arrest a secret from his mother and escaped with just a fine. To prevent his mother finding out about him using prostitutes, he started traveling further away from home to solicit them. Around this time, he also started collecting books and newspaper clippings about murderers who had killed prostitutes. These included works about Arthur Shawcross and the Green River Killer. Two years after his father died, he crossed the line between fantasy and murder.

Murders

Rifkin committed his first murder in 1989, killing a woman at his home in Long Island. He dismembered the body and removed the fingertips and teeth to prevent identification if the body was discovered. The woman's decapitated head was put into a paint can and left in the woods of a New Jersey golf course. Her legs were dumped further north, and the rest of her body went into the East River.

It is believed Rifkin killed another sixteen women over the next four years. The bodies were often placed into objects like boxes and steam trunks before being dumped. At least four of his victims were discovered inside oil drums. How he killed them varied, and some of the bodies showed evidence of being strangled before being cut up and disposed of. Rifkin later admitted he had killed most of them after engaging in sex.

Timeline of known murders:

1989 - Heidi Balch ("Susie"), twenty-five

1990 - Julie Blackbird

July 13, 1991 - Barbara Jacobs, thirty-one

September 1, 1991 - Mary Ellen Deluca, twenty-two

1991 - Yun Lee, thirty-one

December of 1991 - Lorraine Orvieto, twenty-eight

January 2, 1992 - Mary Ann Holloman, thirty-nine

April of 1992 - Iris Sanchez, twenty-five

May 25, 1992 - Anna Lopez, thirty-three

1992 - Violet O'Neill, twenty-one

July of 1992 - Jane Doe

1992 - Jane Doe II

October 2, 1992 - Mary Catherine Williams, thirty-one

November 16, 1992 - Jenny Soto, twenty-three

February 27, 1993 - Leah Evens, twenty-eight

March 2, 1993 - Lauren Marquez, twenty-eight

June 24, 1993 - Tiffany Bresciani, twenty-two

Arrest and Trial

Rifkin came unstuck on June 28, 1993, when he was caught driving without license plates on his truck. Police began chasing Rifkin. The pursuit ended when Rifkin crashed the truck into a utility pole outside the courthouse in Mineola, New York. As police approached the truck to arrest Rifkin, they noticed a terrible smell coming from the back of the truck. They looked inside and found the body of Tiffany Bresciani, a dancer and prostitute.

The initial interrogation lasted for eight hours, during which time Rifkin confessed to killing seventeen women. He provided as much detail about each murder as possible, though sometimes he couldn't remember the victims' names. He even drew maps showing where he had disposed of the victims so police could recover their remains.

The search of Rifkin's home where he lived with his mother turned up a plethora of evidence. In his bedroom they found items belonging to the victims including ID cards, credit cards, driver's licenses, jewelry, clothing, and photographs. The worst discovery was in the garage, where they found a chainsaw and a wheelbarrow stained with human tissue.

When Rifkin went on trial in 1994; he was convicted of nine counts of second-degree murder. He received a sentence of two hundred three years to life with the possibility of parole in the year 2197.

Outcome

In 1994, Rifkin was involved in a prison fight with mass murderer Colin Ferguson. Ferguson had been on the phone and asked Rifkin to be quiet; the situation escalated when Ferguson stated he had killed "six devils" while Rifkin had only killed women. Rifkin then replied that his murder rate was higher, and Ferguson responded by punching him in the mouth.

In 1996, it was decided that Rifkin's presence in the general prison population was disruptive, given the notoriety of his crimes. The corrections department therefore placed him in solitary confinement, where he was only allowed out of his cell for one hour per day. He stayed in solitary confinement for four years until he was transferred to the Clinton Correctional Facility.

Rifkin filed a lawsuit against the corrections department, stating his time in solitary confinement was unconstitutional. But, it was determined his rights had not been violated.

Trivia

–   Tested IQ of 128.
–   In early 1994, it was reported that Rifkin had engaged in a jailhouse scuffle with mass murderer Colin Ferguson. The brawl began when Ferguson asked Rifkin to be quiet while Ferguson was using the telephone. The New York Daily News reported the fight escalated after Ferguson told Rifkin, "I wiped out six devils and you only killed women," to which Rifkin responded, "Yeah, but I had more victims." Ferguson then punched Rifkin in the mouth.

JOHN EDWARD ROBINSON

Date of birth: December 27, 1943

Aliases/Nicknames: John Osborne, The Slave Master, Internet Slavemaster

Characteristics: Rape

Number of victims: 8 +

Date of murders: 1984 - 2000

Date of arrest: June 2, 2000

Murder method: Bludgeoning

Known Victims: Paula Godfrey, 19; Lisa Stasi, 19; Catherine Clampitt, 27; Sheila Dale Faith, 45; Debbie Lynn Faith, 15; Izabela Lewicka, 21; Beverly Bonner, 49; Suzette Trouten, 28

Crime location: Kansas, Missouri

Status: Sentenced to death, awaiting execution.

Background

Robinson's father was an alcoholic and his mother a strict disciplinarian. He was one of five children and was raised in Cicero, Illinois. He became an Eagle Scout in 1957 and was sent with a group to London to perform in front of the Queen, which would have been a huge honor, even for a young boy. That same year he was enrolled at a private boy's school, Quigley Preparatory Seminary, which is where boys were sent if they aspired to become priests. However, there were some disciplinary issues and he left after completing only one year.

Robinson decided to become a medical X-ray technician and enrolled at Morton Junior College in 1961. He only lasted two years though before he dropped out. Three years later he moved to Kansas, where he met his wife Nancy. Their first child, a son, was born a year later, followed by a daughter in 1967 and twins in 1971.

In 1969, Robinson was arrested for embezzlement. He had used fake credentials to gain employment at a medical practice working as an X-ray technician. While employed there, he stole thirty-three thousand dollars and was subsequently sentenced to three years' probation. The following year he violated the terms of his probation by moving away to Chicago without permission. He started working as an insurance salesman and, in 1971, he was in trouble once again for embezzlement. This time he was sent back to Kansas City to serve out his probation order which was extended to take into account the latest embezzlement charge.

Robinson just couldn't keep out of trouble. In 1975, he was arrested for securities fraud as well as mail fraud, after setting up a fake medical consulting company. His probation was extended once again. All throughout this period, Robinson portrayed himself as a good family man and a valuable member of society. He coached baseball, was a scoutmaster, and even helped out as a teacher in Sunday school.

He was able to con his way on to the board of directors of a charity. In this position, he forged letters supposedly from the executive director to the Kansas City mayor and also from the mayor to other community leaders, extolling his wonderful efforts as a volunteer and a member of the community. He even went so far as to host a "Man of the Year" awards banquet and awarded himself the title.

Despite finally finishing his probation in 1979, he still couldn't stop his fraud and forgery habits. He was arrested again in 1980 for check forgery and embezzlement. This time he was sentenced to sixty days behind bars, which he served in 1982. On his release, he created a fake company and scammed a friend out of twenty-five thousand dollars, alleging he could turn a quick profit so the friend could pay for the medical needs of his dying wife.

At the same time, Robinson was becoming a nuisance in the neighborhood. He was sexually propositioning the wives of his neighbors, which led to a physical altercation with a husband. He also claimed he had joined a sadomasochistic cult that was very secretive and called the International Council of Masters. He stated he was the "Slavemaster," and it was his job to lure female victims to gatherings so they could be raped and tortured. His mindset was certainly changing from financial gain to violent fantasy.

Murders

Robinson hired Paula Godfrey in 1984 to work as a sales representative for one of his fraudulent companies. Soon after, he told everyone he had sent her away to do some training. But she was never heard from again. Her disappearance was reported to the police by her parents, who received a typed letter several days later (supposedly written by Godfrey) that stated she was okay and didn't want to have contact with them.

Robinson met Lisa Stasi in a battered women's shelter in Kansas City in 1985. He promised her a job, somewhere to live, and daycare for her baby. He asked her to sign many sheets of blank paper. Robinson contacted his brother a few days later. Because his brother and his wife had been unable to adopt a baby through the regular process, he told them he had one they could adopt. He requested five thousand dollars for legal fees and claimed the mother of the baby had killed herself. The adoption went ahead, and nothing was heard of Lisa Stasi.

Catherine Clampitt moved to Kansas City to find a job in 1987. Robinson hired her, making big promises of travel and wardrobe allowances, and she disappeared in June. Due to being incarcerated for various reasons, Robinson didn't murder again until 1999, when he offered a job to Izabela Lewicka.

When Robinson hired Lewicka, he also offered her a bondage relationship. She moved to Kansas City and was given an engagement ring, despite the fact he was still married. Lewicka signed a slave contract that enabled Robinson to have complete control over her life. She told her parents she had married but didn't tell them to whom. Lewicka disappeared in the summer of 1999.

Robinson's final known victim was nurse Suzette Trouten. She agreed to travel the world with Robinson as his submissive sex slave. Trouten was killed on March 1, 2000, but her parents continued to receive typed letters, telling them about the world travels and experiences she was allegedly having.

Timeline of known murders:

1984 - Paula Godfrey, nineteen

January 10, 1985 - Lisa Stasi, nineteen

June 15, 1987 - Catherine Clampitt, twenty-seven

1993 - Beverly Bonner, forty-nine

Summer, 1994 - Sheila Dale Faith, forty-five

Summer, 1994 - Debbie Lynn Faith, fifteen

Summer, 1999 - Izabela Lewicka, twenty-one

March 1, 2000 - Suzette Trouten, twenty-eight

Arrest and Trial

By 1999, Robinson had become sloppy in his attempts to cover his tracks. The authorities in Kansas and Missouri were taking notice of him because he kept appearing in missing person's reports and investigations.

On June 2, 2000, Robinson was arrested following a complaint of sexual battery and theft against him. Because there had been a theft charge, authorities had the probable cause they needed to search his farm. During the search, two large drums were found containing the decomposing bodies of Lewicka and Trouten.

In Missouri, the authorities searched a storage facility rented by Robinson and found three more large drums. These contained the bodies of Bonner, Sheila Faith, and her daughter Debbie Faith. It was determined that all five victims had died from blows from a blunt instrument to the head.

Robinson went on trial in 2002 for the murders of Trouten, Stasi, and Lewicka. He was convicted on all counts and was given the death penalty for Trouten and Lewicka; he received life imprisonment for Stasi. Another five to twenty-year sentence for arranging the adoption of Trouten's baby was added on.

A deal was proposed for Robinson to get leniency in the murder counts in Missouri if he provided information on where the remains of Stasi, Clampitt, and Godfrey were located. Robinson refused, and so another plea deal was negotiated in October of 2003. Robinson made a statement acknowledging that the prosecution had enough evidence to convict him of the remaining murders. Although technically not a guilty plea, he was convicted of the murders and received a life sentence for each murder.

Outcome

There are long periods of time where Robinson's movements and actions can't be accounted for, and this has led police to think that there may be more victims out there that are yet to be discovered. Robinson remains on death row in Kansas awaiting his execution.

TIAGO GOMES DA ROCHA

Date of birth: 1988

Aliases/Nicknames: The Goiânia Serial Killer

Characteristics: Claimed "rage" killings following abuse as a child

Number of victims: 16 - 39 +

Date of murders: 2011 - 2014

Date of arrest: October 14, 2014

Murder method: Shooting, strangulation, stabbing

Known Victims: Diego Martins Mendes, 16; Bárbara Ribeiro Costa, 14; Beatriz Oliveira Moura, 23; Lílian Mesquita e Silva, 16; Ana Victor Duarte, 27; Wanessa Oliveira Felipe, 51; Janaína de Souza, 24; Bruna de Sousa Gonçalves, 26; Carla Barbosa Araújo, 22; Isadora Cândida dos Reis, 24; Thamara da Conceição Silva, 17; Taynara Rodrigues da Cruz, 13; Rosirene Gualberto da Silva, 29; Juliana Neubia Dias, 22; Ana Lídia Gomes, 14; Arlete dos Anjos Carvalho, 16; Mauro Ferreira Nunes, 51; others unnamed

Crime location: Goiânia, state of Goiás, Brazil

Status: Sentenced to 564 years and 4 months imprisonment.

Background

Rocha has never said a lot about his early life, other than he was raised by his grandparents and suffered sexual abuse at the hands of a neighbor when he was just eleven years old. He also claimed to be a victim of bullying as a child. As a young adult, he began working as a security guard, and he used this job to help him commit robberies.

When he was finally arrested for the murders, he claimed his reason for killing was because no woman had ever loved him.

Murders

Rocha's murders followed no specific patterns; he chose victims randomly and varied the way he killed them. His first known murder was that of Diego Martins Mendes, a homosexual, on November 9, 2011. Rocha lured him into the forest under the pretense of wanting to have sex with him, but strangled him to death instead.

Barbara Costa was killed on January 18, 2014, shot to death as he drove past her on his motorcycle.

She had been waiting in the square for her grandmother. The following day, he shot and killed Beatriz Moura. On February 3, 2014, Rocha killed Lilian Mesquita e Silva as she was on her way to collect her children from school. Quietly walking up to her, he shot her in the chest.

The next victim, Ana Duarte, was standing outside a snack bar when Rocha shot her. A month later, on April 23, he killed Wanessa Felipe by shooting her in the back while she was at a drugstore to purchase medicine. On May 8, he shot Janaína de Souza at a bar; on the same day, he killed Bruna Gonçalves while she was on the street waiting for a bus.

On May 23, he walked up to Carla Barbosa and her sister and asked them to hand over their cellphones. He shot Carla to death right in front of her sister. Isadora dos Reis was killed on June 10 while walking with her boyfriend down the street. Then, Thamara Silva, who was pregnant, was killed on her way to church on June 15. The same day, he shot and killed Taynara Rodrigues da Cruz.

Rosirene de Silva was killed on July 19, and a week later, Juliana Dias was shot while spending time with her boyfriend. The last known victim was Ana Gomes, who was shot to death while waiting for a bus.

Timeline of known murders:

November 9, 2011 - Diego Martins Mendes, sixteen

January 18, 2014 - Barbara Ribeiro Costa, fourteen

January 19, 2014 - Beatriz Cristina Oliveira Moura, twenty-three

January 28, 2014 - Arlete dos Anjos Carvalho, sixteen

February 3, 2014 - Lilian Mesquita e Silva, twenty-seven

February 28, 2014 - Mauro Ferreira Nunes, fifty-one

March 14, 2014 - Ana Maria Victor Duarte, twenty-six

April 23, 2014 - Wanessa Oliveira Felipe, twenty-two

May 8, 2014 - Janaína de Souza, twenty-four

May 8, 2014 - Bruna de Sousa Gonçalves, twenty-six

May 23, 2014 - Carla Barbosa Araújo, twenty-two

June 10, 2014 - Isadora Cândida dos Reis, twenty-four

June 15, 2014 - Thamara da Conceição Silva, seventeen

June 15, 2014 - Taynara Rodrigues da Cruz, thirteen

July 19, 2014 - Rosirene Gualberto da Silva, twenty-nine

July 25, 2014 - Juliana Neubia Dias, twenty-two

August 2, 2014 - Ana Lídia Gomes, fourteen

Arrest and Trial

Within minutes of Gomes' murder, police noticed the license plate on Rocha's motorcycle was stolen. He was eventually found and arrested on October 14, 2014. During the interrogation, Rocha confessed to all of the murders, which surprised the police because they had initially thought the crimes were committed by local gangs or drug cartels.

While searching his house, they found Rocha's gun. Ballistics testing showed it was the same weapon used in the murders.

Rocha was put on trial twenty-six times. He was subsequently convicted of twenty-four murders, as well as illegal possession of a weapon and robbery. There are likely to be more charges placed against him in the future.

Outcome

While incarcerated awaiting his trials, Rocha smashed a light bulb in his cell and used it to cut his wrists. His attempt to commit suicide failed. He was quickly found and treated.

Trivia

–   Police chief Eduardo Prado, one of those in charge of the investigation into the slayings, said: "He asked whether he would face trial if he killed someone else in custody."
–   "He still wants to kill. His attitude is very strange."

DAYTON LEROY ROGERS

Date of birth: September 30, 1953

Aliases/Nicknames: The Molalla Forest Killer

Characteristics: Rape, torture, mutilation

Number of victims: 7 - 8 +

Date of murders: 1983 - 1987

Date of arrest: August 7, 1987

Murder method: Stabbing

Known Victims: Cynthia "Dee Dee" Diane DeVore, 21; Maureen Ann Hodges, 26; Reatha Marie Gyles, 16; Nondace "Noni" Kae Cervantes, 26; Lisa Marie Mock, 23; Christine Lotus Adams, 35; Jennifer Lisa Smith, 25; unidentified victim

Crime location: Clackamas County, Oregon

Status: Sentenced to death, awaiting execution.

Background

Rogers was born in Idaho, and as a child his family moved around a lot. He was one of three children. When his parents adopted another four children, Rogers lost his status as the baby of the family. From a young age, he began committing petty crimes, and in seventh grade he was caught firing a BB gun at cars as they drove past.

In 1972, Rogers was in a relationship with a fifteen-year-old girl. On August 25, he took her into the woods supposedly to have sexual intercourse, but he ended up stabbing her in the abdomen. He told her he couldn't trust her anymore. Immediately afterwards, he asked her to marry him. Then he drove her to the hospital for treatment.

Arrested and charged, he pleaded guilty to second-degree assault and was given a sentence of four years' probation. A year later, he used a broken bottle to attack two fifteen-year-old girls and was charged with assault again. This time he was acquitted by reason of insanity and sent to a state hospital. On December 12, 1974, he was released.

Rogers was charged with first-degree rape in January of 1976 but was found innocent by a jury a few months later. However, in February, while waiting for his trial to start, he raped a high school girl and used a knife to threaten another. Once again, he pleaded innocent by reason of insanity; he was convicted anyway. This time he received a five-year jail sentence. The prosecutor of the case said Rogers was "a murder case looking for a place to happen." Despite this, he was given parole seventeen months into his sentence. He promptly violated his parole and went back to jail for another ten months. Several years later, the prosecutor's prediction came true.

Murders

Rogers was linked to seven murders, his victims often prostitutes, runaways, and drug addicts. The bodies of six of his victims were found together in a dump site on private forest land near Molalla, Oregon.

One of his victims, Jennifer Smith, was working as a prostitute on August 7, 1987, when she was picked up by Rogers. He parked his truck in a lot and then stabbed her eleven times. She suffered stab wounds to her abdomen, breasts, and back. She fell out of the truck and witnesses rushed to her aid, but she later died in the hospital.

After Smith fell out of the truck, witnesses used their cars to block in Rogers' truck. But he managed to escape by driving over the landscaping. One of the witnesses gave chase through Milwaukie, Gladstone, Oregon City, and Canby. When Rogers parked in a driveway, the witness wrote down the address and phoned the police.

Arrest and Trial

Rogers was arrested soon after he killed Smith and was charged with her murder. While he was waiting to go on trial, investigators discovered the remains of seven women in the Molalla Forest. They had all suffered the same savage abuse, including mutilation. Rogers was subsequently charged with eight murders in total.

He was found guilty of murdering Smith and received a life sentence. Then on June 7, 1989, he was convicted of the other seven murders and was sentenced to death.

Outcome

The death penalty for Rogers was overturned by the Supreme Court twice—in 1992 and 2000. In 2012, the death sentence was once again overturned, and a new trial for the appropriate penalty was pending.

On November 16, 2015, Rogers was sentenced to death for the fourth time. For the sentence to be commuted to a whole life sentence, Rogers would have to waive any future appeal options and admit his crimes.

Trivia

– He cut off and took the feet of most of his victims as trophies.

GLEN ROGERS

Date of birth: July 15, 1962

Aliases/Nicknames: The Cross Country Killer, The Casanova Killer

Characteristics: Robbery, rape

Number of victims: 5 +

Date of murders: 1993, 1995

Date of arrest: November 13, 1995

Murder method: Stabbing, strangulation

Known Victims: Mark Peters, 71; Sandra Gallagher, 33; Linda Price, 30s; Tina Marie Cribbs; Andy Jiles Sutton

Crime location: California, Mississippi, Kentucky, Florida, Louisiana

Status: Sentenced to death, awaiting execution.

Background

Rogers came from a large family which included seven children. He was raised in Hamilton, Ohio by his parents Claude and Edna Rogers. Before he had turned sixteen, Rogers was expelled from junior high school, but there is no information as to why. Not long afterwards, his girlfriend Deborah Ann Nix, who was fourteen at the time, became pregnant by another boy. Despite this, they married, and went on to have another child in 1981.

According to Nix, Rogers was physically abusive toward her and she filed for divorce in 1983. Little is known about what happened in Rogers's life between the time of the divorce up to his capture and arrest for murder in 1995. During questioning, he would claim responsibility for nearly seventy murders. But he later changed his story, saying he had just been "joking." However, his jailhouse confessions would lead to many questions being asked, including whether or not it was Rogers who had killed Nicole Simpson and Ron Goldman.

Murders

The body of Mark Peters was discovered on January 10, 1994, in a cabin belonging to Rogers' family. Prior to October of 1993, Peters had given Rogers a place to stay—around the same time Peters was reported missing. Rogers also disappeared, and the police were eventually led to the cabin by Rogers' brother Clay. Peters' skeletal remains were found tied to a chair and hidden beneath a heap of furniture.

Sandra Gallagher met Rogers in a bar in Van Nuys, Los Angeles, on September 28, 1995. Her body was found the next day, strangled and burned, in her car. The car was parked near Rogers' apartment. Rogers moved on, first to Mississippi, then to Louisiana and Florida. He killed a woman in each state he resided in.

Rogers met Linda Price at a beer tent at the Mississippi State Fair, and they ended up sharing an apartment together in Jackson for a while. Her sister went to visit on Halloween, 1995, but Price wouldn't answer the door, and Rogers was nowhere to be seen. Price's body was eventually found dead in the bathtub.

On November 5, 1995, Rogers met Tina Marie Cribbs at a bar in Tampa, Florida. According to the bartender, Rogers asked Cribbs for a ride. Her body was found at a motel two days later, with stab wounds to the buttocks and the chest. The motel clerk confirmed Rogers had arrived at the motel a few days before Cribbs was killed. The day after her body was discovered, her wallet was found at a rest area, and the fingerprints on it matched Rogers.

An acquaintance of Rogers, Andy Jiles Sutton, lived in Bossier City Louisiana. On November 9, 1995, her body was found on her waterbed, with multiple slash wounds. Just a few days later, Rogers' murder spree would come to an end.

Timeline of known murders:

October of 1993 - Mark Peters, seventy-one

September 28, 1995 - Sandra Gallagher, thirty-three

October 30, 1995 - Linda Price

November 5, 1995 - Tina Marie Cribbs, thirty-four

November 9, 1995 - Andy Jiles Sutton, thirty-seven

Arrest and Trial

Rogers was stopped while driving Cribbs' car on November 13, 1995, in Kentucky. He claimed she had lent it to him, but the officers didn't believe him. By now it was known that Rogers was the number one suspect in several murders, and he was promptly arrested and taken in for questioning.

Rogers initially confessed to committing up to seventy murders. But he later changed his story and recanted his statement. He claimed he had only been joking, and that he hadn't committed any murders at all.

When he went on trial though, the jury didn't believe him. Rogers was convicted of killing Tina Marie Cribbs on July 11, 1997, and he was later sentenced to death. On June 22, 1999, he was convicted of murdering Sandra Gallagher. On July 16, he was again sentenced to death.

Outcome

The appeal process has just about run out for Rogers. Unless his final appeal succeeds, he will stay on death row until it's time for his execution.

Trivia

- Was obsessed with redheads

DANNY ROLLING

Date of birth: May 26, 1954

Aliases/Nicknames: The Gainesville Ripper, James R. Kennedy

Characteristics: Rape, necrophilia, mutilation, decapitation

Number of victims: 8

Date of murders: November 4, 1989 – August 27, 1990

Date of arrest: September 8, 1990

Murder method: Stabbing

Known Victims: Julie Grissom, 24; Sean Grissom, 8; William Grissom, 55; Sonja Larson, 18; Christina Powell, 17; Christa Hoyt, 18; Manuel "Manny" Taboada, 23; Tracy Paules, 23

Crime location: Louisiana, Florida

Status: Executed by lethal injection, October 25, 2006.

Background

From the time he was born, Rolling's police officer father James told him he was an unwanted child. The children and their mother suffered terrible abuse from their father. At one point, Rolling's mother went to the local hospital claiming her husband had tried to get her to cut herself. She tried to leave her husband numerous times, but she always went back to him. During one incident, Rolling was handcuffed by his father and then taken away by the police because his father said he was "embarrassed" by his son.

Throughout his teens and into young adulthood, Rolling committed numerous robberies and was arrested multiple times. He also got caught watching a cheerleader get dressed. He had difficulty as an adult holding down a steady job, and he just didn't seem to fit in well with the rest of society. Things started coming to a head in May of 1990, when Rolling tried to kill his father. He was unsuccessful, but his father did lose an ear and an eye.

A few months after the attack on his father, Rolling went on a robbery spree that quickly escalated to murder.

Murders

In Shreveport, on November 4, 1989, William Grissom, his daughter Julie, and his grandson Sean were at home getting ready to have dinner when they were attacked and killed by Rolling. Julie's body suffered mutilation; she had then been cleaned and posed. Rolling has never confessed to these murders, but he wrote about them with details only the killer would know.

During the month of August, 1990, five students were murdered by Rolling while he was on a burglary spree in Florida. The first murders occurred on August 24. Rolling broke into the apartment shared by Christina Powell and Sonja Larson. He came across Powell asleep on the couch, but proceeded upstairs where he found Larson asleep in her room. He put tape over her mouth and stabbed her to death. Then he went back downstairs, taped Powell's mouth, and tied her wrists together. He raped her and stabbed her in the back five times before posing both girls' bodies in provocative poses.

The following day, he broke into Christa Hoyt's apartment and waited for her to return home. He attacked her from behind, choking her until she was subdued, then taped her mouth and bound her wrists. He raped her and stabbed her in the back before decapitating her. He placed her head on a shelf looking toward the corpse.

On Monday, August 27, Rolling broke into the apartment shared by Tracy Paules and Manny Taboada. He struggled with Taboada before killing him; the attack attracted Paules' attention. She tried to barricade her bedroom door, but Rolling broke through it. He taped her mouth and wrists and raped her. Then he stabbed her in the back and posed her dead body.

Timeline of known murders:

November 4, 1989 - William Grissom, fifty-five

November 4, 1989 - Julie Grissom, twenty-four

November 4, 1989 - Sean Grissom, eight

August 24, 1990 - Sonja Larson, seventeen

August 24, 1990 - Christina Powell, seventeen

August 25, 1990 - Christa Hoyt, eighteen

August 27, 1990 - Tracy Paules, twenty-three

August 27, 1990 - Manny Taboada, twenty-three

Arrest and Trial

Rolling was picked up and arrested late in 1990 for a burglary. During that investigation, it was found that his tools matched marks left at the crime scene of the Grissom family murders. They searched the camp where he was living and found recordings of Rolling singing songs he had written that—more or less—were a confession of the murders. In November of 1991, he was charged with several counts of murder.

In 1994, Rolling issued a guilty plea to all charges. He was subsequently sentenced to death for each murder he committed.

Outcome

On October 25, 2006, Rolling was executed by lethal injection. He was pronounced deceased at 6:13 p.m. Before his execution, he had declined to make a last statement but did sing a gospel hymn. He made a written statement before his death in which he confessed to murdering the Grissom family.

Trivia

- While on death row at Florida State Prison, Rolling wrote songs and poems and drew pictures.
- The blockbuster movie *Scream* was inspired by the crimes of Rolling.

ROBERT ROZIER

Date of birth: July 28, 1955

Aliases/Nicknames: Neriah Israel

Characteristics: Member of "the Temple of Love," black supremacist cult - killed on order; mutilation.

Number of victims: 7

Date of murders: 1981 - 1986

Date of arrest: October 31, 1986

Murder method: Stabbing

Known Victims: Raymond Kelly, 61; Cecil Branch, 45; Rudy Broussard, 37; Anthony Brown, 28; others unnamed

Crime location: Florida, New Jersey, Missouri

Status: Plea deal - 22 years for murders, released after 10. Convicted on the Three Strikes law for check fraud, and sentenced to 25 years to life.

Background

Rozier was born in Alaska. But the family moved to California, and he attended Cordova High School in Sacramento. He enrolled at Aberdeen Junior College and then transferred to play for the football team at the University of California at Berkeley. In 1979, he was drafted by the St. Louis Cardinals in the ninth round of the NFL Draft. He only played six games for the Cardinals, however, before being released from his contract. Rumors stated drug issues were the reason.

Rozier began committing petty crimes. After six months in prison, he moved into Yahweh ben Yahweh's "Temple of Love" in 1982. He then decided to change his name to "Neariah Israel," which translates to "child of god."

Murders

Yahweh had a secret group called "The Brotherhood" which Rozier joined in 1985. To gain entrance to this exclusive group, applicants were required to kill a white man and bring a part of their body back. This set Rozier on a deadly path that would see him murder seven innocent people to please the Brotherhood.

One of his first orders he received was to go out and kill a white man to prove his worth. As Rozier walked the streets, he came across Raymond Kelly who had consumed a bit too much alcohol; Kelly was asleep in his car in the parking lot behind the lounge he had been in all evening. Rozier, spotting Kelly, walked up to the car, opened the door and stabbed Kelly over and over with his sword. He had to take back a token of proof, so he cut off one of Kelly's ears. But he dropped it and couldn't find it, so he had to cut off the other one.

Cecil Branch didn't like the harassment he received from cult members on the street, and on one particular day, he pushed a female member out of the way. His license plate number was taken down; three members turned up at his apartment that night, but he scared them off. So the four Death Angels, including Rozier, went back, gagged him, and tied him to a chair. They then stabbed him twenty-five times. His ear was cut off and taken back to Yahweh.

The next targets were Anthony Brown and Rudy Broussard. They were against the cult purchasing their apartment building and they made their opinion known to anyone who listened. So the Death Angels, with Rozier, were sent to sort out the problem on Halloween, 1986. First, they lured Broussard out of the apartment and shot him in the head. Brown tried to escape but was tackled to the ground and shot. This time there were witnesses.

Arrest and Trial

Rozier was arrested that night, October 31, 1986. To help himself, he offered to tell the authorities everything they wanted to know about the crimes being committed by the cult, including the many murders. For the information he gave them, Rozier was put into the witness protection program and given a new identity.

Outcome

Rozier, under his new name Ramses, was arrested for bouncing a bad check on February 5, 1999. Police were able to track down twenty-nine bad checks he had passed which added up to over two thousand dollars. He then told the police his real name, thinking that because he was in the protection program, he couldn't be charged.

But, he was wrong, and he was convicted of fraud. Because he had already spent time in prison, he fell under the Three Strike law in California. He was automatically given a twenty-five to life sentence. He will be eligible for parole in 2024.

MARC SAPPINGTON

Date of birth: February 9, 1978

Aliases/Nicknames: The Kansas City Vampire

Characteristics: Cannibalism, drug addiction, schizophrenia

Number of victims: 4

Date of murders: March - April, 2001

Date of arrest: April 12, 2001

Murder method: Stabbing, shooting

Known Victims: David Mashak; Terry T. Green, 25; Michael Weaver Jr., 22; Alton "Fred" Brown Jr., 16

Crime location: Kansas

Status: Sentenced to life imprisonment.

Background

Sappington was raised by his mother, a single parent who worked hard to support herself and her son. His father had disappeared before he was even born, and they would never meet. To try to keep her son on the straight and narrow without a strong male influence, his mother insisted he attend church every Sunday. Sappington even became a choir boy, which was uncommon in the poverty-stricken neighborhood they lived in full of gangsters and rappers.

Although he wasn't a very good student at school, there was something about Sappington that drew others to him. One young boy who became close with Sappington was sixteen-year-old Alton Brown, whom everyone called Freddie. He saw Sappington as a big brother of sorts and had a lot of admiration for him. But, Sappington wasn't as innocent as he once had been.

As a teenager, Sappington discovered drugs and became particularly fond of PCP - a potent drug that can cause psychotic paranoia. He would smoke cigarettes that had been soaked in embalming fluid and then dried out, commonly referred to as "danks" on the streets. While under the influence, Sappington got into trouble with the local police, typically for minor issues, none of which were violent or crimes against other people.

On March 16, 2001, Sappington's drug use resulted in the brutal and horrific murder of the young man who had considered him a brother.

Murders

Sappington's first involvement in murder was actually a robbery gone wrong. Along with an acquaintance, Gaytan, the two men chose David Mashak as their target. They planned to walk up to him, threaten him with the gun they had, and demand all his money and jewelry. Mashak didn't hesitate to hand everything over. But, for some reason, Sappington opened fire and killed him anyway.

His next victim was his friend, Terry Green. Because they had been friends for a long time, Green wasn't surprised when Sappington arrived on his doorstep on April 7, 2001. According to Sappington, the voices in his head took over, and they instructed him to lure Green down to the basement. There, he attacked him with a knife so ferociously that the walls were splattered with blood. The voices then told Sappington to drink Green's blood, and he obliged by lapping it up. He then disposed of the body.

On April 10, the voices once again took over and told Sappington to find another victim. He saw his friend Michael Weaver sitting outside his house and they began chatting. Sappington suggested they go for a ride in Weaver's car, and they ended up in a dark alley. There he stabbed his friend to death. Though the voices told him to drink Weaver's blood, Sappington was worried about getting caught. He left, with Weaver's body still lying there.

On his way home from killing Weaver, Sappington came across Alton Brown. Obeying the voices, he invited Brown over to his house. This time, instead of stabbing, he killed Brown with a shotgun. He drank his blood, then butchered the body and ate some of the flesh raw. He put what was left of Brown's remains into a trash bag and left the house.

Timeline of known murders:

March 16, 2001 - David Mashak

April 7, 2001 - Terry Green, twenty-five

April 10, 2001 - Michael Weaver, twenty-two

April 10, 2001 - Alton "Fred" Brown, sixteen

Arrest and Trial

Sappington was brought into the police station for questioning after Brown's body was found in the basement of his house, on April 12, 2001. During the interrogation, Sappington was linked to the other murders he had committed.

Initially, he was charged with the murders of Green, Weaver, and Brown. On June 23, 2004, he was found guilty, despite his defense team establishing Sappington had been under the influence of PCP at the time of the murders. He was sentenced to three terms of life imprisonment, as well as thirty-two months for burglary and seventy-nine months for kidnapping. He was later convicted of the robbery and murder of Mashak, and he received another life sentence with the possibility of parole after serving twenty years.

Outcome

Sappington claimed that the voices in his head were telling him that if he didn't drink the blood or eat the flesh of humans, he would die. Many thought this was indicative of insanity, but in actual fact, the hallucinogenic drugs he was abusing most likely caused the auditory hallucinations. It was later discovered he had a fascination with serial killer Jeffrey Dahmer, who was also fond of cannibalism.

Trivia

- During an interview with a homicide detective in Kansas City, Sappington asked if he could "chomp on the cop's leg."
- Officers who interviewed Sappington described him as articulate, funny, and bright.

ARTHUR SHAWCROSS

Date of birth: June 6, 1945

Aliases/Nicknames: The Genesee River Killer, The Monster of the Rivers, The Rochester Strangler

Characteristics: Possible cannibalism

Number of victims: 13

Date of murders: 1972, 1988 - 1990

Date of arrest: January 5, 1990

Murder method: Strangulation, asphyxiation, bludgeoning

Known Victims: Jake Blake, 10; Karen Ann Hill, 8; Patricia Ives, 25; Frances Brown, 22; June Cicero, 34; Darlene Trippi, 32; Anne Marie Steffen, 28; Dorothy Blackburn, 27; Kimberly Logan; June Stotts, 30; Marie Welch, 22; Elizabeth Gibson; Dorothy Keller, 59

Crime location: Monroe and Wayne Counties, New York

Status: Sentenced to life imprisonment without parole. Died from natural causes, November 10, 2008.

Background

Shawcross was born in Maine. When he was still a young child, the family moved to Watertown, New York. According to Shawcross, he was a constant bed-wetter as a child and suffered terrible sexual abuse at the hands of his mother. He alleged she would insert objects into his rectum, and when he was nine years old, she performed oral sex on him. He later admitted to having a sexual relationship with his own sister while he was in junior high school.

Although Shawcross achieved good grades when he first started school, his grades deteriorated after the first two years. Subsequent testing showed his IQ was only 86. This meant he was borderline mentally retarded, but when he was tested again later on in life, the score was a little higher at 105. Shawcross was a bully at school and would lash out violently; he dropped out in 1960.

In 1967, Shawcross was drafted by the Army. Although he was only twenty-one years old, he was already married and had an eighteen-month-old son. When he entered the Army, he divorced his wife and gave up his parental rights to the child, a child he never saw again. During his one tour of the Vietnam War, he claimed to have participated in gruesome acts such as beheading the Vietnamese women. His records, however, showed he never saw any combat.

Following his return from Vietnam, Shawcross was stationed in Oklahoma. There, he married his second wife Linda. She noticed he seemed to get a perverse delight in lighting fires, and a psychiatrist from the Army explained to her that Shawcross derived sexual enjoyment from the fires.

When Shawcross was discharged from the Army, he and his wife moved to Clayton, New York. He started committing crimes including burglary and arson, and he ended up receiving a five-year prison sentence. He was released after serving just twenty-two months, partly because during a prison riot he had helped rescue a guard. After his release, Shawcross, who was divorced yet again, moved back to Watertown. In May of 1972, the community would be rocked by the deaths of two young children and suspicion fell on Shawcross.

Murders

The first murders committed by Shawcross were the terrible killings of two small children. On May 7, 1972, he lured Jack Owen Blake into the woods in Watertown, then raped and killed him. A few months later, on September 2, he did the same with Karen Ann Hill, who was visiting the area for the Labor Day Weekend. Shawcross was quickly arrested in October, and he confessed to the two murders. He negotiated a plea bargain which lowered his charges to manslaughter. He was sentenced to twenty-five years but was released on parole in April, 1987.

For the next series of murders, Shawcross's MO changed completely. Instead of targeting small children, he now focused on adult prostitutes in the area—with the exception of June Stott, who was a local woman. As multiple women were turning up dead, police used aerial surveillance to find missing bodies. On January 3, 1990, they found the body of June Cicero. Nearby, the surveillance team saw Shawcross standing beside his car urinating over the Salmon Creek Bridge, into the water where his last victim had been disposed of.

Timeline of murders:

May 7, 1972 - Jack Owen Blake, ten

September 2, 1972 - Karen Ann Hill, eight

March 18, 1988 - Dorothy "Dotsie" Blackburn, twenty-seven

July 9, 1988 - Anna Marie Steffen, twenty-eight

July 29, 1989 - Dorothy Keeler, fifty-nine

September 29, 1989 - Patricia "Patty" Ives, twenty-five

October 23, 1989 - June Stott, thirty

November 5, 1989 - Marie Welch, twenty-two

November 11, 1989 - Frances "Franny" Brown, twenty-two

November 15, 1989 - Kimberly Logan, thirty

November 25, 1989 - Elizabeth "Liz" Gibson, twenty-nine

December 15, 1989 - Darlene Trippi, thirty-two

December 17, 1989 - June Cicero, thirty-four

December 28, 1989 - Felicia Stephens, twenty

Arrest and Trial

Shawcross was arrested on January 5, 1990. During the interrogation he gave no indication of being responsible for all the murders. They had found enough evidence against him though, and he was charged with eleven murders. Under legal advice, Shawcross pleaded not guilty on all of the charges. A psychiatric assessment was ordered, and numerous tests were given to Shawcross. Although the report found he had a lot of mental issues, he was, by legal definition, sane.

He was found guilty of all charges and sentenced to spend the rest of his life in prison.

Outcome

Shawcross died of natural causes on November 10, 2008. He had been complaining of leg pain and was transported to the Albany Medical Center, where he suffered a cardiac arrest. He was pronounced dead at 9:50 p.m.

Trivia

Psychiatrist's analysis:

–   Dr. Kraus compiled an extensive report which suggested that Arthur Shawcross was "an emotionally unstable, learning disabled, genetically impaired, biochemically disordered, neurologically damaged individual, psychologically alienated from significant others during his entire life, venting his frustration and rage, mixed with fear and defiance in a lifetime of ever more violent and destructive aggression, which ultimately turned to overpowering murderous fury."

Quotes from Shawcross:

–   "I took the right leg of that woman's body, from the knee to the hip took the fat off and ate it while she stared at the other girl. When I bit into it she just urinated right there."
–   "She was giving me oral sex, and she got carried away . . . So I choked her."

HAROLD SHIPMAN

Date of birth: January 14, 1946

Aliases/Nicknames: Dr. Death, The Angel of Death

Characteristics: Poisoning of his patients

Number of victims: 215 - 250 +

Date of murders: 1975 - 1998

Date of arrest: September 7, 1998

Murder method: Poisoning by lethal injection of diamorphine

Known Victims: Marie West, 81; Irene Turner, 67; Lizzie Adams, 77; Jean Lilley, 59; Ivy Lomas, 63; Muriel Grimshaw, 76; Marie Quinn, 67; Laura Kathleen Wagstaff, 81; Bianka Pomfret, 49; Norah Nuttall, 64; Pamela Hillier, 68; Maureen Ward, 57; Winifred Mellor, 73; Joan Melia, 73; Kathleen Grundy, 81; Eva Lyons, 70; Sarah Hannah Marsland, 86; Mary Ellen Jordan, 73; Harold Bramwell, 73; Annie Campbell, 88; Alice Gorton, 76; Jack Shelmerdine, 77; May Slater, 84; Elizabeth Ashworth, 81; Percy Ward, 90; Moira Fox, 77; Dorothy Tucker, 51; Gladys Roberts, 78; Joseph Bardsley, 83; Winifred Arrowsmith, 70; Mary Winterbottom, 76; Ada Ashworth, 87; Joseph Everall, 80; Edith Wibberley, 76; Eileen Cox, 72; Peter Lewis, 41; May Brookes, 74; Ellen Higson, 84; Margaret Conway, 69; Kathleen McDonald, 73; Thomas Moult, 70; Mildred Robinson, 84; Frances Turner, 85; Selina Mackenzie, 77; Vera Bramwell, 79; Fred Kellett, 79; Deborah Middleton, 81; Dorothy Fletcher, 74; Thomas Fowden, 81; Mona White, 63; Mary Tomlin, 73; Beatrice Toft, 59; Lily Broadbent, 75; James Wood, 82; Frank Halliday, 76; Albert Cheetham, 85; Alice Thomas, 83; Jane Frances Rostron, 78; Nancy Anne Brassington, 71; Margaret Townsend, 80; Nellie Bardsley, 69; Elizabeth Ann Rogers, 74; Elizabeth Fletcher, 90; Alice Mary Jones, 83; Dorothea Hill Renwick, 90; Ann Cooper, 93; Jane Jones, 83; Lavinia Robinson, 84; Rose Ann Adshead, 80; Alice Prestwich, 69; Walter Tingle, 85; Harry Stafford, 87; Ethel Bennett, 80; Wilfred Chappell, 80; Mary Emma Hamer, 81; Beatrice Helen Clee, 78; Josephine Hall, 69; Hilda Fitton, 75; Marion Carradice, 80; Elsie Harrop, 82; Elizabeth Mary Burke, 82; Sarah Jane Williamson, 82; John Charlton, 81; George Edgar Vizor, 67; Joseph Frank Wilcockson, 85; Dorothy Rowarth, 56; Mary Rose Dudley, 69; Monica Rene Sparkes, 72; Hilda Mary Couzens, 92; Olive Heginbotham, 86; Amy Whitehead, 82; Mary Emma Andrew, 86; Sarah Ashworth, 74; Marjorie Parker, 74; Nellie Mullen, 77; Edna May Llewellyn, 68; Emily Morgan, 84; Violet May Bird, 60; Jose Kathleen Diana Richards, 74; Edith Calverley, 77; Joseph Leigh, 78; Eileen Robinson, 54; Charles Edward Brocklehurst, 90; Joan Milray Harding, 82; Christine Hancock, 53; Elsie Platt, 73; Mary Alice Smith, 84; Ronnie Devenport, 57; Cicely Sharples, 87; Alice Christine Kitchen, 70; Maria Thornton, 78; Henrietta Walker, 87; Elizabeth Ellen Mellor, 75; John Bennett Molesdale, 81; Alice Kennedy, 88; Lucy Virgin, 70; Netta Ashcroft, 71; Lily Bardsley, 88; Marie Antoinette Fernley, 53; John Crompton, 82; Frank Crompton, 86; Vera Brocklehurst, 70; Angela Philomena Tierney, 71; Edith Scott, 85; Clara Hackney, 84; Renate

342

Eldtraude Overton, 47; Kate Maud Sellors, 75; Clifford Barnes Heapey, 85; Bertha Moss, 68; Brenda Ashworth, 63; Ernest Rudol, 82; Ada Matley Hilton, 88; Irene Aitken, 65; Arthur Henderson Stopford, 82; Geoffrey Bogle, 72; Dora Elizabeth Ashton, 87; Muriel Margaret Ward, 87; Edith Brock, 74; Charles Henry Barlow, 88; Konrad Peter Ovcar-Robinson, 43; Elizabeth Teresa Sigley, 67; Kenneth Wharmby Woodhead, 75; Hilda Mary Hibbert, 81; Erla Copeland, 79; Jane Elizabeth Shelmerdine, 80; John Sheard Greenhalgh, 88; Minnie Doris Irene Galpin, 71; Marjorie Hope Waller, 79; John Stone, 77; Elsie Godfrey, 85; Edith Brady, 72; Valerie Cuthbert, 54; Lilian Cullen, 77; Renee Lacey, 63; Leah Fogg, 82; Gladys Saunders, 82; Nellie Bennett, 86; Margaret Mary Vickers, 81; Tom Balfour Russell, 77; Carrie Leigh, 81; Marion Elizabeth Higham, 84; Elsie Hannible, 85; Elsie Barker, 84; Sidney Arthur Smith, 76; Dorothy Mary Andrew, 85; Anne Lilian Ralphs, 75; Millicent Garside, 76; Irene Heathcote, 76; Samuel Mills, 89; Thomas Cheetham, 78; Kenneth Ernest Smith, 73; Eileen Daphne Crompton, 75; David Alan Harrison, 47; Elsie Lorna Dean, 69; Irene Brooder, 76; Charlotte Bennison, 89; Charles Henry Killan, 90; Betty Royston, 70; Joyce Woodhead, 74; Rose Garlick, 76; May Lowe, 84; Mary Coutts, 80; Elsie Cheetham, 76; Lena Norah Slater, 68; Ethel May Kellet, 74; Doris Earls, 79; Vera Whittingslow, 69; Maureen Lamonnier Jackson, 51; John Louden Livesey, 69; Lily Newby Taylor, 86; Dorothy Doretta Hopkins, 72; Nancy Jackson, 81; Mavis Mary Pickup, 79; Bessie Swann, 79; Enid Otter, 77; Florence Lewis, 79; Mary Walls, 78; Elizabeth Mary Baddeley, 83; Elizabeth Battersby, 70; Alice Black, 73; James Joseph King, 83; Mabel Shawcross, 79; Cissie Davies, 73; Laura Frances Linn, 83; Irene Berry, 74; Joan Edwina Dean, 75; Harold Eddleston, 77; Margaret Anne Waldron, 65; Irene Chapman, 74; Dorothy Long, 84; Lily Higgins, 83; Ada Warburton, 77; Martha Marley, 88

Crime location: West Yorkshire, Greater Manchester, England

Status: Sentenced to life imprisonment. Committed suicide in his cell by hanging on January 13, 2004.

Background

Shipman was born in Nottingham, England, to parents who were devout Methodists. As a youngster, he played in a rugby league and was considered very good at it. He was also an accomplished long-distance runner, and he became the vice-captain of the athletics team in his final year of school.

When Shipman was seven years old, his mother died of lung cancer. Because he had been very close to his mother, her illness and death had a deep effect on him. Toward the end of her life, doctors would come to the home and administer morphine, and Shipman was present to see the effects the drug had on his mother. To him, morphine took away all the pain his mother was suffering, even though her illness was terminal.

Shipman married in 1966, and the marriage produced four children. Four years after the marriage, Shipman graduated from Leeds School of Medicine with a medical degree, and the first few years of his career were spent working at the General Infirmary in Yorkshire. He started working as a general practitioner (GP) in 1974 in West Yorkshire.

Shipman was caught forging prescriptions in 1975. He had been prescribing himself pethidine, also known as Demerol, for his own personal use. He was fined and made to attend a rehabilitation clinic. Two years later, he was a GP again, this time at the Donnybrook Medical Center in Hyde. He stayed with this medical center until 1993, when he started his own practice.

In March of 1998, suspicions arose in the community regarding the high number of patients who were dying under Shipman's care. What started as a general concern grew into a full-blown inquiry, the results of which shocked the nation.

Murders

In March of 1998, Deborah Massey from a local funeral parlor contacted Dr. Linda Reynolds of the Brooke Surgery in Hyde and expressed her concern at the growing number of clients she was receiving from Shipman. The South Manchester District coroner, John Pollard, was also contacted about the high death rate. Of particular note, was the fact that there were a large number of cremation forms for elderly women that Shipman had needed to have countersigned. The police were contacted, but at that time they felt there wasn't enough evidence to charge anyone.

A taxi driver, John Shaw, contacted police in August of 1998, saying he suspected that Shipman may have been murdering a large number of patients. There were also concerns about a will that may not have been authentic. When Angela Woodruff's elderly mother died, she left nothing to her children and family, but she provided a large sum of money (totalling £386,000) to Shipman. They reported their concerns to the police.

The police initiated an investigation and exhumed Woodruff's mother, Kathleen Grundy. Her body was found to contain traces of a drug called diamorphine which is used to control pain in patients who have terminal cancer. There was now a case where charges could be made.

Timeline of known and suspected murders:

March 17, 1975 - Eva Lyons, seventy

August 7, 1978 - Sarah Hannah Marsland, eighty-six

August 30, 1978 - Mary Ellen Jordan, seventy-three

December 7, 1978 - Harold Bramwell, seventy-three

December 20, 1978 - Annie Campbell, eighty-eight

August 10, 1979 - Alice Maude Gorton, seventy-six

November 28, 1979 - Jack Leslie Shelmerdine, seventy-seven

April 18, 1981 - May Slater, eighty-four

August 26, 1981 - Elizabeth Ashworth, eighty-one

January 4, 1983 - Percy Ward, ninety

June 28, 1983 - Moira Ashton Fox, seventy-seven

January 7, 1984 - Dorothy Tucker, fifty-one

February 8, 1984 - Gladys Roberts, seventy-eight

April 15, 1984 - Joseph Bardsley, eighty-three

April 24, 1984 - Winifred Arrowsmith, seventy

September 21, 1984 - Mary Winterbottom, seventy-six

November 27, 1984 - Ada Ashworth, eighty-seven

December 17, 1984 - Joseph Vincent Everall, eighty

December 18, 1984 - Edith Wibberley, seventy-six

December 24, 1984 - Eileen Theresa Cox, seventy-two

January 2, 1985 - Peter Lewis, forty-one

February 1, 1985 - May Brookes, seventy-four

February 4, 1985 - Ellen Higson, eighty-four

February 15, 1985 - Margaret Ann Conway, sixty-nine

February 22, 1985 - Kathleen McDonald, seventy-three

June 26, 1985 - Thomas Moult, seventy

June 26, 1985 - Mildred Robinson, eighty-four

August 23, 1985 - Frances Elizabeth Turner, eighty-five

December 17, 1985 - Selina Mackenzie, seventy-seven

December 20, 1985 - Vera Bramwell, seventy-nine

December 31, 1985 - Fred Kellett, seventy-nine

January 7, 1986 - Deborah Middleton, eighty-one

April 23, 1986 - Dorothy Fletcher, seventy-four

June 6, 1986 - Thomas Fowden, eighty-one

September 15, 1986 - Mona Ashton White, sixty-three

October 7, 1986 - Mary Tomlin, seventy-three

November 17, 1986 - Beatrice Toft, fifty-nine

December 16, 1986 - Lily Broadbent, seventy-five

December 23, 1986 - James Wood, eighty-two

March 30, 1987 - Frank Halliday, seventy-six

April 1, 1987 - Albert Cheetham, eighty-five

April 16, 1987 - Alice Thomas, eighty-three

May 8, 1987 - Jane Frances Rostron, seventy-eight

September 14, 1987 - Nancy Anne Brassington, seventy-one

December 11, 1987 - Margaret Townsend, eighty

December 29, 1987 - Nellie Bardsley, sixty-nine

December 30, 1987 - Elizabeth Ann Rogers, seventy-four

January 5, 1988 - Elizabeth Fletcher, ninety

January 15, 1988 - Alice Mary Jones, eighty-three

February 9, 1988 - Dorothea Hill Renwick, ninety

February 15, 1988 - Ann Cooper, ninety-three

February 15, 1988 - Jane Jones, eighty-three

February 16, 1988 - Lavinia Robinson, eighty-four

September 18, 1988 - Rose Ann Adshead, eighty

October 20, 1988 - Alice Prestwich, sixty-nine

November 6, 1988 - Walter Tingle, eighty-five

December 17, 1988 - Harry Stafford, eighty-seven

December 19, 1988 - Ethel Bennett, eighty

January 31, 1989 - Wilfred Chappell, eighty

March 8, 1989 - Mary Emma Hamer, eighty-one

May 12, 1989 - Beatrice Helen Clee, seventy-eight

June 5, 1989 - Josephine Hall, sixty-nine

July 6, 1989 - Hilda Fitton, seventy-five

August 14, 1989 - Marion Carradice, eighty

September 22, 1989 - Elsie Harrop, eighty-two

September 26, 1989 - Elizabeth Mary Burke, eighty-two

October 15, 1989 - Sarah Jane Williamson, eighty-two

October 16, 1989 - John Charlton, eighty-one

October 18, 1989 - George Edgar Vizor, sixty-seven

November 6, 1989 - Joseph Frank Wilcockson, eighty-five

September 18, 1990 - Dorothy Rowarth, fifty-six

December 30, 1990 - Mary Rose Dudley, sixty-nine

October 7, 1992 - Monica Rene Sparkes, seventy-two

February 24, 1993 - Hilda Mary Couzens, ninety-two

February 24, 1993 - Olive Heginbotham, eighty-six

March 22, 1993 - Amy Whitehead, eighty-two

April 8, 1993 - Mary Emma Andrew, eighty-six

April 17, 1993 - Sarah Ashworth, seventy-four

April 27, 1993 - Marjorie Parker, seventy-four

May 2, 1993 - Nellie Mullen, seventy-seven

May 4, 1993 - Edna May Llewellyn, sixty-eight

May 12, 1993 - Emily Morgan, eighty-four

May 13, 1993 - Violet May Bird, sixty

July 22, 1993 - Jose Kathleen Diana Richards, seventy-four

August 16, 1993 - Edith Calverley, seventy-seven

December 16, 1993 - Joseph Leigh, seventy-eight

December 22, 1993 - Eileen Robinson, fifty-four

December 31, 1993 - Charles Edward Brocklehurst, ninety

January 4, 1994 - Joan Milray Harding, eighty-two

January 13, 1994 - Christine Hancock, fifty-three

February 9, 1994 - Elsie Platt, seventy-three

May 17, 1994 - Mary Alice Smith, eighty-four

May 25, 1994 - Ronnie Devenport, fifty-seven

June 15, 1994 - Cicely Sharples, eighty-seven

June 17, 1994 - Alice Christine Kitchen, seventy

July 27, 1994 - Maria Thornton, seventy-eight

November 25, 1994 - Henrietta Walker, eighty-seven

November 30, 1994 - Elizabeth Ellen Mellor, seventy-five

December 29, 1994 - John Bennett Molesdale, eighty-one

January 9, 1995 - Alice Kennedy, eighty-eight

March 1, 1995 - Lucy Virgin, seventy

March 7, 1995 - Netta Ashcroft, seventy-one

March 7, 1995 - Lily Bardsley, eighty-eight

March 13, 1995 - Marie Antoinette Fernley, fifty-three

March 21, 1995 - John Crompton, eighty-two

March 26, 1995 - Frank Crompton, eighty-six

March 31, 1995 - Vera Brocklehurst, seventy

April 10, 1995 - Angela Philomena Tierney, seventy-one

April 13, 1995 - Edith Scott, eighty-five

April 14, 1995 - Clara Hackney, eighty-four

April 21, 1995 - Renate Eldtraude Overton, forty-seven

May 4, 1995 - Kate Maud Sellors, seventy-five

June 2, 1995 - Clifford Barnes Heapey, eighty-five

June 13, 1995 - Bertha Moss, sixty-eight

June 17, 1985 - Brenda Ashworth, sixty-three

June 29, 1995 - Ernest Rudol, eighty-two

July 12, 1995 - Ada Matley Hilton, eighty-eight

July 31, 1995 - Irene Aitken, sixty-five

August 29, 1995 - Arthur Henderson Stopford, eighty-two

September 14, 1995 - Geoffrey Bogle, seventy-two

September 26, 1995 - Dora Elizabeth Ashton, eighty-seven

October 24, 1995 - Muriel Margaret Ward, eighty-seven

November 8, 1995 - Edith Brock, seventy-four

November 22, 1995 - Charles Henry Barlow, eighty-eight

November 25, 1995 - Konrad Peter Ovcar-Robinson, forty-three

December 14, 1995 - Elizabeth Teresa Sigley, sixty-seven

December 14, 1995 - Kenneth Wharmby Woodhead, seventy-five

January 2, 1996 - Hilda Mary Hibbert, eighty-one

January 11, 1996 - Erla Copeland, seventy-nine

February 21, 1996 - Jane Elizabeth Shelmerdine, eighty

February 27, 1996 - John Sheard Greenhalgh, eighty-eight

March 12, 1996 - Minnie Doris Irene Galpin, seventy-one

April 18, 1996 - Marjorie Hope Waller, seventy-nine

April 24, 1996 - John Stone, seventy-seven

May 7, 1996 - Elsie Godfrey, eighty-five

May 13, 1996 - Edith Brady, seventy-two

May 29, 1996 - Valerie Cuthbert, fifty-four

May 30, 1996 - Lilian Cullen, seventy-seven

June 6, 1996 - Renee Lacey, sixty-three

June 10, 1996 - Leah Fogg, eighty-two

June 17, 1996 - Gladys Saunders, eighty-two

June 25, 1996 - Nellie Bennett, eighty-six

June 25, 1996 - Margaret Mary Vickers, eighty-one

July 2, 1996 - Tom Balfour Russell, seventy-seven

July 11, 1996 - Irene Turner, sixty-seven (CONVICTED)

July 16, 1996 - Carrie Leigh, eighty-one

July 19, 1996 - Marion Elizabeth Higham, eighty-four

July 24, 1996 - Elsie Hannible, eighty-five

July 29, 1996 - Elsie Barker, eighty-four

August 30, 1996 - Sidney Arthur Smith, seventy-six

September 12, 1996 - Dorothy Mary Andrew, eighty-five

September 20, 1996 - Anne Lilian Ralphs, seventy-five

October 23, 1996 - Millicent Garside, seventy-six

November 20, 1996 - Irene Heathcote, seventy-six

November 23, 1996 - Samuel Mills, eighty-nine

December 4, 1996 - Thomas Cheetham, seventy-eight

December 17, 1996 - Kenneth Ernest Smith, seventy-three

January 2, 1997 - Eileen Daphne Crompton, seventy-five

January 3, 1997 - David Alan Harrison, forty-seven

January 8, 1997 - Elsie Lorna Dean, sixty-nine

January 20, 1997 - Irene Brooder, seventy-six

January 27, 1997 - Charlotte Bennison, eighty-nine

February 3, 1997 - Charles Henry Killan, ninety

February 4, 1997 - Betty Royston, seventy

February 23, 1997 - Joyce Woodhead, seventy-four

February 28, 1997 - Lizzie Adams, seventy-seven (CONVICTED)

March 22, 1997 - Rose Garlick, seventy-six

March 27, 1997 - May Lowe, eighty-four

April 21, 1997 - Mary Coutts, eighty

April 25, 1997 - Elsie Cheetham, seventy-six

April 25, 1997 - Jean Lilley, fifty-eight (CONVICTED)

May 2, 1997 - Lena Norah Slater, sixty-eight

May 12, 1997 - Ethel May Kellet, seventy-four

May 21, 1997 - Doris Earls, seventy-nine

May 29, 1997 - Ivy Lomas, sixty-three (CONVICTED)

June 24, 1997 - Vera Whittingslow, sixty-nine

July 7, 1997 - Maureen Lamonnier Jackson, fifty-one

July 14, 1997 - Muriel Grimshaw, seventy-six (CONVICTED)

July 25, 1997 - John Louden Livesey, sixty-nine

July 28, 1997 - Lily Newby Taylor, eighty-six

August 10, 1997 - Dorothy Doretta Hopkins, seventy-two

September 1, 1997 - Nancy Jackson, eighty-one

September 22, 1987 - Mavis Mary Pickup, seventy-nine

September 26, 1997 - Bessie Swann, seventy-nine

September 29, 1997 - Enid Otter, seventy-seven

November 10, 1997 - Florence Lewis, seventy-nine

November 14, 1997 - Mary Walls, seventy-eight

November 21, 1997 - Elizabeth Mary Baddeley, eighty-three

November 24, 1997 - Marie Quinn, sixty-seven (CONVICTED)

December 8, 1997 - Elizabeth Battersby, seventy

December 9, 1997 - Laura Kathleen Wagstaff, eighty-one (CONVICTED)

December 10, 1997 - Bianka Pomfret, forty-nine (CONVICTED)

December 18, 1997 - Alice Black, seventy-three

December 24, 1997 - James Joseph King, eighty-three

January 22, 1998 - Mabel Shawcross, seventy-nine

January 26, 1998 - Norah Nuttall, sixty-four (CONVICTED)

February 2, 1998 - Cissie Davies, seventy-three

February 9, 1998 - Pamela Marguerite Hillier, sixty-eight (CONVICTED)

February 13, 1998 - Laura Frances Linn, eighty-three

February 15, 1998 - Irene Berry, seventy-four

February 18, 1998 - Maureen Alice Ward, fifty-seven (CONVICTED)

February 27, 1998 - Joan Edwina Dean, seventy-five

March 4, 1998 - Harold Eddleston, seventy-seven

March 6, 1998 - Margaret Anne Waldron, sixty-five

March 7, 1998 - Irene Chapman, seventy-four

March 13, 1998 - Dorothy Long, eighty-four

March 17, 1998 - Lily Higgins, eighty-three

March 20, 1998 - Ada Warburton, seventy-seven

March 24, 1998 - Martha Marley, eighty-eight

May 11, 1998 - Winifred Mellor, seventy-three (CONVICTED)

June 12, 1998 - Joan May Melia, seventy-three (CONVICTED)

June 24, 1998 - Kathleen Grundy, eighty-one (CONVICTED)

Arrest and Trial

Shipman was arrested on September 7, 1998. While searching his property, authorities found a typewriter, the same type that was used to type up the forged will of Kathleen Grundy. The police investigated all of the cases where Shipman had signed the death certificates, a total of fifteen cases to begin with.

In each case they discovered a pattern of Shipman administering the Diamorphine, signing the death certificates, and then falsifying the medical records to say the patient had been in poor health. A massive enquiry was undertaken to look at every case Shipman had dealt with and it was discovered there were up to two hundred fifty victims.

On October 5, 1999, Shipman's trial began. He was charged with the murders of Irene Turner, Marie West, Jean Lilley, Lizzie Adams, Ivy Lomas, Marie Quinn, Muriel Grimshaw, Kathleen Wagstaff, Norah Nuttall, Bianka Pomfret, Pamela Hillier, Winifred Mellor, Maureen Ward, Kathleen Grundy, and Joan Melia. The charges were of murder by lethal injection between the years of 1995 and 1998.

At the end of the trial, the jury deliberated for six days. On January 31, 2000, Shipman was found guilty of the fifteen counts of murder and one count of forgery. He received fifteen life sentences, plus four years for the will forgery. In 2002, the Home Secretary confirmed the whole life sentence was appropriate.

Outcome

On January 13, 2004, Shipman took his own life by hanging himself in his cell at Wakefield Prison. He was discovered at 6:20 p.m. and declared dead at 8:10 p.m. He had used his bed sheets and tied them to the bars on the windows of his cell to hang himself. Although some families of his victims were relieved he was dead, others felt as though they had been cheated, as now there would never be a confession or answers given as to why he had killed his patients.

Although it is uncertain as to why he committed suicide, he had mentioned to his probation officer that if he killed himself, his wife would remain financially secure and continue to get his pension. If Shipman lived past the age of sixty, she wouldn't have been entitled to his pension.

Trivia

- For the 2002 movie *Harold Shipman: Doctor Death*, John Hurt was initially offered the lead role. He declined because he thought the project was "distasteful."
- There is a memorial garden for Shipman's victims in Hyde Park called the "Garden of Tranquillity."

DANIEL LEE SIEBERT

Date of birth: June 17, 1954

Aliases/Nicknames: Nil

Characteristics: Rape, robbery

Number of victims: 9 - 12

Date of murders: 1979, 1985 - 1986

Date of arrest: September 4, 1986

Murder method: Strangulation, stabbing

Known Victims: An unnamed homosexual man; Gidget Castro, 28; Nesia McElrath, 23; His girlfriend Sherri Weathers, 24, and her two sons, Chad, 5, and Joseph, 4; Linda Jarman, 33; Linda Faye Odum, 32; Beatrice McDougall, 57

Crime location: California, New Jersey, Alabama

Status: Sentenced to death. Died due to cancer, April 22, 2008.

Background

Siebert was raised in a home that was full of violence, abuse, and domination. His father was a sadistic man who abused Siebert both physically and sexually. According to Siebert, his father had raped him, beaten him, forced him to perform oral sex, and also made him have sex with him. Siebert was also made to put on girl's underwear before having sex with his father. At times he would be gagged and tied up, and he claims his father urinated on him sometimes.

Siebert's father was fond of using a bullwhip on his son, and the physical scars from the beatings remained throughout his life. His mother was so terrified of her husband that she was too afraid to leave or to tell anyone what was going on. She finally got the courage to flee with the kids when Siebert was eleven years old. A year later, his mother became involved with a new man, and Siebert ran away from home. He became involved in the drug and prostitution scene while he was living on the streets.

Siebert decided to straighten himself out in 1972. Using an alias, Daniel Marlow, he managed to enlist with the Marines. Although he thought the disciplinary environment of the Marines would be good for him, he was dishonorably discharged early, though it is not clear why. Within the next two years, Siebert fathered two children; his son would later become a prison inmate as an adult.

In 1979, Siebert was convicted of manslaughter. After his release from prison, he began traveling from state to state under another alias, Danny Spence. In late 1985, he met Donald Hendren who was on his way to Alabama to work at the Institute for the Deaf and Blind. He invited Siebert to go with him, but he declined and they parted ways. However, Hendren called Siebert in January, a month later. This time, Siebert agreed and moved in with Hendren in Talladega, Alabama.

Siebert started volunteering at the Institute as an art teacher, and he was hoping it would become a permanent paid position. But Siebert started dating one of the students, Sherri Weathers, which was against the policy of the school. What happened next would ensure he would never get that position he was hoping for.

Murders

In February of 1986, Sherri Weathers had missed her classes at the Alabama Institute for the Deaf and Blind in Talladega for over a week. When her apartment was searched, they found the dead bodies of Sherri and her two children. All three had been murdered. As they investigated further, they discovered another student was missing, Linda Jarman. They also found her murdered in her apartment.

During the investigation into the students' murders, they questioned an art student called Daniel Spence because people had suggested he was interested in Sherri Weathers. But when they checked his fingerprints, they discovered he was actually Siebert. He had previously been charged with manslaughter, and there was a current warrant for his arrest in an assault case.

Further checks showed he had been dating Linda Odum before she went missing on February 19, 1986. Her body was found a month later, and it was clear she had been murdered. When her stolen was found, there were fingerprints on it that matched Siebert.

Siebert went on the run for the next six months. Then he placed a call to a friend who quickly reported it to the police. The next time he called the friend, it was traced, and police now knew where he was.

Timeline of known murders:

December of 1985 - Gidget Castro, twenty-eight

December of 1985 - Nesia Gail McElrath, twenty-three

February 19, 1986 - Linda Jarman, thirty-three

February 19, 1986 - Sherri Weathers, twenty-four

February 19, 1986 - Chad Weathers, five

February 19, 1986 - Joseph Weathers, four

February 19, 1986 - Linda Faye Odum, thirty-two

March 8, 1986 - Beatrice McDougall, fifty-seven

Arrest and Trial

When Siebert showed up to work on September 4, 1986, he was met by police officers and arrested. While he was being interviewed at the police station, he confessed to committing five murders in Alabama and several others in other states. In total, he believed he had killed twelve people.

When he stood trial, he was found guilty and sentenced to death.

Outcome

Siebert was due to be executed on October 25, 2007. But, just hours beforehand, his execution was delayed. He was suffering from pancreatic cancer at the time and receiving treatment. In December of that year, Siebert was questioned regarding a pornography case, but no charges were filed against him.

On April 22, 2008, at 1:35 p.m., Siebert died from complications of his cancer. By then, he had been awaiting his execution for over twenty-one years.

ROBERT JOSEPH SILVERIA, JR.

Date of birth: March 3, 1959

Aliases/Nicknames: The Boxcar Killer, Sidetrack

Characteristics: Robbery, gang member

Number of victims: 14 +

Date of murders: 1981 - 1996

Date of arrest: March 2, 1996

Murder method: Stabbing, bludgeoning

Known Victims: Anthony Garcia, 62; Darren Royal Miller, 19; Willie Clark, 52; Michael Garfinkle, 20; Roger Bowman, 38; James McLean, 50; Charles Randall Boyd; Paul Wayne Matthews, 43; William Avis Pettit Jr., 39; Michael Clites, 24; Michael Brandolino; others unidentified

Crime location: Several locations in America

Status: Sentenced to life imprisonment without parole.

Background

Despite being born into a middle-class family, Silveria would go on to have a lifelong problem with alcohol and drugs. He used heroin regularly, as well as meth and crack cocaine, and he washed it all down with alcohol. If there was anything he could get high from, he would take it.

Silveria's father got him into many different jobs at the airport where he worked, but he lost each and every one of them due to his substance abuse. He had been married, but his wife left, unable to tolerate the drugs and alcohol and Silveria's habit of wandering off.

At the time, there was a group called the Freight Train Riders of America (FTRA), a group who spent their days and nights riding the box cars of the freight trains. It was originally founded by returned Vietnam War veterans, but before long, others were able to join, including Silveria. To show he was a member, Silveria always carried a bandanna with him as well as a flashback button. This button identified him as being a member of a group called the Wrecking Crew. It was their job to maintain control and order amongst the FTRA members.

The FTRA became associated with multiple crimes on the freight trains, including robbery and assault. And for drug addled Silveria, who suffered from an internal rage he had trouble controlling, these assaults would often go way too far.

Murders

As Silveria rode the freight trains, he found there was a high supply of potential victims for him to choose from. He generally attacked men who were homeless, regardless of their race or age. He preferred to beat his victims to death with his hands and a large stick he called a "Goon Stick." Sometimes they were killed by metal poles or rocks, whatever was at hand at the time. Silveria didn't try to hide or dispose of the bodies after the murders; he just left them beside the railroad.

Once the victim was dead, he would take their belongings, especially items he thought he could use or sell, including money and drugs. He also took the person's identification so he could collect welfare benefits and food stamps.

Silveria was fully aware of the "rage" he had inside him. He would begin by meeting a homeless transient, spend some time partying with them, and then create an excuse to get angry with them. Then he would beat them to death and let all that rage out.

Timeline of known murders:

April 9, 1989 - Anthony Garcia, sixty-two

July 8, 1992 - Darren Royal Miller, nineteen

April 28, 1994 - Willie Clark, fifty-two

August 2, 1994 - Michael Garfinkle, twenty

April 21, 1995 - Roger Bowman, thirty-eight

July 22, 1995 - James McLean, fifty

July 26, 1995 - Charles Randall Boyd

October 1995 - Unidentified drug dealer

October 15, 1995 - Paul Wayne Matthews, forty-three

December 1, 1995 - William Avis Pettit Jr., thirty-nine

December 6, 1995 - Michael A. Cites, twenty-four

December 23, 1995 - Michael A. Brandolino

Arrest and Trial

The body of Michael Cites was found on a train in Oregon, and the detective in charge of the case was able to locate others who had been on the train at the same time. They said that the last person they saw with Cites was "Sidetrack." Others referred to the man as Silveria. The detective initially thought the names referred to two people. According to the witnesses, Silveria and Cites had gone in search of drugs.

Notices were distributed to all law enforcement agencies to try and find Sidetrack or Silveria. On March 2, 1996, Silveria was caught in California and taken in to custody. In the interview room, it was discovered that Sidetrack and Silveria were the same person. Silveria claimed that God told him to surrender and he confessed to the murders of William Pettit and Michael Cites.

Throughout his interrogation, Silveria continued to confess to a number of murders he had committed. He provided drawn maps to show where each murder had taken place and gave details on each killing. This information showed that he had been a part of at least fourteen murders.

Silveria went on three trials for murder. He was found guilty on January 30, 1998, February 17, 1998, and May 20, 1998, of all three murder charges. Because he had agreed to a plea bargain, he received life imprisonment without the possibility of parole.

Outcome

In total, Silveria confessed to committing forty-seven murders. But police suspect he was involved in just fourteen. Because of the nature of the crimes, and the transiency of the people killed as well as the perpetrator, many cases may never be solved.

GEORGE JOSEPH SMITH

Date of birth: January 11, 1872

Aliases/Nicknames: Brides in the Bath Murderer, Oliver George Love, George Rose Smith, Charles Oliver James, John Lloyd, Henry Williams

Characteristics: Bigamy, insurance fraud

Number of victims: 3

Date of murders: 1912 - 1914

Date of arrest: February 1, 1915

Murder method: Drowning

Known Victims: Beatrice "Bessie" Mundy, 31; Alice Burnham, 25; Margaret Elizabeth Lofty, 38

Crime location: England

Status: Executed by hanging on August 13, 1915.

Background

As a child, Smith was no angel. He was sent to a reformatory for boys when he was only nine years old because of his behavior, and he later ended up serving time for theft and swindling. In 1886, he managed to convince a woman to steal some money from her employer so he could open a baker's shop. He got caught and was sentenced to serve twelve months behind bars.

Smith married Caroline Thornhill in 1898, but not under his own name. By then, he was fond of using aliases and he married her as Oliver George Love. They moved from Leicester to London, and while she worked as a maid, she would steal to line her husband's pockets. Eventually, she was caught and convicted and was sentenced to serve twelve months in prison.

When Thornhill was released from prison, she immediately pointed the finger at Smith, claiming he was also involved in the thefts. He was subsequently convicted and sentenced to two years in prison. His wife left the country and moved to Canada. Smith had bigamously married another woman in 1899, and he emptied out her bank accounts and left after his release from prison.

Smith married again in June of 1908, to widow Florence Wilson. The following month he left her, having taken thirty pounds from her bank account and selling off her personal belongings for cash. He married Edith Peglar that same month, after she replied to his advertisement for a housekeeper. None of these marriages were legal, and most were undertaken using false names.

Despite ongoing marriages, Smith always went back to Peglar, bringing his ill-gotten gains with him. In October of 1909, Smith—using the name George Rose Smith—married Sarah Freeman. Once again, he cleared out her finances, and left. The total came to four hundred pounds, which was a vast sum in those days. His next wives were Alice Burnham and Bessie Munday.

Using the alias Charles Oliver James, he married Alice Reid in September of 1914. In total, Smith had entered into seven marriages, all bigamous, between 1908 and 1914; he always left his "wife" after stealing her money. By 1915, suspicions were aroused following the deaths of two women, one of whom was Alice Smith (nee Burnham). The investigation would lead the authorities to Smith.

Murders

Division Detective Inspector Arthur Neil received a letter in January of 1915 from a man who owned a boarding house in Blackpool. The owner, Joseph Crossley, included two newspaper clippings in the letter reporting the deaths of two women in very similar circumstances. The first, Margaret Elizabeth Lloyd, was found dead in the bathtub at her lodgings; she had been discovered by her husband, John Lloyd, and the landlady. The death had occurred just before the end of 1914.

The second clipping was about the death of Alice Smith who had died in 1913 in the bathtub at her boarding house. She had been found by her husband George Smith. Crossley's letter had been written on behalf of his wife and a man named Charles Burnham; they were suspicious of the circumstances of the two deaths, and they urged the police to investigate.

Neil went to the location of Margaret Lloyd's death. When he saw the size of the bathtub, he couldn't believe a grown woman could have drowned in it. He spoke to the coroner and asked about signs of violence, but the only mark that had been found was a bruise above the left elbow. Neil also discovered a will had been made just three hours before her death, and her husband was the sole beneficiary. All of her savings had been withdrawn that day as well.

After he left, the coroner called to say the insurance company had made an inquiry into the death because of the will and insurance policy. Neil told the doctor to delay responding until he could get more information. He then contacted the Blackpool police about the death of Alice Smith. Investigations showed she had also taken out an insurance policy just before her death, and the will favored her husband. Also, when they were looking at moving into the boarding house, Mr. Smith had to inspect the bathtub before they would agree to move in.

Neil contacted the coroner and told him to give a good report to the insurance company so that when the suspect went to claim it at his lawyer's office, they could grab him. His plan worked, and on February 1, the man appeared. Neil asked if he was John Lloyd, to which the man said yes, but when asked if he was George Smith, he denied it. Neil told him he was going to question him about bigamy, and Smith agreed that he was both men.

Arrest and Trial

After he was arrested, more information came out about the murder of Beatrice Munday. She too had died in the bathtub about a year before Alice Smith. Her husband's name was Henry Williams, another alias of Smith.

On June 22, Smith went on trial at the Old Bailey. Because of British law at the time, he could only be charged with the murder of Beatrice Munday. But, the prosecution was able to use the details of the other deaths to establish Smith's pattern of criminal activity. After just twenty minutes of deliberation, Smith was found guilty on July 1. He was sentenced to death.

Outcome

Smith was taken to the gallows and hanged on August 13, 1915. During his trial, the use of "system" came in to play, where other crimes committed could be presented as evidence in murder trials. For example, in cases where there was more than one murder, they could both be used in one trial to show a pattern. This set a precedent for other murder trials later on.

LEMUEL SMITH

Date of birth: July 23, 1941

Aliases/Nicknames: Nil

Characteristics: Rape, mutilation, robbery

Number of victims: 6

Date of murders: 1958, 1976 - 1977, 1981

Date of arrest: August 19, 1977

Murder method: Strangulation, shooting, beating

Known Victims: Dorothy Waterstreet; Robert Hedderman, 48; Hedderman's secretary, Margaret Byron, 59; Joan Richburg, 24; Maralie Wilson, 30; Donna Payant, 31 (female correctional officer)

Crime location: Albany, New York

Status: Sentenced to death but commuted to life imprisonment.

Background

Smith was born into a religious household in New York. He later claimed that he had almost smothered a nine-year-old girl to death when he was just eleven years old, but there is no proof that this happened. Despite being in a family that went to church and practiced religion, Smith had a dark side filled with violence.

When he was sixteen, he was considered a suspect in the robbery and murder of Dorothy Waterstreet on January 21, 1958. There was evidence to suggest Smith was the guilty party, but the case was dropped when the district attorney made mistakes in his rush to try to get a confession. Smith was therefore not formally arrested or charged with the murder.

Not long afterwards, Smith moved to Baltimore, Maryland, to escape the constant pressure he felt he was under from the local police. Before long, he kidnapped a woman and beat her almost to death—fortunately, a witness interrupted him. This time he was arrested and convicted. On April 12, 1959, he was sentenced to twenty years in prison.

Almost ten years later, Smith was given parole in May of 1968. He didn't stay out of trouble for long though. The following May, he kidnapped a woman and sexually assaulted her. She was able to escape from Smith, and that very same day he kidnapped a friend of his mother's and raped her. She convinced Smith to release her, and he was again arrested and convicted, receiving a sentence of up to fifteen years.

Incredibly, Smith had been behind bars for seventeen out of eighteen years until a new law saw him released back into society once again. On October 5, 1976, Smith walked out of the prison a free man. By the end of the next month, he had committed his most violent crimes yet - murder.

Murders

A month after Smith was released from prison, on November 24, the bodies of Robert Hedderman and his secretary Margaret Byron were found in the back of Hedderman's religious store in Albany. The evidence was contaminated by human feces, which actually turned out to be forensically useful in detecting a suspect.

On December 23, Joan Richburg was attacked in her car at a mall in Colonie. She was raped, murdered, and mutilated. Hair was found at the scene which matched Smith, but he remained free while police continued their investigations.

Maralie Wilson was found strangled to death and mutilated on July 22, 1977, near train tracks in Schenectady, New York. The mutilation this time was much more severe than in the previous murders. She was found in an area where Smith was known to frequent, and the witness descriptions fit, so Smith became the prime suspect.

Then, on August 19, 1977, Smith abducted Marianne Maggio, eighteen, and raped her. He forced her to drive toward Albany. When the car was stopped by police, he was arrested.

Timeline of known murders:

January 21, 1958 - Dorothy Waterstreet

November 24, 1976 - Robert Hedderman, forty-eight

November 24, 1976 - Margaret Byron, fifty-nine

December 23, 1976 - Joan Richburg, twenty-four

July 22, 1977 - Maralie Wilson, thirty

May 15, 1981 - Donna Payant, thirty-one

Arrest and Trial

While investigating Smith, Police Lt. Don Pinto was looking at crime scene photos of Maralie Wilson when he noticed what looked like a bite mark on her nose. They exhumed her body and the bite mark was matched to Smith's bite pattern.

Late in October, a lineup was created with Smith and four other men, and they were placed behind individual screens at the end of Bleecker Stadium. Officers then gave a police dog the scent of the clothing stained with feces from the Hedderman store murders. The dog went directly to Smith. They rearranged the men again, and the dog went to Smith a second time.

When the bite mark evidence was produced to Smith on March 5, 1978, he confessed to committing five murders. He also claimed to have multiple personality disorder, and he said he was controlled by his dead brother's spirit. Despite his attempts to be considered insane, he was eventually found guilty of rape on March 9, 1978. He received ten to twenty years in prison.

A four-day bench trial on July 21, 1978, resulted in Smith being found guilty of kidnapping, and he received twenty-five years to life. On February 2, 1979 he was found guilty of the double murder at Hedderman's store and received fifty years to life.

Smith was originally indicted for the murders of Wilson and Richburg, but because he was never going to be released from prison due to his previous convictions, the indictments were dismissed.

Outcome

Smith committed the murder of a corrections officer while he was incarcerated. Subsequently, he was put into solitary confinement for nearly twenty years because of the serious risk he posed to other inmates and staff. At that time, it was the longest time any prisoner had spent in solitary confinement.

MORRIS SOLOMON JR.

Date of birth: March 15, 1944

Aliases/Nicknames: The Sacramento Slayer

Characteristics: Rape, prostitutes

Number of victims: 6 - 7

Date of murders: June 1986 – April 1987

Date of arrest: April 22, 1987

Murder method: Undetermined due to level of decomposition

Known Victims: Yolanda Johnson, 22; Angela Polidori, 25; Maria Apodaca, 18; Cherie Washington, 16; Linda Vitela, 24; Sheila Jacox, 17; Sharon Massey, 29

Crime location: Sacramento, California

Status: Sentenced to death, awaiting execution.

Background

Brought up in a violent and abusive household, Solomon was raised by his grandmother who doled out harsh beatings for the slightest misdoings. Solomon was regularly beaten for wetting the bed or for saying words incorrectly. Even crying while he was being beaten would make her fiercer in her discipline. There were times where Solomon and his brother were beaten for no apparent reason at all.

As a young boy, Solomon's grandmother would put him over her knee and hit him. Other times, she would make him strip off his clothes and stand on a stool in the corner so she could beat him with switches or electrical cords. He was beaten so badly he often bled from his wounds. If he tried to back away from her, she would tie him to the bedpost with an extension cord.

Solomon had barely known his parents. But he was reunited with them when he was thirteen after he moved to Isleton with his grandmother, near where his parents lived. It was a poor part of town often called "Cannery Row" or "Tinpan Alley," and his parents regularly beat each other or sexually assaulted one another in front of the children. Now it wasn't just his grandmother beating him; his mother would beat him as well, and she took great delight in abusing him verbally when they were out in public.

When he finished high school, Solomon went to classes at the community college, and he managed to work in a variety of jobs including driving buses and carpentry. He went into the Army and served in the Vietnam War for a year in 1966. Afterwards, he went back to Isleton, and his fiancé broke off their engagement. This event prompted him to move to the San Francisco Bay area. There, he met another woman, married, and a daughter was born.

Following their divorce, Solomon moved back to Sacramento and started working as a handyman. The first time Solomon crossed paths with the police was when he reported finding a dead woman's body. But he wasn't the good citizen reporting a crime they initially thought he was.

Murders

The body of Yolanda Johnson was found on June 18, 1986, after her murder was reported to the police by Solomon. The known prostitute and drug user was partially nude and bound. When Angela Polidori was found on July 20, she was also bound and partially nude.

Marie Apodaca, another prostitute and drug user, and was killed on March 19, 1987. Her body was wrapped up in bedding and buried. The next victim was Cherie Washington, who was killed on April 20, 1987. A possible prostitute and drug user, she was found nude, bound, and wrapped up in bedding.

Another prostitute and drug user, Linda Vitela, was murdered on April 22, 1987. She was also nude and wrapped up in bedding—the same with Sheila Jacox and Sharon Massey. All of these women fit a pattern, and their cases were almost identical.

When Solomon reported the death of Johnson, he had to submit a blood sample and his fingerprints were taken. Although his statements were inconsistent, he wasn't arrested or charged. He was questioned again after the discovery of Apodaca's body and again he gave false statements. He tried to explain that this was because he thought he had some outstanding misdemeanor warrants.

Solomon gave permission for the police to search his car on April 20, 1987. It was parked on a lot, and while they were there, they noticed the soil seemed to be depressed in one area. They got hold of a shovel, started digging, and found the body of Washington. Two days later, they found the bodies of Jacox and Vitela at another property linked to Solomon. Later, they found the body of Massey at the same place they had found Apodaca's.

Timeline of known murders - dates bodies found:

June 18, 1986 - Yolanda Johnson, twenty-two

July 20, 1986 - Angela Polidori, twenty-five

March 19, 1987 - Maria Apodaca, eighteen

April 20, 1987 - Cherie Washington, twenty-six

April 22, 1987 - Linda Vitela, twenty-four

April 22, 1987 - Sheila Jacox, seventeen

April 29, 1987 - Sharon Massey, twenty-nine

Arrest and Trial

Solomon was arrested on April 22, 1987 and questioned about the murders. He was charged with all seven murders, but the charges for the murder of Polidori were eventually dropped. The defense team tried to convince the court that Solomon was suffering from mental issues due to childhood abuse, his cocaine use, and his experiences fighting in the Vietnam War. However, he was convicted of the six remaining murders he had been charged with and sentenced to death.

Outcome

Solomon remains on death row awaiting his execution.

ANTHONY SOWELL

Date of birth: August 19, 1949

Aliases/Nicknames: The Cleveland Strangler, The Imperial Avenue Murderer

Characteristics: Kidnapping, rape, necrophilia

Number of victims: 11

Date of murders: May 2007 - September 2009

Date of arrest: October 31, 2009

Murder method: Strangulation with objects

Known Victims: Crystal Dozier, 38; Tishana Culver, 31; Leshanda Long, 25; Michelle Mason, 45; Tonia Carmichael, 53; Nancy Cobbs, 43; Amelda Hunter, 47; Telacia Fortson, 31; Janice Webb, 49; Kim Yvette Smith, 44; Diane Turner, 38

Crime location: Cleveland, Ohio

Status: Sentenced to death, awaiting execution.

Background

Sowell was one of seven children born to Claudia Garrison, a single mother. His sister also had seven children, and following her death due to illness, they all lived in the house with Sowell, his mother, and his siblings. Garrison would abuse these children but not her own; Garrison's children would watch while she whipped the others. Sowell's niece was once forced to take off all her clothes, and she was then whipped with an electrical cord by Garrison until her wounds bled. She was also raped by Sowell nearly every day for around two years, starting when she was just eleven years old.

Sowell enlisted with the Marines when he was nineteen, in 1978. He trained as an electrician in the Marines, and in 1980, he spent a year with the 3rd Force Service Support Group overseas. When he returned, he spent time at Cherry Point. In 1984, he was sent to the Marine Corps Base Camp Butler in Japan. The following year, he spent three days at Camp Pendleton in California, and he was discharged from the military on January 18, 1985.

Sowell received a number of awards while in the service, including a Sea Service Deployment Ribbon, a Good Conduct Medal with one service star, a Meritorious Mast, two Letters of Appreciation, and a Certificate of Commendation.

Sowell attacked a pregnant woman in 1989, choking her and tying her up with a belt. She managed to get away, and he was charged with attempted rape, receiving a fifteen-year prison sentence. He served the full time and was released from prison in 2005.

For the next two years he worked in a factory. But, he stopped working and started claiming unemployment benefits in 2007. He would make extra money from selling scrap metal. He joined an online dating service, and his profile stated he was a master looking for a submissive woman so he could "train her." Around this time, the neighbors started to notice a terrible smell in the area, and the health department received a number of complaints. Sowell claimed it was coming from the sausage shop next door to his house. But soon it would be discovered where the stench was really coming from.

Murders

Sowell invited a woman back to his place for a drink in September of 2009. On September 22, she went to the police and claimed that after they had a few drinks, he became angry and hit her before choking her and raping her while she was passed out. The police went to Sowell's home on October 29 with an arrest warrant, but he wasn't there. They did, however, find two dead bodies on the living room floor.

As they investigated the home, they found four more bodies in the crawl spaces and one body buried in the basement in a shallow grave. Outside, they found three more bodies and a fourth set of partial remains. A skull was found in a bucket. Altogether, they had found the remains of eleven victims. The majority of them had been strangled, and some still had ligatures around their necks.

Timeline of known murders:

November 10, 2008 - Tonia Carmichael, fifty-three

May 17, 2007 - Crystal Dozier, thirty-five

June of 2008 - Tishana Culver, thirty-three

August of 2008 - Leshanda Long, seventeen

October 8, 2008 - Michelle Mason, forty-five

January 17, 2009 - Kim Y. Smith, forty-four

April 24, 2009 - Nancy Cobb, forty-four

Spring of 2009- Amelda (Amy) Hunter, forty-seven

June of 2009 - Janice Webb, forty-nine

June 3, 2009 - Telacia Fortson, thirty-one

September of 2009 - Diane Turner, thirty-eight

Arrest and Trial

Sowell was located and arrested on October 31, 2009. He was charged with the murders and his bond was set at five million dollars. After numerous delays, Sowell went on trial on June 6, 2011. In addition to the eleven counts of aggravated murder, there were seventy additional charges related to rape, kidnapping, abuse of a corpse, and tampering with evidence. Initially, he pleaded not guilty by reason of insanity. But he later changed it to not guilty. On July 22, he was found guilty of all but two counts.

Sentencing took place on August 12, and Sowell was sentenced to death.

Outcome

Despite launching multiple lawsuits and appeals, Sowell's death sentence remained in place. He is still awaiting his execution date, and he has been on death row since September 14, 2011.

TIMOTHY WILSON SPENCER

Date of birth: March 17, 1962

Aliases/Nicknames: The Southside Strangler, The Southside Slayer, The Southside Rapist

Characteristics: Rape

Number of victims: 5

Date of murders: 1984, 1987 – 1988

Date of arrest: January 20, 1988

Murder method: Strangulation by ligature

Known Victims: Carol Hamm; Debbie Dudley Davis, 35; Dr. Susan Hellams; Diane Cho, 15; Susan Tucker, 44

Crime location: Arlington County, Virginia

Status: Executed by electric chair, April 27, 1994.

Background

Spencer was raised in Green Valley, Arlington, considered to be one of the "toughest black neighborhoods" in the area. He was well-known to the police for committing multiple burglaries throughout his youth. He later became the first murderer to be convicted in the United States based purely on DNA evidence. This would also lead to an innocent man being exonerated for a crime he didn't commit.

Murders

It is believed that Spencer's first murder victim was Carol Hamm in 1984. David Vasquez was originally tried and convicted of this murder. He was later exonerated when Spencer was arrested for the other murders.

Debbie Dudley Davie was murdered sometime between September 18 and September 19, 1987. Her body was found naked on the bed in her apartment by the police. A ligature was around her neck with a ratchet-type device attached to it. Her cause of death was determined to be strangulation by ligature.

On October 2, 1987, Dr. Susan Hellams was killed in her home. Her husband came home and found her dead on the floor of the bedroom closet, partially clothed. She had two belts fastened around her neck; her death was caused by ligature strangulation.

The next victim was Diane Cho, a high school student, who was murdered on November 22, 1987. She was found in the family home, and she had been raped before being strangled to death. The last known victim of Spencer was Susan Tucker. She was raped and murdered in her home on November 27, 1987. She wasn't found until December 1. Although she lived in a different area, the similarities between the murders made it clear they were all committed by the same person.

Timeline of known murders:

1984 - Carol Hamm

September 18, 1987 - Debbie Dudley Davis, thirty-five

October 2, 1987 - Dr. Susan Hellams

November 22, 1987 - Diane Cho, fifteen

November 27, 1987 - Susan Tucker, forty-four

Arrest and Trial

Spencer was arrested on January 20, 1988, in Arlington County for the rape and murder of Tucker. Spencer had traveled to Arlington from Richmond to have Thanksgiving with his mother who lived close to Tucker.

He was later charged with the murders of Davis, Hellams, and Cho in Richmond. He had been living within walking distance of the homes of both Davis and Hellams at the time of their murders. Forensic testing was undertaken on the biological samples found at the crime scenes. The DNA results linked Spencer to the murder of Tucker, and it was the first time DNA had been used in a Virginia criminal case. Spencer's DNA was also a match to samples found at the murders of Davis, Hellams, and Hamm.

His Arlington trial for the rape, murder, and burglary of Tucker began on July 11, 1988. With the help of the DNA evidence, he was convicted and sentenced to death. He then went on trial in Richmond, for the murder, rape, and burglary of Davis. Again, the DNA evidence was paramount, and he was convicted.

At his next trial on January 17, 1989, for the murder, rape, and burglary of Hellams, he was found guilty. He was also found guilty of the charges in the Cho murder.

Outcome

Spencer was executed by electric chair at Greensville Correctional Center on April 27, 1994, and he was declared deceased at 11:13 p.m. He received four rounds of electricity, the first of which made his body clench. He declined to donate his organs, and he made no final statement before his death.

The man originally convicted for the murder of Carol Hamm, David Vasquez was granted an unconditional pardon on January 4, 1989. By that time, he had served five years of his thirty-five-year sentence. He became the very first American exonerated on the basis of DNA evidence.

Trivia

- The electric chair used in Spencer's execution was built by inmates during the 1960s.

CARY STAYNER

Date of birth: August 13, 1961

Aliases/Nicknames: The Yosemite Killer

Characteristics: Decapitation, rape

Number of victims: 4

Date of murders: February of 1999, July of 1999

Date of arrest: July 24, 1999

Murder method: Throat cutting, strangulation

Known Victims: Carole Sund, 42, her daughter, Juli, 15, and their Argentine friend, Silvina Pelosso, 16; Joie Ruth Armstrong, 26

Crime location: Mariposa County, California

Status: Sentenced to death, awaiting execution.

Background

Stayner's childhood was rocked by the loss of his younger brother in 1972. Steven was abducted by Kenneth Parnell, a child molester, and held captive for a staggering seven years before he escaped. Stayner later said he had felt as though he was neglected and ignored by his parents during his brother's captivity, as they were grieving, believing Steven had been murdered. Stayner also claimed that his uncle had molested him when he was eleven years old.

When his brother Steven miraculously returned to the family in 1980, it was a major media event that resulted in a book and a movie being made for television. Both of these were called *I Know My First Name Is Steven*, a statement he first made when questioned by the authorities after he had escaped from Parnell.

Nine years after the escape, Steven was killed in a motorcycle accident. In 1990, a year later, Stayner's uncle was murdered. Stayner had been staying with the uncle at the time of the murder. The following year, Stayner tried to commit suicide but survived. Then, in 1997, he was arrested for the possession of methamphetamine and marijuana. But these charges were dropped. That same year he started working at the Cedar Lodge Motel as a handyman, near the Yosemite National Park entrance. He was still working here in 1999, when the bodies of two women were found in the trunk of a burned out car nearby.

Murders

While working as a handyman at the Cedar Lodge Motel in El Portal, near the entrance to Yosemite National Park, Stayner murdered four women between February and July of 1999. The first two victims were Silvina Pelosso and Carole Sund. Their bodies were found burned beyond recognition in the trunk of Sund's rental car. They were identified using dental records.

The police received a note with a map drawn showing where the body of Juli Sund could be found. At the top of the note, the killer had written, "we had fun with this one." Investigators rushed to the location indicated and found Juli with her throat cut.

Because three of the victims had been staying at the motel, the employees were interviewed, including Stayner. At that point he wasn't considered a suspect, and he had no prior criminal history. However, when the decapitated body of Joie Armstrong was found, witnesses reported seeing a blue 1979 International Scout (the car belonging to Stayner) parked outside the same cabin Armstrong had been renting.

Arrest and Trial

Stayner fled. But he was found staying at a nudist resort in Wilton and was promptly arrested. Evidence in his vehicle linked him to Armstrong's murder, and while he was being interrogated, he confessed to all of the murders. He claimed he had been fantasizing about committing murders of women since he was seven years old.

When Stayner stood trial, he pleaded not guilty by reason of insanity. An psychological assessment deemed him sane, and he was subsequently convicted.

Outcome

Stayner was convicted of four counts of first-degree murder and was sentenced to death in 2001. He is still awaiting his execution, and there are appeals pending.

Trivia

- Stayner asked for child pornography in exchange for his confession.
- Stayner suffered from obsessive-compulsive disorder.

PETER SUTCLIFFE

Date of birth: June 2, 1946

Aliases/Nicknames: The Yorkshire Ripper, Peter William Coonan

Characteristics: Claimed to hear voices - targeted prostitutes

Number of victims: 13

Date of murders: 1975 - 1980

Date of arrest: January 2, 1981

Murder method: Stabbing, striking with hammer

Known Victims: Wilma McCann, 28; Emily Jackson, 42; Irene Richardson, 28; Patricia Atkinson, 32; Jayne MacDonald, 16; Jean Jordan, 20; Yvonne Pearson, 21; Helen Rytka, 18; Vera Millward, 40; Josephine Whitaker, 19; Barbara Leach, 20; Marguerite Walls, 47; Jacqueline Hill, 20

Crime location: West Yorkshire, England

Status: Sentenced to life imprisonment without parole.

Background

Sutcliffe was raised in a Catholic family in Yorkshire by parents John and Kathleen. At fifteen, he left school and worked in a number of jobs considered menial, including that of being a gravedigger in the 1960s. From November of 1971 until April of 1973, he worked on the packaging line at a local factory, but he left after being offered the job of traveling salesman.

In 1975, Sutcliffe voluntarily took redundancy from his job and used the money to train as an HGV driver. He completed his license and started working for a tire company as a driver in September of 1975. Within a year, he was fired for stealing tires, and he remained unemployed until he found more driving work in October of 1976.

Sutcliffe married Sonia Szurma in August of 1974. Despite all efforts, she suffered multiple miscarriages before they were told she could never have children. She went back to training as a teacher, during which time she had an affair, yet the couple remained together. In 1977, they bought a house using her salary as a teacher in Heaton, Bradford, where they would remain until the police came looking for Sutcliffe.

Murders

After numerous random and violent attacks on women, Sutcliffe graduated to murder in 1975. The first victim, Wilma McCann, was killed on October 30. She was hit with a hammer twice and stabbed a total of fifteen times, in the chest, abdomen, and neck.

The next victim was Emily Jackson, who was killed in January of 1976. She was hit in the head with a hammer and stabbed with a sharpened screwdriver. She had been stabbed in the chest, abdomen, and neck, and Sutcliffe had stomped on her thigh so hard he left a boot impression.

Irene Richardson was bludgeoned to death on February 5, 1977. Sutcliffe had beaten her with a hammer and used a knife to mutilate her body. Then, on April 23, Patricia Atkinson was killed in her flat in Bradford. Sutcliffe's murderous urges were escalating, and he was killing more frequently now.

Jayne McDonald, sixteen, was murdered on June 26, 1977. On October 1, Sutcliffe murdered Jean Jordan, a prostitute. Her body wasn't found until ten days after the murder, and investigators determined her body had been moved after she had died. According to Sutcliffe, he had given Jordan a new five-pound note. Worried it could be traceable, he went back to her body to retrieve it. He then mutilated the body and shifted it.

In January of 1978, Yvonne Pearson was killed. Sutcliffe hid her body beneath an old sofa that had been thrown out, and it remained hidden until March. He then killed prostitute Helen Rytka on January 31, and her body was discovered three days later. The next victim, Vera Millward, was murdered on May 16 in the parking lot of the Manchester Royal Infirmary, a major hospital in Manchester.

Sutcliffe murdered Josephine Whitaker on April 4, 1979, as she was walking home. Then, on September 1, he killed Barbara Leach and dumped her body behind a building, beneath a pile of bricks. Marguerite Walls was murdered on August 20, and Jacqueline Hill was killed on November 17.

Timeline of murders:

October 30, 1975 - Wilma McCann, twenty-eight

January of 1976 - Emily Jackson, forty-two

February 5, 1977 - Irene Richardson, twenty-eight

April 23, 1977- Patricia Atkinson, thirty-two

June 26, 1977 - Jayne MacDonald, sixteen

October 1, 1977 - Jean Jordan, twenty

January of 1978 - Yvonne Pearson, twenty-one

January 31, 1978 - Helen Rytka, eighteen

May 16, 1978 - Vera Millward, forty

April 4, 1979 - Josephine Whitaker, nineteen

September 1, 1979 - Barbara Leach, twenty

August 20, 1980 - Marguerite Walls, forty-seven

November 17, 1980 - Jaqueline Hill, twenty

Arrest and Trial

Throughout the investigations into the murders, Sutcliffe had been interviewed numerous times. But he wasn't considered a suspect. On January 2, 1981, however, he was pulled over by the police. He had a prostitute, Olivia Reivers, in the car with him. The license plates on his car were false, so he was arrested and taken back to the station.

Sutcliffe matched many of the physical characteristics of the Yorkshire Ripper, and so he was questioned again about the murders. The following day, police went back to where he had been arrested and found a hammer, knife, and rope he had dumped when he told the arresting officer he was "busting to go to the toilet." At the police station, they found another knife hidden in the toilet cistern.

Police obtained a search warrant for his home. While they were doing that, Sutcliffe was subjected to a strip search. They discovered he was wearing a V-neck sweater inverted under his pants. The sleeves of the sweater were over his legs, with the V-neck exposing his genitals.

Sutcliffe was questioned for two days before he finally confessed that he was the Ripper on January 4, 1981. He then spent the next day describing all of the attacks and murders in detail. On January 5, he was formally charged with thirteen counts of murder.

When Sutcliffe went on trial, he pleaded not guilty to murder, though he did plead guilty of the lesser charge of manslaughter due to diminished responsibility. He claimed he was instructed by God to murder prostitutes. The diminished responsibility plea was subsequently quashed by the judge, and the full trial was set to start on May 5, 1981.

After two weeks on trial, Sutcliffe was found guilty on all counts of murder and was sentenced to twenty sentences of life imprisonment. Initially, it was recommended he serve at least thirty years, but later the High Court issued Sutcliffe a whole life sentence.

Outcome

Sutcliffe was assaulted by fellow inmate James Costello while incarcerated at Parkhurst Prison on January 10, 1983. Costello struck Sutcliffe twice in the face with a broken coffee jar, and Sutcliffe required thirty stitches to repair the four lacerations the jar caused.

In 1984, Sutcliffe was sectioned under the Mental Health Act and sent to Broadmoor Hospital. He was once again attacked by a fellow inmate, Paul Wilson, on February 23, 1996. Wilson attempted to strangle Sutcliffe with a headphone cable. He was saved when two convicted murderers, Jamie Devitt and Kenneth Erskine, came to his assistance after hearing him scream.

On March 10, 1997, Sutcliffe was attacked by inmate Ian Kay, which resulted in him losing his vision in one eye and suffering severe damage to the other. He was attacked again on December 22, 2007, by Patrick Sureda, who lunged at him with a knife. Sutcliffe managed to move away quickly enough to save his remaining working eye, but he was stabbed in the cheek.

Trivia

— Sutcliffe was later diagnosed as having paranoid schizophrenia

JAMES SWANN

Date of birth: 1964
Aliases/Nicknames: The Shotgun Stalker
Characteristics: Paranoid schizophrenia, drive-by shootings
Number of victims: 4
Date of murders: February - April of 1993
Date of arrest: April 19, 1993
Murder method: Shooting
Known Victims: Julius Bryant, 58; Elizabeth Hutson, 28; Edward Fleming, 35; Nello Hughes, 61
Crime location: Washington
Status: Found not guilty by reason of insanity. Held at a psychiatric facility.

Background

Swann was born and raised in Iselin, New Jersey, and it wasn't until his teenage years that he started showing signs of suffering from some form of mental illness. He was seen and heard talking to himself all the time, and sometimes he would burst into laughter for no apparent reason. Little is known about his parents and family situation other than that his father, James, had been a former Navy man and had worked at the Treasury Department.

As an adult, Swann occasionally worked as a security guard, despite having a mental illness. He was eventually fired, however, after insisting on walking backwards while on patrol. He later moved to Oxon Hill to live with his sister, but she kicked him out of the home in early 1993 after an argument. From then onwards, Swann would move between New Jersey, New York, and Pennsylvania.

That same year, 1993, the voices in his head were becoming more and more demanding, and Swann could no longer ignore them.

Murders

Swann's first murder victim was shot and killed in a barbershop. Swann purposely entered the shop and killed a client while he was sitting in the barber chair. Police at first assumed it was a drug-related shooting. Then, six days later, Swann killed Elizabeth "Bessie" Hutson as she was walking her dogs. On April 10, he fired randomly at pedestrians, killing Edward Fleming, and injuring two others.

On April 19, Swann opened fire on a group of pedestrians again, and this time he killed Nello Hughes. Somehow, he missed all of the other pedestrians. This was his last murder. Immediately after the murder of Hughes, Swann caught the attention of the police when he ran through a red light. An officer followed Swann until he stopped near a building and tried to run. The officer caught him and placed him under arrest.

Timeline of known murders:

February 26, 1993 - Julius Bryant, fifty-eight

March 23, 1993 - Elizabeth Hutson, twenty-eight

April 10, 1993 - Edward Fleming, thirty-five

April 19, 1993 - Nello Hughes, sixty-one

Arrest and Trial

In Swann's car was a 20-gauge shotgun, similar to the weapon used in the shooting spree. Swann was charged with the murders and the attempted murders of those who were injured. He went on trial and was found not guilty by reason of insanity on September 27, 1994. It was determined by psychiatrists that he had been suffering from paranoid schizophrenia at the time of the shootings.

Outcome

Swann was sent to St. Elizabeth's Hospital, a psychiatric hospital with a maximum security unit. During his incarceration at the hospital, Swann has managed to earn an associate's degree in computer science. Despite his good behavior at St. Elizabeth's and his lack of psychotic episodes since 2003, any requests made by Swann to leave have been denied.

Trivia

- While incarcerated, Swann would often be seen wearing a T-shirt that said "thrill to kill" - given to him by his father.
- He has subsequently been diagnosed with narcissistic personality disorder as well as the paranoid schizophrenia.

VASILE TCACIUC

Date of birth: circa 1900
Aliases/Nicknames: The Butcher of Iasi
Characteristics: Robbery
Number of victims: 21 - 26 +
Date of murders: 1917 - 1935
Date of arrest: 1935
Murder method: Axe
Known Victims: Unknown
Crime location: Iasi, Romania
Status: Shot and killed by police during an attempted escape.

Background

Very little is known about the background and childhood of Romanian killer Vasile Tcaciuc. He was in police custody for burglary and robbery charges when the actions of a dog lead to the discovery of bodies buried beneath Tcaciuc's home. Following the unearthing of the bodies, Tcaciuc explained how he had built a special axe to use purely for committing the murders.

Murders

Tcaciuc's motive for committing murder was predominantly for financial gain. He would kill his victim and then rob them of any money or valuables they had. When his victims were discovered, all showed signs of having been hit by an object that was most an axe.

Arrest and Trial

Tcaciuc was taken out of the jail to help reconstruct his crimes, having confessed to committing twenty-six murders. During the excursion, he attempted to escape. Shot by a policeman, he was killed on the spot. The real reason behind Tcaciuc's crimes remains unknown.

JOHN FLOYD THOMAS

Date of birth: July 26, 1936

Aliases/Nicknames: The Westside Rapist, The Southland Strangler, Willie Eugene Wilson

Characteristics: Rape

Number of victims: 7 - 15 +

Date of murders: 1972 - 1986

Date of arrest: March 31, 2009

Murder method: Asphyxiation

Known Victims: Ethel Sokoloff, 68; Elizabeth McKeown, 67; Cora Perry, 79; Maybelle Hudson; Miriam McKinley; Evalyn Bunner; Adrian Askew, 85

Crime location: Los Angeles

Status: Sentenced to life imprisonment without parole.

Background

Thomas' mother died when he was was twelve years old. He was subsequently raised by his godmother and aunt, moving between the two homes. He attended public schools in Los Angeles before joining the Air Force in 1956. During his service, a superior officer once noted that Thomas was often late and was "slovenly" in his appearance. He received a dishonorable discharge from the Air Force after serving for a short period of time.

After he left the military, Thomas was arrested for attempted rape and burglary. He was found guilty and sentenced to six years in prison. Because he later violated his parole twice, he remained in prison until 1966. It is believed he started raping and killing during the 1970s, but he wouldn't be arrested until 2009, thanks in part to DNA evidence.

Murders

In the mid-1970s, the Westside Rapist was terrorizing elderly women in Los Angeles who lived by themselves. He would break into their homes, rape them, and then choke them until they died or passed out. There were at least seventeen victims, and they were usually found with their faces covered by blankets or pillows. Then, a decade after this spate of killings, five elderly women were found dead in Claremont. They too had their faces covered with blankets or pillows.

In October of 2008, Thomas was asked to provide a DNA sample for an offender database the state of

California was trying to put together. Because he had been charged twice before for sexual crimes, he was of particular interest. This DNA sample led to a huge break in the hunt for the Westside Rapist, as Thomas was now identified as the killer.

Timeline of known murders:

1972 - Ethel Sokoloff, sixty-eight

1976 - Elizabeth McKeown, sixty-seven

September 20, 1975 - Cora Perry, seventy

April of 1976 - Maybelle Hudson

June of 1976 - Miriam McKinley

October of 1976 - Evalyn Brunner

June of 1986 - Adrian Askew

Arrest and Trial

Thomas was arrested on March 31, 2009, and questioned about the murders of the elderly women over the previous thirty years. On April 2, he was formally charged with the murders of Ethel Sokoloff and Elizabeth McKeown. By September 23, he was charged with five more murders, those of Cora Perry, Maybelle Hudson, Miriam McKinley, Evalyn Bunner, and Adrian Askew.

At his first court appearance, Thomas pleaded not guilty to the seven charges of murder. On April 1, 2011, he changed his plea to guilty to the seven counts of murder as part of a plea deal so he could avoid the death sentence for the murder of Adrian Askew. He was subsequently sentenced to life imprisonment without the possibility of parole.

Outcome

Initially, Thomas was charged with two murders. But eventually he was charged with killing seven women. The prosecution officials stated they had DNA evidence linking him to the murders. Authorities also believe he may be responsible for up to thirty unsolved homicides. Most likely, he had killed for over forty years.

Dubbed the "Westside Rapist" because it was thought his crimes only centered on the Westside area of Los Angeles, it is now believed he may have been preying on women in other areas, including Claremont, Lennox, Pomona, and Inglewood.

PETER TOBIN

Date of birth: August 27, 1946

Aliases/Nicknames: Peter Wilson, James Kelly, Paul Semple, John Tobin, Peter Proban, Pat McLaughlin

Characteristics: Rape

Number of victims: 3 +

Date of murders: February 10, 1991; August, 1991; September 24, 2006

Date of arrest: October 3, 2006

Murder method: Stabbing

Known Victims: Vicky Hamilton, 15; Dinah McNicol; Angelika Kluk, 23

Crime location: Scotland, England

Status: Sentenced to life imprisonment without parole.

Background

Tobin, one of eight children in the family, was described as a "difficult" child and was sent off to a special school in 1953, when he was seven years old. Later, he was sent to a young offender institution, and eventually he was charged and convicted of forgery and burglary and sentenced to prison in 1970.

After his release, he moved to Brighton in Sussex along with his girlfriend, Margaret Louise Robertson Mountney, who was only seventeen at the time. They were married in August of 1970, but divorced a year later in 1971. Tobin married again in 1973, to Sylvia Jeffries, a thirty-year old nurse. They had two children. But, unfortunately, the second child died soon after she was born. This marriage was violent, and in 1976, Sylvia fled the home with their son.

In 1987, Tobin had another child with Cathy Wilson, who was only fifteen at the time, and they married in 1989. Three years later, they moved to Bathgate, but the relationship ended soon after. All three of Tobin's wives claimed he had been charming right up until they married; at that point, he would then become a sadistic and violent psychopath.

Tobin moved to Margate in May of 1991 to be closer to his youngest son. In August of 1993, two teenage girls were attacked in his flat in Leigh Park, Havant. The fourteen-year-olds had tried to visit Tobin's neighbor who wasn't home at the time, and they asked if they could wait in his flat until their friend returned home. Once inside, Tobin produced a knife and threatened the girls, forcing them to drink alcohol until they were intoxicated. He then raped both girls and stabbed one of them, all while his child was in the flat. Tobin then turned the gas taps on, thinking they would die, but they both survived.

Tobin went on the run and tried to hide among a religious sect, the Jesus Fellowship, in Coventry. He was later caught when his vehicle was located. He was convicted and given a fourteen-year sentence in May of 1994. But he only served eight years, getting released in 2004 when he was fifty-eight years old. But that wasn't to be the end of Tobin's reign of terror. Many would later suspect he could possibly have been Bible John.

Murders

Vicky Hamilton disappeared while waiting for a bus ride home on February 10, 1991. In June of 2007, Tobin's old residence in Margate was searched in relation to the murder of Vicky, and her body was found buried in the garden.

Dinah McNicol had been hitchhiking home from a music festival on August 5, 1991, when she disappeared. Her boyfriend had been with her, but she continued on in the car with the stranger after he was dropped off. A body was found on November 16, 2007, and it later was identified as McNichol.

Tobin was working as a handyman for the St. Patrick's Roman Catholic Church in Glasgow in September of 2006, under the false name of Pat McLaughlin. This was because he was still on the sex offender register and he didn't want anyone to know. He had left Paisley without notifying the police, so there was a warrant for his arrest.

Polish student Angelika Kluk was working as a cleaner at the church to make some money and was staying at the presbytery. The last time she was seen alive, on September 24, 2006, she had been in the company of Tobin. Her body was found on September 29 beneath the floor in the confessional. She had been raped, beaten, and stabbed to death. Tobin was arrested soon afterwards on October 3.

Timeline of known murders:

February 10, 1991 - Vicky Hamilton, fifteen

August 5, 1991 - Dinah McNicol, eighteen

September 24, 2006 - Angelika Kluk, twenty-three

Arrest and Trial

After his arrest on October 3, 2006, Tobin was heavily questioned about the murders of Hamilton and McNicol. He was formally charged with the murder of Angelika Kluk and his trial was set to take place in March of 2007.

The trial lasted for six weeks, ending on May 4, 2007. Tobin denied being responsible for the murder of Kluk and the rape, but he was found guilty of the crimes. He was sentenced to life imprisonment with a minimum sentence of twenty-one years.

After the bodies of Hamilton and McNicol were found in his garden, Tobin was formally arrested for their murders on July 21, 2007. The first trial was for the murder of Vicky Hamilton. After a month, he was convicted on December 2, 2008. He was again sentenced to life imprisonment.

Tobin was charged with McNicol's murder on September 1, 2008. The trial started in June of 2009, but it had to be postponed due to the poor health of Tobin, who was awaiting surgery. The trial resumed on December 14, 2009. On December 16, after a deliberation of just fifteen minutes, the jury found him guilty. He received a third life sentence and the judge recommended he should never be released.

Outcome

Tobin suffered chest pains on August 9, 2012, and was taken to the Edinburgh Royal Infirmary with a suspected heart attack. He survived and returned to prison. In February of 2016, he once again was sent to the hospital with a suspected stroke. He remains in prison and is unlikely to ever be released.

The British Police created a task force called "Operation Anagram" which focuses solely on the movements of Tobin before his arrest. The purpose of the operation is to investigate the possibility of Tobin being responsible for dozens of murders across Britain. Police forces across the country are involved. Through Operation Anagram, the bodies of two victims (Dinah McNicol and Vicky Hamilton) were located. In June of 2011, the operation was wound down due to their inability to locate or identify any further victims.

After Tobin was convicted of the murders, the similarities between his physical appearance, the locations he had lived in, and his methods of killing led to speculation that he may have been the killer known as Bible John, a serial killer that had been operating in Glasgow. Interestingly, Tobin moved away from Glasgow at the same time that the murders stopped. Tobin looked very similar to the identikit pictures provided by witnesses. One witness statement said the killer had a tooth missing in the upper-right area of his mouth. Dental records showed the Tobin had had a tooth removed in the same area in the late 1960s.

MAURY TRAVIS

Date of birth: October 25, 1965

Aliases/Nicknames: Nil

Characteristics: Rape

Number of victims: 12 - 17 +

Date of murders: 2001 - 2002

Date of arrest: June 7, 2002

Murder method: Strangulation by ligature

Known Victims: Brenda Beasley, 33; Yvonne Crues, 50; Verona Thompson, 36; suspected - Betty James, 46; Teresa Wilson, 36; Alysa Greenwade, 34; Mary Shields, 61; others unidentified

Crime location: Ferguson, Missouri

Status: Committed suicide by hanging in the police cell before going to trial, June 10, 2002.

Background

Everything about Travis' background seems to have been "normal" and ordinary. His neighbors, teachers at school, and more or less everyone who knew Travis, described him as polite, helpful, and quiet. His parents had divorced in 1978, and although his mother remarried and later divorced again, there is no record of this having a major impact on Travis.

He was so ordinary, in fact, that many of his former classmates at school couldn't even remember him. He is not even identifiable in any yearbook photographs from his time at school. One teacher did remember him as a student and described Travis as being very reserved and withdrawn but not a problem in class. There is also no record of any type of violence or abuse in the household when he was growing up. And there nothing to suggest he indulged in torturing or killing animals as a child, which is a common predictor of a burgeoning killer.

When he was twenty-two, Travis attended college in Atlanta. During his time at the school he developed a cocaine addiction. He went home for spring break in March of 1988 and, desperate for money to feed his cocaine habit, he robbed several shoe stores over an eight-day spree. He was arrested and subsequently convicted. By the time sentencing came around, he told the judge he had attended rehabilitation and was no longer using drugs. There were multiple letters of support for Travis asking for leniency in the sentencing, and he ended up being sentenced to fifteen years of imprisonment.

Despite receiving thirteen conduct violation reports during his imprisonment, Travis only served five years and a few months of his sentence. These violations were not considered serious enough to affect his parole and he was released on June 14, 1994. It was then that he moved into a duplex home on Lucas & Hunt Road. Travis would serve two more sentences for drug charges in the following years. During the summers of 2000 and 2001, he worked at the Mayfair Hotel restaurant as a waiter.

One of his co-workers at the restaurant was Dave Wucher, who later stated Travis constantly—almost obsessively—talked about his car. During a conversation between the two men one day, Wucher had told Travis about a friend's car that was stolen and set on fire in East St. Louis. In response, Travis stated that East St. Louis was a "good place to dump things because there's not many police around."

Wucher's girlfriend at the time, Julie Kroenig, was working at a news channel as an intern. Travis asked her one day if the station had done a story on prostitutes in the area that were being murdered. He told her he had heard from friends that bodies had been dumped there. She checked with the station boss, but no information could be found related to Travis' story. Three months later, the police released details about a serial killer murdering prostitutes in the area, and Kroenig finally realized the truth behind what Travis had told her.

Murders

Not long after Travis was released from prison in March of 2001, the bodies of women who had been strangled started to appear around Ferguson, Missouri. Each of the bodies bore signs of being tortured before death, and most of the victims were prostitutes.

Travis was on the suspect list early on, largely because of his criminal history. But there was no evidence to arrest him for the murders. Travis tried to be clever with the authorities, however, which backfired on him and led to his capture.

The police received a letter on May 21, 2002, written by the serial killer. Included in the letter was a map showing where the body of the latest victim had been disposed of. Police searched the area shown on the map and found the remains of a murdered woman. At this time, the investigators took a good look at the map and realized it had been downloaded from the internet.

What Travis didn't know, was that when he downloaded the map, the IP address of his computer was stored electronically. Therefore, when police contacted the source of the map, they were able to retrieve the address where the computer was located. And it led straight to Travis.

Timeline of murders (identified victims):

July 31, 2000 - Mary Shields, sixty

April 1, 2001 - Alysa Greenwade, thirty-four

May 15, 2001-Teresa Wilson, thirty-six

May 23, 2001 - Betty James, forty-six

June 29, 2001- Verona Thompson, thirty-six

August 25, 2001- Yvonne Crues, fifty

October 8, 2001 - Brenda Beasley, thirty-three

January 30, 2002 - unidentified female remains found

March 11, 2002 - unidentified female remains found

March 28, 2002 - unidentified female remains found

Arrest and Trial

On June 7, 2002, policed arrested Travis and took him in to custody. When they searched his house, they found a huge collection of video tapes showing the torture, rape, and murder of many of the victims. There was no doubt they had captured the right man.

However, while Travis was in custody at the St. Louis County jail, he took steps to ensure he would never stand trial for the multiple murders.

Outcome

Travis committed suicide by hanging himself on June 10, 2002, while in jail awaiting his trial for the murders. He should have been put on suicide watch, but the officers who had been trained in it didn't show up for duty.

HENRY LOUIS WALLACE

Date of birth: November 4, 1965

Aliases/Nicknames: The Taco Bell Strangler

Characteristics: Rape

Number of victims: 9 +

Date of murders: 1990 - 1994

Date of arrest: March 12, 1994

Murder method: Stabbing, strangulation

Known Victims: Caroline Love; Shawna Hawk; Audrey Ann Spain; Valencia M. Jumper; Michelle Stinson; Vanessa Little Mack; Betty Jean Baucom; Brandi June Henderson; Deborah Slaughter; Tashonda Bethea

Crime location: Charlotte, North Carolina

Status: Sentenced to death, awaiting execution.

Background

Wallace was the product of an affair between his mother Lottie Mae Wallace and a school teacher, who promptly ended the affair as soon as he discovered she was pregnant. His mother was therefore a single parent, and she was known to be very harsh when it came to disciplining her son. Wallace was criticized by his mother for any mistake he made, even if it was minor.

Wallace graduated from high school in 1983, and he attended multiple colleges until 1985, when he enlisted in the Navy. That same year, he also married Maretta Brabham, who had been his high school sweetheart. He remained with the Navy until he received an honorable discharge in 1992.

While Wallace was in the Navy, he used a variety of drugs; his criminal career started around the same time. He began committing burglaries around Seattle, and in January of 1988, he was arrested after breaking into a store. As a result, he was sentenced to two years of supervised probation. But, he failed to turn up to most of his mandatory meetings. Burglary was just the start of things to come, however. In 1990, he committed his first murder.

Murders

Unlike most serial killers who kill random strangers, Wallace focused largely on women he knew. They were friends of his girlfriend, co-workers, employees, and friends of Wallace's sister. Somehow,

Wallace wasn't linked to the murders until he had committed eleven. This seems quite remarkable, considering he was very much in the picture at the funerals and work places of the victims.

Tashonda Bethea was Wallace's first known victim. He murdered her in early 1990 and dumped her body in a lake. Her body wasn't discovered until weeks after her death. During the investigation, Wallace was questioned about her disappearance and murder but no charges were filed.

Wallace picked up Sharon Nance, a prostitute and known drug dealer, in May of 1992. When it came time to pay her, Wallace beat her to death and then dumped her body by the railroad tracks, where it was found a few days later.

The next month, Caroline Love was raped and strangled at her apartment. She was a friend of Wallace's girlfriend, and he was with her sister when she filed the missing person's report. Wallace disposed of her body in a wooded area in Charlotte, and she wouldn't be found for two years.

On February 19, 1993, Wallace had sex with Shawna Hawk at her home before he killed her. He was her supervisor at work and even attended her funeral. Another co-worker, Audrey Spain, was raped and strangled by Wallace on June 22.

Wallace raped and strangled a friend of his sister, Valencia M. Jumper, on August 10, 1993. To cover up the murder, he set her body on fire. He accompanied his sister to the funeral a few days later. In September, he went to the home of a friend from work, Michelle Stinson. He raped her, then later strangled and stabbed her in front of one of her children.

The next murder occurred on February 20, 1994, when Wallace killed another one of his employees. Vanessa Little Mack was killed in her apartment. Weeks later, on March 8, he strangled Betty Baucom. After she was dead, he robbed her house of any valuables and left in her car, which he later abandoned at a shopping center. Baucom was a co-worker of Wallace's girlfriend.

The same night, he went back to the same apartment complex and murdered his friend's girlfriend, Brandi June Henderson. He raped her first, while she was holding on to her baby, and then strangled her. Though he attempted to strangle her son, he managed to survive. Wallace robbed the apartment before leaving.

His final victim was Deborah Ann Slaughter, another co-worker of his girlfriend, around March 12. He strangled her to death before he stabbed her in the chest and stomach thirty-eight times.

Timeline of murders:

1990 - Tashonda Bethea

May of 1992 - Sharon Nance

June of 1992 - Caroline Love

February 19, 1993 - Shawna Hawk

June 22, 1993 - Audrey Spain

August 10, 1993 - Valencia M. Jumper

September of 1993 - Michelle Stinson

February 20, 1994 - Vanessa Little Mack

March 8, 1994 - Betty Jean Baucom

March 8, 1994 - Brandi June Henderson

March 12, 1994 - Deborah Ann Slaughter

Arrest and Trial

Wallace was arrested on March 13, 1994. Over a period of twelve hours, he confessed to murdering ten women in Charlotte, describing each murder in detail. He was charged with the murders and held in custody to await his trial.

The trial was delayed a number of times over the next two years due to the choice of venue, jury selection, and DNA evidence. It finally began in September of 1996. In an attempt to avoid the death penalty, his defense attorney tried to blame Wallace's actions on mental illness.

The defense plan failed, and on January 7, 1997, Wallace was convicted of nine murders and sentenced to nine death sentences.

Outcome

While incarcerated, Wallace got married on June 5, 1998, to Rebeca Torrijas who had been a former nurse at the prison. The wedding ceremony took place next to the execution chamber, and the manager of the Death Row unit attended.

Wallace appealed his death sentence on a number of grounds, including his claims that his confessions were coerced. He also claimed the investigating officers had violated his constitutional rights. So far, his appeals have failed, and he is still awaiting an execution date.

FARYION WARDRIP

Date of birth: March 6, 1959

Aliases/Nicknames: Nil

Characteristics: Rape

Number of victims: 5

Date of murders: 1984 - 1986

Date of arrest: May 6, 1986; February 14, 1999

Murder method: Stabbing, asphyxiation, strangulation

Known Victims: Terry Lee Sims, 20; Toni Jean Gibbs, 24; Debra Taylor, 25; Ellen Blau, 21; Tina Elizabeth Kimbrew, 22

Crime location: Wichita County, Texas

Status: Sentenced to death, awaiting execution.

Background

Wardrip was born in Salem in 1959, to parents George and Diana. He didn't do well in school, receiving poor grades, and he left before he had finished the twelfth grade. In 1978, he joined the Army National Guard. As far as anybody was aware, he had settled into his role well.

In 1983, he married his first wife, and he worked as a janitor for the local hospital. That same year, he was promoted at work and became an orderly. The following year, he received a less-than-honorable discharge from the National Guard for drug use, unlawful absences, and misconduct.

In 1984, Wardrip was also arrested for rape and murder and was sent to prison. He served eleven years before getting released on parole. His first marriage had ended in 1985 and he married his second wife following his release. It was now 1997, and it would be another two years before Wardrip would be linked—through DNA evidence—to a string of murders that had occurred in the 1980s.

Murders

The first known murder victim of Wardrip was Terry Lee Sims. In 1984, her body was found at home, having been sexually assaulted and then stabbed to death. She had tried to stop Wardrip from entering her home, but he broke down the door. Because she was resistant, he tied her hands together with an electrical cord. He later said he killed her for no apparent reason at all.

386

On January 19, 1985, Toni Gibbs disappeared. She had been working at Wichita General Hospital at the time, and two days after she went missing, her car was found a few miles away. Her body was located in a field on February 15, and a postmortem revealed she had been sexually assaulted and stabbed to death.

Debra Taylor was killed on March 24, 1985, in Fort Worth Texas. She met Wardrip at a bar after her husband had gone home, and he offered to drive her home. According to Wardrip, he made some advances toward her and she rejected him, so he killed her. Her body was found a week later at a construction site.

The murder of Ellen Blau occured on September 20, 1985, after she had left work that night. Wardrip forced her to drive to an area that was secluded and then strangled her to death, though he also stated once that he broken her neck. He took her car and purse and abandoned them in Wichita Falls.

Tina Elizabeth Kimbrew was killed in her apartment on May 6, 1986. Wardrip later said he killed her because she reminded him of his former wife. Kimbrew was suffocated to death with a pillow. After her body was discovered, her neighbors reported they had seen a tall man, white, with brown hair leaving her apartment.

On May 9, Wardrip phoned the police and confessed that he was responsible for the murder of Kimbrew. He was subsequently sentenced to serve thirty-five years in prison, but he was paroled in 1997. He seemed to turn his life around at this point, having remarried and gotten a job in a factory in Olney.

Meanwhile, a cold case investigation was underway in Wichita Falls to investigate the murders of Sims, Gibbs, Blau, and Taylor. At two of the crime scenes, the murder site of Sims and Gibbs, DNA had been found and the samples from each site matched. It was now clear they were dealing with a serial killer.

As they investigated, a link was made between Blau and Wardrip. While Wardrip was on trial for Kimbrew's murder, he had stated he had known Blau, but nobody followed up on it. Further evidence was then found linking Wardrip to the murders. They needed a DNA sample from him though, and to get it, they approached his work and asked for the paper cup he had been drinking out of. So that there would be no suspicion, the officer said he needed it to spit his chewing tobacco into.

Analysis was done on the DNA right away, and it came back positive in the cases of Gibbs and Sims.

Timeline of murders:

1984 - Terry Lee Sims, twenty

January 19, 1985 - Toni Jean Gibbs, twenty-three

March 24, 1985 - Debra Taylor, twenty-five

September 20, 1985 - Ellen Blau, twenty-one

May 6, 1986 - Tina Elizabeth Kimbrew, twenty-one

Arrest and Trial

Wardrip was arrested on February 14, 1999, and he confessed to the murders of Sims, Blau, Taylor, and Gibbs. His trial took place the same year, and he was found guilty of all charges. Wardrip was sentenced to death.

Outcome

Wardrip received the death penalty for murdering Sims. But in 2008, nine years after sentencing, a federal magistrate recommended that Wardrip's death sentence should be overturned due to his defense being ineffective throughout his trial. In June of 2011, the Circuit Court of Appeals ordered the State of Texas to either change the sentence to life or embark on a new sentencing trial.

The case is under review by the US District Court. In the meantime, Wardrip is still on death row.

CARL "CORAL" WATTS

Date of birth: November 7, 1953

Aliases/Nicknames: Coral, The Sunday Morning Slasher

Characteristics: Stalking, torture

Number of victims: 22 - 100

Date of murders: 1974 - 1982

Date of arrest: May 23, 1982

Murder method: Strangulation, stabbing, drowning, slashing, bludgeoning

Known Victims: Jeanne Clyne, 35; Linda Tilley, 22; Elizabeth Montgomery, 25; Phyllis Tamm, 27; Margaret Fossi, 25; Elena Semander, 20; Emily LaQua,14; Edith Leder, 34; Yolanda Gracia, 21; Carrie Jefferson, 32; Suzanne Searles, 25; Michelle Maday, 20; Helen Dutcher, 36; Gloria Steele, 19; others unidentified

Crime location: Michigan, Texas

Status: Sentenced to life imprisonment without parole. Died from prostate cancer, September 21, 2007.

Background

Watts' father was a private in the Army and his mother was an art teacher at a kindergarten when Watts was born in 1953. The family lived in Killeen Texas, and when he was two, his parents separated and Watts remained in the care of his mother. They then moved to Michigan. His mother remarried in 1962, and two daughters were born.

According to Watts, he first started to fantasize about murder and torture when he was just twelve years old. As a teenager, he enjoyed stalking girls and young women in his neighborhood. It was later suspected that his first murder was committed when he was only fifteen years old.

Watts contracted meningitis when he was thirteen, and had to be kept back in the eighth grade at school. He found it hard to keep up with his fellow students, and he failed most of his grades. By the time he was sixteen, he could only read at a third-grade level, and he suffered from severe bullying by his peers.

The first time he came into contact with law enforcement was in June of 1969, when he was arrested for sexual assault on Joan Gave, twenty-six. Instead of going to prison, he was sentenced to the mental hospital in Detroit, the Lafayette Clinic. He was found to have a very low IQ of just 75, which is classified as mild mental retardation. The psychiatrists also found he had a delusional thought process.

One of the arresting police officers, however, thought he had an excellent memory and seemed very intelligent.

Watts was released from the clinic in November of 1969, and went back to high school. He managed to graduate in 1973, despite his appalling grades, and was given a football scholarship to Lane College in Jackson, Tennessee. However, he only lasted three months before he was expelled for assaulting and stalking women. At the time, he was also implicated in the murder of a female student, but there wasn't enough evidence to charge him.

Watts moved to Houston, Texas, and had a daughter with his girlfriend Deloris. In 1979, he married another woman, Valeria Goodwill, but they divorced several months later in May of 1980. By then, he had already become a serial killer. But two more years would pass before he was caught.

Murders

When Watts was twenty years old, he began killing women. He would kidnap them from their homes, inflict torture on them, and then murder them. He targeted women between the ages of fourteen and forty-four, and he killed them in a variety of ways. The methods he used were strangling, bludgeoning, drowning, and stabbing.

Watts managed to stay undetected for a very long time for a number of reasons. He always killed in different places, such as different states and jurisdictions, so the murders were less likely to be linked together. He rarely engaged in sexual acts with his victims, so he wouldn't leave his DNA behind.

Not all of his attacks were fatal, however. A large number of women received vicious injuries, some so severe that they were almost lethal. Later, after his arrest, Watts claimed he had killed around forty women. When combined with the nonfatal attacks, the number was around eighty.

Identified victim's timeline:

1979 - Helen Dutcher

October 31, 1979 - Jeanne Clyne, thirty-five

September 5, 1981- Linda Tilley, twenty-two

September 12, 1981 - Elizabeth Montgomery, twenty-five

January 4, 1982 - Phyllis Tamm, twenty-seven

January 17, 1982 - Margaret Fossi, twenty-five

February 7, 1982 - Elena Semander, twenty

March 20, 1982 - Emily LaQua, fourteen

March 27, 1982 - Edith Ledet, thirty-four

April 15, 1982 - Yolanda Gracia, twenty-one

April 16, 1982 - Carrie Jefferson, thirty-two

April 21, 1982 - Suzanne Searles, twenty-five

May 23, 1982 - Michelle Maday, twenty

Arrest and Trial

Watts' last attempt to commit murder occurred on May 22, 1982, when he broke into the home of two women. This time, he was caught and arrested and taken back to the police station to be interviewed.

As he was questioned, a number of things urged police to look at other murders. Eventually, they were able to link them back to Watts. In the early months of 1981, he had lived in Michigan, and the investigators believed he was the man behind at least ten murders of women there. He had been questioned about the murders in 1975, but there hadn't been enough evidence back then to charge him.

The prosecutors didn't think they could convict Watts with the evidence they had, so the only alternative was to offer him a plea bargain. In 1982, they told Watts that if he confessed to all of his murders and gave the full details of each crime, he wouldn't be charged with murder. Instead, he would be charged with burglary with the intent to murder, which was a sixty-year sentence.

Watts agreed to the deal and confessed to committing twelve murders in the state of Texas. The authorities in Michigan didn't want to go in on the deal, so those cases remained open. Watts received the sixty-year sentence as promised. But, because of a technicality, he was reclassified as nonviolent. This meant he could have been eligible for an early parole.

The Michigan Attorney General made a plea on national television in 2004, asking for information to help prosecute Watts for murder. A witness claimed he had seen Watts murder Helen Dutcher in 1979, and he subsequently positively identified him. Even though he had immunity in Texas for the murders he had confessed to, no such immunity existed for Watts in Michigan.

Watts was charged with the murder of Helen Dutcher, and he went on trial later that year. On November 17, 2004, he was convicted of the murder. On December 7, he received a life sentence. Two days after his sentencing, Watts was charged with the murder of Gloria Steele, who had been killed in 1974.

The trial for this murder started on July 25, 2007. Two days later, he was found guilty and sentenced to life imprisonment without parole.

Outcome

On September 21, 2007, Watts died as a result of prostate cancer.

Watts was suspected of being responsible for ninety murders in total.

FRED WEST AND ROSEMARY WEST

Date of birth: September 29, 1941; November 29, 1953

Aliases/Nicknames: The Gloucester House of Horrors

Characteristics: Incest, torture, rape, dismemberment, mutilation

Number of victims: 11 - 13 +

Date of murders: 1971 - 1987

Date of arrest: February 25, 1994

Murder method: Asphyxiation, strangulation

Known Victims: Charmaine West, 8; Catherine Bernadette "Rena" West, 27; Lynda Carole Gough, 19; Carol Ann Cooper, 15; Lucy Katherine Partington, 21; Theresa Siegenthaler, 21; Shirley Hubbard, 15; Juanita Marion Mott, 18; Shirley Anne Robinson, 18; Alison Jane Chambers, 16; Heather Ann West, 16

Crime location: Gloucestershire, England

Status: Fred committed suicide by hanging while on remand. Rose was sentenced to life imprisonment.

Background

Fred West

The deeply disturbing environment West was raised in most likely played a large part in what he would become infamous for later on in his life. He was born into a poor family, his parents Walter and Daisy both being farm workers in Much Marcle, Herefordshire. There were six children in the family, and West later claimed that his father had incestuous relationships with all of his daughters. It seems that incest was acceptable to the family, and West's father was also the person who introduced West to bestiality. He would say to his son that he could do what he wanted, as long as he didn't get caught. West also claimed to have been sexually abused by his mother from the age of twelve years.

West did not do well in academic subjects at school, but he was very good at art and woodwork. He left school in December of 1956, at the age of 15. In 1958, he was involved in a motorcycle accident and received fractures in his skull, arm, and leg. He remained in a coma for just over a week. After the accident, he tended to suffer from sudden fits of anger and rage. He suffered another head injury two years later, after falling from a fire escape, and he remained unconscious for twenty-four hours.

When West was twenty, he was arrested and charged with the molestation of a thirteen-year-old girl. Despite being convicted, he managed to escape being sent to prison. From then onwards, his family more or less disowned him. After all, his father had told him repeatedly not to get caught.

Rosemary West

Rosemary was born to William and Daisy Letts following a very difficult pregnancy. Her mother had suffered from bouts of depression throughout the pregnancy and even received electroconvulsive therapy at one point. It was later suspected that perhaps this treatment had damaged West's brain while she was in the womb. She grew up to be particularly moody as a teenager and didn't do well at school.

Her parents divorced when she was a teenager and she lived with her mother for a time before moving into her father's home when she was sixteen. This was surprising, as her father repeatedly sexually abused her and was a violent man. She met Fred West around this time and they started dating. Her father was not happy about this at all. He threatened Fred and also threatened to call social services.

Eventually, Rosemary moved in with Fred at the Lake House Hotel Caravan Park. She started taking care of Fred's daughter Anne-Marie (a child from his previous marriage to Rena Costello) and his stepdaughter, Charmaine, who was the daughter of Rena and another man. In 1970, Rosemary discovered she was pregnant, and the family moved to a house on Midland Road, Gloucester.

In January of 1973, a young woman named Caroline Roberts escaped the home of Rosemary and Fred and reported the couple to the police for sexual assault. They were convicted of indecent assault and received only a fine.

Rosemary often worked as a prostitute, and when she brought men home, Fred would watch. Disturbingly, one of the most regular visitors was Rosemary's own father, and he continued to indulge in sex with her even after the birth of her fourth child. He also raped Anne-Marie, Fred's daughter. Rosemary went on to give birth to eight children, only five of whom were fathered by Fred.

Fred made films of himself raping his daughter, and she told some of her school friends about it. This led to a parent informing the police. Fred was charged on August 6, 1992, and Rosemary was also charged with being an accomplice. Rosemary received other charges including child cruelty, and the children were taken away and put into foster care. The whole case collapsed, however, when two witnesses refused to testify and they walked free.

By now rumors were starting to circulate about the disappearance of their daughter Heather. It was during this investigation that Fred and Rosemary's Gloucester House of Horrors was finally discovered.

Murders

Fred and Rosemary killed at least eight women over a six-year period. Some came to the house at 25 Cromwell Street as lodgers, and some worked for the family as child minders or housekeepers. Lynda Gough was killed in April of 1973; she was known to Fred and Rosemary as she worked as a seamstress.

In November of 1973, Carol Ann Cooper went missing while walking home from the cinema; she was later confirmed to be a victim of the Wests. Lucy Katherine Partington was on her way home in December of that year and was waiting at a bus stop when she was abducted by the Wests. For over a week they kept her captive, raping her and inflicting terrible torture on her body before they killed her.

Over the next five years, another five more women were killed by the couple. They most likely continued to kill after 1979, as people like the Wests don't just stop. But no other bodies were found on the property at Cromwell Street. Except for their daughter Heather. Fred started abusing Heather, and when she refused, she was forced to comply. In June of 1987, things went too far, and she was strangled to death. Afterwards, they cut up her body and buried it in the garden.

Timeline of murders:

Summer of 1967 - Anne McFall

June of 1971 - Charmaine West, eight

August of 1971 - Catherine Bernadette "Rena" West, twenty-seven

April of 1973 - Lynda Carole Gough, nineteen

November of 1973 - Carol Ann Cooper, fifteen

December of 1973 - Lucy Katherine Partington, twenty-one

April of 1974 - Theresa Siegenthaler, twenty-one

November of 1974 - Shirley Hubbard, fifteen

April of 1975 - Juanita Marion Mott, eighteen

May of 1978 - Shirley Anne Robinson, eighteen

August of 1979 - Alison Jane Chambers, sixteen

June of 1987 - Heather Ann West, sixteen

Arrest and Trial

In May of 1992, Fred filmed himself raping his own daughter on three occasions, and his daughter told her school friends what had happened. One of the friends told her mother, who went straight to the police on August 4 and reported it. Two days later, the police investigated, and both Fred and Rosemary were arrested for committing rape.

In addition to being charged as an accomplice, Rosemary was also charged with child cruelty. The children were all put into foster care for their protection. The rape trial for Fred and Rosemary was meant to go ahead on June 7, 1993, but two of the witnesses refused to testify and the case collapsed.

Meanwhile, police were still trying to find out what had happened to Heather. On speaking to the social workers, they were told that the children had said Fred used to say that if they didn't behave, they would "end up under the patio like Heather." This was enough to get a search warrant, which was granted in February of 1994, and they began excavating the property on February 24.

Fred was arrested on February 25, and human bones were found. Fred subsequently confessed to killing Heather. He then retracted his confession and confessed again, saying that Rosemary hadn't been involved. As the excavation continued, more bodies were found buried on the property. On March 4, Fred finally confessed that—in addition to Heather—he had committed another nine murders.

Both Fred and Rosemary were brought before the court on June 30, 1994. Fred was charged with committing eleven murders and Rosemary was charged with ten. Fred was arrested again immediately afterwards for the murder of Ann McFall; he was charged on July 3.

Rosemary wouldn't confess to committing any murders, and the evidence the prosecutors had was circumstantial at best. However, at her trial in October of 1995, she was found guilty of all ten murders and received a life sentence. It was recommended she never be released.

Outcome

While Fred West was on remand, he hanged himself in his cell on January 1, 1995. A funeral was held, with only three people in attendance, and his body was cremated. In October of 1996, the house in Gloucester where the atrocities had taken place was demolished, and a pathway was created instead. The rubble from the house was completely destroyed to ensure souvenir hunters stayed away.

NATHANIEL WHITE

Date of birth: July 28, 1960

Aliases/Nicknames: Nil

Characteristics: Rape

Number of victims: 6

Date of murders: 1991 - 1992

Date of arrest: August 2, 1992

Murder method: Stabbing, beating

Known Victims: Juliana R. Frank, 28; Christine M. Klebbe, 14; Laurette Huggins Reviere, 34; Angelina Hopkins, 23; Brenda L. Whiteside, 20; Adriane M. Hunter, 27

Crime location: Orange County, New York

Status: Sentenced to 150 years to life.

Background

White was born in 1960, and that's about all the information that is available regarding his childhood. As an adult in the 1990s, he murdered several people in the Hudson Valley area of New York. He had served a one-year prison sentence for the abduction of a sixteen-year-old girl, and he started killing just a few months after he was released. After he was apprehended for murder, a lot of controversy sprang up surrounding his previous short sentence and early parole. White had agreed to plead guilty to a misdemeanor as part of a plea bargain, instead of a felony charge, which is why he received such a light sentence.

He later claimed to hear voices, but he was never diagnosed with any form of mental illness. He also claimed that one of his murders mimicked a scene he had seen in the movie *Robocop*.

Murders

The first murder committed by White was that of a pregnant woman, Juliana Frank, on March 25, 1991. After he killed her, White left her naked body near railroad tracks in Middleton. His next victim was Christine Klebbe, who was only fourteen years old. She disappeared on June 29, 1991, and her body was discovered on August 4.

On July 10, 1992, White murdered Laurette Huggins Reviere in her own home in Middleton. Ten days later, White met Angela Hopkins and Brenda Whiteside at a tavern; both women were last seen getting into his pickup truck. Their bodies were found at the same time as Klebbe's, on August 4. The cause of death for Hopkins and Whiteside was blunt trauma to the head.

In the early hours of July 30, 1992, Adriane Hunter was brutally stabbed to death. Her body was found the same day, in Goshen.

Angela Hopkins sister Cecilia had seen Hopkins and Whiteside leave the bar with four men the night she disappeared. On August 2, Cecilia saw White back at the same bar, and she notified the police.

Timeline of murders:

March 25, 1991 - Juliana Frank, twenty-nine

June 29, 1991 - Christine Klebbe, fourteen

July 10, 1992 - Laurette Huggins Reviere

July 20, 1992 - Angela Hopkins

July 20, 1992 - Brenda L. Whiteside

July 30, 1992 - Adriane Hunter, twenty-seven

Arrest and Trial

White was arrested on August 2, 1992. During his interview, he confessed to the murders and showed the police his dumping ground in Goshen. His arraignment for the murder of Klebbe took place on August 7. On September 9, five more murders were added to the indictment, meaning White was charged with a total of six murders.

Outcome

Although White did plead not guilty by reason of insanity, he was declared sane at the time of the murders. He was sentenced to one hundred fifty years to life in prison, and he started his incarceration on May 27, 1993 at the Great Meadow Correctional Facility.

The New York governor George Pataki cited White's crimes as a push to get the death penalty reinstated.

WAYNE WILLIAMS

Date of birth: May 27, 1958

Aliases/Nicknames: The Atlanta Child Killer

Characteristics: Child murderer

Number of victims: 2 - 31

Date of murders: 1979 - 1981

Date of arrest: June 21, 1981

Murder method: Asphyxiation, strangulation

Known Victims: Nathaniel Cater, 28; Jimmy Ray Payne, 21; Alfred Evans, 13; Yusef Bell, 9; Eric Middlebrooks, 14; Christopher Richardson, 12; Aaron Wyche, 10; Anthony Carter, 9; Earl Terrell, 11; Clifford Jones, 13; Charles Stephens, 12; Aaron Jackson, 9; Patrick Rogers, 16; Lubie Geter, 14; Terry Pue, 15; Patrick Baltazar, 11; Curtis Walker, 13; Jo Jo Bell, 15; Timothy Hill, 13; Eddie Duncan, 21; Larry Rogers, 20; Michael McIntosh, 23; John Porter, 28; William Barrett, 17

Crime location: Atlanta, Georgia

Status: Sentenced to life imprisonment.

Background

Born and raised in Dixie Hills, Atlanta, Williams was considered a bit of a dreamer and a liar who would come up with incredible stories about himself that were too ridiculous to be true. He wanted to be a DJ and actually ran an amateur radio station from his parents' home. Williams was known in the area for being a musician scout, and he was particularly fond of scouting teenage musicians.

Though rumors circulated around the neighborhood that Williams was gay, this was never proven. In 1976, he had impersonated a police officer and was arrested but not charged. This was the only time he came into contact with the police before he was arrested on suspicion of murdering children.

Murders

Between 1979 and 1981, a multitude of young African-American boys were turning up dead in Atlanta. By May of 1981, twenty-nine had been killed, and most had died in the same manner - by strangulation or asphyxiation. Included in the victims were two older men - Jimmy Ray Payne and Nathaniel Cater.

The FBI entered the investigation in 1980. In May of 1981, Williams' car was seen on a bridge when a loud splash occurred in the river below. In an effort to catch the killer, the bridge and the river were being staked out at the time. Advice had been given that the killer was most likely going to dispose of his next victim in water because the bodies were being found too quickly.

The police stopped Williams who claimed he was on his way out of town for a young singer's audition. When police looked into his alibi, however, much of the information he had given—such as the address and phone number—was wrong.

The naked body of Nathaniel Cater was found in the river three days later. The postmortem indicated he had most likely died due to asphyxia. Because Williams had been seen on the bridge a few days earlier, police became suspicious. They brought him in for further questioning and made him take a polygraph test, which he failed.

When police searched his home and car, they found a number of fibers and hairs that were similar to those found on the bodies of some of the victims. Witnesses came forward saying they had seen Williams with scratches on his arms and face when some of the murders had occurred. Trying to plead his innocence, Williams conducted a press conference outside the home of his parents. But his words fell on deaf ears.

Timeline of murders:

July 28, 1979 - Edward Hope Smith, fourteen

July 28, 1979 - Alfred Evans, fourteen

September 4, 1979 - Milton Harvey, fourteen

October 21, 1979 - Yusuf Bell, nine

March 4, 1980 - Angel Lenair, twelve

March 11, 1980 - Jeffrey Mathis, eleven

May 18, 1980 - Eric Middlebrooks, fourteen

June 9, 1980 - Christopher Richardson, twelve

June 22, 1980 - Latonya Wilson, seven

June 23, 1980 - Aaron Wyche, ten

July of 1980 - Anthony Carter, nine

July of 1980 - Earl Terrell, eleven

August - November 1980 - Clifford Jones, thirteen

August - November 1980 - Charles Stephens, twelve

August - November 1980 - Aaron Jackson, nine

August - November 1980 - Patrick Rogers, sixteen

January 3, 1981 - Lubie Geter, fourteen

January of 1981 - Terry Pue, fifteen

February of 1981 - Patrick Baltazar, eleven

February of 1981 - Curtis Walker, thirteen

March of 1981 - Jo Jo Bell, fifteen

March of 1981 - Timothy Hill, thirteen

March of 1981 - Eddie Duncan, twenty-one

March of 1981 - Michael McIntosh, twenty-three

April of 1981 - Larry Rogers, twenty

April of 1981 - John Porter, twenty-eight

April of 1981 - Jimmy Ray Payne, twenty-one

May of 1981 - William Barrett, seventeen

May of 1981 - Nathaniel Cater, twenty-seven

Arrest and Trial

On June 21, 1981, Williams was arrested and charged with the murders of Cater and Payne, but he wasn't charged with the murders of the boys. His trial began on January 6, 1982, and the prosecution relied on circumstantial evidence, which isn't great, but they did have a lot of it.

The trial lasted two months, with many pieces of forensic evidence being produced in court. In addition to the fibers and hairs from his dog, they also found blood in his car that matched some of the victims. Some witnesses testified that Williams was a pedophile who liked black boys.

On February 27, the jury spent ten hours deliberating before finding him guilty of the murders of Payne and Cater. He was sentenced to two terms of life to be served consecutively.

Outcome

There has been a lot of controversy surrounding Williams' conviction. Many people, particularly those from his community, do not believe he committed the murders. Four of the murder cases were reopened in DeKalb County in May of 2005, but authorities in nearby Fulton County have not reopened any of their cases. The authorities in DeKalb later closed the cases again due to lack of new evidence.

John E. Douglas, former FBI profiler and author of the book *Mindhunter*, stated that while he believes Williams committed some of the murders, he doesn't believe he was responsible for all of them. In his book, he says he believes the authorities have an idea who the other killers are. In his words, "it isn't a single offender and the truth isn't pleasant."

Trivia

– During the investigation, Charles Sanders, a member of the Ku Klux Klan, was suspected of being involved in the murders of at least some of the boys. But, he later passed lie detector tests and was eliminated from the enquiry.

RANDALL WOODFIELD

Date of birth: December 26, 1950

Aliases/Nicknames: The I-5 Bandit, The I-5 Killer

Characteristics: Rape, robbery

Number of victims: 3 - 18 +

Date of murders: October of 1979 - February of 1981

Date of arrest: March 7, 1981

Murder method: Shooting

Known Victims: Darci Fix; Doug Altic; Shari Hull; Julie Reitz; others unnamed or not confirmed

Crime location: Washington, California, Oregon

Status: Sentenced to life imprisonment plus ninety years.

Background

Born in Salem, Oregon, Woodfield's early childhood seemed to be normal; he grew up in a regular middle-class family with no history or signs of any form of dysfunction. He was popular at school and with his friends, and while he attended Newport High school, he was a football star. He went on to attend Portland State University, where he continued to play football.

During his teen years though, Woodfield started to exhibit some sexual behaviors that were considered to be antisocial. He had a habit of exposing himself, and his first arrest for this occurred while he was still in high school. Being a much-needed football player though, his coaches kept these transgressions quiet so he could remain on the team.

In the early 1970s, Woodfield was arrested three times for public indecency and vandalism, but he still managed to get drafted by the Green Bay Packers. By 1974, he had been arrested over a dozen times for indecent exposure and he was dismissed from the team. The next year, he went on a spree of sexual assault and robbery, using a knife to threaten his victims. He was caught and convicted, but only for second degree robbery. Sentenced to ten years, he served only four.

Woodfield continued his crimes after his release from prison. Beginning in 1979, he spent the next two years robbing gas stations, homes, and ice cream parlors. If his victims were female, he would sexually assault them and sometimes murder them. Woodfield came under investigation for murder in 1981, following the shooting death of a woman in Beaverton, Oregon, who just happened to be an acquaintance of Woodfield.

Murders

In November of 1980, Darci Fix and Doug Altic were both shot to death in Fix's home in North Portland. It appeared they had been killed execution style, with gunshots to the head, and a revolver belonging to Fix was missing. Although Fix was acquainted with Woodfield through a friend, the police didn't consider the possibility of Woodfield being involved in the murders.

On January 18, 1981, Shari Hull and Beth Wilmot were sexually abused by a man who entered their office building while they were working. He killed Hull and believed he had also killed Wilmot, but she survived. The next victim was Julie Reitz who was shot and killed in Oregon on February 15, 1981. Sylvia Durante was strangled to death in Seattle in December of 1979.

The bodies of Marsha Weatter and her friend Kathy Allen were found together in May of 1980.

Bodies belonging to Donna Eckard and her daughter were found on February 3, 1981. They were in a bed together and both had received multiple gunshots to the head. Postmortem examinations revealed the young girl had been sodomized before she was killed.

Timeline of murders:

November of 1980 - Darci Fix

November of 1980 - Doug Altic

January 18, 1981 - Shari Hull

February 15, 1981 - Julie Reitz

Suspected:

December of 1979 - Sylvia Durante, twenty-one

May of 1980 - Marsha Weatter, nineteen

May of 1980 - Kathy Allen, eighteen

February 3, 1981 - Donna Eckard, thirty-seven

February 3, 1981 - daughter of Donna Eckard, fourteen

Arrest and Trial

During the investigation into the shooting death in Beaverton, police came across Woodfield, who was an acquaintance of the murder victim. Police had enough grounds to search his property. There, they located evidence of his involvement in this murder and the attempted murders of two women.

On March 7, 1981, Woodfield was arrested and charged with three murders - the murder in Beaverton and the murders of the mother and daughter in California.

His trial took place in October of 1981, and he was also charged with the murder of Shari Hull. He was convicted and sentenced to life imprisonment plus ninety years.

Outcome

While incarcerated, Woodfield got married three times and divorced twice. By 1990, he was suspected in forty-four murders. DNA testing later linked him to two murders from the early 1980s in Oregon.

Trivia

Written by Woodfield on his MySpace account:

- "I'm Randy, I'm 55. I spend the remainder of my days in prison because I have committed a murder along with many other crimes. I once tried out for the Green Bay Packers. The only reason I didn't make it is because the skills I had to offer they didn't need at the time."

STEVEN WRIGHT

Date of birth: April 24, 1958

Aliases/Nicknames: Suffolk Strangler, Ipswich Ripper

Characteristics: Killed prostitutes

Number of victims: 5

Date of murders: October - December 2006

Date of arrest: December 19, 2006

Murder method: Strangulation, asphyxiation

Known Victims: Tania Nicol, 19; Gemma Adams, 25; Anneli Alderton, 24; Annette Nicholls, 29; Paula Clennell, 24

Crime location: Ipswich, Suffolk, England

Status: Sentenced to life imprisonment with the recommendation he never be released.

Background

The son of a military policeman, Wright was born in Erpingham, Norfolk. During his father's service, the family had also lived in Singapore and Malta. When Wright was eight years old, his mother left the family, and they divorced in 1977. The children stayed with their father, who later remarried and had two more children.

After he finished school in 1974, Wright joined the Merchant Navy and became a chef working on the ferries. He married Angela O'Donovan in 1978, and they had a child, Michael. In 1987, they separated and eventually divorced. Wright worked as a steward on the liner QE2 for a while, before taking on a variety of jobs such as bartending and driving trucks and forklifts.

He married Diane Cassell in 1987, but they separated in July of 1988. At that time, Wright was a landlord at a pub. A year later he became involved with Sarah Whiteley, and they had a daughter in 1992. Due to heavy drinking and gambling, Wright was eventually fired from his position as pub landlord. In 2001, he was convicted of stealing eighty pounds. He continued to rack up huge gambling debts and at one point was declared bankrupt.

Twice, Wright had tried to kill himself. The first attempt took place in the mid-1990s. He had tried to gas himself by carbon monoxide poisoning but failed. Then, in 2000, he took an overdose of pills.

Once again, he survived. In 2001, he met Pamela Wright (coincidental surname) and they moved in together in 2004. When she started working night shifts, however, their intimate relationship began to fail. As he had during his time in the Navy, Wright again turned to the services of prostitutes. It wasn't until the later months of 2006 that some of these prostitutes started to turn up dead and Wright came under suspicion.

Murders

Wright targeted women working as prostitutes in Ipswich, Suffolk. His first victim, Tania Nicol, was killed on October 30, 2006. Her body was discovered on December 8 in a river near Copdock Mill. The autopsy could not determine the exact cause of death, and there were no indications of sexual assault.

On November 15, 2006, Gemma Rose Adams disappeared from West End Road in Ipswich. On December 2, her naked body was found in a river at Hintlesham. The autopsy, however, showed no evidence that she had been sexually assaulted. Adams had been working as a prostitute to fund her drug habit.

The third victim, a pregnant woman named Anneli Alderton, went missing on December 3 after taking a train to Ipswich. Her body was found seven days later in the woods in front of Amberfield School in Nacton. This time, the cause of death was identified as asphyxiation. Alderton was left naked, like the other victims, but she had been posed, with her body in the position of a crucifix.

Annette Nicholls went missing on December 8 from the town center in Ipswich. She was also working as a prostitute so she could pay for her drug habit. Her naked body was discovered on December 12, near Levington, and she had been posed in the crucifix position. According to her postmortem, she hadn't been sexually assaulted. Although the cause of death wasn't clear, she had suffered from some kind of disruption to her breathing.

Wright's last known victim was Paula Clennell who went missing on December 10; her unclothed body was found near Levington two days later, the same day Nicholls' body was found. Clennell's her autopsy revealed that her throat had been compressed, causing her death. Like the other women, she hadn't been sexually assaulted.

Timeline of murders:

October 30, 2006 - Tania Nicol, nineteen

November 15, 2006 - Gemma Rose Adams, twenty-five

December 3, 2006 - Anneli Alderton, twenty-four

December 8, 2006 - Annette Nicholls, twenty-nine

December 10, 2006 - Paula Clennell, twenty-four

Arrest and Trial

As police investigated the murders—which they believed were all linked—they decided to look at CCTV footage from the date and place of the victims' disappearances. This involved painstakingly sorting through hours and hours of footage. But, they eventually noticed that one particular vehicle was on camera at each occasion. They traced the license plate back to Wright.

Forensic testing revealed the presence of Wright's DNA on three of the victims; this was enough to enable them to get an arrest warrant. Wright was arrested on December 19, 2006. While he was being interviewed, he refused to answer any questions other than to say "no comment."

Wright was formally charged with the five murders. At the end of his trial, on February 21, 2008, he was found guilty of all charges. He was sentenced to life imprisonment, and the judge recommended he remain in prison for the rest of his life, without parole.

Outcome

Despite lodging numerous appeals against his convictions and sentence, Wright decided to halt all appeals on his behalf on February 2, 2009. Because the judge recommended he never be released, Wright is most likely going to spend the rest of his living days behind bars.

Trivia

- Quote by his father on learning of his son's arrest for the murders: "He's just not the type. Steve is soft! He's daft. He wouldn't even know how to kill five people, take them and distribute their bodies all over Suffolk."

AILEEN CAROL WUORNOS

Date of birth: February 29, 1956

Aliases/Nicknames: Sandra Kretsch, Susan Lynn Blahovec, Lee Blahovec, Cammie Marsh Greene, Lori Kristine Grody

Characteristics: Prostitution, robbery

Number of victims: 7

Date of murders: 1989 - 1990

Date of arrest: January 1, 1991

Murder method: Shooting

Known Victims: Richard Mallory, 51; Dick Humphreys, 56; Troy Burress, 50; David Spears, 43; Walter Gino Antonio, 62; Peter Siems, 65; Charles Carskaddon, 40

Crime location: Florida

Status: Executed by lethal injection, October 9, 2002.

Background

Wuornos' fifteen-year-old mother had already filed for divorce from her husband Leo Pittman just a couple of months before Wuornos' birth. Leo had been arrested and convicted of the rape and attempted murder of a seven-year-old girl when Wuornos was born, and she never met him. A diagnosed schizophrenic, he was in and out of prison regularly for various sex crimes against children before he hanged himself while incarcerated in 1969.

When Wuornos was around four years old, her mother took off, leaving the children with their grandparents, who subsequently adopted Wuornos and her brother in March of 1960. By the time she was eleven years old, Wuornos had already learned how to trade sexual favors for food, drugs, and cigarettes—even at school. Her brother was no exception, and she claimed to have been involved in sexual activities with him as well.

She later stated that her grandfather was an alcoholic who had beaten and sexually assaulted her. Wuornos was raped by a friend of her grandfather when she was just fourteen years old, which resulted in a pregnancy. She was then placed in a home for unwed mothers and the baby was put up for adoption. Following the death of their grandmother a few months later, Wuornos and her brother were temporarily made wards of the court. Around this same time, she also dropped out of school. When her grandfather later kicked her out of the house, Wuornos started living in the woods nearby and worked as a prostitute to support herself.

In May of 1974, Wuornos was arrested for driving under the influence, firing a pistol from a moving vehicle, and disorderly conduct. She failed to appear at her court appearances. In 1976, she hitchhiked her way to Florida and met Lewis Gratz Fell, a sixty-nine-year-old yacht club president. The two married, but Wuornos wound up constantly getting involved in confrontations at a bar, and she was sent to prison for assault. She assaulted her husband with his own walking cane as well, and he filed a restraining order against her.

Wuornos went back to Michigan but soon got into trouble again. She was arrested for assault on July 14, 1976, after throwing a cue ball at the head of a bartender. Three days later, her brother Keith from cancer, and she received a payment of ten thousand dollars from his insurance. Her marriage to Fell was annulled the same month.

From then onwards, Wuornos was constantly in trouble with the law for a variety of crimes, including grand theft auto, obstruction of justice, resisting arrest, firearms possession, forgery, and robbery. In 1986, she met a hotel maid named Tyria Moore at a gay bar in Daytona, Florida. A relationship ensued and they moved in together. Trouble continued. Accusations of assault were made against Wuornos with Moore often acting as a witness in her defense. Ironically, years later, Moore would once again be a witness in a case against Wuornos. But this time it would be for the prosecution.

Murders

Richard Mallory, a convicted rapist, was shot and killed by Wuornos on November 30, 1989, in what she later claimed to be self-defense. His body was located on December 13 in the woods in Clearwater, Florida. He had been shot multiple times, with two bullets to his lung causing his death.

On June 1, 1990, the naked body of David Spears was found beside the highway in Citrus County, Florida. Wuornos had shot him six times. Her next victim was Charles Carskaddon, whom she shot nine times on May 31, 1990. His body was found in Pasco County, Florida, on June 6, 1990. Peter Siems went missing in June of 1990; his car was later found on July 4 in Orange Springs. Witnesses had seen Wuornos and Moore abandon the car, and a palm print belonging to Wuornos was found on the door handle. The body of Peter Siems has never been found.

Troy Burress was reported missing on July 31, 1990. His body was found in the woods beside State Road 19, Marion County, on August 4. On September 11, Charles "Dick" Humphreys was shot six times in the torso and head. His body was discovered the next day in Marion County, and his car was later located in Suwannee County.

The last known victim of Wuornos was Walter Jeno Antonia. He was shot and killed on November 1. His nearly nude body was found by a logging road in Dixie County. Police located his car five days later in Brevard County.

Timeline of murders:

November 30, 1989— Richard Mallory, fifty-one

June 1, 1990 - David Spears, forty-three

May 31, 1990 - Charles Carskaddon, forty

June 1990 - Peter Siems, sixty-five

July 31, 1990 - Troy Burress, fifty

September 11, 1990 - Charles "Dick" Humphreys, fifty-six

November 19, 1990 - Walter Jeno Antonia, sixty-two

Arrest and Trial

After Wuornos and Moore dumped Siems' car, the witnesses provided their descriptions and names to the police, who embarked on a media campaign to try to find the two women. Property belonging to the victims was discovered in pawn shops, and police were able to lift fingerprints off some of the items. Because Wuornos had been arrested before, her fingerprints were on file, and a match was made.

Police arrested Wuornos on on an outstanding warrant on January 9, 1991. Moore was found the following day, and she agreed to get a confession out of Wuornos in exchange for immunity. Accompanied by the police, she left Pennsylvation to return to Florida, where they placed her in a motel. She then made a number of phone calls to Wuornos asking her to help her clear her name. On January 16, Wuornos confessed to committing the murders, allegedly out of self-defense against them trying to rape her.

Wuornos went on trial for the murder of Mallory on January 14, 1992. Under Florida's Williams Rule, the prosecution was allowed to present evidence from Wuornos' previous crimes during the trial in order to show a pattern of illegal activity.

The trial ended on January 27, 1992, and Wuornos was found guilty of Mallory's murder. She was sentenced to death four days later.

Outcome

Wuornos petitioned the Supreme Court to allow her to fire her legal counsel and stop the appeal process. Her reasoning was as follows: "I killed those men, robbed them as cold as ice. And I'd do it again, too. There's no chance in keeping me alive or anything, because I'd kill again. I have hate crawling through my system...I am so sick of hearing this 'she's crazy' stuff. I've been evaluated so many times. I'm competent, sane, and I'm trying to tell the truth. I'm one who seriously hates human life and would kill again."

This resulted in the governor instructing three psychiatrists to evaluate Wuornos to ensure she was competent to make such a decision. They all concluded she was mentally fit and understood that she was going to die by execution.

While awaiting her execution date, Wuornos started to make wild accusations. A prison matron, she claimed, had been abusing her. She also claimed her food was tainted with spit, dirt, and urine. She also said she had overheard conversations where prison staff were planning to push her over the "brink" so she would commit suicide. She further declared that they were "wishing to rape me before execution." She started to complain about everything—the handcuffs (they were too tight and left bruises), the strip searches, the frequency of window checks, mildew, and low water pressure in the showers.

Wuornos was provided KFC for her last meal, and she was taken to the death chamber on October 9, 2002. Her last words were: "Yes, I would just like to say I'm sailing with the rock, and I'll be back, like Independence Day with Jesus. June 6, like the movie. Big mother ship and all, I'll be back, I'll be back." She was pronounced deceased at 9:47 a.m.

Wuornos was cremated and her ashes were given to her old friend Dawn Botkins, who spread them underneath a tree in Michigan. She had requested Natalie Merchant's song "Carnival" to be played at her funeral.

Trivia

- Tenth woman executed in America since 1976.
- Second woman ever executed in Florida.

YANG XINHAI

Date of birth: July 17, 1968

Aliases/Nicknames: The Monster Killer

Characteristics: Rape

Number of victims: 67

Date of murders: 2000 - 2003

Date of arrest: November 3, 2003

Murder method: Beating to death with a hammer

Known Victims: Unnamed children, women, men

Crime location: Henan, China

Status: Executed by gunshot to the head on February 14, 2004.

Background

Yang was born into an extremely poor family in Henan Province, China, in 1968. His family, in fact, was one of the most poverty-stricken in the village where they lived. Yang was described as intelligent but introverted, and he left school in 1985 when he was seventeen years old. He refused to go back to the family home and instead traveled around China to find work as a laborer.

Yang was convicted of theft in both 1988 and 1991, and he was sent to labor camps to serve his sentences. In 1996, he was arrested for attempted rape and was sent to prison for five years. He had only served 3 years however, when he was released in 1999. This was the same year his gruesome killing spree began—with each crime more brutal than the one before it. And he would continue to kill until at least sixty-seven people had died at his hands.

Murders

Yang went on a murder spree between 1999 and 2003, in the Hebei, Shandong, Anhui, and Henan provinces. He would enter homes at night and kill everyone who occupied the property. Most of the victims were farmers, and if a whole family was present, he would kill them all.

His preferred method was to hack and bash them to death with hammers, axes, and shovels. He always wore large shoes, so if forensic prints were taken, they wouldn't match his actual shoe size. He also wore new clothes at each murder to reduce the amount of forensic transfer as he went from crime scene to crime scene.

One of his most brutal murders occurred in October of 2002. He broke into a home and killed the father, raped the mother, who was pregnant, and killed their six year old child. Incredibly, the woman survived the attack with serious head injuries.

Timeline of known murders:

September 19, 2000 - Guozhuang Village, two Murders

October 1, 2000 - Chunshuzhuang, Xiaoying Village, three murders, one rape

August 15, 2001 - Fangcheliu Village, three murders, one rape

Autumn of 2001 - Kanglou Township, two Murders

Winter of 2001 - Henan Province, two Murders

January 27, 2002 - Tongxu County, three murders, one rape

June 30, 2002 - Chaigang Township, four murders, one rape

July 28, 2002 - Dengzhou City, four murders, two rapes

October 22, 2002 - Zhaihu Village, two murders, one rape, one seriously injured

November 8, 2002 - Gaoli Village, four murders, two rapes, one seriously injured

November 16, 2002 - Liuzhuang Village, two murders, one rape

November 19, 2002 - Shiguai Village, two Murders

December 1, 200 2 - Yanwan Village, two murders, one rape, one seriously injured

December 6, 2002 - Liuzhuang Village, five murders, one rape

December 13, 2002 - Sijia Village, two Murders

December 15, 2002 - Xiaolizhuang, Miaocha Town, three murders, one rape

February 5, 2003 - Kuzhuang Township, three murders, one rape, one seriously injured

February 18, 2003 - Chiying Township, four murders, two rapes

March 23, 2003 - Chengguan Town, four murders, one rape

April 2, 2003 - Sanlizhai Village, two Murders

August 5, 2003 - Lidao Village, three Murders

August 8, 2003 - Dongliangxiang Village, five Murders

Arrest and Trial

On November 3, 2003, Yang was seen acting suspiciously in Hebei, and he was detained by the police. During questioning, police discovered Yang was wanted for murder in four separate provinces. He subsequently confessed to committing sixty-five murders, twenty-three rapes, and five attacks that resulted in serious injury. His DNA was also matched to several of the crime scenes.

Yang went on trial, and on February 1, 2004, he was found guilty of all charges and sentenced to death.

Outcome

Yang's execution was carried out swiftly following sentencing. He was sentenced on February 1, and executed just thirteen days later, on February 14, 2004. The execution was carried out by a gunshot to the head.

Trivia

- "When I killed people I had a desire. This inspired me to kill more. I don't care whether they deserve to live or not. It is none of my concern...I have no desire to be part of society. Society is not my concern."

ROBERT LEE YATES

Date of birth: May 27, 1952

Aliases/Nicknames: Spokane Serial Killer

Characteristics: Rape

Number of victims: 16 - 18 +

Date of murders: 1975; 1988; 1996 - 1998

Date of arrest: April 20, 2000

Murder method: Shooting

Known Victims: Patrick Oliver, 21; Susan Savage, 22; Stacy Hawn, 23; Shannon Zielinski, 39; Patricia Barnes, 60; Heather Hernandez, 20; Jennifer Joseph, 16; Darla Scott, 28; Melinda Mercer, 24; Shawn Johnson, 36; Laurie Wason, 31; Sunny Oster, 41; Linda Maybin, 34; Melody Murfin, 43; Michelyn Derning, 47; Connie Ellis, 35; Shawn McClenahan, 39

Crime location: Washington

Status: Sentenced to death, awaiting execution.

Background

Yates was brought up in a religious middle-class family in Oak Harbor, Washington. He completed high school in 1970. And in 1975, he started working as a prison guard at the Washington State Penitentiary. Six months later, he enlisted in the Army and trained to fly civilian helicopters and transport planes. During his time in the Army he was stationed in a number of countries, including Germany and Somalia.

Yates was in the military for nineteen years, during which time he earned a number of medals and military awards. These included three Army commendation medals, three Army achievement medals, three meritorious service medals, and two Armed Forces expeditionary medals. Despite his distinguished military career, there was a very dark side to Yates. Unbeknownst to the Army, he had killed two people while on active duty. Even worse, he would go on to murder many more following his discharge from the Army.

Murders

Yates murdered numerous women over a two year period between 1996 and 1998 in Spokane. He would go to the "Skid Row" area where the prostitutes could be found and solicit them. Then, after having sex with them, he would kill them. The bodies were always dumped in rural areas where there were less people around.

Yates killed each victim by shooting them in the head. He disposed of all the bodies in much the same manner, except for Melody Murfin. After he killed her, he buried her outside his home's bedroom window.

Dates victims were discovered:

July 13, 1975 - Patrick Oliver, twenty-one

July 13, 1975 - Susan Savage, twenty-two

December 28, 1988 - Stacy E. Hawn twenty-three

June 14, 1996 - Shannon Zielinski, thirty-nine

August 25, 1996 - Patricia Barnes, sixty

August 26, 1997 - Heather Hernandez, twenty

August 26, 1997 - Jennifer Joseph, sixteen

November 5, 1997 - Darla Scott, twenty-eight

December 7, 1997 - Melinda Mercer, twenty-four

December 18, 1997 - Shawn Johnson, thirty-six

December 26, 1997 - Laurie Wason, thirty-one

December 26, 1997 - Shawn McClenaghan, thirty-nine

February 8, 1998 - Sunny Oster, forty-one

April 1, 1998 - Linda Daveys (Maybin), thirty-four

May 12, 1998 - Melody Murfin, forty-three

July 7, 1998 - Michelyn Derning, forty-seven

October 13, 1998 - Connie LaFontaine Ellis, thirty-five

Arrest and Trial

Witnesses had come forward saying they had seen a very specific looking car picking up the victims on the nights they were murdered. The car was a 1977 white Corvette, which wasn't a common vehicle. It was soon established that Yates had owned that particular model of car. Rather than arrest him right away, they surveilled him for a couple days so they could make sure they had the evidence they needed to charge him.

Yates was arrested on April 18, 1999. Initially, he was charged with the murder of Jennifer Joseph. A search warrant was issued to search the Corvette he had previously owned. Inside they found blood that matched to both Joseph and Yates. They then matched Yates' DNA to the other twelve victims.

In 2000, Yates was convicted of thirteen counts of first-degree murder and one count of attempted murder. To avoid the death penalty, he made a deal and confessed to the murders. He received a sentence of four hundred eight years.

A year later, Yates was charged with the murders of Melinda L. Mercer and Connie Ellis. In October of 2002, he was found guilty. This time he was given the death penalty.

Outcome

His first execution date was scheduled for September 19, 2008. On September 11, however, he was granted a stay of execution to allow his defense team the time they needed to file more appeals. Today he is still sitting on death row.

Trivia

- Robert Lee Yates worked as a prison guard in Walla Walla, Washington.
- Quote by Yates: "Every life has meaning."

YOO YOUNG-CHUL

Date of birth: April 18, 1970
Aliases/Nicknames: Raincoat Killer
Characteristics: Cannibalism, mutilation
Number of victims: 20
Date of murders: 2003 - 2004
Date of arrest: July 17, 2004
Murder method: Beating to death with a hammer
Known Victims: Unnamed wealthy men, prostitutes
Crime location: Seoul, South Korea
Status: Sentenced to death, awaiting execution.

Background

Yoo was a criminal from a young age, having been arrested and convicted of a number of crimes from the age of eighteen years. These were predominantly theft charges in the early years, and they didn't take on a more violent note until the year 2000. His early crimes were as follows:

1988   Theft

1991   Theft (ten months in prison)

1993   Theft (eight months in prison)

1995   Sale of illegal pornography

1998   Theft, identity theft, forgery (two years in prison)

2000   Rape and sexual abuse of a child (three years, six months in prison)

Yoo married his girlfriend in 1993, and their son was born in October of 1994. Following his arrest in 2000, she divorced him. He was released from prison on September 11, 2003. Less than two weeks later, he killed his first victim.

Murders

Yoo went on a horrendous murder spree between September of 2003 and July of 2004. He proclaimed to be a cannibal, and he targeted wealthy men and prostitutes. At least eleven of his victims were mutilated and burned, and he confessed to eating the livers from some of the victims.

Killing spree timeline:

September 24, 2003 - Two victims, aged sixty-seven and seventy-two. One victim was stabbed and struck by a 4 kg hammer; the other was killed with the hammer.

October 9, 2003 - Three victims, aged eighty-five, thirty-five, and sixty. All three were killed with the hammer.

October 16, 2003 - One victim, aged sixty. Killed with the hammer; they survived for a few hours before dying.

November 18, 2003 - Three victims: two were aged eighty-seven and fifty-three, and the third was a baby. The adults were killed with the hammer, and the house was set on fire to try to hide any evidence.

March 16, 2004 - One victim, a female escort, aged twenty-three. Strangled then mutilated; the remains were dumped on a trail near the local University.

April - May of 2004 - Unknown female escort. Struck with the hammer and then decapitated. The mutilated remains were dumped on a construction site near a temple.

May of 2004 - One victim, aged twenty-five. Killed in the same manner as the previous victim—strangled, and then mutilated and decapitated.

June 1, 2004 - One victim, aged thirty-five. By now he had a signature and was killing each victim in the same manner.

June of 2004 - Unknown female victim.

June 9, 2004 - One victim, aged twenty-six.

June 18, 2004 - One female victim, aged twenty-seven.

June 25, 2004 - One victim, aged twenty-eight.

July 2, 2004 - One victim, aged twenty-six.

July 9, 2004 - One female escort victim, aged twenty-four.

July 13, 2004 - Another female escort, aged twenty-seven.

Arrest and Trial

Yoo was arrested on July 17, 2004, two days after his last victim was killed. He confessed to killing twenty-one people. But when he went on trial, he was convicted of only twenty murders. One of the cases was dropped because of a technicality.

He was sentenced to death on June 19, 2005.

Outcome

Although capital punishment had not been carried out in South Korea since 1997, the extreme nature of Yoo's crimes resulted in him receiving the death penalty.

Yoo is currently awaiting his execution.

Trivia

Quote:

- "Women shouldn't be sluts, and the rich should know what they've done."

ZODIAC KILLER

Date of birth: Unknown

Aliases/Nicknames: Red Phantom

Characteristics: Called the police after the attacks

Number of victims: 5 - 37

Date of murders: 1960s - 1970s

Date of arrest: Never apprehended

Murder method: Shooting, stabbing

Known Victims: Confirmed: David Faraday, 17; Betty Lou Jensen, 16; Darlene Ferrin, 22; Cecelia Shepard, 22; Paul Stine, 29; Suspected: Robert Domingos, 18; Linda Edwards, 17; Cheri Jo Bates, 18; Donna Lass, 25

Crime location: California

Status: Unknown

Background

The "Zodiac Killer," who terrorized California for a number of years, has never been identified. Some clues surfaced as to his true identity, but there was never enough information gathered to point the finger at a specific person. There have been a great number of theories and speculations, but nothing concrete has been established.

The Zodiac Killer has intrigued millions of people for decades, largely due to the cryptic clues he sent to the local news media during his prolific killing period in the 1960s and 1970s. Experts tried tirelessly to solve all the puzzles, but to no avail. The story of the Zodiac Killer is still in the forethought of many today. This is partly thanks to books and movies that have been made about the case. But it is also partly due to fear stemming from the fact that he has never been apprehended.

Who was the Zodiac Killer? And the number one question that has been asked all along: Why did he stop killing? Or did he…?

Murders

The Zodiac's first known murders occurred on December 20, 1968, in California. Teenagers David Faraday and Betty Lou Jensen were both shot and killed with a .22-caliber pistol. No further known murders occurred until July 4, 1969. Michael Mageau and Darlene Ferrin were sitting in a parked car in the Blue Rock Springs Park parking lot in Vallejo when the Zodiac killer appeared and fired at them. Ferrin was killed; Mageau survived, albeit with severe injuries.

The next two victims were attacked by the Zodiac at Lake Berryessa on September 27. Bryan Hartnell and Cecelia Shepard were tied up before getting stabbed. Shepard was able to give a description of the attacker, before she died a few days later. Hartnell survived the attack.

The last murder definitively ascribed to the Zodiac killer occurred on October 11. The killer had taken a ride in a taxi driven by Paul Stine in Presidio Heights, San Francisco. For some reason, the Zodiac Killer shot and killed Stine, taking a small piece of his shirt with him to send in a letter.

Timeline of murders:

December 20, 1968 - David Arthur Faraday, seventeen

December 20, 1968 - Betty Lou Jensen, sixteen

July 4, 1969 - Darlene Elizabeth Ferrin, twenty-two

September 27, 1969 - Cecelia Ann Shepard, twenty-two

October 11, 1969 - Paul Lee Stine, twenty-nine

Suspected:

June 4, 1963 - Robert Domingos, eighteen

June 4, 1963 - Linda Edwards, seventeen

October 30, 1966 - Cheri Jo Bates, eighteen

September 6, 1970 - Donna Lass, twenty-five

Letters

Three letters allegedly prepared by the Zodiac Killer were sent to the *Vallejo Times Herald*, the *San Francisco Examiner*, and the *San Francisco Chronicle*, on August 1, 1969. In the letters, which were almost identical, the killer claimed responsibility for the murders at Blue Rock Springs and Herman Road. Each of the letters also contained one-third of a cryptogram, made up of four hundred eight symbols, that the killer claimed would reveal his identity when solved. The killer demanded the letters be printed on the front page of each paper or he would kill again.

Another letter arrived at the *San Francisco Examiner* on August 7, 1969. The letter contained details of the murders that had not been made public knowledge, as well as the writer's assertion that when the code was cracked, they would know who he was.

The cryptogram was solved by Donald and Bettye Harden on August 8, 1969. The misspelled message read as follows:

"I LIKE KILLING PEOPLE BECAUSE IT IS SO MUCH FUN IT IS MORE FUN THAN KILLING WILD GAME IN THE FORREST BECAUSE MAN IS THE MOST DANGEROUE ANAMAL OF ALL TO KILL SOMETHING GIVES ME THE MOST THRILLING EXPERENCE IT IS EVEN BETTER THAN GETTING YOUR ROCKS OFF WITH A GIRL THE BEST PART OF IT IS THAE WHEN I DIE I WILL BE REBORN IN PARADICE AND THEI HAVE KILLED WILL BECOME MY SLAVES I WILL NOT GIVE YOU MY NAME BECAUSE YOU WILL TRY TO SLOI DOWN OR ATOP MY COLLECTIOG OF SLAVES FOR MY AFTERLIFE EBEORIETEMETHHPITI"

The last part is indecipherable, but perhaps that is the real clue to the whole puzzle.

Suspects

Description:

Approximately five feet eight inches to five feet ten inches in height.

Curly brown or light reddish brown hair worn in a crew cut.

Wore horn-rimmed eyeglasses. Usually wore dark clothing—usually wool trousers and a dark navy blue or black windbreaker jacket with distinctive military chukka boots known as a "Wing walkers."

Medium or slightly stocky build.

Odd gait

Shoeprints were size ten and a half.

Glove size seven.

Slow, monotone voice.

Suspect - Louie Myers

1951 - 2002

- Confessed on his deathbed that he was the Zodiac Killer.
- Attended the same schools as the first victims.
- Worked at the same place as the second female victim.
- Able to access military boots through his father's work.
- Served in the Army.
- Long haul truck driver.
- Petty theft and disorderly conduct charges and convictions.
- Stationed in Germany at a military base during the period the Zodiac Killer wasn't killing.

Problem - did not fit the physical description.

Suspect - Richard "Rick" Marshall

1928 - 2008

- Had training in code.
- Navy sailor.
- Movie buff and projectionist at a theater.
- Ham radio enthusiast.
- Bad temper, especially with women.

Problem - not enough potential evidence.

Suspect - Jack Tarrance

1928 - 2006

- Former enlistee with the Air Force and Navy.
- Ham radio operator.
- Worked for a steel company.
- Foreman at General Electric.
- Attendant at a laundromat.

Tarrance's stepson reported him as a possible suspect after he found a number of pieces of "evidence" that he thought indicated his stepfather was the Zodiac Killer. Items he handed over to the authorities included the following:

- Handwriting samples.
- A hood similar to one reported by surviving victims.
- Knife with bloodstains.
- Undeveloped film with gruesome images.
- Taped phone conversation where Tarrance hints he may have been the Zodiac.

Problem - Hoping to either incriminate him or rule him out as a suspect, the FBI conducted DNA testing. Unfortunately, the results came back as inconclusive.

Suspect - Arthur Leigh Allen

1933 - 1992

- Considered to be the prime suspect.
- Was dishonorably discharged from the Navy.
- Worked as a teacher at an Elementary School.
- Sail maker.
- Lifeguard.
- Had bloodstained knives but claimed the blood was from a chicken.
- Jailed for child molestation during the period the Zodiac Killer ceased killing.
- Survivor Michael Mageau identified Allen as the Zodiac Killer during a photo lineup in 1991.

Problem - Fingerprints and handwriting samples were not a match. DNA testing was done using stamps from an envelope and this came back negative. It was known, however, that Allen did not like licking stamps because the taste of the glue made him feel sick.

For references and mugshots of the serial killer profiles you've read about, go to http://jackrosewood.com/mugshots

To complete this A to Z reference book of serial killers, we have included an additional chapter called The Making of a Serial Killer on the next page.

THE MAKING OF A SERIAL KILLER

"I was born with the devil in me," said H.H. Holmes who, in 1893, took advantage of the World's Fair – and the extra room he rented out in his Chicago mansion – to kill at least twenty-seven people without attracting much attention.

"I could not help the fact that I was a murderer, no more than the poet can help the inspiration to sing. I was born with the evil one standing as my sponsor beside the bed where I was ushered into the world, and he has been with me since," Holmes said.

The idea of "I can't help it" is one of the hallmarks of many serial killers, along with an unwillingness to accept responsibility for their actions and a refusal to acknowledge that they themselves chose to commit their dreadful deeds of their own free will.

"Yes, I did it, but I'm a sick man and can't be judged by the standards of other men," said Juan Corona, who killed twenty-five migrant workers in California in the late 1960s and early 1970s, burying them in the very fruit orchards where they'd hoped to build a better life for their families.

Dennis Rader, who called himself the BTK Killer (Bind, Torture, Kill), also blamed some unknown facet of his personality, something he called Factor X, for his casual ability to kill one family, and then go home to his own, where he was a devoted family man.

"When this monster entered my brain, I will never know, but it is here to stay. How does one cure himself? I can't stop it, the monster goes on, and hurts me as well as society. Maybe you can stop him. I can't," said Rader, who said he realized he was different than the other kids before he entered high school. "I actually think I may be possessed with demons."

But again, he blamed others for not stopping him from making his first murderous move.

"You know, at some point in time, someone should have picked something up from me and identified it," he later said.

Rader is not the only serial killer to place the blame far away from himself.

William Bonin actually took offense when a judge called him "sadistic and guilty of monstrous criminal conduct."

"I don't think he had any right to say that to me," Bonin later whined. "I couldn't help myself. It's not my fault I killed those boys."

This leaves us always asking, "Why?"

For those of us who are not serial killers, the questions of "why" and "how" almost always come to mind, so ill-equipped are we to understand the concept of murder on such a vast scale.

"Some nights I'd lie awake asking myself, 'Who the hell is this BTK?'" said FBI profiler John Douglas. He worked the Behavioral Science Unit at Quantico before writing several best-selling books, including *Mindhunter: Inside the FBI's Elite Serial Crime Unit,* and *Obsession: The FBI's Legendary Profiler Probes the Psyches of Killers, Rapists, and Stalkers and Their Victims and Tells How to Fight Back.*

These questions were never far from his mind - "What makes a guy like this do what he does? What makes him tick?" It's the kind of thing that keeps profilers and police up at night, worrying, wondering, and waiting for answers that are not always so easily forthcoming.

Another leader into the study of madmen, the late FBI profiler Robert Ressler - who coined the terms serial killer and criminal profiling – also spent sleepless nights trying to piece together a portrait of many a killer, something that psychiatrist James Brussel did almost unfailingly well in 1940, when a pipe bomb killer enraged at Con Edison was terrorizing New York City.

(Brussel told police what the killer would be wearing when they arrested him. Although he was caught at home late at night, wearing his pajamas, when police asked him to dress, he emerged from his room wearing a double-breasted suit, exactly as Brussel had predicted.)

"What is this force that takes a hold of a person and pushes them over the edge?" wondered Ressler, who interviewed scores of killers over the course of his illustrious career.

In an effort to infiltrate the minds of serial killers, Douglas and Ressler embarked on a mission to interview some of the most deranged serial killers in the country. They started their journey in California, which "has always had more than its share of weird and spectacular crimes," Douglas said.

In their search for a pattern, they determined that there are essentially two types of serial killers: organized and disorganized.

Organized killers

Organized killers are revealed through their crime scenes, which are neat, controlled, and meticulous, with effort taken both in the crime and with their victims. Organized killers also take care to leave behind few clues once they're done.

Dean Corll was an organized serial killer. He tortured his victims overnight, carefully collecting blood and bodily fluids on a sheet of plastic before rolling them up and burying them and their possessions, most beneath the floor of a boat shed he'd rented. He went there late at night under the cover of darkness.

Disorganized killers

On the flip side of the coin, disorganized killers grab their victims indiscriminately, or act on the spur of the moment, allowing victims to collect evidence beneath their fingernails when they fight back. Oftentimes they leave behind numerous clues including weapons.

"The disorganized killer has no idea of, or interest in, the personalities of his victims," Ressler wrote in his book *Whoever Fights Monsters*, one of several detailing his work as a criminal profiler. "He does not want to know who they are, and many times takes steps to obliterate their personalities by quickly knocking them unconscious or covering their faces or otherwise disfiguring them."

Cary Stayner – also known as the Yosemite Killer – became a disorganized killer during his last murder, which occurred on the fly when he was unable to resist a pretty park educator.

Luckily for other young women in the picturesque park, he left behind a wide range of clues, including four unmatched tire tracks from his aging 1979 International Scout.

"The crime scene is presumed to reflect the murderer's behavior and personality in much the same way as furnishings reveal the homeowner's character," Douglas and Ressler later wrote, expanding on their findings as they continued their interview sessions.

Serial killers think they're unique – but they're not

Dr. Helen Morrison – a long time fixture in the study of serial killers who keeps the brain of the Clown Killer, John Wayne Gacy, in her basement (after Gacy's execution she sent the brain away for an analysis that proved it to be completely normal) – said that at their core, most serial killers are essentially the same.

While psychologists still haven't determined the motives behind what drives serial killers to murder, there are certain characteristics they have in common, said Morrison, who has studied or interviewed scores of serial killers and wrote about her experiences in *My Life Among the Serial Killers*.

Most often men, serial killers tend to be talkative hypochondriacs who develop a remorseless addiction to the brutality of murder.

They are able to see their victims as inanimate objects, playthings, if you will, around simply for their amusement.

Empathy? Not on your life.

"They have no appreciation for the absolute agony and terror and fear that the victim is demonstrating," said Morrison. "They just see the object in front of them. A serial murderer has no feelings. Serial killers have no motives. They kill only to kill an object."

In doing so, they satisfy their urges and quiet the tumultuous turmoil inside of them.

"You say to yourself, 'How could anybody do this to another human being?'" Morrison said. "Then you realize they don't see them as humans. To them, it's like pulling the wings off a fly or the legs off a daddy longlegs.... You just want to see what happens. It's the most base experiment."

Nature vs. nurture?

For many serial killers, the desire to kill is as innate as their hair or eye color and out of control. But most experts say that childhood trauma is an experience shared by them all.

In 1990, Colin Wilson and Donald Seaman conducted a study of serial killers behind bars and found that childhood problems were the most influential factors that led serial killers down their particular path of death and destruction.

Former FBI profiler Robert Ressler – who coined the terms serial killer and criminal profiling – goes so far as to say that 100 percent of all serial killers experienced childhoods that were not filled with happy memories of camping trips or fishing on the lake.

According to Ressler, of all the serial killers he interviewed or studied, each had suffered some form of abuse as a child – whether it be sexual, physical, or emotional abuse, neglect or rejection by their parents, or humiliation, including instances that occurred at school.

For those who are already hovering psychologically on edge the due to unfortunate genetics, such events become focal points that drive a killer to act on seemingly insane instincts.

Because there is often no solid family unit – parents are missing or more focused on drugs and alcohol, sexual abuse goes unnoticed, physical abuse is commonplace – the child's development becomes stunted. They can either develop deep-seated rage or create for themselves a fantasy world where everything is perfect, and they are essentially the kings of their self-made castle.

That was the world of Jeffrey Dahmer, who recognized his need for control much later, after hours spent in analysis where he learned the impact of a sexual assault as a child as well as his parents' messy, rage-filled divorce.

"After I left the home, that's when I started wanting to create my own little world, where I was the one who had complete control," Dahmer said. "I just took it way too far."

Dahmer's experiences suggest that psychopathic behavior likely develops in childhood, when, due to neglect and abuse, children revert to a place of fantasy, a world where the victimization of the child shifts toward others.

"The child becomes sociopathic because the normal development of the concepts of right and wrong and empathy towards others is retarded because the child's emotional and social development occurs within his self-centered fantasies. A person can do no wrong in his own world and the pain of others is of no consequence when the purpose of the fantasy world is to satisfy the needs of one person," one expert said.

As the lines between fantasy and reality become blurred, fantasies that on their own are harmless become real, and monsters like Dean Corll find themselves strapping young boys down to a wooden board, raping them, torturing them, and listening to them scream, treating the act like little more than a dissociative art project that ends in murder.

Going inside the mind: Psychopathy and other mental illnesses

While not all serial killers are psychopaths – many compulsive killers do feel some sense of remorse, such as Green River Killer Gary Ridgeway did when he cried in court after one victim's father offered Ridgeway his forgiveness – those who are, Morrison said, are unable to feel a speck of empathy for their victims.

Their focus is entirely on themselves and the power they are able to assert over others, especially in the case of a psychopath.

Psychopaths are charming – think Ted Bundy, who had no trouble luring young women into his car by eliciting sympathy with a faked injury – and have the skills to easily manipulate their victims, or in some cases, their accomplices.

Dean Corll was called a Svengali – a name taken from a fictional character in George du Maurier's 1895 novel *Trilby* who seduces, dominates, and exploits the main character, a young girl – for being able to enlist the help of several neighborhood boys who procured his youthful male victims without remorse, even when the teens were their friends.

Some specific traits of serial killers, determined through years of profiling, include:

- **Smooth talking but insincere.** Ted Bundy was a charmer, the kind of guy that made it easy for people to be swept into his web. "I liked him immediately, but people like Ted can fool you completely," said Ann Rule, author of the best-selling book *Stranger Beside Me,* which is about her experiences with Bundy, a man she considered a friend. "I'd been a cop, had all that psychology — but his mask was perfect. I say that long acquaintance can help you know someone. But you can never be really sure. Scary."

- **Egocentric and grandiose.** Jack the Ripper thought the world of himself and felt he would outsmart police, so much so that he sent letters taunting the London officers. "Dear Boss," he wrote, "I keep on hearing the police have caught me but they won't fix me just yet. I have laughed when they look so clever and talk about being on the right track. That joke about Leather Apron gave me real fits. I am down on whores and I shan't quit ripping them till I do get buckled. Grand work the last job was. I gave the lady no time to squeal. How can they catch me now? I love my work and want to start again. You will soon hear of me with my funny little games. I saved some of the proper red stuff in a ginger beer bottle over the last job to write with but it went thick like glue and I can't use it. Red ink is fit enough I hope ha. ha. The next job I do I shall clip the lady's ears off and send to the police officers ... My knife's so nice and sharp I want to get to work right away if I get a chance. Good luck."

- **Lack of remorse or guilt.** Joel Rifkin was filled with self-pity after he was convicted of killing and dismembering at least nine women. He called his conviction a tragedy, but later, in prison, he got into an argument with mass murderer Colin Ferguson over whose killing spree was more important. When Ferguson taunted him for only killing women, Rifkin said, "Yeah, but I had more victims."

- **Lack of empathy.** Andrei Chikatilo, who feasted on bits of genitalia both male and female after his kills, thought nothing of taking a life, no matter how torturous it was for his victims. "The whole thing - the cries, the blood, the agony - gave me relaxation and a certain pleasure," he said.

- **Deceitful and manipulative.** John Wayne Gacy refused to take responsibility for the twenty-eight boys buried beneath his house, even though he also once said that clowns can get away with murder. "I think after 14 years under truth serum had I committed the crime I would have known it," said the man the neighbors all claimed to like. "There's got to be something that would... would click in my mind. I've had photos of 21 of the victims and I've looked at them all over the years here and I've never recognized anyone of them."

- **Shallow emotions.** German serial killer Rudolph Pliel, who was convicted of killing ten people and who later took his own life in prison, compared his "hobby" of murder to playing cards. He later told police, "What I did is not such a great harm, with all these surplus women nowadays. Anyway, I had a good time."

- **Impulsive.** Tommy Lynn Sells, who claimed responsibility for dozens of murders throughout the Midwest and South, saw a woman at a convenience store and followed her home, an impulse he was unable to control. He waited until the house went dark, then "I went into this house. I go to the first bedroom I see...I don't know whose room it is and, and, and, and I start stabbing." The victim was the woman's young son.

- **Poor behavior controls.** "I wished I could stop but I could not. I had no other thrill or happiness," said UK killer Dennis Nilsen, who killed at least twelve young men via strangulation, then bathed and dressed their bodies before disposing of them, often by burning them.

- **Need for excitement.** For Albert Fish - a masochistic killer with a side of sadism that included sending a letter to the mother of one of his victims, describing in detail how he cut, cooked, and ate her daughter - even the idea of his own death was one he found particularly thrilling. "Going to the electric chair will be the supreme thrill of my life," he said.

- **Lack of responsibility.** "I see myself more as a victim rather than a perpetrator," said Gacy, in a rare moment when he admitted to the murders. "I was cheated out of my childhood. I should never have been convicted of anything more serious than running a cemetery without a license. They were just a bunch of worthless little queers and punks."

- **Early behavior problems.** "When I was a boy I never had a friend in the world," said German serial killer Heinrich Pommerencke, who began raping and murdering girls as a teen.

- **Adult antisocial behavior.** Gary Ridgeway pleaded guilty to killing forty-eight women, mostly prostitutes, who were easy prey and were rarely reported missing – at least not immediately. "I don't believe in man, God nor Devil. I hate the whole damned human race, including myself... I preyed upon the weak, the harmless and the unsuspecting. This lesson I was taught by others: Might makes right."

"I felt like it"

Many psychopaths will say after a crime, "I did it because I felt like it," with a certain element of pride.

That's how BTK killer Dennis Rader felt. And, because he had no sense of wrong regarding his actions, he was able to carry on with his normal life with his wife and children with ease.

Someone else's demeanor might have changed. They may have become jittery or anxious, and they would have been caught.

Many serial killers are so cold they are can pop into a diner right after a murder, never showing a sign of what they've done.

"Serial murderers often seem normal," according to the FBI. "They have families and/or a steady job."

"They're so completely ordinary," Morrison added. "That's what gets a lot of victims in trouble."

That normalcy is often what allows perpetrators to get away with their crimes for so long.

Unlike mass murderers, such as terrorists, who generally drop off the radar before perpetrating their event, serial killers blend in. They might seem a bit strange – neighbors noticed that Ed Gein wasn't too big on personal hygiene, and neighbors did think it was odd that William Bonin hung out with such young boys - but not so much so that anyone would ask too many questions.

"That's why so many people often say "I had no idea" or "He was such a nice guy" after a friend or neighbor is arrested.

And it's also why people are so very, very stunned when they see stories of serial killers dominating the news.

"For a person with a conscience, Rader's crimes seem hideous, but from his point of view, these are his greatest accomplishments and he is anxious to share all of the wonderful things he has done," said Jack Levin, PhD, director of the Brudnick Center on Violence and Conflict at Northeastern University in Boston and the author of *Extreme Killings*.

A new take on psychopathy

Psychopathy is now diagnosed as antisocial personality disorder, a prettier spin on an absolutely horrifying diagnosis.

According to studies, almost 50 percent of men in prison and 21 percent of women in prison have been diagnosed with antisocial personality disorder.

Of serial killers, Ted Bundy (who enjoyed sex with his dead victims), John Wayne Gacy, and Charles Manson (who encouraged others to do his dirty work which included the murder of pregnant Sharon Tate) were all diagnosed with this particular affliction, which allowed them to carry out their crimes with total disregard toward others or toward the law.

They showed no remorse.

Schizophrenia

Many known serial killers were later diagnosed with some other form of mental illness, including schizophrenia. Examples include: David Berkowitz (he said his neighbor's dog told him to kill his six victims in the 1970s), Ed Gein (whose grisly saving of skin, bones, and various female sex parts was a desperate effort to resurrect his dead mother), and Richard Chase (the vampire of Sacramento who killed six people in California in order to drink their blood).

Schizophrenia includes a wide range of symptoms, ranging from hallucinations and delusions to living in a catatonic state.

Borderline personality disorder

Borderline personality disorder – which is characterized by intense mood swings, problems with interpersonal relationships, and impulsive behaviors – is also common in serial killers.

Some diagnosed cases of borderline personality disorder include Aileen Wuornos, a woman whose horrific childhood and numerous sexual assaults led her to murder one of her rapists, after which she spiraled out of control and killed six other men who picked her up along with highway in Florida, nurse Kristen H. Gilbert, who killed four patients at a Virginia hospital with overdoses of epinephrine, and Dahmer, whose murder count rose to seventeen before he was caught.

With a stigma still quite present regarding mental illness, it's likely we will continue to diagnose serial killers and mass murderers after the fact—too late to protect their victims.

Top signs of a serial killer

While there is still no simple thread of similarities – which is why police and the FBI have more trouble in real life solving crimes than they do on shows like *Criminal Minds* – there are some things to look for, experts say.

- **Antisocial Behavior.** Psychopaths tend to be loners, so if a child that was once gregarious and outgoing becomes shy and antisocial, this could be an issue. Jeffrey Dahmer was a social, lively child until his parents moved to Ohio for his father's new job. There, he regressed – allegedly after being sexually molested – and began focusing his attentions on dissecting road kill rather than developing friendships.

- **Arson.** Fire is power, and power and control are part of the appeal for serial killers, who enjoy having their victims at their mercy. David Berkowitz was a pyromaniac as a child – his classmates called him Pyro as a nickname, so well-known was he for his fire obsession - and he reportedly started more than one thousand fires in New York before he became the Son of Sam killer.

- **Torturing animals.** Serial killers often start young and test boundaries with animals, including family or neighborhood pets. According to studies, 70 percent of violent offenders have episodes of animal abuse in their childhood histories, compared to just 6 percent of nonviolent offenders. Albert DeSalvo – better known as the Boston Strangler – would capture cats and dogs as a child and trap them in boxes, shooting arrows at the defenseless animals for sport.

- **A troubled family history.** Many serial killers come from families with criminal or psychiatric histories or alcoholism. Edmund Kemper killed his grandparents to see what it would be like, and later – after he murdered a string of college students – he killed his alcoholic mother, grinding her vocal chords in the garbage disposal in an attempt to erase the sound of her voice.

- **Childhood abuse.** William Bonin – who killed at least twenty-one boys and young men – was abandoned as a child, sent to live in a group home where he himself was sexually assaulted. The connections suggest either a rage that can't be erased – Aileen Wuornos, a rare female serial killer, was physically and sexually abused throughout her childhood, resulting in a distrust of others and a pent-up rage that exploded during a later rape - or a disassociation of sorts, refusing to connect on a human level with others for fear of being rejected yet again.

- **Substance abuse.** Many serial killers use drugs or alcohol. Jeffrey Dahmer was discharged from the Army due to a drinking problem he developed in high school, and he used alcohol to lure his victims to his apartment, where he killed them in a fruitless effort to create a zombie-like sex slave who would never leave him.

- **Voyeurism.** When Ted Bundy was a teen, he spent his nights as a Peeping Tom, hoping to get a glimpse of one of the neighborhood girls getting undressed in their bedrooms.

- **Serial killers are usually smart.** While their IQ is not usually the reason why serial killers elude police for so long, many have very high IQs. Edmund Kemper was very close to being considered a genius (his IQ was 136, just four points beneath the 140 mark that earns genius status), and he used his intelligence to create complex cons that got him released from prison early after killing his grandparents, allowing eight more women to die.

- **Can't keep a job.** Serial killers often have trouble staying employed, either because their off-hours activities take up a lot of time (Jeffrey Dahmer hid bodies in his shower, the shower he used every morning before work, because he was killing at such a fast rate) or because their obsessions have them hunting for victims when they should be on the clock.

Trademarks of a serial killer

While what we know helps us get a better understanding of potential serial killers – and perhaps take a closer look at our weird little neighbors – it is still tricky for police and FBI agents to track down serial killers without knowing a few tells.

The signature

While serial killers like to stake a claim over their killings – "Serial killers typically have some sort of a signature," according to Dr. Scott Bonn, a professor at Drew University in New Jersey – they are usually still quite neat, and a signature does not necessarily mean evidence.

"Jack the Ripper, of course, his signature was the ripping of the bodies," said Bonn.

While there are multiple theories, Jack the Ripper has yet to be identified, despite the similarities in his murders.

The Happy Face Killer, Keith Hunter Jespersen – whose childhood was marked by alcoholic parents, teasing at school, and a propensity to abuse small animals - drew happy faces on the numerous letters he sent to both media and authorities, teasing them a bit with a carrot on a string.

"If the forensic evidence itself - depending upon the bones or flesh or whatever is left - if it allows for that sort of identification, that would be one way of using forensic evidence to link these murders," Bonn said.

The cooling-off period

Organized killers are so neat, tidy, and meticulous that they may never leave clues, even if they have a signature.

And if there's a long cooling-off period between crimes, tracking the killer becomes even more of a challenge.

After a murder – which could be compared to a sexual experience or getting high on drugs – the uncontrollable urges that led the killer to act dissipate, at least temporarily.

But, according to Ressler, serial killers are rarely satisfied with their kills, and each one increases desire to murder – in the same way a porn addiction can start with the pages of Playboy and then turn into BDSM videos or other fetishes when the magazine pictorials are no longer satisfying.

"I was literally singing to myself on my way home, after the killing. The tension, the desire to kill a woman had built up in such explosive proportions that when I finally pulled the trigger, all the pressures, all the tensions, all the hatred, had just vanished, dissipated, but only for a short time," said David Berkowitz, better known as the Son of Sam.

Afterwards, the memory of the murder, or mementos from the murder (such as the skulls Jeffrey Dahmer retained, the scalps collected by David Gore, or the box of vulvas Ed Gein kept in his kitchen) no longer become enough. The killers must kill again, creating a "serial" cycle.

That window between crimes usually becomes smaller, however, which allows authorities to notice similarities in murder scenes or methodology, making tracking easier.

In the case of William Bonin, there were months between his first few murders. But, toward the end, he sometimes killed two young men a day to satisfy his increasingly uncontrollable urges.

"Sometimes… I'd get tense and think I was gonna go crazy if I couldn't get some release, like my head would explode. So I'd go out hunting. Killing helped me… It was like... needing to go gambling or getting drunk. I had to do it," Bonin said.

Hunting in pairs

Some serial killers – between 10 and 25 percent - find working as a team more efficient, and they use their charm as the hook to lure in accomplices.

Ed Gein may never have killed anyone had his accomplice, a mentally challenged man who helped Gein dig up the graves of women who resembled his mother, not been sent to a nursing home, leaving Gein unable to dig up the dead on his own.

Texas killer Dean Corll used beer, drugs, money, and candy to bribe neighborhood boys to bring him their friends for what they were promised was a party but instead would turn to torture and murder. He would have killed many more if one of his accomplices had not finally shot him to prevent another night of death.

William Bonin also liked to work with friends, and he enticed boys who were reportedly on the low end of the IQ scale to help him sadistically rape and torture his victims.

Other red flags

According to the FBI's Behavioral Science Unit – founded by Robert Ressler - 60 percent of murderers whose crimes involved sex were childhood bed-wetters who sometimes carried the habit into adulthood. One such serial killer, Alton Coleman, regularly wet his pants, earning the humiliating nickname "Pissy."

Sexual arousal over violent fantasies during puberty can also play a role in a serial killer's future.

Jeffrey Dahmer hit puberty about the same time he was dissecting road kill. So, in some way, his wires became crossed and twisted, and sex and death aroused him.

Brain damage? Maybe

Helen Morrison's test found that John Wayne Gacy's brain was normal. And Jeffrey Dahmer's father never had the opportunity to have his son's brain studied, although both he and Jeffrey had wanted the study. There is some evidence, however, that some serial killers have brain damage that impact their ability to exact rational control.

"Normal parents? Normal brains? I think not," said Dr. Jonathan Pincus, a neurologist and author of the book *Base Instincts: What Makes Killers Kill*.

"Abusive experiences, mental illnesses and neurological deficits interplayed to produce the tragedies reported in the newspapers. The most vicious criminals have also been, overwhelmingly, people who have been grotesquely abused as children and have paranoid patterns of thinking," said Pincus in his book, adding that childhood traumas can impact the developmental anatomy and functioning of the brain.

***

So what do we know?

Serial killers can be either uber-smart or brain damaged, completely people savvy or totally awkward, high functioning and seemingly normal or unable to hold down a job.

But essentially, regardless of their back story, their modus operandi, or their style, "they're evil," said criminal profiler Pat Brown.

And do we need to know anything more than that?

MORE BOOKS BY JACK ROSEWOOD

From rampage killers to hunters that seek out human prey in the shadows of the night, this anthology is a collection of serial killer horror stories. Collectively, these men were responsible for hundreds of deaths, and they all belong in the realm of the worst serial killers to date. Delve into eight different cases and explore the heinous deeds committed, the background of each killer, and the apparent motives for their crimes.

There are those who went on deadly rampages, such as Cho Seung-Hui and George Hennard, men who decided to inflict as much terror in one day as they possibly could. Famous serial killers are included, such as the Hillside Stranglers, Kenneth Bianchi and Angelo Buono, and the Beast of the Ukraine, Anatoly Onoprienko. There are also lesser-known murderers such as Fritz Haarmann and Ronald Dominique who preyed on young men for their own deviant pleasures.

Each of these true murder stories will leave you with a sense of horror and perhaps a little fear. David Parker Ray's surviving victims still live in fear today, and this notorious true crime story is one of the most sadistic and disturbing. With tales of torture, mind control, and violence, very few survived their time in Ray's toy box.

The true crime stories in this book have been selected because of the horrendous nature of the killer's actions and the sheer volume of victims they slaughtered. Innocent people, going about their daily business or asleep in their beds, all make up these serial killers true crime stories.

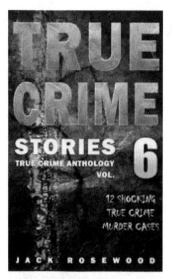

In the following true crime anthology, you will read about twelve true crime stories that have baffled investigators and captured the imagination of the public for years. Among some of the more shocking stories is a trio of mass murder cases from around the world. You will be intrigued to read about how Ronald DeFeo Junior mercilessly gunned down six members of his family in cold blood. And you will be equally intrigued to learn about and how two other cases of mass murder shocked the small countries where they took place. You will also follow the criminal investigations of some high-profile cases, such as that of best-selling author Michael Peterson, and see how they were resolved.

Some of the true crime murder cases profiled in this volume can only be described as bizarre. You will be introduced to Elifasi Msomi, a failed Zulu witch doctor who became a serial killer notorious for keeping some of his victims' blood for various rituals. You will also read about two potential curses that sent many of the people involved with their respective cases to early graves. Finally, the strange case of Robert Dirscherl is profiled. The authorities initially ruled Dirscherl's death a suicide, but after several decades it now appears that the death may be a case of true murder and not suicide.

If you are interested in learning more about man's dark side, then open the pages of this book. But be warned, some of the murder stories you will read about will be shocking and disturbing. Despite being disturbed by many of these cases, you will also find this volume extremely intriguing and exciting!

GET THESE BOOKS FOR FREE

Go to www.jackrosewood.com/free and get these E-Books for free!

A NOTE FROM THE AUTHOR

Hello, this is Jack Rosewood. Thank you for reading this book. I hope you enjoyed the read. If you did, I'd appreciate if you would take a few moments to post a review wherever you got the book.

I would also love if you'd sign up to my newsletter to receive updates on new releases, promotions, and a FREE copy of my Herbert Mullin E-Book, www.jackrosewood.com/free

Thanks again for reading this book, and make sure to follow me on Facebook.

Best Regards,
Jack Rosewood